PostGIS Cookbook
Second Edition

Store, organize, manipulate, and analyze spatial data

Mayra Zurbarán
Pedro M. Wightman
Paolo Corti
Stephen Vincent Mather
Thomas J Kraft
Bborie Park

BIRMINGHAM - MUMBAI

PostGIS Cookbook
Second Edition

Copyright © 2018 Packt Publishing

Commissioning Editor: Merint Mathew
Acquisition Editors: Nitin Dasan, Shriram Shekhar
Content Development Editor: Nikhil Borkar
Technical Editor: Subhalaxmi Nadar
Copy Editor: Safis Editing
Project Coordinator: Ulhas Kambali
Proofreader: Safis Editing
Indexer: Mariammal Chettiyar
Graphics: Tania Dutta
Production Coordinator: Shantanu Zagade

First published: January 2014
Second edition: March 2018

Production reference: 1270318

Published by Packt Publishing Ltd.
Livery Place
35 Livery Street
Birmingham
B3 2PB, UK.

ISBN 978-1-78829-932-9

www.packtpub.com

`mapt.io`

Mapt is an online digital library that gives you full access to over 5,000 books and videos, as well as industry leading tools to help you plan your personal development and advance your career. For more information, please visit our website.

Why subscribe?

- Spend less time learning and more time coding with practical eBooks and Videos from over 4,000 industry professionals

- Improve your learning with Skill Plans built especially for you

- Get a free eBook or video every month

- Mapt is fully searchable

- Copy and paste, print, and bookmark content

PacktPub.com

Did you know that Packt offers eBook versions of every book published, with PDF and ePub files available? You can upgrade to the eBook version at `www.PacktPub.com` and as a print book customer, you are entitled to a discount on the eBook copy. Get in touch with us at `service@packtpub.com` for more details.

At `www.PacktPub.com`, you can also read a collection of free technical articles, sign up for a range of free newsletters, and receive exclusive discounts and offers on Packt books and eBooks.

Contributors

About the authors

Mayra Zurbarán is a Colombian geogeek currently pursuing her PhD in geoprivacy. She has a BS in computer science from Universidad del Norte and is interested in the intersection of ethical location data management, free and open source software, and GIS. She is a Pythonista with a marked preference for the PostgreSQL database. Mayra is a member of the **Geomatics and Earth Observation laboratory (GEOlab)** at Politecnico di Milano and is also a contributor to the FOSS community.

I would like to thank my mother for her patience and support, and my father and grandmother for their love and for teaching me awesome life skills. To Jota, the kindest person I have met and whose faith in me continues to push me forward. Thanks to Stephen for passing on the task. To my adviser, coauthor, and friend Pedro, and to Jorge Martinez for his help.

Pedro M. Wightman is an associate professor at the Systems Engineering Department of Universidad del Norte, Barranquilla, Colombia. With a PhD in computer science from the University of South Florida, he's a researcher in location-based information systems, wireless sensor networks, and virtual and augmented reality, among other fields. Father of two beautiful and smart girls, he's also a rookie writer of short stories, science fiction fan, time travel enthusiast, and is worried about how to survive apocalyptic solar flares.

Thank you to my family and all the special people in my life for their love, support, and sacrifice; without them, this wouldn't have been possible. Thanks to my doctoral student for all effort and energy in her research and in life. Thanks to Universidad del Norte for their support in this project. Finally, thanks to my cat for hours of fun (and scratches) that make me forget bad times when things don't go as expected.

Paolo Corti is an environmental engineer with 20 years of experience in the GIS field, currently working as a Geospatial Engineer Fellow at the Center for Geographic Analysis at Harvard University. He is an advocate of open source geospatial technologies and Python, an OSGeo Charter member, and a member of the pycsw and GeoNode Project Steering Committees. He is a coauthor of the first edition of this book and the reviewer for the first and second editions of the *Mastering QGIS* book by *Packt*.

Stephen Vincent Mather has worked in the geospatial industry for 15 years, having always had a flair for geospatial analyses in general, especially those at the intersection of Geography and Ecology. His work in open-source geospatial databases started 5 years ago with PostGIS and he immediately began using PostGIS as an analytic tool, attempting a range of innovative and sometimes bleeding-edge techniques (although he admittedly prefers the cutting edge).

Thomas J Kraft is currently a Planning Technician at Cleveland Metroparks after beginning as a GIS intern in 2011. He graduated with Honors from Cleveland State University in 2012, majoring in Environmental Science with an emphasis on GIS. When not in front of a computer, he spends his weekends landscaping and in the outdoors in general.

Bborie Park has been breaking (and subsequently fixing) computers for most of his life. His primary interests involve developing end-to-end pipelines for spatial datasets. He is an active contributor to the PostGIS project and is a member of the PostGIS Steering Committee. He happily resides with his wife Nicole in the San Francisco Bay Area.

Packt is searching for authors like you

Table of Contents

Preface

How close is the nearest hospital from my children's school? Where were the property crimes in my city for the last three months? What is the shortest route from my home to my office? What route should I prescribe for my company's delivery truck to maximize equipment utilization and minimize fuel consumption? Where should the next fire station be built to minimize response times?

People ask these questions, and others like them, every day all over this planet. Answering these questions requires a mechanism capable of thinking in two or more dimensions. Historically, desktop GIS applications were the only ones capable of answering these questions. This method—though completely functional—is not viable for the average person; most people do not need all the functionalities that these applications can offer, or they do not know how to use them. In addition, more and more location-based services offer the specific features that people use and are accessible even from their smartphones. Clearly, the massification of these services requires the support of a robust backend platform to process a large number of geographical operations.

Since scalability, support for large datasets, and a direct input mechanism are required or desired, most developers have opted to adopt spatial databases as their support platform. There are several spatial database software available, some proprietary and others open source. PostGIS is an open source spatial database software available, and probably the most accessible of all spatial database software.

PostGIS runs as an extension to provide spatial capabilities to PostgreSQL databases. In this capacity, PostGIS permits the inclusion of spatial data alongside data typically found in a database. By having all the data together, questions such as "What is the rank of all the police stations, after taking into account the distance for each response time?" are possible. New or enhanced capabilities are possible by building upon the core functions provided by PostGIS and the inherent extensibility of PostgreSQL. Furthermore, this book also includes an invitation to include location privacy protection mechanisms in new GIS applications and in location-based services so that users feel respected and not necessarily at risk for sharing their information, especially information as sensitive as their whereabouts.

PostGIS Cookbook, Second Edition uses a problem-solving approach to help you acquire a solid understanding of PostGIS. It is hoped that this book provides answers to some common spatial questions and gives you the inspiration and confidence to use and enhance PostGIS in finding solutions to challenging spatial problems.

Who this book is for

This book is written for those who are looking for the best method to solve their spatial problems using PostGIS. These problems can be as simple as finding the nearest restaurant to a specific location, or as complex as finding the shortest and/or most efficient route from point A to point B.

For readers who are just starting out with PostGIS, or even with spatial datasets, this book is structured to help them become comfortable and proficient at running spatial operations in the database. For experienced users, the book provides opportunities to dive into advanced topics such as point clouds, raster map-algebra, and PostGIS programming.

What this book covers

Chapter 1, *Moving Data In and Out of PostGIS*, covers the processes available for importing and exporting spatial and non-spatial data to and from PostGIS. These processes include the use of utilities provided by PostGIS and by third parties, such as GDAL/OGR.

Chapter 2, *Structures That Work*, discusses how to organize PostGIS data using mechanisms available through PostgreSQL. These mechanisms are used to normalize potentially unclean and unstructured import data.

Chapter 3, *Working with Vector Data – The Basics*, introduces PostGIS operations commonly done on vectors, known as geometries and geographies in PostGIS. Operations covered include the processing of invalid geometries, determining relationships between geometries, and simplifying complex geometries.

Chapter 4, *Working with Vector Data – Advanced Recipes*, dives into advanced topics for analyzing geometries. You will learn how to make use of KNN filters to increase the performance of proximity queries, create polygons from LiDAR data, and compute Voronoi cells usable in neighborhood analyses.

Chapter 5, *Working with Raster Data*, presents a realistic workflow for operating on rasters in PostGIS. You will learn how to import a raster, modify the raster, conduct analysis on the raster, and export the raster in standard raster formats.

Chapter 6, *Working with pgRouting*, introduces the pgRouting extension, which brings graph traversal and analysis capabilities to PostGIS. The recipes in this chapter answer real-world questions of conditionally navigating from point A to point B and accurately modeling complex routes, such as waterways.

Chapter 7, *Into the Nth Dimension*, focuses on the tools and techniques used to process and analyze multidimensional spatial data in PostGIS, including LiDAR-sourced point clouds. Topics covered include the loading of point clouds into PostGIS, creating 2.5D and 3D geometries from point clouds, and the application of several photogrammetry principles.

Chapter 8, *PostGIS Programming*, shows how to use the Python language to write applications that operate on and interact with PostGIS. The applications written include methods to read and write external datasets to and from PostGIS, as well as a basic geocoding engine using OpenStreetMap datasets.

Chapter 9, *PostGIS and the Web*, presents the use of OGC and REST web services to deliver PostGIS data and services to the web. This chapter discusses providing OGC, WFS, and WMS services with MapServer and GeoServer, and consuming them from clients such as OpenLayers and Leaflet. It then shows how to build a web application with GeoDjango and how to include your PostGIS data in a Mapbox application.

Chapter 10, *Maintenance, Optimization, and Performance Tuning*, takes a step back from PostGIS and focuses on the capabilities of the PostgreSQL database server. By leveraging the tools provided by PostgreSQL, you can ensure the long-term viability of your spatial and non-spatial data, and maximize the performance of various PostGIS operations. In addition, it explores new features such as geospatial sharding and parallelism in PostgreSQL.

Chapter 11, *Using Desktop Clients*, tells you about how spatial data in PostGIS can be consumed and manipulated using various open source desktop GIS applications. Several applications are discussed so as to highlight the different approaches to interacting with spatial data and help you find the right tool for the task.

Chapter 12, *Introduction to Location Privacy Protection Mechanisms*, provides an introductory approximation to the concept of location privacy and presents the implementation of two different location privacy protection mechanisms that can be included in commercial applications to give a basic level of protection to the user's location data.

To get the most out of this book

Before going further into this book, you will want to install latest versions of PostgreSQL and PostGIS (9.6 or 103 and 2.3 or 2.41, respectively). You may also want to install pgAdmin (1.18) if you prefer a graphical SQL tool. For most computing environments (Windows, Linux, macOS X), installers and packages include all required dependencies of PostGIS. The minimum required dependencies for PostGIS are PROJ.4, GEOS, libjson and GDAL.
A basic understanding of the SQL language is required to understand and adapt the code found in this book's recipes.

Download the example code files

You can download the example code files for this book from your account at www.packtpub.com. If you purchased this book elsewhere, you can visit www.packtpub.com/support and register to have the files emailed directly to you.

You can download the code files by following these steps:

1. Log in or register at www.packtpub.com.
2. Select the **SUPPORT** tab.
3. Click on **Code Downloads & Errata**.
4. Enter the name of the book in the **Search** box and follow the onscreen instructions.

Once the file is downloaded, please make sure that you unzip or extract the folder using the latest version of:

- WinRAR/7-Zip for Windows
- Zipeg/iZip/UnRarX for Mac
- 7-Zip/PeaZip for Linux

The code bundle for the book is also hosted on GitHub at https://github.com/PacktPublishing/PostGIS-Cookbook-Second-Edition. In case there's an update to the code, it will be updated on the existing GitHub repository.

We also have other code bundles from our rich catalog of books and videos available at https://github.com/PacktPublishing/. Check them out!

Download the color images

We also provide a PDF file that has color images of the screenshots/diagrams used in this book. You can download it here: `https://www.packtpub.com/sites/default/files/downloads/PostGISCookbookSecondEdition_ColorImages.pdf`.

Conventions used

There are a number of text conventions used throughout this book.

`CodeInText`: Indicates code words in text, database table names, folder names, filenames, file extensions, pathnames, dummy URLs, user input, and Twitter handles. Here is an example: "We will import the `firenews.csv` file that stores a series of web news collected from various RSS feeds."

A block of code is set as follows:

```
SELECT ROUND(SUM(chp02.proportional_sum(ST_Transform(a.geom,3734), b.geom,
b.pop))) AS population
    FROM nc_walkzone AS a, census_viewpolygon as b
    WHERE ST_Intersects(ST_Transform(a.geom, 3734), b.geom)
    GROUP BY a.id;
```

When we wish to draw your attention to a particular part of a code block, the relevant lines or items are set in bold:

```
SELECT ROUND(SUM(chp02.proportional_sum(ST_Transform(a.geom,3734), b.geom,
b.pop))) AS population
    FROM nc_walkzone AS a, census_viewpolygon as b
    WHERE ST_Intersects(ST_Transform(a.geom, 3734), b.geom)
    GROUP BY a.id;
```

Any command-line input or output is written as follows:

```
> raster2pgsql -s 4322 -t 100x100 -F -I -C -Y
C:\postgis_cookbook\data\chap5\PRISM\us_tmin_2012.*.asc chap5.prism | psql
-d postgis_cookbook
```

Bold: Indicates a new term, an important word, or words that you see onscreen. For example, words in menus or dialog boxes appear in the text like this. Here is an example: "Clicking the **Next** button moves you to the next screen."

Warnings or important notes appear like this.

 Tips and tricks appear like this.

Sections

In this book, you will find several headings that appear frequently (*Getting ready, How to do it..., How it works..., There's more...,* and *See also*).

To give clear instructions on how to complete a recipe, use these sections as follows:

Getting ready

This section tells you what to expect in the recipe and describes how to set up any software or any preliminary settings required for the recipe.

How to do it...

This section contains the steps required to follow the recipe.

How it works...

This section usually consists of a detailed explanation of what happened in the previous section.

There's more...

This section consists of additional information about the recipe in order to make you more knowledgeable about the recipe.

See also

This section provides helpful links to other useful information for the recipe.

Get in touch

Feedback from our readers is always welcome.

General feedback: Email feedback@packtpub.com and mention the book title in the subject of your message. If you have questions about any aspect of this book, please email us at questions@packtpub.com.

Errata: Although we have taken every care to ensure the accuracy of our content, mistakes do happen. If you have found a mistake in this book, we would be grateful if you would report this to us. Please visit www.packtpub.com/submit-errata, selecting your book, clicking on the Errata Submission Form link, and entering the details.

Piracy: If you come across any illegal copies of our works in any form on the internet, we would be grateful if you would provide us with the location address or website name. Please contact us at copyright@packtpub.com with a link to the material.

If you are interested in becoming an author: If there is a topic that you have expertise in and you are interested in either writing or contributing to a book, please visit authors.packtpub.com.

Reviews

Please leave a review. Once you have read and used this book, why not leave a review on the site that you purchased it from? Potential readers can then see and use your unbiased opinion to make purchase decisions, we at Packt can understand what you think about our products, and our authors can see your feedback on their book. Thank you!

For more information about Packt, please visit packtpub.com.

Moving Data In and Out of PostGIS

1

In this chapter, we will cover:

- Importing nonspatial tabular data (CSV) using PostGIS functions
- Importing nonspatial tabular data (CSV) using GDAL
- Importing shapefiles with shp2pgsql
- Importing and exporting data with the ogr2ogr GDAL command
- Handling batch importing and exporting of datasets
- Exporting data to a shapefile with the pgsql2shp PostGIS command
- Importing OpenStreetMap data with the osm2pgsql command
- Importing raster data with the raster2pgsql PostGIS command
- Importing multiple rasters at a time
- Exporting rasters with the gdal_translate and gdalwarp GDAL commands

Introduction

PostGIS is an open source extension for the PostgreSQL database that allows support for geographic objects; throughout this book you will find recipes that will guide you step by step to explore the different functionalities it offers.

The purpose of the book is to become a useful tool for understanding the capabilities of PostGIS and how to apply them in no time. Each recipe presents a preparation stage, in order to organize your workspace with everything you may need, then the set of steps that you need to perform in order to achieve the main goal of the task, that includes all the external commands and SQL sentences you will need (which have been tested in Linux, Mac and Windows environments), and finally a small summary of the recipe. This book will go over a large set of common tasks in geographical information systems and location-based services, which makes it a must-have book in your technical library.

In this first chapter, we will show you a set of recipes covering different tools and methodologies to import and export geographic data from the PostGIS spatial database, given that pretty much every common action to perform in a GIS starts with inserting or exporting geospatial data.

Importing nonspatial tabular data (CSV) using PostGIS functions

There are a couple of alternative approaches to importing a **Comma Separated Values (CSV)** file, which stores attributes and geometries in PostGIS. In this recipe, we will use the approach of importing such a file using the PostgreSQL COPY command and a couple of PostGIS functions.

Getting ready

We will import the firenews.csv file that stores a series of web news collected from various RSS feeds related to forest fires in Europe in the context of the **European Forest Fire Information System (EFFIS)**, available at http://effis.jrc.ec.europa.eu/.

For each news feed, there are attributes such as place name, size of the fire in hectares, URL, and so on. Most importantly, there are the x and y fields that give the position of the geolocalized news in decimal degrees (in the WGS 84 spatial reference system, SRID = 4326).

For Windows machines, it is necessary to install OSGeo4W, a set of open source geographical libraries that will allow the manipulation of the datasets. The link is:
`https://trac.osgeo.org/osgeo4w/`

In addition, include the OSGeo4W and the Postgres binary folders in the Path environment variable to be able to execute the commands from any location in your PC.

How to do it...

The steps you need to follow to complete this recipe are as shown:

1. Inspect the structure of the CSV file, `firenews.csv`, which you can find within the book dataset (if you are on Windows, open the CSV file with an editor such as Notepad).

```
$ cd ~/postgis_cookbook/data/chp01/
$ head -n 5 firenews.csv
```

The output of the preceding command is as shown:

```
Chapter 1 — bash — 80×26
x,y,place,size,update,startdate,enddate,title,url
-8.2499,42.37657,Avión,52,2011/03/07,2011/03/05,2011/03/06,Dos incendios calcina
n 74 hectáreas el fin de semana,http://www.laregion.es/noticia/145578/incendios/
calcinan/hectareas/semana/
-8.1013,42.13924,Quintela de Leirado,22,2011/03/07,2011/03/06,2011/03/06,Dos inc
endios calcinan 74 hectáreas el fin de semana,http://www.laregion.es/noticia/145
578/incendios/calcinan/hectareas/semana/
3.48159,43.99156,Arrigas,4,2011/03/06,2011/03/05,2011/03/05,"À Arrigas, la forêt
 sous la menace d'un feu",http://www.midilibre.com/articles/2011/03/06/NIMES-A-A
rrigas-la-foret-sous-la-menace-d-39-un-feu-1557923.php5
6.1672,44.96038,Vénéon,9,2011/03/06,2011/03/06,2011/03/06,Isère Spectaculaire in
cendie dans la vallée du Vénéon,http://www.ledauphine.com/isere-sud/2011/03/i
sere-spectaculaire-incendie-dans-la-vallee-du-veneon
bash-3.2$ 
```

2. Connect to PostgreSQL, create the chp01 SCHEMA, and create the following table:

```
$ psql -U me -d postgis_cookbook
postgis_cookbook=> CREATE EXTENSION postgis;
postgis_cookbook=> CREATE SCHEMA chp01;
postgis_cookbook=> CREATE TABLE chp01.firenews
(
  x float8,
  y float8,
  place varchar(100),
  size float8,
  update date,
  startdate date,
  enddate date,
  title varchar(255),
  url varchar(255),
  the_geom geometry(POINT, 4326)
);
```

We are using the psql client for connecting to PostgreSQL, but you can use your favorite one, for example, pgAdmin.

Using the psql client, we will not show the host and port options as we will assume that you are using a local PostgreSQL installation on the standard port.

If that is not the case, please provide those options!

3. Copy the records from the CSV file to the PostgreSQL table using the COPY command (if you are on Windows, use an input directory such as c:\temp instead of /tmp) as follows:

```
postgis_cookbook=> COPY chp01.firenews (
  x, y, place, size, update, startdate,
  enddate, title, url
) FROM '/tmp/firenews.csv' WITH CSV HEADER;
```

Make sure that the firenews.csv file is in a location accessible from the PostgreSQL process user. For example, in Linux, copy the file to the /tmp directory.

If you are on Windows, you most likely will need to set the encoding to UTF-8 before copying: postgis_cookbook=# set client_encoding to 'UTF-8'; and remember to set the full path, 'c:\\tmp\firenews.csv'.

4. Check all of the records have been imported from the CSV file to the PostgreSQL table:

```
postgis_cookbook=> SELECT COUNT(*) FROM chp01.firenews;
```

The output of the preceding command is as follows:

```
● ● ●                    Chapter 1 — psql — 80×26
bash-3.2$ psql -d postgis_cookbook
psql (9.6.3)
Type "help" for help.

postgis_cookbook=# SELECT COUNT(*) FROM chp01.firenews;
 count
──────────
  3006
(1 row)

postgis_cookbook=#
```

5. Check a record related to this new table is in the PostGIS `geometry_columns` metadata view:

```
postgis_cookbook=# SELECT f_table_name,
f_geometry_column, coord_dimension, srid, type
FROM geometry_columns where f_table_name = 'firenews';
```

The output of the preceding command is as follows:

```
● ● ●                    Chapter 1 — psql — 80×26
postgis_cookbook=# SELECT f_table_name, f_geometry_column, coord_dimension, srid
, type FROM geometry_columns where f_table_name = 'firenews';
 f_table_name | f_geometry_column | coord_dimension | srid | type
──────────────┼───────────────────┼─────────────────┼──────┼───────
 firenews     | the_geom          |               2 | 4326 | POINT
(1 row)

postgis_cookbook=#
```

Before PostGIS 2.0, you had to create a table containing spatial data in two distinct steps; in fact, the `geometry_columns` view was a table that needed to be manually updated. For that purpose, you had to use the `AddGeometryColumn` function to create the column. For example, this is for this recipe:

```
postgis_cookbook=> CREATE TABLE chp01.firenews(
x float8,
y float8,
place varchar(100),
size float8,
update date,
startdate date,
enddate date,
title varchar(255),
url varchar(255))
WITHOUT OIDS;postgis_cookbook=> SELECT
AddGeometryColumn('chp01', 'firenews', 'the_geom', 4326,
'POINT', 2);
chp01.firenews.the_geom SRID:4326 TYPE:POINT DIMS:2
```

In PostGIS 2.0, you can still use the `AddGeometryColumn` function if you wish; however, you need to set its `use_typmod` parameter to `false`.

6. Now, import the points in the geometric column using the `ST_MakePoint` or `ST_PointFromText` functions (use one of the following two update commands):

```
postgis_cookbook=> UPDATE chp01.firenews
SET the_geom = ST_SetSRID(ST_MakePoint(x,y), 4326);
postgis_cookbook=> UPDATE chp01.firenews
SET the_geom = ST_PointFromText('POINT(' || x || ' ' || y || ')',
                                4326);
```

7. Check how the geometry field has been updated in some records from the table:

```
postgis_cookbook=# SELECT place, ST_AsText(the_geom) AS wkt_geom
FROM chp01.firenews ORDER BY place LIMIT 5;
```

The output of the preceding comment is as follows:

```
● ● ●                       Chapter 1 — psql — 103×26
postgis_cookbook=# SELECT place, ST_AsText(the_geom) AS wkt_geom FROM chp01.firenews ORDER BY place LIM
IT 5;
              place              |              wkt_geom
---------------------------------+------------------------------------
 'Ain Abid, Constantine, DZ | POINT(6.95 36.2333)
 A Coruña                         | POINT(-8.4283 43.36)
 A Fonsagrada                     | POINT(-7.0696263128 43.1247538232)
 A Guarda                         | POINT(-8.87237 41.90273)
 A Gudiña                         | POINT(-7.1376758921 42.0617733251)
(5 rows)

postgis_cookbook=#
```

8. Finally, create a spatial index for the geometric column of the table:

```
postgis_cookbook=> CREATE INDEX idx_firenews_geom
ON chp01.firenews USING GIST (the_geom);
```

How it works...

This recipe showed you how to load nonspatial tabular data (in CSV format) in PostGIS using the COPY PostgreSQL command.

After creating the table and copying the CSV file rows to the PostgreSQL table, you updated the geometric column using one of the geometry constructor functions that PostGIS provides (ST_MakePoint and ST_PointFromText for bi-dimensional points).

These geometry constructors (in this case, ST_MakePoint and ST_PointFromText) must always provide the **spatial reference system identifier (SRID)** together with the point coordinates to define the point geometry.

Each geometric field added in any table in the database is tracked with a record in the geometry_columns PostGIS metadata view. In the previous PostGIS version (< 2.0), the geometry_fields view was a table and needed to be manually updated, possibly with the convenient AddGeometryColumn function.

For the same reason, to maintain the updated `geometry_columns` view when dropping a geometry column or removing a spatial table in the previous PostGIS versions, there were the `DropGeometryColumn` and `DropGeometryTable` functions. With PostGIS 2.0 and newer, you don't need to use these functions any more, but you can safely remove the column or the table with the standard `ALTER TABLE`, `DROP COLUMN`, and `DROP TABLE` SQL commands.

In the last step of the recipe, you have created a spatial index on the table to improve performance. Please be aware that as in the case of alphanumerical database fields, indexes improve performances only when reading data using the `SELECT` command. In this case, you are making a number of updates on the table (`INSERT`, `UPDATE`, and `DELETE`); depending on the scenario, it could be less time consuming to drop and recreate the index after the updates.

Importing nonspatial tabular data (CSV) using GDAL

As an alternative approach to the previous recipe, you will import a CSV file to PostGIS using the `ogr2ogr` GDAL command and the **GDAL OGR virtual format**. The **Geospatial Data Abstraction Library (GDAL)** is a translator library for raster geospatial data formats. OGR is the related library that provides similar capabilities for vector data formats.

This time, as an extra step, you will import only a part of the features in the file and you will reproject them to a different spatial reference system.

Getting ready

You will import the `Global_24h.csv` file to the PostGIS database from NASA's **Earth Observing System Data and Information System (EOSDIS)**.

You can copy the file from the dataset directory of the book for this chapter.

This file represents the active hotspots in the world detected by the **Moderate Resolution Imaging Spectroradiometer (MODIS)** satellites in the last 24 hours. For each row, there are the coordinates of the hotspot (latitude, longitude) in decimal degrees (in the WGS 84 spatial reference system, SRID = 4326), and a series of useful fields such as the `acquisition date`, `acquisition time`, and `satellite type`, just to name a few.

You will import only the active fire data scanned by the satellite type marked as *T* (Terra MODIS), and you will project it using the **Spherical Mercator** projection coordinate system (EPSG:3857; it is sometimes marked as EPSG:900913, where the number 900913 represents Google in 1337 speak, as it was first widely used by Google Maps).

How to do it...

The steps you need to follow to complete this recipe are as follows:

1. Analyze the structure of the Global_24h.csv file (in Windows, open the CSV file with an editor such as Notepad):

```
$ cd ~/postgis_cookbook/data/chp01/
$ head -n 5 Global_24h.csv
```

The output of the preceding command is as follows:

```
Chapter 1 — bash — 103×26
bash-3.2$ head -n 5 Global_24h.csv
latitude,longitude,brightness,scan,track,acq_date,acq_time,satellite,confidence,version,bright_t31,frp
-23.386,-46.197,307.5,1.1,1,2012-08-20, 0140,T,54,5.0      ,285.7,16.5
-22.952,-47.574,330.1,1.2,1.1,2012-08-20, 0140,T,100,5.0    ,285.2,53.9
-23.726,-56.108,333.3,4.7,2,2012-08-20, 0140,T,100,5.0     ,283.5,404.1
-23.729,-56.155,311.8,4.7,2,2012-08-20, 0140,T,61,5.0      ,272,143.1
bash-3.2$
```

2. Create a GDAL virtual data source composed of just one layer derived from the Global_24h.csv file. To do so, create a text file named global_24h.vrt in the same directory where the CSV file is and edit it as follows:

```
<OGRVRTDataSource>
  <OGRVRTLayer name="Global_24h">
    <SrcDataSource>Global_24h.csv</SrcDataSource>
    <GeometryType>wkbPoint</GeometryType>
    <LayerSRS>EPSG:4326</LayerSRS>
      <GeometryField encoding="PointFromColumns"
        x="longitude" y="latitude"/>
  </OGRVRTLayer>
</OGRVRTDataSource>
```

3. With the `ogrinfo` command, check if the virtual layer is correctly recognized by GDAL. For example, analyze the schema of the layer and the first of its features (`fid=1`):

```
$ ogrinfo global_24h.vrt Global_24h -fid 1
```

The output of the preceding command is as follows:

```
●●●                    Chapter 1 — bash — 91×44
bash-3.2$ ogrinfo global_24h.vrt Global_24h -fid 1
INFO: Open of `global_24h.vrt'
      using driver `OGR_VRT' successful.

Layer name: Global_24h
Geometry: Point
Feature Count: 30326
Extent: (-155.284000, -40.751000) - (177.457000, 70.404000)
Layer SRS WKT:
GEOGCS["WGS 84",
    DATUM["WGS_1984",
        SPHEROID["WGS 84",6378137,298.257223563,
            AUTHORITY["EPSG","7030"]],
        AUTHORITY["EPSG","6326"]],
    PRIMEM["Greenwich",0,
        AUTHORITY["EPSG","8901"]],
    UNIT["degree",0.0174532925199433,
        AUTHORITY["EPSG","9122"]],
    AUTHORITY["EPSG","4326"]]
latitude: String (0.0)
longitude: String (0.0)
brightness: String (0.0)
scan: String (0.0)
track: String (0.0)
acq_date: String (0.0)
acq_time: String (0.0)
satellite: String (0.0)
confidence: String (0.0)
version: String (0.0)
bright_t31: String (0.0)
frp: String (0.0)
OGRFeature(Global_24h):1
  latitude (String) = -23.386
  longitude (String) = -46.197
  brightness (String) = 307.5
  scan (String) = 1.1
  track (String) = 1
  acq_date (String) = 2012-08-20
  acq_time (String) =  0140
  satellite (String) = T
  confidence (String) = 54
  version (String) = 5.0
  bright_t31 (String) = 285.7
  frp (String) = 16.5
```

You can also try to open the virtual layer with a desktop GIS supporting a GDAL/OGR virtual driver such as **Quantum GIS (QGIS)**. In the following screenshot, the Global_24h layer is displayed together with the shapefile of the countries that you can find in the dataset directory of the book:

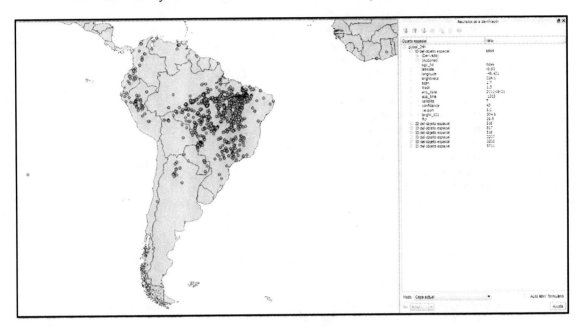

The global_24h dataset over the countries layers and information of the selected features

4. Now, export the virtual layer as a new table in PostGIS using the ogr2ogr GDAL/OGR command (in order for this command to become available, you need to add the GDAL installation folder to the PATH variable of your OS). You need to use the -f option to specify the output format, the -t_srs option to project the points to the EPSG:3857 spatial reference, the -where option to load only the records from the MODIS Terra satellite type, and the -lco layer creation option to provide the schema where you want to store the table:

```
$ ogr2ogr -f PostgreSQL -t_srs EPSG:3857
PG:"dbname='postgis_cookbook' user='me' password='mypassword'"
-lco SCHEMA=chp01 global_24h.vrt -where "satellite='T'"
-lco GEOMETRY_NAME=the_geom
```

5. Check how the `ogr2ogr` command created the table, as shown in the following command:

```
$ pg_dump -t chp01.global_24h --schema-only -U me postgis_cookbook

CREATE TABLE global_24h (
  ogc_fid integer NOT NULL,
  latitude character varying,
  longitude character varying,
  brightness character varying,
  scan character varying,
  track character varying,
  acq_date character varying,
  acq_time character varying,
  satellite character varying,
  confidence character varying,
  version character varying,
  bright_t31 character varying,
  frp character varying,
  the_geom public.geometry(Point,3857)
);
```

6. Now, check the record that should appear in the `geometry_columns` metadata view:

```
postgis_cookbook=# SELECT f_geometry_column, coord_dimension,
srid, type FROM geometry_columns
WHERE f_table_name = 'global_24h';
```

The output of the preceding command is as follows:

```
Chapter 1 — psql — 91×29
postgis_cookbook=# SELECT f_geometry_column, coord_dimension, srid, type FROM geometry_colu
mns WHERE f_table_name = 'global_24h'
;
 f_geometry_column | coord_dimension | srid | type
-------------------+-----------------+------+-------
 the_geom          |               2 | 3857 | POINT
(1 row)

postgis_cookbook=#
```

7. Check how many records have been imported in the table:

```
postgis_cookbook=# SELECT count(*) FROM chp01.global_24h;
```

The output of the preceding command is as follows:

```
● ● ●                          Chapter 1 — psql — 91×29
postgis_cookbook=# SELECT count(*) FROM chp01.global_24h;
 count

  9190
(1 row)

postgis_cookbook=#
```

8. Note how the coordinates have been projected from EPSG:4326 to EPSG:3857:

```
postgis_cookbook=# SELECT ST_AsEWKT(the_geom)
FROM chp01.global_24h LIMIT 1;
```

The output of the preceding command is as follows:

```
● ● ●                          Chapter 1 — psql — 91×29
postgis_cookbook=# SELECT ST_AsEWKT(the_geom) FROM chp01.global_24h LIMIT 1;
                    st_asewkt

 SRID=3857;POINT(-5142626.51617686 -2678766.03496892)
(1 row)

postgis_cookbook=#
```

How it works...

As mentioned in the GDAL documentation:

> *"OGR Virtual Format is a driver that transforms features read from other drivers based on criteria specified in an XML control file."*

GDAL supports the reading and writing of nonspatial tabular data stored as a CSV file, but we need to use a virtual format to derive the geometry of the layers from attribute columns in the CSV file (the longitude and latitude coordinates for each point). For this purpose, you need to at least specify in the driver the path to the CSV file (the SrcDataSource element), the geometry type (the GeometryType element), the spatial reference definition for the layer (the LayerSRS element), and the way the driver can derive the geometric information (the GeometryField element).

There are many other options and reasons for using OGR virtual formats; if you are interested in developing a better understanding, please refer to the GDAL documentation available at http://www.gdal.org/drv_vrt.html.

After a virtual format is correctly created, the original flat nonspatial dataset is spatially supported by GDAL and software-based on GDAL. This is the reason why we can manipulate these files with GDAL commands such as ogrinfo and ogr2ogr, and with desktop GIS software such as QGIS.

Once we have verified that GDAL can correctly read the features from the virtual driver, we can easily import them in PostGIS using the popular ogr2ogr command-line utility. The ogr2ogr command has a plethora of options, so refer to its documentation at http://www.gdal.org/ogr2ogr.html for a more in-depth discussion.

In this recipe, you have just seen some of these options, such as:

- -where: It is used to export just a selection of the original feature class
- -t_srs: It is used to reproject the data to a different spatial reference system
- -lco layer creation: It is used to provide the schema where we would want to store the table (without it, the new spatial table would be created in the public schema) and the name of the geometry field in the output layer

Importing shapefiles with shp2pgsql

If you need to import a shapefile in PostGIS, you have at least a couple of options such as the `ogr2ogr` GDAL command, as you have seen previously, or the `shp2pgsql` PostGIS command.

In this recipe, you will load a shapefile in the database using the `shp2pgsql` command, analyze it with the `ogrinfo` command, and display it in QGIS desktop software.

How to do it...

The steps you need to follow to complete this recipe are as follows:

1. Create a shapefile from the virtual driver created in the previous recipe using the `ogr2ogr` command (note that in this case, you do not need to specify the `-f` option as the shapefile is the default output format for the `ogr2ogr` command):

   ```
   $ ogr2ogr global_24h.shp global_24h.vrt
   ```

2. Generate the SQL dump file for the shapefile using the `shp2pgsql` command. You are going to use the `-G` option to generate a PostGIS spatial table using the geography type, and the `-I` option to generate the spatial index on the geometric column:

   ```
   $ shp2pgsql -G -I global_24h.shp
     chp01.global_24h_geographic > global_24h.sql
   ```

3. Analyze the `global_24h.sql` file (in Windows, use a text editor such as Notepad):

   ```
   $ head -n 20 global_24h.sql
   ```

The output of the preceding command is as follows:

```
bash-3.2$ head -n 20 global_24h.sql
SET CLIENT_ENCODING TO UTF8;
SET STANDARD_CONFORMING_STRINGS TO ON;
BEGIN;
CREATE TABLE "chp01"."global_24h_geographic" (gid serial,
"latitude" varchar(80),
"longitude" varchar(80),
"brightness" varchar(80),
"scan" varchar(80),
"track" varchar(80),
"acq_date" varchar(80),
"acq_time" varchar(80),
"satellite" varchar(80),
"confidence" varchar(80),
"version" varchar(80),
"bright_t31" varchar(80),
"frp" varchar(80),
"geog" geography(POINT,4326));
ALTER TABLE "chp01"."global_24h_geographic" ADD PRIMARY KEY (gid);
INSERT INTO "chp01"."global_24h_geographic" ("latitude","longitude","brightness","scan","tr
ack","acq_date","acq_time","satellite","confidence","version","bright_t31","frp",geog) VALU
ES ('-23.386','-46.197','307.5','1.1','1','2012-08-20','0140','T','54','5.0','285.7','16.5'
,'0101000020E6100000F0A7C64B371947C0894160E5D06237C0');
INSERT INTO "chp01"."global_24h_geographic" ("latitude","longitude","brightness","scan","tr
ack","acq_date","acq_time","satellite","confidence","version","bright_t31","frp",geog) VALU
ES ('-22.952','-47.574','330.1','1.2','1.1','2012-08-20','0140','T','100','5.0','285.2','53
.9','0101000020E6100000B6F3FDD478C947C0C1CAA145B6F336C0');
bash-3.2$ 
```

4. Run the `global_24h.sql` file in PostgreSQL:

   $ psql -U me -d postgis_cookbook -f global_24h.sql

   If you are on Linux, you may concatenate the commands from the last two
   steps in a single line in the following manner:
   $ shp2pgsql -G -I global_24h.shp
   chp01.global_24h_geographic | psql -U me -d
   postgis_cookbook

5. Check if the metadata record is visible in the `geography_columns` view (and not
   in the `geometry_columns` view, as with the -G option of the `shp2pgsql`
   command, we have opted for a `geography` type):

   **postgis_cookbook=# SELECT f_geography_column,   coord_dimension,
   srid, type FROM geography_columns
   WHERE f_table_name = 'global_24h_geographic';**

The output of the preceding command is as follows:

```
● ● ●                        Chapter 1 — psql — 91×29
postgis_cookbook=# SELECT f_geography_column,   coord_dimension, srid, type FROM geography_
columns   WHERE f_table_name = 'global_24h_geographic';
 f_geography_column | coord_dimension | srid | type
--------------------+-----------------+------+-------
 geog               |               2 | 4326 | Point
(1 row)

postgis_cookbook=#
```

6. Analyze the new PostGIS table with `ogrinfo` (use the `-fid` option just to display one record from the table):

```
$ ogrinfo PG:"dbname='postgis_cookbook' user='me'
    password='mypassword'" chp01.global_24h_geographic -fid 1
```

The output of the preceding command is as follows:

```
● ● ●                        Chapter 1 — bash — 91×29
Layer name: chp01.global_24h_geographic
Geometry: Point
Feature Count: 30326
Extent: (-155.284000, -40.751000) - (177.457000, 70.404000)
Layer SRS WKT:
GEOGCS["WGS 84",
    DATUM["WGS_1984",
        SPHEROID["WGS 84",6378137,298.257223563,
            AUTHORITY["EPSG","7030"]],
        AUTHORITY["EPSG","6326"]],
    PRIMEM["Greenwich",0,
        AUTHORITY["EPSG","8901"]],
    UNIT["degree",0.0174532925199433,
        AUTHORITY["EPSG","9122"]],
    AUTHORITY["EPSG","4326"]]
FID Column = gid
Geometry Column = geog
latitude: String (80.0)
longitude: String (80.0)
brightness: String (80.0)
scan: String (80.0)
track: String (80.0)
acq_date: String (80.0)
acq_time: String (80.0)
satellite: String (80.0)
confidence: String (80.0)
version: String (80.0)
bright_t31: String (80.0)
frp: String (80.0)
```

Now, open QGIS and try to add the new layer to the map. Navigate to **Layer** | **Add Layer** | **Add PostGIS layers** and provide the connection information, and then add the layer to the map as shown in the following screenshot:

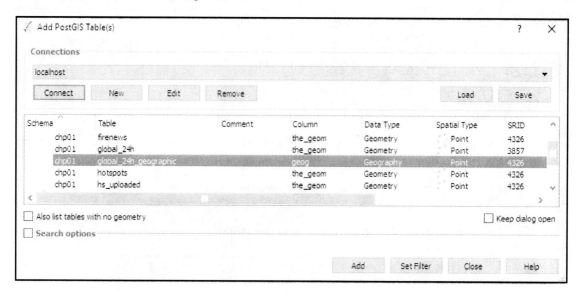

How it works...

The PostGIS command, `shp2pgsql`, allows the user to import a shapefile in the PostGIS database. Basically, it generates a PostgreSQL dump file that can be used to load data by running it from within PostgreSQL.

The SQL file will be generally composed of the following sections:

- The `CREATE TABLE` section (if the `-a` option is not selected, in which case, the table should already exist in the database)
- The `INSERT INTO` section (one `INSERT` statement for each feature to be imported from the shapefile)
- The `CREATE INDEX` section (if the `-I` option is selected)

 Unlike `ogr2ogr`, there is no way to make spatial or attribute selections (`-spat`, `-where ogr2ogr` options) for features in the shapefile to import. On the other hand, with the `shp2pgsql` command, it is possible to import the *m* coordinate of the features too (`ogr2ogr` only supports *x*, *y*, and *z* at the time of writing).

To get a complete list of the `shp2pgsql` command options and their meanings, just type the command name in the shell (or in the command prompt, if you are on Windows) and check the output.

There's more...

There are GUI tools to manage data in and out of PostGIS, generally integrated into GIS desktop software such as QGIS. In the last chapter of this book, we will take a look at the most popular one.

Importing and exporting data with the ogr2ogr GDAL command

In this recipe, you will use the popular `ogr2ogr` GDAL command for importing and exporting vector data from PostGIS.

Firstly, you will import a shapefile in PostGIS using the most significant options of the `ogr2ogr` command. Then, still using `ogr2ogr`, you will export the results of a spatial query performed in PostGIS to a couple of GDAL-supported vector formats.

How to do it...

The steps you need to follow to complete this recipe are as follows:

1. Unzip the `wborders.zip` archive to your working directory. You can find this archive in the book's dataset.
2. Import the world countries shapefile (`wborders.shp`) in PostGIS using the `ogr2ogr` command. Using some of the options from `ogr2ogr`, you will import only the features from SUBREGION=2 (Africa), and the ISO2 and NAME attributes, and rename the feature class to `africa_countries`:

```
$ ogr2ogr -f PostgreSQL -sql "SELECT ISO2,
NAME AS country_name FROM wborders WHERE REGION=2" -nlt
MULTIPOLYGON PG:"dbname='postgis_cookbook' user='me'
password='mypassword'" -nln africa_countries
-lco SCHEMA=chp01 -lco GEOMETRY_NAME=the_geom wborders.shp
```

3. Check if the shapefile was correctly imported in PostGIS, querying the spatial table in the database or displaying it in a desktop GIS.

4. Query PostGIS to get a list of the 100 active hotspots with the highest brightness temperature (the `bright_t31` field) from the `global_24h` table created in the previous recipe:

```
postgis_cookbook=# SELECTST_AsText(the_geom) AS the_geom, bright_t31
FROM chp01.global_24h
ORDER BY bright_t31 DESC LIMIT 100;
```

The output of the preceding command is as follows:

```
● ● ●                      Chapter 1 — more — 91×33
postgis_cookbook=# SELECT
postgis_cookbook-# ST_AsText(the_geom) AS the_geom, bright_t31
postgis_cookbook-# FROM chp01.global_24h
postgis_cookbook-# ORDER BY bright_t31 DESC LIMIT 100;
                   the_geom                   |  bright_t31
-----------------------------------------------+-------------
 POINT(-13361233.2019535 4991419.20457202)    |   360.6
 POINT(-13161080.7575072 8624445.64118912)    |   359.6
 POINT(-13359897.3680639 4991124.84275376)    |   357.4
 POINT(-13159077.0066729 8624904.79861514)    |   351.3
 POINT(-13360120.0070455 4989800.32453147)    |   347.7
 POINT(-13161859.9939427 8619855.65609598)    |   344.3
 POINT(-13361455.840935 4990094.64636667)     |   338.3
 POINT(-13359674.7290824 4992449.54093155)    |   332.2
 POINT(-13160635.479544 8618020.47050205)     |   331.5
 POINT(-13361010.5629719 4992743.942751)      |   330
 POINT(5311052.90574708 3695374.96924629)     |   328
 POINT(-13361121.8824627 4988623.12600837)    |   326
 POINT(5519665.63149368 3125470.87992288)     |   325.8
 POINT(-695524.178476373 5200607.76532119)    |   325.5
 POINT(5268083.58230088 3601878.73296264)     |   325.1
 POINT(5518552.43658574 3125595.83504836)     |   325
 POINT(5269642.05517199 3617174.6454432)      |   325
 POINT(5268083.58230088 3610561.39379457)     |   324.7
 POINT(8043835.08523116 5919740.7848368)      |   324.4
 POINT(-5933885.45673545 -1627849.34544934)   |   324.1
 POINT(5267526.98484691 3591778.16979249)     |   324.1
 POINT(5269085.45771802 3591648.728413)       |   324
 POINT(4936351.49973692 4236551.70176014)     |   324
 POINT(-13359786.0485731 4988328.84857754)    |   323.7
 POINT(8573938.50038872 5453224.87938544)     |   323.6
 POINT(5269976.01364437 3591130.97629928)     |   323.5
:
```

5. You want to figure out in which African countries these hotspots are located. For this purpose, you can do a spatial join with the `africa_countries` table produced in the previous step:

```
postgis_cookbook=# SELECT ST_AsText(f.the_geom)
AS the_geom, f.bright_t31, ac.iso2, ac.country_name
FROM chp01.global_24h as f
JOIN chp01.africa_countries as ac
ON ST_Contains(ac.the_geom, ST_Transform(f.the_geom, 4326))
ORDER BY f.bright_t31 DESCLIMIT 100;
```

The output of the preceding command is as follows:

```
● ● ●                        Chapter 1 — more — 104×33
postgis_cookbook=# SELECT
postgis_cookbook-# ST_AsText(f.the_geom) AS the_geom,    f.bright_t31, ac.iso2, ac.country_name
postgis_cookbook-# FROM chp01.global_24h as f
postgis_cookbook-# JOIN chp01.africa_countries as ac
postgis_cookbook-# ON ST_Contains(ac.the_geom, ST_Transform(f.the_geom,    4326))
postgis_cookbook-# ORDER BY f.bright_t31 DESC
postgis_cookbook-# LIMIT 100;
                the_geom              | bright_t31 | iso2 |       country_name
--------------------------------------+------------+------+-------------------------
 POINT(2297856.92895475 -1156211.27087933) | 316.1    | AO   | Angola
 POINT(3635694.56930832 -868851.746537112) | 315.4    | TZ   | United Republic of Tanzania
 POINT(2299860.67978903 -1163793.36952541) | 315      | AO   | Angola
 POINT(-626728.73316613 4186462.82578735)  | 314.9    | MA   | Morocco
 POINT(2299304.08233507 -1156437.57872925) | 314.7    | AO   | Angola
 POINT(-625281.579785818 4186054.31484101) | 314.6    | MA   | Morocco
 POINT(2298524.84589951 -1157003.35465544) | 314.1    | AO   | Angola
 POINT(3191863.75951553 -2855246.3351064)  | 314.1    | ZA   | South Africa
 POINT(3421738.50800364 -483589.255881647) | 313.9    | TZ   | United Republic of Tanzania
 POINT(3094459.20507142 -1438946.78512311) | 313.8    | ZM   | Zambia
 POINT(3640592.62690322 -951168.957166242) | 313.8    | TZ   | United Republic of Tanzania
 POINT(1900780.30529515 -1873614.98065512) | 313.8    | AO   | Angola
 POINT(3517807.22855824 -1173188.3759633)  | 313.7    | ZM   | Zambia
 POINT(2298636.16539031 -1155758.65949881) | 313.6    | AO   | Angola
 POINT(578861.352125023 4366594.3451834)   | 313.2    | DZ   | Algeria
 POINT(2301307.83316934 -1164019.72578116) | 313.2    | AO   | Angola
 POINT(3563225.58080189 -923375.606508147) | 313      | TZ   | United Republic of Tanzania
 POINT(773113.863559285 4361611.57547542)  | 313      | DZ   | Algeria
 POINT(172433.891238781 4289344.1566943)   | 312.9    | DZ   | Algeria
 POINT(487468.050183745 4412239.11061166)  | 312.8    | DZ   | Algeria
 POINT(2159375.48240792 -1213513.85253403) | 312.6    | AO   | Angola
 POINT(2089912.12015292 -1796386.26248973) | 312.6    | AO   | Angola
 POINT(3562112.38589396 -923263.118552325) | 312.4    | TZ   | United Republic of Tanzania
:
```

You will now export the result of this query to a vector format supported by GDAL, such as GeoJSON, in the WGS 84 spatial reference using `ogr2ogr`:

```
$ ogr2ogr -f GeoJSON -t_srs EPSG:4326 warmest_hs.geojson
PG:"dbname='postgis_cookbook' user='me' password='mypassword'" -sql "
SELECT f.the_geom as the_geom, f.bright_t31,
       ac.iso2, ac.country_name
FROM chp01.global_24h as f JOIN chp01.africa_countries as ac
ON ST_Contains(ac.the_geom, ST_Transform(f.the_geom, 4326))
ORDER BY f.bright_t31 DESC LIMIT 100"
```

6. Open the GeoJSON file and inspect it with your favorite desktop GIS. The following screenshot shows you how it looks with QGIS:

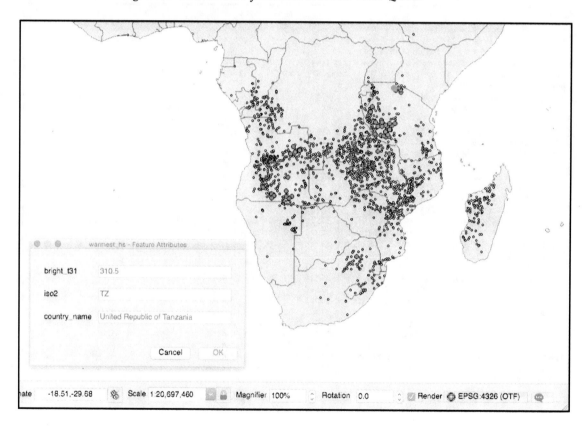

7. Export the previous query to a CSV file. In this case, you have to indicate how the geometric information must be stored in the file; this is done using the -lco GEOMETRY option:

```
$ ogr2ogr -t_srs EPSG:4326 -f CSV -lco GEOMETRY=AS_XY
-lco SEPARATOR=TAB warmest_hs.csv PG:"dbname='postgis_cookbook'
 user='me' password='mypassword'" -sql "
SELECT f.the_geom, f.bright_t31,
  ac.iso2, ac.country_name
FROM chp01.global_24h as f JOIN chp01.africa_countries as ac
ON ST_Contains(ac.the_geom, ST_Transform(f.the_geom, 4326))
ORDER BY f.bright_t31 DESC  LIMIT 100"
```

How it works...

GDAL is an open source library that comes together with several command-line utilities, which let the user translate and process raster and vector geodatasets into a plethora of formats. In the case of vector datasets, there is a GDAL sublibrary for managing vector datasets named OGR (therefore, when talking about vector datasets in the context of GDAL, we can also use the expression **OGR dataset**).

When you are working with an OGR dataset, two of the most popular OGR commands are ogrinfo, which lists many kinds of information from an OGR dataset, and ogr2ogr, which converts the OGR dataset from one format to another.

It is possible to retrieve a list of the supported OGR vector formats using the -formats option on any OGR commands, for example, with ogr2ogr:

```
$ ogr2ogr --formats
```

The output of the preceding command is as follows:

```
● ● ●                          Chapter 1 — bash — 104×38
Supported Formats:
  PCIDSK -raster,vector- (rw+v): PCIDSK Database File
  netCDF -raster,vector- (rw+s): Network Common Data Format
  JP2OpenJPEG -raster,vector- (rwv): JPEG-2000 driver based on OpenJPEG library
  JPEG2000 -raster,vector- (rwv): JPEG-2000 part 1 (ISO/IEC 15444-1), based on Jasper library
  ESRI Shapefile -vector- (rw+v): ESRI Shapefile
  MapInfo File -vector- (rw+v): MapInfo File
  UK .NTF -vector- (ro): UK .NTF
  OGR_SDTS -vector- (ro): SDTS
  S57 -vector- (rw+v): IHO S-57 (ENC)
  DGN -vector- (rw+): Microstation DGN
  OGR_VRT -vector- (rov): VRT - Virtual Datasource
  REC -vector- (ro): EPIInfo .REC
  Memory -vector- (rw+): Memory
  BNA -vector- (rw+v): Atlas BNA
  CSV -vector- (rw+v): Comma Separated Value (.csv)
  NAS -vector- (ro): NAS - ALKIS
  GML -vector- (rw+v): Geography Markup Language (GML)
  GPX -vector- (rw+v): GPX
  LIBKML -vector- (rw+v): Keyhole Markup Language (LIBKML)
  KML -vector- (rw+v): Keyhole Markup Language (KML)
  GeoJSON -vector- (rw+v): GeoJSON
  Interlis 1 -vector- (rw+): Interlis 1
  Interlis 2 -vector- (rw+): Interlis 2
  OGR_GMT -vector- (rw+): GMT ASCII Vectors (.gmt)
  GPKG -raster,vector- (rw+vs): GeoPackage
  SQLite -vector- (rw+v): SQLite / Spatialite
  OGR_DODS -vector- (ro): OGR_DODS
  ODBC -vector- (rw+): ODBC
  WAsP -vector- (rw+v): WAsP .map format
  MSSQLSpatial -vector- (rw+): Microsoft SQL Server Spatial Database
  OGR_OGDI -vector- (ro): OGDI Vectors (VPF, VMAP, DCW)
  PostgreSQL -vector- (rw+): PostgreSQL/PostGIS
  OpenFileGDB -vector- (rov): ESRI FileGDB
  XPlane -vector- (rov): X-Plane/Flightgear aeronautical data
  DXF -vector- (rw+v): AutoCAD DXF
  Geoconcept -vector- (rw+): Geoconcept
  GeoRSS -vector- (rw+v): GeoRSS
```

Note that some formats are read-only, while others are read/write.

PostGIS is one of the supported read/write OGR formats, so it is possible to use the OGR API or any OGR commands (such as `ogrinfo` and `ogr2ogr`) to manipulate its datasets.

The `ogr2ogr` command has many options and parameters; in this recipe, you have seen some of the most notable ones such as `-f` to define the output format, `-t_srs` to reproject/transform the dataset, and `-sql` to define an (eventually spatial) query in the input OGR dataset.

When using `ogrinfo` and `ogr2ogr` together with the desired option and parameters, you have to define the datasets. When specifying a PostGIS dataset, you need a connection string that is defined as follows:

```
PG:"dbname='postgis_cookbook' user='me' password='mypassword'"
```

See also

You can find more information about the `ogrinfo` and `ogr2ogr` commands on the GDAL website available at `http://www.gdal.org`.

If you need more information about the PostGIS driver, you should check its related documentation page available at `http://www.gdal.org/drv_pg.html`.

Handling batch importing and exporting of datasets

In many GIS workflows, there is a typical scenario where subsets of a PostGIS table must be deployed to external users in a filesystem format (most typically, shapefiles or a spatialite database). Often, there is also the reverse process, where datasets received from different users have to be uploaded to the PostGIS database.

In this recipe, we will simulate both of these data flows. You will first create the data flow for processing the shapefiles out of PostGIS, and then the reverse data flow for uploading the shapefiles.

You will do it using the power of bash scripting and the `ogr2ogr` command.

Getting ready

If you didn't follow all the other recipes, be sure to import the hotspots (Global_24h.csv) and the countries dataset (countries.shp) in PostGIS. The following is how to do it with ogr2ogr (you should import both the datasets in their original SRID, 4326, to make spatial operations faster):

1. Import in PostGIS the Global_24h.csv file, using the global_24.vrt virtual driver you created in a previous recipe:

```
$ ogr2ogr -f PostgreSQL PG:"dbname='postgis_cookbook'
user='me' password='mypassword'" -lco SCHEMA=chp01 global_24h.vrt
-lco OVERWRITE=YES -lco GEOMETRY_NAME=the_geom -nln hotspots
```

2. Import the countries shapefile using ogr2ogr:

```
$ ogr2ogr -f PostgreSQL -sql "SELECT ISO2, NAME AS country_name
FROM wborders" -nlt MULTIPOLYGON PG:"dbname='postgis_cookbook'
user='me' password='mypassword'" -nln countries
-lco SCHEMA=chp01 -lco OVERWRITE=YES
-lco GEOMETRY_NAME=the_geom wborders.shp
```

If you already imported the hotspots dataset using the 3857 SRID, you can use the PostGIS 2.0 method that allows the user to modify the geometry type column of an existing spatial table. You can update the SRID definition for the hotspots table in this way thanks to the support of typmod on geometry objects:

```
postgis_cookbook=# ALTER TABLE chp01.hotspots
ALTER COLUMN the_geom
SET DATA TYPE geometry(Point, 4326)
USING ST_Transform(the_geom, 4326);
```

How to do it...

The steps you need to follow to complete this recipe are as follows:

1. Check how many hotspots there are for each distinct country by using the following query:

```
postgis_cookbook=> SELECT c.country_name, MIN(c.iso2)
as iso2, count(*) as hs_count FROM chp01.hotspots as hs
JOIN chp01.countries as c ON ST_Contains(c.the_geom, hs.the_geom)
GROUP BY c.country_name ORDER BY c.country_name;
```

The output of the preceding command is as follows:

```
●  ●  ●                      Chapter 1 — more — 104×38
postgis_cookbook=# SELECT c.name, MIN(c.iso2) as iso2, count(*) as hs_count
FROM chp01.hotspots as hs JOIN chp01.countries as c ON ST_Contains(c.the_geom, hs.the_geom) GROUP BY c.n
ame ORDER BY c.name;
              name                | iso2 | hs_count
----------------------------------+------+----------
 Albania                          | AL   |       68
 Algeria                          | DZ   |      358
 Angola                           | AO   |     4555
 Argentina                        | AR   |       94
 Australia                        | AU   |     2272
 Austria                          | AT   |        8
 Belarus                          | BY   |        3
 Belgium                          | BE   |        2
 Bolivia                          | BO   |       54
 Bosnia and Herzegovina           | BA   |       61
 Botswana                         | BW   |       41
 Brazil                           | BR   |     4954
 Brunei Darussalam                | BN   |        1
 Bulgaria                         | BG   |       32
 Burundi                          | BI   |       11
 Cambodia                         | KH   |        7
 Canada                           | CA   |      657
 Chile                            | CL   |        2
 China                            | CN   |      197
 Colombia                         | CO   |       31
 Congo                            | CG   |      414
 Costa Rica                       | CR   |        3
 Cote d'Ivoire                    | CI   |        3
 Croatia                          | HR   |        1
 Cuba                             | CU   |        1
 Cyprus                           | CY   |        1
 Czech Republic                   | CZ   |        1
 Democratic Republic of the Congo | CD   |     3227
 Dominican Republic               | DO   |        8
 Ecuador                          | EC   |       34
 Egypt                            | EG   |        5
 Ethiopia                         | ET   |        8
```

2. Using the same query, generate a CSV file using the PostgreSQL COPY command or the `ogr2ogr` command (in the first case, make sure that the Postgre service user has full write permission to the output directory). If you are following the COPY approach and using Windows, be sure to replace `/tmp/hs_countries.csv` with a different path:

```
$ ogr2ogr -f CSV hs_countries.csv
PG:"dbname='postgis_cookbook' user='me' password='mypassword'"
-lco SCHEMA=chp01 -sql "SELECT c.country_name, MIN(c.iso2) as iso2,
count(*) as hs_count FROM chp01.hotspots as hs
JOIN chp01.countries as c ON ST_Contains(c.the_geom, hs.the_geom)
GROUP BY c.country_name ORDER BY c.country_name"
postgis_cookbook=> COPY (SELECT c.country_name, MIN(c.iso2) as iso2,
count(*) as hs_count  FROM chp01.hotspots as hs
JOIN chp01.countries as c  ON ST_Contains(c.the_geom, hs.the_geom)
```

```
GROUP BY c.country_name   ORDER BY c.country_name)
TO '/tmp/hs_countries.csv' WITH CSV HEADER;
```

3. If you are using Windows, go to step 5. With Linux, create a bash script named `export_shapefiles.sh` that iterates each record (country) in the `hs_countries.csv` file and generates a shapefile with the corresponding hotspots exported from PostGIS for that country:

```
#!/bin/bash
while IFS="," read country iso2 hs_count
do
   echo "Generating shapefile $iso2.shp for country
   $country ($iso2) containing $hs_count features."
   ogr2ogr out_shapefiles/$iso2.shp
   PG:"dbname='postgis_cookbook' user='me' password='mypassword'"
   -lco SCHEMA=chp01 -sql "SELECT ST_Transform(hs.the_geom, 4326),
   hs.acq_date, hs.acq_time, hs.bright_t31
   FROM chp01.hotspots as hs JOIN chp01.countries as c
   ON ST_Contains(c.the_geom, ST_Transform(hs.the_geom, 4326))
   WHERE c.iso2 = '$iso2'" done < hs_countries.csv
```

4. Give execution permissions to the `bash` file, and then run it after creating an output directory (`out_shapefiles`) for the shapefiles that will be generated by the script. Then, go to *step 7*:

```
chmod 775 export_shapefiles.sh
mkdir out_shapefiles
$ ./export_shapefiles.sh
Generating shapefile AL.shp for country
   Albania (AL) containing 66 features.
Generating shapefile DZ.shp for country
   Algeria (DZ) containing 361 features.
...
Generating shapefile ZM.shp for country
   Zambia (ZM) containing 1575 features.
Generating shapefile ZW.shp for country
   Zimbabwe (ZW) containing 179 features.
```

If you get the output `ERROR: function getsrid(geometry) does not exist LINE 1: SELECT getsrid("the_geom") FROM (SELECT, ...,` you will need to load legacy support in PostGIS, for example, in a Debian Linux box:
`psql -d postgis_cookbook -f /usr/share/postgresql/9.1/contrib/postgis-2.1/legacy.sql`

5. If you are using Windows, create a batch file named `export_shapefiles.bat` that iterates each record (country) in the `hs_countries.csv` file and generates a shapefile with the corresponding hotspots exported from PostGIS for that country:

```
@echo off
for /f "tokens=1-3 delims=, skip=1" %%a in (hs_countries.csv) do (
   echo "Generating shapefile %%b.shp for country %%a
        (%%b) containing %%c features"
   ogr2ogr .\out_shapefiles\%%b.shp
   PG:"dbname='postgis_cookbook' user='me' password='mypassword'"
   -lco SCHEMA=chp01 -sql "SELECT ST_Transform(hs.the_geom, 4326),
   hs.acq_date, hs.acq_time, hs.bright_t31
   FROM chp01.hotspots as hs JOIN chp01.countries as c
   ON ST_Contains(c.the_geom, ST_Transform(hs.the_geom, 4326))
   WHERE c.iso2 = '%%b'"
)
```

6. Run the batch file after creating an output directory (`out_shapefiles`) for the shapefiles that will be generated by the script:

```
>mkdir out_shapefiles
>export_shapefiles.bat
"Generating shapefile AL.shp for country
 Albania (AL) containing 66 features"
"Generating shapefile DZ.shp for country
 Algeria (DZ) containing 361 features"
...
"Generating shapefile ZW.shp for country
 Zimbabwe (ZW) containing 179 features"
```

7. Try to open a couple of these output shapefiles in your favorite desktop GIS. The following screenshot shows you how they look in QGIS:

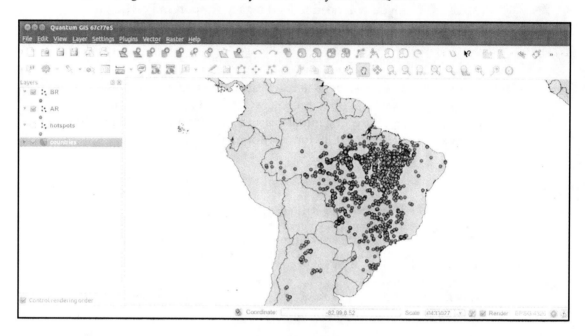

8. Now, you will do the return trip, uploading all of the generated shapefiles to PostGIS. You will upload all of the features for each shapefile and include the upload datetime and the original shapefile name. First, create the following PostgreSQL table, where you will upload the shapefiles:

```
postgis_cookbook=# CREATE TABLE chp01.hs_uploaded
(
  ogc_fid serial NOT NULL,
  acq_date character varying(80),
  acq_time character varying(80),
  bright_t31 character varying(80),
  iso2 character varying,
  upload_datetime character varying,
  shapefile character varying,
  the_geom geometry(POINT, 4326),
  CONSTRAINT hs_uploaded_pk PRIMARY KEY (ogc_fid)
);
```

9. If you are using Windows, go to step 12. With OS X, you will need to install `findutils` with `homebrew` and run the script for Linux:

```
$ brew install findutils
```

10. With Linux, create another bash script named `import_shapefiles.sh`:

```
#!/bin/bash
for f in `find out_shapefiles -name \*.shp -printf "%f\n"`
do
   echo "Importing shapefile $f to chp01.hs_uploaded PostGIS
     table..." #, ${f%.*}"
   ogr2ogr -append -update  -f PostgreSQL
   PG:"dbname='postgis_cookbook' user='me'
   password='mypassword'" out_shapefiles/$f
   -nln chp01.hs_uploaded -sql "SELECT acq_date, acq_time,
   bright_t31, '${f%.*}' AS iso2, '`date`' AS upload_datetime,
   'out_shapefiles/$f' as shapefile FROM ${f%.*}"
done
```

11. Assign the execution permission to the bash script and execute it:

```
$ chmod 775 import_shapefiles.sh
$ ./import_shapefiles.sh
Importing shapefile DO.shp to chp01.hs_uploaded PostGIS table
. . .
Importing shapefile ID.shp to chp01.hs_uploaded PostGIS table
. . .
Importing shapefile AR.shp to chp01.hs_uploaded PostGIS table
. . . . . .
```

   Now, go to *step 14*.

12. If you are using Windows, create a batch script named `import_shapefiles.bat`:

```
@echo off
for %%I in (out_shapefiles\*.shp*) do (
   echo Importing shapefile %%~nxI to chp01.hs_uploaded
   PostGIS table...

   ogr2ogr -append -update  -f PostgreSQL
   PG:"dbname='postgis_cookbook' user='me'
   password='password'" out_shapefiles/%%~nxI
```

```
-nln chp01.hs_uploaded -sql "SELECT acq_date, acq_time,
bright_t31, '%%~nI' AS iso2, '%date%' AS upload_datetime,
'out_shapefiles/%%~nxI' as shapefile FROM %%~nI"
)
```

13. Run the batch script:

```
>import_shapefiles.bat
Importing shapefile AL.shp to chp01.hs_uploaded PostGIS table...
Importing shapefile AO.shp to chp01.hs_uploaded PostGIS table...
Importing shapefile AR.shp to chp01.hs_uploaded PostGIS table......
```

14. Check some of the records that have been uploaded to the PostGIS table by using SQL:

```
postgis_cookbook=# SELECT upload_datetime,
shapefile, ST_AsText(wkb_geometry)
FROM chp01.hs_uploaded WHERE ISO2='AT';
```

The output of the preceding command is as follows:

```
● ● ●                              Chapter 1 — psql — 104×38
postgis_cookbook=# SELECT upload_datetime, shapefile, ST_AsText(the_geom) FROM chp01.hs_uploaded WHERE I
SO2='AT';
        upload_datetime      |        shapefile       |       st_astext
-----------------------------+------------------------+---------------------
 Fri Jun 23 11:27:48 COT 2017 | out_shapefiles/AT.shp | POINT(14.333 48.279)
 Fri Jun 23 11:27:48 COT 2017 | out_shapefiles/AT.shp | POINT(14.347 48.277)
 Fri Jun 23 11:27:48 COT 2017 | out_shapefiles/AT.shp | POINT(14.327 48.277)
 Fri Jun 23 11:27:48 COT 2017 | out_shapefiles/AT.shp | POINT(14.349 48.272)
 Fri Jun 23 11:27:48 COT 2017 | out_shapefiles/AT.shp | POINT(14.345 48.275)
 Fri Jun 23 11:27:48 COT 2017 | out_shapefiles/AT.shp | POINT(14.333 48.269)
 Fri Jun 23 11:27:48 COT 2017 | out_shapefiles/AT.shp | POINT(14.343 48.275)
 Fri Jun 23 11:27:48 COT 2017 | out_shapefiles/AT.shp | POINT(14.329 48.271)
(8 rows)

postgis_cookbook=#
```

15. Check the same query with `ogrinfo` as well:

```
$ ogrinfo PG:"dbname='postgis_cookbook' user='me'
password='mypassword'"
chp01.hs_uploaded -where "iso2='AT'"
```

The output of the preceding command is as follows:

```
● ● ●                                    Chapter 1 — bash — 104×38
Layer name: chp01.hs_uploaded
Geometry: Point
Feature Count: 8
Extent: (-155.284000, -40.751000) - (177.457000, 70.404000)
Layer SRS WKT:
GEOGCS["WGS 84",
    DATUM["WGS_1984",
        SPHEROID["WGS 84",6378137,298.257223563,
            AUTHORITY["EPSG","7030"]],
        AUTHORITY["EPSG","6326"]],
    PRIMEM["Greenwich",0,
        AUTHORITY["EPSG","8901"]],
    UNIT["degree",0.0174532925199433,
        AUTHORITY["EPSG","9122"]],
    AUTHORITY["EPSG","4326"]]
FID Column = ogc_fid
Geometry Column = the_geom
acq_date: String (80.0)
acq_time: String (80.0)
bright_t31: String (80.0)
iso2: String (0.0)
upload_datetime: String (0.0)
shapefile: String (0.0)
OGRFeature(chp01.hs_uploaded):4706
  acq_date (String) = 2012-08-20
  acq_time (String) = 0110
  bright_t31 (String) = 292.7
  iso2 (String) = AT
  upload_datetime (String) = Fri Jun 23 11:27:48 COT 2017
  shapefile (String) = out_shapefiles/AT.shp
  POINT (14.333 48.279)

OGRFeature(chp01.hs_uploaded):4707
  acq_date (String) = 2012-08-20
  acq_time (String) = 0110
  bright_t31 (String) = 291.8
  iso2 (String) = AT
  upload_datetime (String) = Fri Jun 23 11:27:48 COT 2017
```

How it works...

You could implement both the data flows (processing shapefiles out from PostGIS, and then into it again) thanks to the power of the `ogr2ogr` GDAL command.

You have been using this command in different forms and with the most important input parameters in other recipes, so you should now have a good understanding of it.

Here, it is worth mentioning the way OGR lets you export the information related to the current datetime and the original shapefile name to the PostGIS table. Inside the `import_shapefiles.sh` (Linux, OS X) or the `import_shapefiles.bat` (Windows) scripts, the core is the line with the `ogr2ogr` command (here is the Linux version):

```
ogr2ogr -append -update  -f PostgreSQL PG:"dbname='postgis_cookbook'
user='me' password='mypassword'" out_shapefiles/$f -nln chp01.hs_uploaded -
sql "SELECT acq_date, acq_time, bright_t31, '${f%.*}' AS iso2, '`date`' AS
upload_datetime, 'out_shapefiles/$f' as shapefile FROM ${f%.*}"
```

Thanks to the -sql option, you can specify the two additional fields, getting their values from the system date command and the filename that is being iterated from the script.

Exporting data to a shapefile with the pgsql2shp PostGIS command

In this recipe, you will export a PostGIS table to a shapefile using the pgsql2shp command that is shipped with any PostGIS distribution.

How to do it...

The steps you need to follow to complete this recipe are as follows:

1. In case you still haven't done it, export the countries shapefile to PostGIS using the ogr2ogr or the shp2pgsql commands. The shp2pgsql approach is as shown:

```
$ shp2pgsql -I -d -s 4326 -W LATIN1 -g the_geom countries.shp
chp01.countries > countries.sql
$ psql -U me -d postgis_cookbook -f countries.sql
```

2. The ogr2ogr approach is as follows:

```
$ ogr2ogr -f PostgreSQL PG:"dbname='postgis_cookbook' user='me'
password='mypassword'"
-lco SCHEMA=chp01 countries.shp -nlt MULTIPOLYGON -lco OVERWRITE=YES
-lco GEOMETRY_NAME=the_geom
```

3. Now, query PostGIS in order to get a list of countries grouped by the subregion field. For this purpose, you will merge the geometries for features having the same subregion code, using the ST_Union PostGIS geometric processing function:

```
postgis_cookbook=> SELECT subregion,
  ST_Union(the_geom) AS the_geom, SUM(pop2005) AS pop2005
  FROM chp01.countries GROUP BY subregion;
```

4. Execute the `pgsql2shp` PostGIS command to export into a shapefile the result of the given query:

```
$ pgsql2shp -f subregions.shp -h localhost -u me -P mypassword
postgis_cookbook "SELECT MIN(subregion) AS subregion,
ST_Union(the_geom) AS the_geom, SUM(pop2005) AS pop2005
FROM chp01.countries GROUP BY subregion;"

Initializing...
Done (postgis major version: 2).
Output shape: Polygon
Dumping: X [23 rows].
```

5. Open the shapefile and inspect it with your favorite desktop GIS. This is how it looks in QGIS after applying a graduated classification symbology style based on the aggregated population for each subregion:

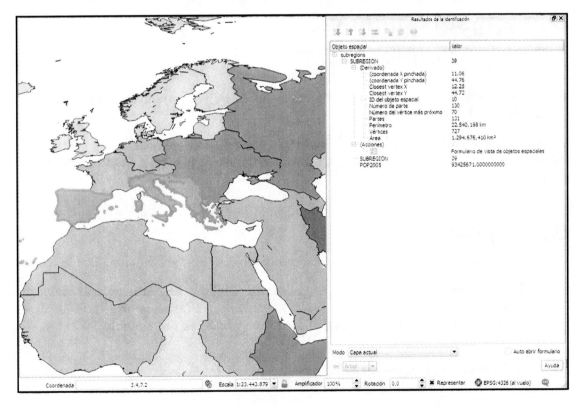

Visualization in QGIS of the classification of subregions based on population and information of the selected feature

How it works...

You have exported the results of a spatial query to a shapefile using the `pgsql2shp` PostGIS command. The spatial query you have used aggregates fields using the `SUM` PostgreSQL function for summing country populations in the same subregion, and the `ST_Union` PostGIS function to aggregate the corresponding geometries as a geometric union.

The `pgsql2shp` command allows you to export PostGIS tables and queries to shapefiles. The options you need to specify are quite similar to the ones you use to connect to PostgreSQL with `psql`. To get a full list of these options, just type `pgsql2shp` in your command prompt and read the output.

Importing OpenStreetMap data with the osm2pgsql command

In this recipe, you will import **OpenStreetMap (OSM)** data to PostGIS using the `osm2pgsql` command.

You will first download a sample dataset from the OSM website, and then you will import it using the `osm2pgsql` command.

You will add the imported layers in GIS desktop software and generate a view to get subdatasets, using the `hstore` PostgreSQL additional module to extract features based on their tags.

Getting ready

We need the following in place before we can proceed with the steps required for the recipe:

1. Install `osm2pgsql`. If you are using Windows, follow the instructions available at `http://wiki.openstreetmap.org/wiki/Osm2pgsql`. If you are on Linux, you can install it from the preceding website or from packages. For example, for Debian distributions, use the following:

    ```
    $ sudo apt-get install osm2pgsql
    ```

2. For more information about the installation of the `osm2pgsql` command for other Linux distributions, macOS X, and MS Windows, please refer to the `osm2pgsql` web page available at http://wiki.openstreetmap.org/wiki/Osm2pgsql.

3. It's most likely that you will need to compile `osm2pgsql` yourself as the one that is installed with your package manager could already be obsolete. In my Linux Mint 12 box, this was the case (it was `osm2pgsql` v0.75), so I have installed Version 0.80 by following the instructions on the `osm2pgsql` web page. You can check the installed version just by typing the following command:

```
$ osm2pgsqlosm2pgsql SVN version 0.80.0 (32bit id space)
```

4. We will create a different database only for this recipe, as we will use this OSM database in other chapters. For this purpose, create a new database named `rome` and assign privileges to your user:

```
postgres=# CREATE DATABASE rome OWNER me;
postgres=# \connect rome;
rome=# create extension postgis;
```

5. You will not create a different schema in this new database, though, as the `osm2pgsql` command can only import OSM data in the public schema at the time of writing.

6. Be sure that your PostgreSQL installation supports `hstore` (besides `PostGIS`). If not, download and install it; for example, in Debian-based Linux distributions, you will need to install the `postgresql-contrib-9.6` package. Then, add `hstore` support to the `rome` database using the CREATE EXTENSION syntax:

```
$ sudo apt-get update
$ sudo apt-get install postgresql-contrib-9.6
$ psql -U me -d romerome=# CREATE EXTENSION hstore;
```

How to do it...

The steps you need to follow to complete this recipe are as follows:

1. Download an .osm file from the OpenStreetMap website (https://www. openstreetmap.org/#map=5/21.843/82.795).

   1. Go to the OpenStreetMap website.

2. Select the area of interest for which you want to export data. You should not select a large area, as the live export from the website is limited to 50,000 nodes.

If you want to export larger areas, you should consider downloading the whole database, built daily at `planet.osm` (250 GB uncompressed and 16 GB compressed). At `planet.osm`, you may also download extracts that contain OpenstreetMap data for individual continents, countries, and metropolitan areas.

3. If you want to get the same dataset used for this recipe, just copy and paste the following URL in your browser:
   `http://www.openstreetmap.org/export?lat=41.88745&lon=12.4899&` `zoom=15&layers=M`; or, get it from the book datasets (`chp01/map.osm` file).
4. Click on the **Export** link.
5. Select **OpenStreetMap XML Data** as the output format.
6. Download the `map.osm` file to your working directory.

2. Run `osm2pgsql` to import the OSM data in the PostGIS database. Use the `−hstore` option, as you wish to add tags with an additional `hstore` (key/value) column in the PostgreSQL tables:

```
$ osm2pgsql -d rome -U me --hstore map.osm
osm2pgsql SVN version 0.80.0 (32bit id space)Using projection
SRS 900913 (Spherical Mercator)Setting up table:
planet_osm_point...All indexes on planet_osm_polygon created
in 1sCompleted planet_osm_polygonOsm2pgsql took 3s overall
```

3. At this point, you should have the following geometry tables in your database:

```
rome=# SELECT f_table_name, f_geometry_column,
coord_dimension, srid, type FROM geometry_columns;
```

The output of the preceding command is shown here:

f_table_name	f_geometry_column	coord_dimension	srid	type
planet_osm_roads	way	2	900913	LINESTRING
planet_osm_point	way	2	900913	POINT
planet_osm_polygon	way	2	900913	GEOMETRY
planet_osm_line	way	2	900913	LINESTRING
(4 rows)				

4. Note that the `osm2pgsql` command imports everything in the public schema. If you did not deal differently with the command's input parameter, your data will be imported in the Mercator Projection (`3857`).

5. Open the PostGIS tables and inspect them with your favorite desktop GIS. The following screenshot shows how it looks in QGIS. All the different thematic features are mixed at this time, so it looks a bit confusing:

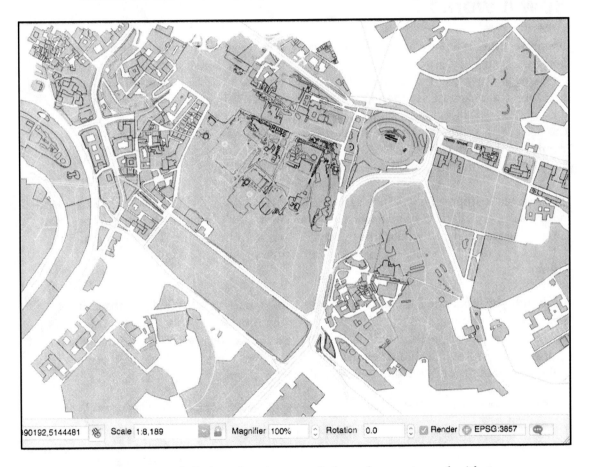

6. Generate a PostGIS view that extracts all the polygons tagged with `trees` as `land cover`. For this purpose, create the following view:

```
rome=# CREATE VIEW rome_trees AS SELECT way, tags
FROM planet_osm_polygon WHERE (tags -> 'landcover') = 'trees';
```

7. Open the view with a desktop GIS that supports PostGIS views, such as QGIS, and add your `rome_trees` view. The previous screenshot shows you how it looks.

How it works...

OpenStreetMap is a popular collaborative project for creating a free map of the world. Every user participating in the project can edit data; at the same time, it is possible for everyone to download those datasets in `.osm` datafiles (an XML format) under the terms of the **Open Data Commons Open Database License (ODbL)** at the time of writing.

The `osm2pgsql` command is a command-line tool that can import `.osm` datafiles (eventually zipped) to the PostGIS database. To use the command, it is enough to give the PostgreSQL connection parameters and the `.osm` file to import.

It is possible to import only features that have certain tags in the spatial database, as defined in the `default.style` configuration file. You can decide to comment in or out the OSM tagged features that you would like to import, or not, from this file. The command by default exports all the nodes and ways to linestring, point, and geometry PostGIS geometries.

It is highly recommended to enable `hstore` support in the PostgreSQL database and use the `-hstore` option of `osm2pgsql` when importing the data. Having enabled this support, the OSM tags for each feature will be stored in a `hstore` PostgreSQL data type, which is optimized for storing (and retrieving) sets of key/values pairs in a single field. This way, it will be possible to query the database as follows:

```
SELECT way, tags FROM planet_osm_polygon WHERE (tags -> 'landcover') =
'trees';
```

Importing raster data with the raster2pgsql PostGIS command

PostGIS 2.0 now has full support for raster datasets, and it is possible to import raster datasets using the `raster2pgsql` command.

In this recipe, you will import a raster file to PostGIS using the `raster2pgsql` command. This command, included in any PostGIS distribution from version 2.0 onward, is able to generate an SQL dump to be loaded in PostGIS for any GDAL raster-supported format (in the same fashion that the `shp2pgsql` command does for shapefiles).

After loading the raster to PostGIS, you will inspect it both with SQL commands (analyzing the raster metadata information contained in the database), and with the `gdalinfo` command-line utility (to understand the way the input `raster2pgsql` parameters have been reflected in the PostGIS import process).

You will finally open the raster in a desktop GIS and try a basic spatial query, mixing vector and raster tables.

Getting ready

We need the following in place before we can proceed with the steps required for the recipe:

1. From the worldclim website, download the current raster data (`http://www.worldclim.org/current`) for min and max temperatures (only the raster for max temperatures will be used for this recipe). Alternatively, use the ones provided in the book datasets (`data/chp01`). Each of the two archives (`data/tmax_10m_bil.zip` and `data/tmin_10m_bil.zip`) contain 12 rasters in the BIL format, one for each month. You can look for more information at `http://www.worldclim.org/formats`.
2. Extract the two archives to a directory named `worldclim` in your working directory.
3. Rename each raster dataset to a name format with two digits for the month, for example, `tmax1.bil` and `tmax1.hdr` will become `tmax01.bil` and `tmax01.hdr`.
4. If you still haven't loaded the countries shapefile to PostGIS from a previous recipe, do it using the `ogr2ogr` or `shp2pgsql` commands. The following is the `shp2pgsql` syntax:

```
$ shp2pgsql -I -d -s 4326 -W LATIN1 -g the_geom countries.shp
chp01.countries > countries.sql
$ psql -U me -d postgis_cookbook -f countries.sql
```

How to do it...

The steps you need to follow to complete this recipe are as follows:

1. Get information about one of the rasters using the `gdalinfo` command-line tool as follows:

```
$ gdalinfo worldclim/tmax09.bil

Driver: EHdr/ESRI .hdr Labelled
Files: worldclim/tmax9.bil
       worldclim/tmax9.hdr
Size is 2160, 900
Coordinate System is:
GEOGCS[""WGS 84"",
  DATUM[""WGS_1984"",
    SPHEROID[""WGS 84"",6378137,298.257223563,
      AUTHORITY[""EPSG"",""7030""]],
    TOWGS84[0,0,0,0,0,0,0],
    AUTHORITY[""EPSG"",""6326""]],
  PRIMEM[""Greenwich"",0,
    AUTHORITY[""EPSG"",""8901""]],
  UNIT[""degree"",0.0174532925199433,
  AUTHORITY[""EPSG"",""9108""]],
AUTHORITY[""EPSG"",""4326""]]
Origin = (-180.000000000000057,90.000000000000000)
Pixel Size = (0.166666666666667,-0.166666666666667)
Corner Coordinates:
  Upper Left  (-180.0000000,  90.0000000) (180d 0' 0.00""W, 90d
                                          0' 0.00""N)
  Lower Left  (-180.0000000, -60.0000000) (180d 0' 0.00""W, 60d
                                          0' 0.00""S)
  Upper Right ( 180.0000000,  90.0000000) (180d 0' 0.00""E, 90d
                                          0' 0.00""N)
  Lower Right ( 180.0000000, -60.0000000) (180d 0' 0.00""E, 60d
                                          0' 0.00""S)
  Center      ( 0.0000000,   15.0000000) ( 0d 0' 0.00""E, 15d
                                          0' 0.00""N)
Band 1 Block=2160x1 Type=Int16, ColorInterp=Undefined
Min=-153.000 Max=441.000
NoData Value=-9999
```

2. The `gdalinfo` command provides a lot of useful information about the raster, for example, the GDAL driver being used to read it, the files composing it (in this case, two files with `.bil` and `.hdr` extensions), the size in pixels (2160 x 900), the spatial reference (WGS 84), the geographic extents, the origin, and the pixel size (needed to correctly georeference the raster), and for each raster band (just one in the case of this file), some statistical information like the min and max values (-153.000 and 441.000, corresponding to a temperature of -15.3 °C and 44.1 °C. Values are expressed as temperature * 10 in °C, according to the documentation available at http://worldclim.org/).

3. Use the `raster2pgsql` file to generate the `.sql` dump file and then import the raster in PostGIS:

```
$ raster2pgsql -I -C -F -t 100x100 -s 4326
worldclim/tmax01.bil chp01.tmax01 > tmax01.sql
$ psql -d postgis_cookbook -U me -f tmax01.sql
```

If you are in Linux, you may pipe the two commands in a unique line:

```
$ raster2pgsql -I -C -M -F -t 100x100 worldclim/tmax01.bil
chp01.tmax01 | psql -d postgis_cookbook -U me -f tmax01.sql
```

4. Check how the new table has been created in PostGIS:

```
$ pg_dump -t chp01.tmax01 --schema-only -U me postgis_cookbook
...
CREATE TABLE tmax01 (
  rid integer NOT NULL,
  rast public.raster,
  filename text,
  CONSTRAINT enforce_height_rast CHECK (
    (public.st_height(rast) = 100)
  ),
  CONSTRAINT enforce_max_extent_rast CHECK (public.st_coveredby
    (public.st_convexhull(rast), ''0103...''::public.geometry)
  ),
  CONSTRAINT enforce_nodata_values_rast CHECK (
    ((public._raster_constraint_nodata_values(rast)
      )::numeric(16,10)[] = ''{0}''::numeric(16,10)[])
    ),
  CONSTRAINT enforce_num_bands_rast CHECK (
    (public.st_numbands(rast) = 1)
```

```
  ),
  CONSTRAINT enforce_out_db_rast CHECK (
    (public._raster_constraint_out_db(rast) = ''{f}''::boolean[])
    ),
  CONSTRAINT enforce_pixel_types_rast CHECK (
    (public._raster_constraint_pixel_types(rast) =
    ''{16BUI}''::text[])
    ),
  CONSTRAINT enforce_same_alignment_rast CHECK (
    (public.st_samealignment(rast, ''01000...''::public.raster)
  ),
  CONSTRAINT enforce_scalex_rast CHECK (
    ((public.st_scalex(rast))::numeric(16,10) =
      0.166666666666667::numeric(16,10))
    ),
  CONSTRAINT enforce_scaley_rast CHECK (
    ((public.st_scaley(rast))::numeric(16,10) =
      (-0.166666666666667)::numeric(16,10))
    ),
  CONSTRAINT enforce_srid_rast CHECK ((public.st_srid(rast) = 0)),
  CONSTRAINT enforce_width_rast CHECK ((public.st_width(rast) = 100))
);
```

5. Check if a record for this PostGIS raster appears in the `raster_columns`
   metadata view, and note the main metadata information that has been stored
   there, such as schema, name, raster column name (default is raster), SRID, scale
   (for *x* and *y*), block size (for *x* and *y*), band numbers (1), band types (`16BUI`), zero
   data values (0), and `db` storage type (`out_db` is `false`, as we have stored the
   raster bytes in the database; you could have used the `-R` option to register the
   raster as an out-of-db filesystem):

```
postgis_cookbook=# SELECT * FROM raster_columns;
```

6. If you have followed this recipe from the beginning, you should now have 198
   rows in the raster table, with each row representing one raster block size (100 x
   100 pixels blocks, as indicated with the `-t raster2pgsql` option):

```
postgis_cookbook=# SELECT count(*) FROM chp01.tmax01;
```

The output of the preceding command is as follows:

```
count
-------
198
(1 row)
```

7. Try to open the raster table with `gdalinfo`. You should see the same information you got from `gdalinfo` when you were analyzing the original BIL file. The only difference is the block size, as you moved to a smaller one (100 x 100) from the original (2160 x 900). That's why the original file has been split into several datasets (198):

```
gdalinfo PG":host=localhost port=5432 dbname=postgis_cookbook
user=me password=mypassword schema='chp01' table='tmax01'"
```

8. The `gdalinfo` command reads the PostGIS raster as being composed of multiple raster subdatasets (198, one for each row in the table). You still have the possibility of reading the whole table as a single raster, using the `mode=2` option in the PostGIS raster connection string (`mode=1` is the default). Check the difference:

```
gdalinfo PG":host=localhost port=5432 dbname=postgis_cookbook
user=me password=mypassword schema='chp01' table='tmax01' mode=2"
```

9. You can easily obtain a visual representation of those blocks by converting the extent of all the 198 rows in the `tmax01` table (each representing a raster block) to a shapefile using `ogr2ogr`:

```
$ ogr2ogr temp_grid.shp PG:"host=localhost port=5432
dbname='postgis_cookbook' user='me' password='mypassword'"
-sql "SELECT rid, filename, ST_Envelope(rast) as the_geom
FROM chp01.tmax01"
```

10. Now, try to open the raster table with QGIS (at the time of writing, one of the few desktop GIS tools that has support for it) together with the blocks shapefile generated in the previous steps (`temp_grid.shp`). You should see something like the following screenshot:

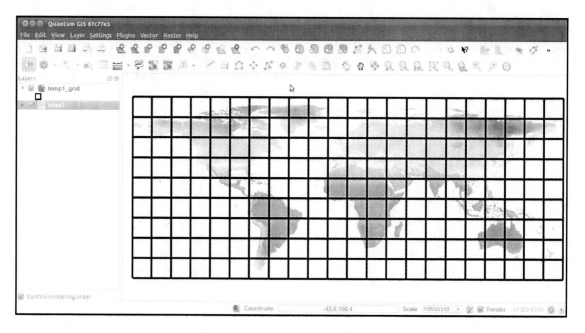

If you are using QGIS 2.6 or higher, you can see the layer in the **DB Manager** under the **Database** menu and drag it to the **Layers** panel.

11. As the last bonus step, you will select the 10 countries with the lowest average max temperature in January (using the centroid of the polygon representing the country):

```
SELECT * FROM (
  SELECT c.name, ST_Value(t.rast,
    ST_Centroid(c.the_geom))/10 as tmax_jan FROM chp01.tmax01 AS t
  JOIN chp01.countries AS c
  ON ST_Intersects(t.rast, ST_Centroid(c.the_geom))
) AS foo
ORDER BY tmax_jan LIMIT 10;
```

The output is as follows:

```
name                                        | tmax_jan
--------------------------------------------+----------
Greenland                                   |    -29.8
  ...
Korea                                       |     -8.5
Democratic People's Republic of Kyrgyzstan  |     -7.9
Finland                                     |     -6.8
(10 rows)
```

How it works...

The `raster2pgsql` command is able to load any raster formats supported by GDAL in PostGIS. You can have a format list supported by your GDAL installation by typing the following command:

```
$ gdalinfo --formats
```

In this recipe, you have been importing one raster file using some of the most common `raster2pgsql` options:

```
$ raster2pgsql -I -C -F -t 100x100 -s 4326 worldclim/tmax01.bil
chp01.tmax01 > tmax01.sql
```

The -I option creates a GIST spatial index for the raster column. The -C option will create the standard set of constraints after the rasters have been loaded. The -F option will add a column with the filename of the raster that has been loaded. This is useful when you are appending many raster files to the same PostGIS raster table. The -s option sets the raster's SRID.

If you decide to include the -t option, then you will cut the original raster into tiles, each inserted as a single row in the raster table. In this case, you decided to cut the raster into 100 x 100 tiles, resulting in 198 table rows in the raster table.

Another important option is -R, which will register the raster as out-of-db; in such a case, only the metadata will be inserted in the database, while the raster will be out of the database.

The raster table contains an identifier for each row, the raster itself (eventually one of its tiles, if using the -t option), and eventually the original filename, if you used the -F option, as in this case.

You can analyze the PostGIS raster using SQL commands or the gdalinfo command. Using SQL, you can query the raster_columns view to get the most significant raster metadata (spatial reference, band number, scale, block size, and so on).

With gdalinfo, you can access the same information, using a connection string with the following syntax:

```
gdalinfo PG":host=localhost port=5432 dbname=postgis_cookbook user=me
password=mypassword schema='chp01' table='tmax01' mode=2"
```

The mode parameter is not influential if you loaded the whole raster as a single block (for example, if you did not specify the -t option). But, as in the use case of this recipe, if you split it into tiles, gdalinfo will see each tile as a single subdataset with the default behavior (mode=1). If you want GDAL to consider the raster table as a unique raster dataset, you have to specify the mode option and explicitly set it to 2.

Importing multiple rasters at a time

This recipe will guide you through the importing of multiple rasters at a time.

You will first import some different single band rasters to a unique single band raster table using the raster2pgsql command.

Then, you will try an alternative approach, merging the original single band rasters in a virtual raster, with one band for each of the original rasters, and then load the multiband raster to a raster table. To accomplish this, you will use the GDAL gdalbuildvrt command and then load the data to PostGIS with raster2pgsql.

Getting ready

Be sure to have all the original raster datasets you have been using for the previous recipe.

How to do it...

The steps you need to follow to complete this recipe are as follows:

1. Import all the maximum average temperature rasters in a single PostGIS raster table using `raster2pgsql` and then `psql` (eventually, pipe the two commands if you are in Linux):

```
$ raster2pgsql -d -I -C -M -F -t 100x100 -s 4326
worldclim/tmax*.bil chp01.tmax_2012 > tmax_2012.sql
$ psql -d postgis_cookbook -U me -f tmax_2012.sql
```

2. Check how the table was created in PostGIS, querying the `raster_columns` table. Here we are querying only some significant fields:

```
postgis_cookbook=# SELECT r_raster_column, srid,
ROUND(scale_x::numeric, 2) AS scale_x,
ROUND(scale_y::numeric, 2) AS scale_y, blocksize_x,
blocksize_y, num_bands, pixel_types, nodata_values, out_db
FROM raster_columns where r_table_schema='chp01'
AND r_table_name ='tmax_2012';
```

r_raster_column	srid	scale_x	scale_y	blocksize_x	blocksize_y	num_bands	pixel_types	nodata_values	out_db
rast	4326	0.17	-0.17	100	100	1	{16BSI}	{-9999}	{f}
(1 row)									

3. Check some raster statistics using the `ST_MetaData` function:

```
SELECT rid, (foo.md).*
FROM (SELECT rid, ST_MetaData(rast) As md
FROM chp01.tmax_2012) As foo;
```

Moving Data In and Out of PostGIS

 Note that there is different metadata for each raster record loaded in the table.

The output of the preceding command is as shown here:

rid	upperleftx	upperlefty	width	height	scalex	scaley	skewx	skewy	srid	numbands
1	-180	90	100	100	0.166666666666667	-0.166666666666667	0	0	4326	1
2	-163.333333333333	90	100	100	0.166666666666667	-0.166666666666667	0	0	4326	1
3	-146.666666666667	90	100	100	0.166666666666667	-0.166666666666667	0	0	4326	1
4	-130	90	100	100	0.166666666666667	-0.166666666666667	0	0	4326	1
5	-113.333333333333	90	100	100	0.166666666666667	-0.166666666666667	0	0	4326	1
6	-96.6666666666666	90	100	100	0.166666666666667	-0.166666666666667	0	0	4326	1
7	-79.9999999999999	90	100	100	0.166666666666667	-0.166666666666667	0	0	4326	1
8	-63.3333333333332	90	100	100	0.166666666666667	-0.166666666666667	0	0	4326	1
9	-46.6666666666665	90	100	100	0.166666666666667	-0.166666666666667	0	0	4326	1
10	-29.9999999999998	90	100	100	0.166666666666667	-0.166666666666667	0	0	4326	1
11	-13.3333333333331	90	100	100	0.166666666666667	-0.166666666666667	0	0	4326	1
12	3.33333333333363	90	100	100	0.166666666666667	-0.166666666666667	0	0	4326	1

4. If you now query the table, you would be able to derive the month for each raster row only from the `original_file` column. In the table, you have imported 198 distinct records (rasters) for each of the 12 original files (we divided them into 100 x 100 blocks, if you remember). Test this with the following query:

```
postgis_cookbook=# SELECT COUNT(*) AS num_raster,
MIN(filename) as original_file FROM chp01.tmax_2012
GROUP BY filename ORDER BY filename;
```

```
 num_raster | original_file
------------+---------------
        198 | tmax01.bil
        198 | tmax02.bil
        198 | tmax03.bil
        198 | tmax04.bil
        198 | tmax05.bil
        198 | tmax06.bil
        198 | tmax07.bil
        198 | tmax08.bil
        198 | tmax09.bil
        198 | tmax10.bil
        198 | tmax11.bil
        198 | tmax12.bil
(12 rows)
```

5. With this approach, using the `filename` field, you could use the `ST_Value` PostGIS raster function to get the average monthly maximum temperature of a certain geographic zone for the whole year:

```
SELECT REPLACE(REPLACE(filename, 'tmax', ''), '.bil', '') AS month,
(ST_VALUE(rast, ST_SetSRID(ST_Point(12.49, 41.88), 4326))/10) AS tmax
FROM chp01.tmax_2012
WHERE rid IN (
  SELECT rid FROM chp01.tmax_2012
  WHERE ST_Intersects(ST_Envelope(rast),
      ST_SetSRID(ST_Point(12.49, 41.88), 4326))
)
ORDER BY month;
```

The output of the preceding command is as shown here:

month	tmax
01	11.8
02	13.2
03	15.3
04	18.5
05	22.9
06	27
07	30
08	29.8
09	26.4
10	21.7
11	16.6
12	12.9
(12 rows)	

6. A different approach is to store each month value in a different raster band. The `raster2pgsql` command doesn't let you load to different bands in an existing table. But, you can use GDAL by combining the `gdalbuildvrt` and the `gdal_translate` commands. First, use `gdalbuildvrt` to create a new virtual raster composed of 12 bands, one for each month:

```
$ gdalbuildvrt -separate tmax_2012.vrt worldclim/tmax*.bil
```

7. Analyze the `tmax_2012.vrt` XML file with a text editor. It should have a virtual band (`VRTRasterBand`) for each physical raster pointing to it:

```
<VRTDataset rasterXSize="2160" rasterYSize="900">
  <SRS>GEOGCS...</SRS>
  <GeoTransform>
    -1.8000000000000006e+02, 1.6666666666666699e-01, ...
  </GeoTransform>
  <VRTRasterBand dataType="Int16" band="1">
    <NoDataValue>-9.99900000000000E+03</NoDataValue>
    <ComplexSource>
      <SourceFilename relativeToVRT="1">
        worldclim/tmax01.bil
      </SourceFilename>
      <SourceBand>1</SourceBand>
      <SourceProperties RasterXSize="2160" RasterYSize="900"
       DataType="Int16" BlockXSize="2160" BlockYSize="1" />
      <SrcRect xOff="0" yOff="0" xSize="2160" ySize="900" />
      <DstRect xOff="0" yOff="0" xSize="2160" ySize="900" />
      <NODATA>-9999</NODATA>
    </ComplexSource>
  </VRTRasterBand>
<VRTRasterBand dataType="Int16" band="2">
...
```

8. Now, with `gdalinfo`, analyze this output virtual raster to check if it is effectively composed of 12 bands:

```
$ gdalinfo tmax_2012.vrt
```

The output of the preceding command is as follows:

```
Driver: VRT/Virtual Raster
Files: tmax_2012.vrt
        worldclim/tmax01.bil
        worldclim/tmax02.bil
        worldclim/tmax03.bil
        worldclim/tmax04.bil
        worldclim/tmax05.bil
        worldclim/tmax06.bil
        worldclim/tmax07.bil
        worldclim/tmax08.bil
        worldclim/tmax09.bil
        worldclim/tmax10.bil
        worldclim/tmax11.bil
        worldclim/tmax12.bil
Size is 2160, 900
Coordinate System is:
GEOGCS["WGS 84",
    DATUM["WGS_1984",
        SPHEROID["WGS 84",6378137,298.257223563,
            AUTHORITY["EPSG","7030"]],
        AUTHORITY["EPSG","6326"]],
    PRIMEM["Greenwich",0,
        AUTHORITY["EPSG","8901"]],
    UNIT["degree",0.0174532925199433,
        AUTHORITY["EPSG","9122"]],
    AUTHORITY["EPSG","4326"]]
Origin = (-180.000000000000057,90.000000000000000)
Pixel Size = (0.166666666666667,-0.166666666666667)
Corner Coordinates:
Upper Left  (-180.0000000,  90.0000000) (180d 0' 0.00"W, 90d 0' 0.00"N)
Lower Left  (-180.0000000, -60.0000000) (180d 0' 0.00"W, 60d 0' 0.00"S)
Upper Right ( 180.0000000,  90.0000000) (180d 0' 0.00"E, 90d 0' 0.00"N)
Lower Right ( 180.0000000, -60.0000000) (180d 0' 0.00"E, 60d 0' 0.00"S)
Center      (   0.0000000,  15.0000000) (  0d 0' 0.00"E, 15d 0' 0.00"N)
Band 1 Block=128x128 Type=Int16, ColorInterp=Undefined
  Min=-478.000 Max=418.000
```
...

9. Import the virtual raster composed of 12 bands, each referring to one of the 12 original rasters, to a PostGIS raster table composed of 12 bands. For this purpose, you can use the `raster2pgsql` command:

```
$ raster2pgsql -d -I -C -M -F -t 100x100 -s 4326 tmax_2012.vrt
chp01.tmax_2012_multi > tmax_2012_multi.sql
$ psql -d postgis_cookbook -U me -f tmax_2012_multi.sql
```

10. Query the `raster_columns` view to get some indicators for the imported raster. Note that the `num_bands` is now 12:

```
postgis_cookbook=# SELECT r_raster_column, srid, blocksize_x,
blocksize_y, num_bands, pixel_types
from raster_columns where r_table_schema='chp01'
AND r_table_name ='tmax_2012_multi';
```

```
 r_raster_column | srid | blocksize_x | blocksize_y | num_bands |                                    pixel_types
-----------------+------+-------------+-------------+-----------+--------------------------------------------------------------------------------------
 rast            | 4326 |         100 |         100 |        12 | {16BSI,16BSI,16BSI,16BSI,16BSI,16BSI,16BSI,16BSI,16BSI,16BSI,16BSI,16BSI}
```

11. Now, let's try to produce the same output as the query using the previous approach. This time, given the table structure, we keep the results in a single row:

```
postgis_cookbook=# SELECT
 (ST_VALUE(rast, 1, ST_SetSRID(ST_Point(12.49, 41.88), 4326))/10)
AS jan,
 (ST_VALUE(rast, 2, ST_SetSRID(ST_Point(12.49, 41.88), 4326))/10)
AS feb,
 (ST_VALUE(rast, 3, ST_SetSRID(ST_Point(12.49, 41.88), 4326))/10)
AS mar,
 (ST_VALUE(rast, 4, ST_SetSRID(ST_Point(12.49, 41.88), 4326))/10)
AS apr,
 (ST_VALUE(rast, 5, ST_SetSRID(ST_Point(12.49, 41.88), 4326))/10)
AS may,
 (ST_VALUE(rast, 6, ST_SetSRID(ST_Point(12.49, 41.88), 4326))/10)
AS jun,
 (ST_VALUE(rast, 7, ST_SetSRID(ST_Point(12.49, 41.88), 4326))/10)
AS jul,
 (ST_VALUE(rast, 8, ST_SetSRID(ST_Point(12.49, 41.88), 4326))/10)
AS aug,
 (ST_VALUE(rast, 9, ST_SetSRID(ST_Point(12.49, 41.88), 4326))/10)
AS sep,
 (ST_VALUE(rast, 10, ST_SetSRID(ST_Point(12.49, 41.88), 4326))/10)
AS oct,
 (ST_VALUE(rast, 11, ST_SetSRID(ST_Point(12.49, 41.88), 4326))/10)
AS nov,
 (ST_VALUE(rast, 12, ST_SetSRID(ST_Point(12.49, 41.88), 4326))/10)
AS dec
FROM chp01.tmax_2012_multi WHERE rid IN (
   SELECT rid FROM chp01.tmax_2012_multi
   WHERE ST_Intersects(rast, ST_SetSRID(ST_Point(12.49, 41.88), 4326))
   );
```

The output of the preceding command is as follows:

```
 jan  |  feb  |  mar  |  apr  |  maj  |  jun  | jul  |  aug  |  sep  |  oct  |  nov  |  dec
------+-------+-------+-------+-------+------+------+-------+-------+-------+-------+------
 11.8 | 13.2  | 15.3  | 18.5  | 22.9  |  27  |  30  | 29.8  | 26.4  | 21.7  | 16.6  | 12.9
(1 row)
```

How it works...

You can import raster datasets in PostGIS using the `raster2pgsql` command.

The GDAL PostGIS raster so far does not support writing operations; therefore, for now, you cannot use GDAL commands such as `gdal_translate` and `gdalwarp`.
This is going to change in the near future, so you may have such an extra option when you are reading this chapter.

In a scenario where you have multiple rasters representing the same variable at different times, as in this recipe, it makes sense to store all of the original rasters as a single table in PostGIS. In this recipe, we have the same variable (average maximum temperature) represented by a single raster for each month. You have seen that you could proceed in two different ways:

1. Append each single raster (representing a different month) to the same PostGIS single band raster table and derive the information related to the month from the value in the filename column (added to the table using the `-F raster2pgsql` option).
2. Generate a multiband raster using `gdalbuildvrt` (one raster with 12 bands, one for each month), and import it in a single multiband PostGIS table using the `raster2pgsql` command.

Exporting rasters with the gdal_translate and gdalwarp GDAL commands

In this recipe, you will see a couple of main options for exporting PostGIS rasters to different raster formats. They are both provided as command-line tools, `gdal_translate` and `gdalwarp`, by GDAL.

Getting ready

You need the following in place before you can proceed with the steps required for the recipe:

1. You need to have gone through the previous recipe and imported `tmax` 2012 datasets (12 `.bil` files) as a single multiband (12 bands) raster in PostGIS.

2. You must have the PostGIS raster format enabled in GDAL. For this purpose, check the output of the following command:

   ```
   $ gdalinfo --formats | grep -i postgis
   ```

   The output of the preceding command is as follows:

   ```
   PostGISRaster (rw): PostGIS Raster driver
   ```

3. You should have already learned how to use the GDAL PostGIS raster driver in the previous two recipes. You need to use a connection string composed of the following parameters:

   ```
   $ gdalinfo PG:"host=localhost port=5432
   dbname='postgis_cookbook' user='me' password='mypassword'
   schema='chp01' table='tmax_2012_multi' mode='2'"
   ```

4. Refer to the previous two recipes for more information about the preceding parameters.

How to do it...

The steps you need to follow to complete this recipe are as follows:

1. As an initial test, you will export the first six months of the `tmax` for 2012 (the first six bands in the `tmax_2012_multi` PostGIS raster table) using the `gdal_translate` command:

```
$ gdal_translate -b 1 -b 2 -b 3 -b 4 -b 5 -b 6
PG:"host=localhost port=5432 dbname='postgis_cookbook'
user='me' password='mypassword' schema='chp01'
table='tmax_2012_multi' mode='2'" tmax_2012_multi_123456.tif
```

2. As the second test, you will export all of the bands, but only for the geographic area containing Italy. Use the `ST_Extent` command to get the geographic extent of that zone:

```
postgis_cookbook=# SELECT ST_Extent(the_geom)
FROM chp01.countries WHERE name = 'Italy';
```

The output of the preceding command is as follows:

```
                             st_extent
------------------------------------------------------------------
 BOX(6.61975999999996 36.6491620000001,18.512218 47.0016630000001)
(1 row)
```

3. Now use the `gdal_translate` command with the `-projwin` option to obtain the desired purpose:

```
$ gdal_translate -projwin 6.619 47.095 18.515 36.649
PG:"host=localhost port=5432 dbname='postgis_cookbook'
user='me' password='mypassword' schema='chp01'
table='tmax_2012_multi' mode='2'" tmax_2012_multi.tif
```

4. There is another GDAL command, `gdalwarp`, that is still a convert utility with reprojection and advanced warping functionalities. You can use it, for example, to export a PostGIS raster table, reprojecting it to a different spatial reference system. This will convert the PostGIS raster table to GeoTiff and reproject it from `EPSG:4326` to `EPSG:3857`:

```
gdalwarp -t_srs EPSG:3857 PG:"host=localhost port=5432
dbname='postgis_cookbook' user='me' password='mypassword'
schema='chp01' table='tmax_2012_multi' mode='2'"
tmax_2012_multi_3857.tif
```

How it works...

Both `gdal_translate` and `gdalwarp` can transform rasters from a PostGIS raster to all GDAL-supported formats. To get a complete list of the supported formats, you can use the `--formats` option of GDAL's command line as follows:

```
$ gdalinfo --formats
```

For both these GDAL commands, the default output format is GeoTiff; if you need a different format, you must use the `-of` option and assign to it one of the outputs produced by the previous command line.

In this recipe, you have tried some of the most common options for these two commands. As they are complex tools, you may try some more command options as a bonus step.

See also

To get a better understanding, you should check out the excellent documentation on the GDAL website:

- Information about the `gdal_translate` command is available at
  http://www.gdal.org/gdal_translate.html
- Information about the `gdalwarp` command is available at
  http://www.gdal.org/gdalwarp.html

Structures That Work

2

In this chapter, we will cover:

- Using geospatial views
- Using triggers to populate the geometry column
- Structuring spatial data with table inheritance
- Extending inheritance – table partitioning
- Normalizing imports
- Normalizing internal overlays
- Using polygon overlays for proportional census estimates

Introduction

This chapter focuses on ways to structure data using the functionality provided by the combination of PostgreSQL and PostGIS. These will be useful approaches for structuring and cleaning up imported data, converting tabular data into spatial data *on the fly* when it is entered, and maintaining relationships between tables and datasets using functionality endemic to the powerful combination of PostgreSQL and PostGIS. There are three categories of techniques with which we will leverage these functionalities: automatic population and modification of data using views and triggers, object orientation using PostgreSQL table inheritance, and using PostGIS functions (stored procedures) to reconstruct and normalize problematic data.

Automatic population of data is where the chapter begins. By leveraging PostgreSQL views and triggers, we can create ad hoc and flexible solutions to create connections between and within the tables. By extension, and for more formal or structured cases, PostgreSQL provides table inheritance and table partitioning, which allow for explicit hierarchical relationships between tables. This can be useful in cases where an object inheritance model enforces data relationships that either represent the data better, thereby resulting in greater efficiencies, or reduce the administrative overhead of maintaining and accessing the datasets over time. With PostGIS extending that functionality, the inheritance can apply not just to the commonly used table attributes, but to leveraging spatial relationships between tables, resulting in greater query efficiency with very large datasets. Finally, we will explore PostGIS SQL patterns that provide table normalization of data inputs, so datasets that come from flat filesystems or are not normalized can be converted to a form we would expect in a database.

Using geospatial views

Views in PostgreSQL allow the ad hoc representation of data and data relationships in alternate forms. In this recipe, we'll be using views to allow for the automatic creation of point data based on tabular inputs. We can imagine a case where the input stream of data is non-spatial, but includes longitude and latitude or some other coordinates. We would like to automatically show this data as points in space.

Getting ready

We can create a view as a representation of spatial data pretty easily. The syntax for creating a view is similar to creating a table, for example:

```
CREATE VIEW viewname AS
    SELECT...
```

In the preceding command line, our SELECT query manipulates the data for us. Let's start with a small dataset. In this case, we will start with some random points, which could be real data.

First, we create the table from which the view will be constructed, as follows:

```
-- Drop the table in case it exists
DROP TABLE IF EXISTS chp02.xwhyzed CASCADE;
CREATE TABLE chp02.xwhyzed
-- This table will contain numeric x, y, and z values
(
  x numeric,
  y numeric,
  z numeric
)
WITH (OIDS=FALSE);
ALTER TABLE chp02.xwhyzed OWNER TO me;
-- We will be disciplined and ensure we have a primary key
ALTER TABLE chp02.xwhyzed ADD COLUMN gid serial;
ALTER TABLE chp02.xwhyzed ADD PRIMARY KEY (gid);
```

Now, let's populate this with the data for testing using the following query:

```
INSERT INTO chp02.xwhyzed (x, y, z)
  VALUES (random()*5, random()*7, random()*106);
INSERT INTO chp02.xwhyzed (x, y, z)
  VALUES (random()*5, random()*7, random()*106);
INSERT INTO chp02.xwhyzed (x, y, z)
  VALUES (random()*5, random()*7, random()*106);
INSERT INTO chp02.xwhyzed (x, y, z)
  VALUES (random()*5, random()*7, random()*106);
```

How to do it...

Now, to create the view, we will use the following query:

```
-- Ensure we don't try to duplicate the view
DROP VIEW IF EXISTS chp02.xbecausezed;
-- Retain original attributes, but also create a point   attribute from x
and y
CREATE VIEW chp02.xbecausezed AS
SELECT x, y, z, ST_MakePoint(x,y)
FROM chp02.xwhyzed;
```

How it works...

Our view is really a simple transformation of the existing data using PostGIS's `ST_MakePoint` function. The `ST_MakePoint` function takes the input of two numbers to create a PostGIS point, and in this case our view simply uses our x and y values to populate the data. Any time there is an update to the table to add a new record with x and y values, the view will populate a point, which is really useful for data that is constantly being updated.

There are two disadvantages to this approach. The first is that we have not declared our spatial reference system in the view, so any software consuming these points will not know the coordinate system we are using, that is, whether it is a geographic (latitude/longitude) or a planar coordinate system. We will address this problem shortly. The second problem is that many software systems accessing these points may not automatically detect and use the spatial information from the table. This problem is addressed in the *Using triggers to populate the geometry column* recipe.

The **spatial reference system identifier** (**SRID**) allows us to specify the coordinate system for a given dataset. The numbering system is a simple integer value to specify a given coordinate system. SRIDs are derived originally from the **European Petroleum Survey Group** (**EPSG**) and are now maintained by the Surveying and Positioning Committee of the International Association of **Oil and Gas Producers** (**OGP**). Useful tools for SRIDs are spatial reference (http://spatialreference.org) and Prj2EPSG (http://prj2epsg.org/search).

There's more...

To address the first problem mentioned in the *How it works...* section, we can simply wrap our existing `ST_MakePoint` function in another function specifying the SRID as `ST_SetSRID`, as shown in the following query:

```
-- Ensure we don't try to duplicate the view
DROP VIEW IF EXISTS chp02.xbecausezed;
-- Retain original attributes, but also create a point    attribute from x
and y
CREATE VIEW chp02.xbecausezed AS
  SELECT x, y, z, ST_SetSRID(ST_MakePoint(x,y), 3734) -- Add ST_SetSRID
  FROM chp02.xwhyzed;
```

See also

- The *Using triggers to populate the geometry column* recipe

Using triggers to populate the geometry column

In this recipe, we imagine that we have ever increasing data in our database, which needs spatial representation; however, in this case we want a hardcoded geometry column to be updated each time an insertion happens on the database, converting our x and y values to geometry as and when they are inserted into the database.

The advantage of this approach is that the geometry is then registered in the geometry_columns view, and therefore this approach works reliably with more PostGIS client types than creating a new geospatial view. This also provides the advantage of allowing for a spatial index that can significantly speed up a variety of queries.

Getting ready

We will start by creating another table of random points with x, y, and z values, as shown in the following query:

```
DROP TABLE IF EXISTS chp02.xwhyzed1 CASCADE;
CREATE TABLE chp02.xwhyzed1
(
   x numeric,
   y numeric,
   z numeric
)
WITH (OIDS=FALSE);
ALTER TABLE chp02.xwhyzed1 OWNER TO me;
ALTER TABLE chp02.xwhyzed1 ADD COLUMN gid serial;
ALTER TABLE chp02.xwhyzed1 ADD PRIMARY KEY (gid);

INSERT INTO chp02.xwhyzed1 (x, y, z)
   VALUES (random()*5, random()*7, random()*106);
INSERT INTO chp02.xwhyzed1 (x, y, z)
   VALUES (random()*5, random()*7, random()*106);
INSERT INTO chp02.xwhyzed1 (x, y, z)
   VALUES (random()*5, random()*7, random()*106);
```

```
INSERT INTO chp02.xwhyzed1 (x, y, z)
  VALUES (random()*5, random()*7, random()*106);
```

How to do it...

Now we need a geometry column to populate. By default, the geometry column will be populated with null values. We populate a geometry column using the following query:

```
SELECT AddGeometryColumn ('chp02','xwhyzed1','geom',3734,'POINT',2);
```

We now have a column called geom with an SRID of 3734; that is, a point geometry type in two dimensions. Since we have x, y, and z data, we could, in principle, populate a 3D point table using a similar approach.

Since all the geometry values are currently null, we will populate them using an UPDATE statement as follows:

```
UPDATE chp02.xwhyzed1
  SET the_geom = ST_SetSRID(ST_MakePoint(x,y), 3734);
```

The query here is simple when broken down. We update the xwhyzed1 table and set the the_geom column using ST_MakePoint, construct our point using the x and y columns, and wrap it in an ST_SetSRID function in order to apply the appropriate spatial reference information. So far, we have just set the table up. Now, we need to create a trigger in order to continue to populate this information once the table is in use. The first part of the trigger is a new populated geometry function using the following query:

```
CREATE OR REPLACE FUNCTION chp02.before_insertXYZ()
  RETURNS trigger AS
$$
BEGIN

if NEW.geom is null then
   NEW.geom = ST_SetSRID(ST_MakePoint(NEW.x,NEW.y), 3734);
end if;
RETURN NEW;
END;

$$
LANGUAGE 'plpgsql';
```

In essence, we have created a function that does exactly what we did manually: update the table's geometry column with the combination of ST_SetSRID and ST_MakePoint, but only to the new registers being inserted, and not to all the table.

There's more...

While we have a function created, we have not yet applied it as a trigger to the table. Let us do that here as follows:

```
CREATE TRIGGER popgeom_insert
  BEFORE INSERT ON chp02.xwhyzed1
  FOR EACH ROW EXECUTE PROCEDURE chp02.before_insertXYZ();
```

Let's assume that the general geometry column update has not taken place yet, then the original five registers still have their geometry column in null. Now, once the trigger has been activated, any inserts into our table should be populated with new geometry records. Let us do a test insert using the following query:

```
INSERT INTO chp02.xwhyzed1 (x, y, z)
  VALUES (random()*5, random()*7, 106),
  (random()*5, random()*7, 107),
  (random()*5, random()*7, 108),
  (random()*5, random()*7, 109),
  (random()*5, random()*7, 110);
```

Check the rows to verify that the geom columns are updated with the command:

```
SELECT * FROM chp02.xwhyzed1;
```

Or use pgAdmin:

x numeric	y numeric	z numeric	gid [PK] integer	geom geometry
4.67860845383257	6.45900910301134	85.2110590171069	1	[null]
3.63836708012968	3.47429635189474	36.4363031163812	2	[null]
0.985967454034835	3.52874203631654	19.2578147305176	3	[null]
1.7305088089779	4.95445863297209	22.9104127548635	4	[null]
3.65890902932733	4.32095986232162	106	5	0101000020960E0000F9FFDF1872450D400500C0B3A9481140
0.742483325302601	6.26183870760724	107	6	0101000020960E000001 0000646CC2E73F010038721F0C1940
1.09579629963264	0.518613429740071	108	7	0101000020960E0000060060B36188F13FFDFFFF307B98E03F
0.317031748127192	1.32443253044039	109	8	0101000020960E0000FBFF7F873F4AD43F0000402AE030F53F
2.05664261709899	4.71963535342366	110	9	0101000020960E00000700600B0174004006001017E8E01240

After applying the general update, then all the registers will have a value on their geom column:

x numeric	y numeric	z numeric	gid [PK] integer	geom geometry
4.67860845383257	6.45900910301134	85.2110590171069	1	0101000020960E000004007022E5B612400000787B06D61940
3.63836708012968	3.47429635189474	36.4363031163812	2	0101000020960E0000F9FF1F33601B0D400800C0E25BCB0B40
0.905967454034835	3.52874203631654	19.2578147305176	3	0101000020960E0000FFFF3F9E0B8DEF3FF7FFCF1ADD3A0C40
1.7305088089779	4.95445863297209	22.9104127548635	4	0101000020960E0000F7FF3F012A80FB3FFEFF979A5DD11340
3.65890902932733	4.32095936232162	106	5	0101000020960E0000F9FFDF1872450D400500C0B3A9481140
0.742483325302601	6.26183870760724	107	6	0101000020960E0000010000646CC2E73F010038721F0C1940
1.09579629968264	0.518613429740071	108	7	0101000020960E00000060060B36188F13FFDFFFF307698E03F
0.317031743127192	1.32443253044039	109	8	0101000020960E0000FBFF7F873F4AD43F0000402AE030F53F
2.05664261709899	4.71963535342366	110	9	0101000020960E00000700600B0174004006001017E8E01240

Extending further...

So far, we've implemented an insert trigger. What if the value changes for a particular row? In that case, we will require a separate update trigger. We'll change our original function to test the UPDATE case, and we'll use WHEN in our trigger to constrain updates to the column being changed.

Also, note that the following function is written with the assumption that the user wants to always update the changing geometries based on the changing values:

```
CREATE OR REPLACE FUNCTION chp02.before_insertXYZ()
  RETURNS trigger AS
$$
BEGIN
if (TG_OP='INSERT') then
  if (NEW.geom is null) then
    NEW.geom = ST_SetSRID(ST_MakePoint(NEW.x,NEW.y), 3734);
  end if;
ELSEIF (TG_OP='UPDATE') then
  NEW.geom = ST_SetSRID(ST_MakePoint(NEW.x,NEW.y), 3734);
end if;
```

```
RETURN NEW;
END;

$$
LANGUAGE 'plpgsql';

CREATE TRIGGER popgeom_insert
  BEFORE INSERT ON chp02.xwhyzed1
  FOR EACH ROW EXECUTE PROCEDURE chp02.before_insertXYZ();

CREATE trigger popgeom_update
  BEFORE UPDATE ON chp02.xwhyzed1
  FOR EACH ROW
  WHEN (OLD.X IS DISTINCT FROM NEW.X OR OLD.Y IS DISTINCT FROM
    NEW.Y)
  EXECUTE PROCEDURE chp02.before_insertXYZ();
```

See also

- The *Using geospatial views* recipe

Structuring spatial data with table inheritance

An unusual and useful property of the PostgreSQL database is that it allows for object inheritance models as they apply to tables. This means that we can have parent/child relationships between tables and leverage that to structure the data in meaningful ways. In our example, we will apply this to hydrology data. This data can be points, lines, polygons, or more complex structures, but they have one commonality: they are explicitly linked in a physical sense and inherently related; they are all about water. Water/hydrology is an excellent natural system to model this way, as our ways of modeling it spatially can be quite mixed depending on scales, details, the data collection process, and a host of other factors.

Getting ready

The data we will be using is hydrology data that has been modified from engineering *blue lines* (see the following screenshot), that is, hydrologic data that is very detailed and is meant to be used at scales approaching 1:600. The data in its original application aided, as breaklines, in detailed digital terrain modeling.

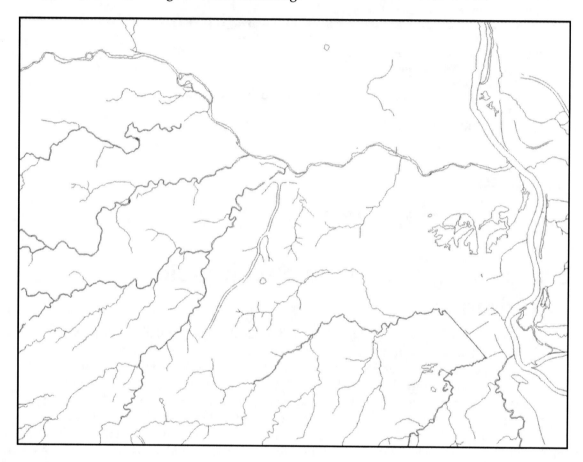

While useful in itself, the data was further manipulated, separating the linear features from area features, with additional polygonization of the area features, as shown in the following screenshot:

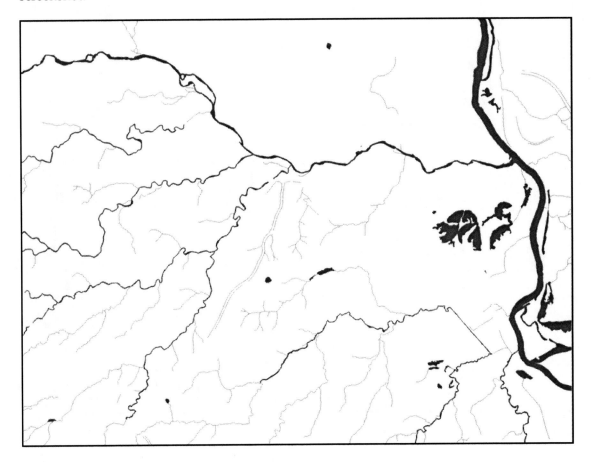

Finally, the data was classified into basic waterway categories, as follows:

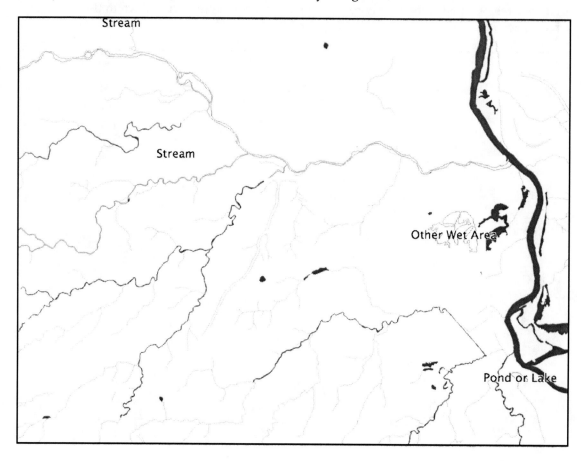

In addition, a process was undertaken to generate centerlines for polygon features such as streams, which are effectively linear features, as follows:

Hence, we have three separate but related datasets:

- cuyahoga_hydro_polygon
- cuyahoga_hydro_polyline
- cuyahoga_river_centerlines

Now, let us look at the structure of the tabular data. Unzip the hydrology file from the book repository and go to that directory. The `ogrinfo` utility can help us with this, as shown in the following command:

```
> ogrinfo cuyahoga_hydro_polygon.shp -al -so
```

The output is as follows:

```
                                    Chapter 1 — bash — 114×28
INFO: Open of `cuyahoga_hydro_polygon.shp'
      using driver `ESRI Shapefile' successful.

Layer name: cuyahoga_hydro_polygon
Geometry: Polygon
Feature Count: 579
Extent: (2142566.039992, 591583.960120) — (2178951.930105, 627276.599084)
Layer SRS WKT:
PROJCS["NAD_1983_StatePlane_Ohio_North_FIPS_3401_Feet",
    GEOGCS["GCS_North_American_1983",
        DATUM["North_American_Datum_1983",
            SPHEROID["GRS_1980",6378137.0,298.257222101]],
        PRIMEM["Greenwich",0.0],
        UNIT["Degree",0.0174532925199433]],
    PROJECTION["Lambert_Conformal_Conic_2SP"],
    PARAMETER["False_Easting",1968500.0],
    PARAMETER["False_Northing",0.0],
    PARAMETER["Central_Meridian",-82.5],
    PARAMETER["Standard_Parallel_1",40.43333333333333],
    PARAMETER["Standard_Parallel_2",41.7],
    PARAMETER["Latitude_Of_Origin",39.66666666666666],
    UNIT["Foot_US",0.3048006096012192]]
Name: String (30.0)
AREA: Real (19.11)
PERIMETER: Real (19.11)
hyd_type: String (50.0)
geom_type: String (15.0)
bash-3.2$
```

Executing this query on each of the shapefiles, we see the following fields that are common to all the shapefiles:

- `name`
- `hyd_type`
- `geom_type`

It is by understanding our common fields that we can apply inheritance to completely structure our data.

How to do it...

Now that we know our common fields, creating an inheritance model is easy. First, we will create a parent table with the fields common to all the tables, using the following query:

```
CREATE TABLE chp02.hydrology (
  gid SERIAL PRIMARY KEY,
  "name"      text,
  hyd_type    text,
  geom_type   text,
  the_geom    geometry
);
```

If you are paying attention, you will note that we also added a geometry field as all of our shapefiles implicitly have this commonality. With inheritance, every record inserted in any of the child tables will also be saved in our parent table, only these records will be stored without the extra fields specified for the child tables.

To establish inheritance for a given table, we need to declare only the additional fields that the child table contains using the following query:

```
CREATE TABLE chp02.hydrology_centerlines (
  "length"    numeric
) INHERITS (chp02.hydrology);

CREATE TABLE chp02.hydrology_polygon (
  area      numeric,
  perimeter   numeric
) INHERITS (chp02.hydrology);

CREATE TABLE chp02.hydrology_linestring (
  sinuosity   numeric
) INHERITS (chp02.hydrology_centerlines);
```

Now, we are ready to load our data using the following commands:

- shp2pgsql -s 3734 -a -i -I -W LATIN1 -g the_geom cuyahoga_hydro_polygon chp02.hydrology_polygon | psql -U me -d postgis_cookbook

- shp2pgsql -s 3734 -a -i -I -W LATIN1 -g the_geom cuyahoga_hydro_polyline chp02.hydrology_linestring | psql -U me -d postgis_cookbook

- shp2pgsql -s 3734 -a -i -I -W LATIN1 -g the_geom cuyahoga_river_centerlines chp02.hydrology_centerlines | psql -U me -d postgis_cookbook

If we view our parent table, we will see all the records in all the child tables. The following is a screenshot of fields in `hydrology`:

gid [PK] integer	name text	hyd_type text	geom_type text	the_geom geometry
1	1	Lake Isaac	Pond or Lake	multipolygon	010600002...
2	2 [null]	Stream	multipolygon	010600002...
3	3 [null]	Stream	multipolygon	010600002...
4	4	Beyer's Pond	Pond or Lake	multipolygon	010600002...
5	5 [null]	Other Wet Area	multipolygon	010600002...
6	6 [null]	Other Wet Area	multipolygon	010600002...
7	7 [null]	Other Wet Area	multipolygon	010600002...
8	8 [null]	Other Wet Area	multipolygon	010600002...
9	9 [null]	Other Wet Area	multipolygon	010600002...
10	10 [null]	Other Wet Area	multipolygon	010600002...
11	11 [null]	Other Wet Area	multipolygon	010600002...
12	12 [null]	Pond or Lake	multipolygon	010600002...
13	13 [null]	Other Wet Area	multipolygon	010600002...
14	14 [null]	Other Wet Area	multipolygon	010600002...
15	15 [null]	Other Wet Area	multipolygon	010600002...
16	16 [null]	Pond or Lake	multipolygon	010600002...
17	17 [null]	Other Wet Area	multipolygon	010600002...
18	18 [null]	Other Wet Area	multipolygon	010600002...
19	19 [null]	Other Wet Area	multipolygon	010600002...
20	20 [null]	Other Wet Area	multipolygon	010600002...
21	21 [null]	Pond or Lake	multipolygon	010600002...
22	22 [null]	Other Wet Area	multipolygon	010600002...
23	23 [null]	Stream	multipolygon	010600002...
24	24 [null]	Other Wet Area	multipolygon	010600002...

Compare that to the fields available in `hydrology_linestring` that will reveal specific fields of interest:

	gid integer	name text	hyd_type text	geom_type text	the_geom geometry	length numeric	sinuosity numeric
1	580	[null]	Non-Stream Waterway	linestring	01050000E...	4039134630	00000000000
2	581	[null]	Non-Stream Waterway	linestring	01050000E...	9732715200	83613023587
3	582	[null]	Non-Stream Waterway	linestring	01050000E...	9742916700	99929583918
4	583	[null]	Non-Stream Waterway	linestring	01050000E...	2665436700	91803563396
5	584	[null]	Ditch	linestring	01050000E...	8303417700	99967999563
6	585	[null]	Ditch	linestring	01050000E...	8326783600	99929628256
7	586	[null]	Ditch	linestring	01050000E...	3971908500	99264311873
8	587	[null]	Ditch	linestring	01050000E...	5216740200	95220213360
9	588	[null]	Non-Stream Waterway	linestring	01050000E...	4463251100	96285677485
10	589	[null]	Non-Stream Waterway	linestring	01050000E...	4663221200	99751447311
11	590	[null]	Non-Stream Waterway	linestring	01050000E...	8777600900	98541087641
12	591	[null]	Non-Stream Waterway	linestring	01050000E...	7702293700	99901740366
13	592	[null]	Non-Stream Waterway	linestring	01050000E...	0697353920	97550639773
14	593	[null]	Non-Stream Waterway	linestring	01050000E...	4175308400	99972032150
15	594	[null]	Ditch	linestring	01050000E...	8966233330	99821067158
16	595	[null]	Non-Stream Waterway	linestring	01050000E...	7897864400	98636052492
17	596	[null]	Non-Stream Waterway	linestring	01050000E...	8968107330	99785430938
18	597	[null]	Ditch	linestring	01050000E...	8705548360	99983846322
19	598	[null]	Ditch	linestring	01050000E...	1769298810	99784885844
20	599	[null]	Ditch	linestring	01050000E...	9435483960	99999932726
21	600	[null]	Ditch	linestring	01050000E...	8006629180	99878874084
22	601	[null]	Non-Stream Waterway	linestring	01050000E...	9314161920	99420687124
23	602	[null]	Non-Stream Waterway	linestring	01050000E...	5607016130	99921978125

How it works...

PostgreSQL table inheritance allows us to enforce essentially hierarchical relationships between tables. In this case, we leverage inheritance to allow for commonality between related datasets. Now, if we want to query data from these tables, we can query directly from the parent table as follows, depending on whether we want a mix of geometries or just a targeted dataset:

```
SELECT * FROM chp02.hydrology
```

From any of the child tables, we could use the following query:

```
SELECT * FROM chp02.hydrology_polygon
```

See also

It is possible to extend this concept in order to leverage and optimize storage and querying by using the CHECK constrains in conjunction with inheritance. For more info, see the *Extending inheritance – table partitioning* recipe.

Extending inheritance – table partitioning

Table partitioning is an approach specific to PostgreSQL that extends inheritance to model tables that typically do not vary from each other in the available fields, but where the child tables represent logical partitioning of the data based on a variety of factors, be it time, value ranges, classifications, or in our case, spatial relationships. The advantages of partitioning include improved query performance due to smaller indexes and targeted scans of data, bulk loads, and deletes that bypass the costs of vacuuming. It can thus be used to put commonly used data on faster and more expensive storage, and the remaining data on slower and cheaper storage. In combination with PostGIS, we get the novel power of spatial partitioning, which is a really powerful feature for large datasets.

Getting ready

We could use many examples of large datasets that could benefit from partitioning. In our case, we will use a contour dataset. Contours are useful ways to represent terrain data, as they are well established and thus commonly interpreted. Contours can also be used to compress terrain data into linear representations, thus allowing it to be shown in conjunction with other data easily.

The problem is, the storage of contour data can be quite expensive. Two-foot contours for a single US county can take 20 to 40 GB, and storing such data for a larger area such as a region or nation can become quite prohibitive from the standpoint of accessing the appropriate portion of the dataset in a performant way.

How to do it...

The first step in this case may be to prepare the data. If we had a monolithic contour table called `cuy_contours_2`, we could choose to clip the data to a series of rectangles that will serve as our table partitions; in this case, `chp02.contour_clip`, using the following query:

```
CREATE TABLE chp02.contour_2_cm_only AS
  SELECT contour.elevation, contour.gid, contour.div_10, contour.div_20,
contour.div_50,
  contour.div_100, cc.id, ST_Intersection(contour.the_geom, cc.the_geom) AS
the_geom FROM
    chp02.cuy_contours_2 AS contour, chp02.contour_clip as cc
  WHERE ST_Within(contour.the_geom, cc.the_geom
    OR
    ST_Crosses(contour.the_geom, cc.the_geom);
```

We are performing two tests here in our query. We are using `ST_Within`, which tests whether a given contour is entirely within our area of interest. If so, we perform an intersection; the resultant geometry should just be the geometry of the contour.

The `ST_Crosses` function checks whether the contour crosses the boundary of the geometry we are testing. This should capture all the geometries lying partially inside and partially outside our areas. These are the ones that we will truly intersect to get the resultant shape.

In our case, it is easier and we don't require this step. Our contour shapes are already individual shapefiles clipped to rectangular boundaries, as shown in the following screenshot:

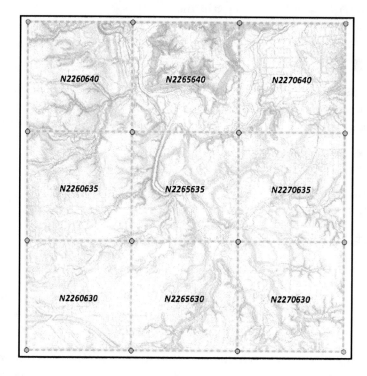

Since the data is already clipped into the chunks needed for our partitions, we can just continue to create the appropriate partitions.

Much like with inheritance, we start by creating our parent table using the following query:

```
CREATE TABLE chp02.contours
(
  gid serial NOT NULL,
  elevation integer,
  __gid double precision,
  the_geom geometry(MultiLineStringZM,3734),
  CONSTRAINT contours_pkey PRIMARY KEY (gid)
)
WITH (
  OIDS=FALSE
);
```

Here again, we maintain our constraints, such as PRIMARY KEY, and specify the geometry type (MultiLineStringZM), not because these will propagate to the child tables, but for any client software accessing the parent table to anticipate such constraints.

Now we may begin to create tables that inherit from our parent table. In the process, we will create a CHECK constraint specifying the limits of our associated geometry using the following query:

```
CREATE TABLE chp02.contour_N2260630
  (CHECK
    (ST_CoveredBy(the_geom, ST_GeomFromText
      ('POLYGON((2260000, 630000, 2260000 635000, 2265000 635000,
                2265000 630000, 2260000 630000))',3734)
    )
  )) INHERITS (chp02.contours);
```

We can complete the table structure for partitioning the contours with similar CREATE TABLE queries for our remaining tables, as follows:

```
CREATE TABLE chp02.contour_N2260635
  (CHECK
    (ST_CoveredBy(the_geom, ST_GeomFromText
      ('POLYGON((2260000 635000, 2260000 640000,
                2265000 640000, 2265000 635000, 2260000 635000))', 3734)
    )
  )) INHERITS (chp02.contours);
CREATE TABLE chp02.contour_N2260640
  (CHECK
    (ST_CoveredBy(the_geom, ST_GeomFromText
      ('POLYGON((2260000 640000, 2260000 645000, 2265000 645000,
                2265000 640000, 2260000 640000))', 3734)
    )
  )) INHERITS (chp02.contours);
CREATE TABLE chp02.contour_N2265630
  (CHECK
    (ST_CoveredBy(the_geom, ST_GeomFromText
      ('POLYGON((2265000 630000, 2265000 635000, 2270000 635000,
                2270000 630000, 2265000 630000))', 3734)
    )
  )) INHERITS (chp02.contours);
CREATE TABLE chp02.contour_N2265635
  (CHECK
    (ST_CoveredBy(the_geom, ST_GeomFromText
      ('POLYGON((2265000 635000, 2265000 640000, 2270000 640000,
                2270000 635000, 2265000 635000))', 3734)
    )
  )) INHERITS (chp02.contours);
```

```
CREATE TABLE chp02.contour_N2265640
  (CHECK
    (ST_CoveredBy(the_geom, ST_GeomFromText
      ('POLYGON((2265000 640000, 2265000 645000, 2270000 645000,
                2270000 640000, 2265000 640000))', 3734)
    )
  )) INHERITS (chp02.contours);
CREATE TABLE chp02.contour_N2270630
  (CHECK
    (ST_CoveredBy(the_geom, ST_GeomFromText
      ('POLYGON((2270000 630000, 2270000 635000, 2275000 635000,
                2275000 630000, 2270000 630000))', 3734)
    )
  )) INHERITS (chp02.contours);
CREATE TABLE chp02.contour_N2270635
  (CHECK
    (ST_CoveredBy(the_geom, ST_GeomFromText
      ('POLYGON((2270000 635000, 2270000 640000, 2275000 640000,
                2275000 635000, 2270000 635000))', 3734)
    )
  )) INHERITS (chp02.contours);
CREATE TABLE chp02.contour_N2270640
  (CHECK
    (ST_CoveredBy(the_geom, ST_GeomFromText
      ('POLYGON((2270000 640000, 2270000 645000, 2275000 645000,
                2275000 640000, 2270000 640000))', 3734)
    )
  )) INHERITS (chp02.contours);
```

And now we can load our contours shapefiles found in the `contours1` ZIP file into each of our child tables, using the following command, by replacing the filename. If we wanted to, we could even implement a trigger on the parent table, which would place each insert into its correct child table, though this might incur performance costs:

```
shp2pgsql -s 3734 -a -i -I -W LATIN1 -g the_geom N2265630
chp02.contour_N2265630 | psql -U me -d postgis_cookbook
```

How it works...

The CHECK constraint in combination with inheritance is all it takes to build a table partitioning. In this case, we're using a bounding box as our CHECK constraint and simply inheriting the columns from the parent table. Now that we have this in place, queries against the parent table will check our CHECK constraints first before employing a query.

This also allows us to place any of our lesser-used contour tables on cheaper and slower storage, thus allowing for cost-effective optimizations of large datasets. This structure is also beneficial for rapidly changing data, as updates can be applied to an entire area; the entire table for that area can be efficiently dropped and repopulated without traversing across the dataset.

See also

For more on table inheritance in general, particularly the flexibility associated with the usage of alternate columns in the child table, see the previous recipe, *Structuring spatial data with table inheritance.*

Normalizing imports

Often, data used in a spatial database is imported from other sources. As such, it may not be in a form that is useful for our current application. In such a case, it may be useful to write functions that will aid in transforming the data into a form that is more useful for our application. This is particularly the case when going from flat file formats, such as shapefiles, to relational databases such as PostgreSQL.

A shapefile is a de facto as well as a format specification for the storage of spatial data, and is probably the most common delivery format for spatial data. A shapefile, in spite of its name, is never just one file, but a collection of files. It consists of at least *.shp (which contains geometry), *.shx (an index file), and *.dbf (which contains the tabular information for the shapefile). It is a powerful and useful format, but as a flat file, it is inherently non-relational. Each geometry is associated in a one-to-one relationship with each row in a table.

There are many structures that might serve as a proxy for relational stores in a shapefile. We will explore one here: a single field with delimited text for multiple relations. This is a not-too-uncommon hack to encode multiple relationships into a flat file. The other common approach is to create multiple fields to store what in a relational arrangement would be a single field.

Getting ready

The dataset we will be working with is a trails dataset that has linear extents for a set of trails in a park system. The data is the typical data that comes from the GIS world; as a flat shapefile, there are no explicit relational constructs in the data.

First, unzip the `trails.zip` file and use the command line to go into it, then load the data using the following command:

```
shp2pgsql -s 3734 -d -i -I -W LATIN1 -g the_geom trails chp02.trails | psql
-U me -d postgis_cookbook
```

Looking at the linear data, we have some categories for the use type:

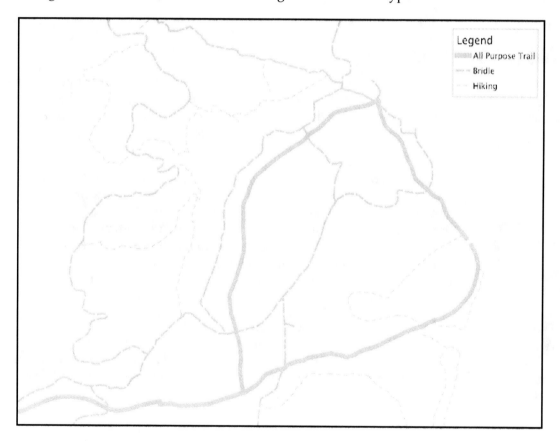

We want to retain this information as well as the name. Unfortunately, the `label_name` field is a messy field with a variety of related names concatenated with an ampersand (`&`), as shown in the following query:

```
SELECT DISTINCT label_name FROM chp02.trails
  WHERE label_name LIKE '%&%' LIMIT 10;
```

It will return the following output:

```
                  🔅 may — bash — 80×24
postgis_cookbook=# SELECT DISTINCT label_name FROM chp02.trails
  WHERE label_name LIKE '%&%' LIMIT 10;
                        label_name
-------------------------------------------------------------
 All Purpose Trail & Buckeye Trail & Sagamore Creek Loop Trail
 NC1 & NC2
 BR3 & BR4 & Buckeye Trail
 Hemlock Trail & NC2
 Lake Isaac Trail & Lake to Lake Trail
 BR4 & Deer Lick Cave Loop Trail
 Bridle Trail & Deer Lick Cave Loop Trail & Hemlock Loop Trail
 Towpath Trail & Buckeye Trail
 Bridle Trail & Connector Trail
 BR3 & BR4 & Deer Lick Cave Loop Trail
(10 rows)

postgis_cookbook=# ▊
```

This is where the normalization of our table will begin.

How to do it...

The first thing we need to do is find all the fields that don't have ampersands and use those as our unique list of available trails. In our case, we can do this, as every trail has at least one segment that is uniquely named and not associated with another trail name. This approach will not work with all datasets, so be careful in understanding your data before applying this approach to that data.

To select the fields ordered without ampersands, we use the following query:

```
SELECT DISTINCT label_name, res
  FROM chp02.trails
  WHERE label_name NOT LIKE '%&%'
  ORDER BY label_name, res;
```

It will return the following output:

```
● ● ●                        ⬆ may — bash — 91×34
postgis_cookbook=# SELECT DISTINCT label_name, res
postgis_cookbook-#    FROM chp02.trails
postgis_cookbook-#   WHERE label_name NOT LIKE '%&%'
postgis_cookbook-#   ORDER BY label_name, res;
             label_name                        |                res
-----------------------------------------------+-----------------------------------
 All Purpose Trail                             | Bedford Reservation
 All Purpose Trail                             | Big Creek Reservation
 All Purpose Trail                             | Bradley Woods Reservation
 All Purpose Trail                             | Brecksville Reservation
 All Purpose Trail                             | Brookside Reservation
 All Purpose Trail                             | Cuyahoga Valley National Park
 All Purpose Trail                             | Euclid Creek Reservation
 All Purpose Trail                             | Garfield Park Reservation
 All Purpose Trail                             | Hinckley Reservation
 All Purpose Trail                             | Huntington Reservation
 All Purpose Trail                             | Mill Stream Run Reservation
 All Purpose Trail                             | North Chagrin Reservation
 All Purpose Trail                             | Ohio and Erie Canal Reservation
 All Purpose Trail                             | Rocky River Reservation
 All Purpose Trail                             | South Chagrin Reservation
 All Purpose Trail                             | Washington Reservation
 Arboretum Loop Trail                          | South Chagrin Reservation
 BR1                                           | Brecksville Reservation
 BR2                                           | Brecksville Reservation
 BR3                                           | Brecksville Reservation
 BR4                                           | Brecksville Reservation
 Bedford Reservation Physical Fitness Trail    | Bedford Reservation
 Bluebird Box Trail                            | North Chagrin Reservation
 Bluebird Box Trail                            | South Chagrin Reservation
 Bonnie Park Loop Trail                        | Mill Stream Run Reservation
 Bridle Connector Trail                        | Rocky River Reservation
 Bridle Trail                                  | Bedford Reservation
:
```

Next, we want to search for all the records that match any of these unique trail names. This will give us the list of records that will serve as relations. The first step in doing this search is to append the percent (%) signs to our unique list in order to build a string on which we can search using a LIKE query:

```
SELECT '%' || label_name || '%' AS label_name, label_name as   label, res
FROM
   (SELECT DISTINCT label_name, res
     FROM chp02.trails
     WHERE label_name NOT LIKE '%&%'
     ORDER BY label_name, res
   ) AS label;
```

Finally, we'll use this in the context of a WITH block to do the normalization itself. This will provide us with a table of unique IDs for each segment in our first column, along with the associated label column. For good measure, we will do this as a CREATE TABLE procedure, as shown in the following query:

```
CREATE TABLE chp02.trails_names AS WITH labellike AS
(
SELECT '%' || label_name || '%' AS label_name, label_name as   label, res
FROM
   (SELECT DISTINCT label_name, res
     FROM chp02.trails
     WHERE label_name NOT LIKE '%&%'
     ORDER BY label_name, res
   ) AS label
)
SELECT t.gid, ll.label, ll.res
   FROM chp02.trails AS t, labellike AS ll
   WHERE t.label_name LIKE ll.label_name
   AND
   t.res = ll.res
   ORDER BY gid;
```

If we view the first rows of the table created, `trails_names`, we have the following output with `pgAdmin`:

gid integer	label character varying	res character varying
1	All Purpose Trail	Bradley Woods Re...
2	All Purpose Trail	Bradley Woods Re...
3	Swamp Forest Lo...	Bradley Woods Re...
4	Swamp Forest Lo...	Bradley Woods Re...
5	Swamp Forest Lo...	Bradley Woods Re...
6	Swamp Forest Lo...	Bradley Woods Re...
7	Swamp Forest Lo...	Bradley Woods Re...
8	Swamp Forest Lo...	Bradley Woods Re...
9	Swamp Forest Lo...	Bradley Woods Re...
10	Swamp Forest Lo...	Bradley Woods Re...
11	Swamp Forest Lo...	Bradley Woods Re...
12	All Purpose Trail	Bradley Woods Re...
13	All Purpose Trail	Bradley Woods Re...
14	Quarry Loop Trail	Bradley Woods Re...
15	All Purpose Trail	Bradley Woods Re...

Now that we have a table of the relations, we need a table of the geometries associated with `gid`. This, in comparison, is quite easy, as shown in the following query:

```
CREATE TABLE chp02.trails_geom AS
  SELECT gid, the_geom
  FROM chp02.trails;
```

How it works...

In this example, we have generated a unique list of possible records in conjunction with a search for the associated records, in order to build table relationships. In one table, we have the geometry and a unique ID of each spatial record; in another table, we have the names associated with each of those unique IDs. Now we can explicitly leverage those relationships.

First, we need to establish our unique IDs as primary keys, as follows:

```
ALTER TABLE chp02.trails_geom ADD PRIMARY KEY (gid);
```

Now we can use that `PRIMARY KEY` as a `FOREIGN KEY` in our `trails_names` table using the following query:

```
ALTER TABLE chp02.trails_names ADD FOREIGN KEY (gid) REFERENCES
chp02.trails_geom(gid);
```

This step isn't strictly necessary, but does enforce referential integrity for queries such as the following:

```
SELECT geo.gid, geo.the_geom, names.label FROM
  chp02.trails_geom AS geo, chp02.trails_names AS names
  WHERE geo.gid = names.gid;
```

The output is as follows:

gid integer	the_geom geometry	label character varying
1	01050000...	All Purpose Trail
2	01050000...	All Purpose Trail
3	01050000...	Swamp Forest Loo...
4	01050000...	Swamp Forest Loo...
5	01050000...	Swamp Forest Loo...
6	01050000...	Swamp Forest Loo...
7	01050000...	Swamp Forest Loo...
8	01050000...	Swamp Forest Loo...
9	01050000...	Swamp Forest Loo...
10	01050000...	Swamp Forest Loo...

There's more...

If we had multiple fields we wanted to normalize, we could write `CREATE TABLE` queries for each of them.

It is interesting to note that the approach framed in this recipe is not limited to cases where we have a delimited field. This approach can provide a relatively generic solution to the problem of normalizing flat files. For example, if we have a case where we have multiple fields to represent relational info, such as `label1`, `label2`, `label3`, or similar multiple attribute names for a single record, we can write a simple query to concatenate them together before feeding that info into our query.

Normalizing internal overlays

Data from an external source can have issues in the table structure as well as in the topology, endemic to the geospatial data itself. Take, for example, the problem of data with overlapping polygons. If our dataset has polygons that overlap with internal overlays, then queries for area, perimeter, and other metrics may not produce predictable or consistent results.

There are a few approaches that can solve the problem of polygon datasets with internal overlays. The general approach presented here was originally proposed by *Kevin Neufeld* of *Refractions Research*.

Over the course of writing our query, we will also produce a solution for converting polygons to linestrings.

Getting ready

First, unzip the `use_area.zip` file and go into it using the command line; then, load the dataset using the following command:

```
shp2pgsql -s 3734 -d -i -I -W LATIN1 -g the_geom cm_usearea_polygon
chp02.use_area | psql -U me -d postgis_cookbook
```

How to do it...

Now that the data is loaded into a table in the database, we can leverage PostGIS to flatten and get the union of the polygons, so that we have a normalized dataset. The first step in doing so using this approach will be to convert the *polygons* to *linestrings*. We can then link those *linestrings* and convert them back to *polygons*, representing the union of all the *polygon* inputs. We will perform the following tasks:

1. Convert polygons to linestrings
2. Convert linestrings back to polygons
3. Find the center points of the resultant polygons
4. Use the resultant points to query tabular relationships

To convert polygons to linestrings, we'll need to extract just the portions of the polygons we want using `ST_ExteriorRing`, convert those parts to points using `ST_DumpPoints`, and then connect those points back into lines like a connect-the-dots coloring book using `ST_MakeLine`.

Breaking it down further, ST_ExteriorRing (the_geom) will grab just the outer boundary of our polygons. But ST_ExteriorRing returns polygons, so we need to take that output and create a line from it. The easiest way to do this is to convert it to points using ST_DumpPoints and then connect those points. By default, the Dump function returns an object called a geometry_dump, which is not just simple geometry, but the geometry in combination with an array of integers. The easiest way to return the geometry alone is the leverage object notation to extract just the geometry portion of geometry_dump, as follows:

```
(ST_DumpPoints(geom)).geom
```

Piecing the geometry back together with ST_ExteriorRing is done using the following query:

```
SELECT (ST_DumpPoints(ST_ExteriorRing(geom))).geom
```

This should give us a listing of points in order from the exterior rings of all the points from which we want to construct our lines using ST_MakeLine, as shown in the following query:

```
SELECT ST_MakeLine(geom) FROM (
    SELECT (ST_DumpPoints(ST_ExteriorRing(geom))).geom) AS linpoints
```

Since the preceding approach is a process we may want to use in many other places, it might be prudent to create a function from this using the following query:

```
CREATE OR REPLACE FUNCTION chp02.polygon_to_line(geometry)
    RETURNS geometry AS
$BODY$

    SELECT ST_MakeLine(geom) FROM (
        SELECT (ST_DumpPoints(ST_ExteriorRing((ST_Dump($1)).geom))).geom

    ) AS linpoints
$BODY$
    LANGUAGE sql VOLATILE;
ALTER FUNCTION chp02.polygon_to_line(geometry)
    OWNER TO me;
```

Now that we have the polygon_to_line function, we still need to force the linking of overlapping lines in our particular case. The ST_Union function will aid in this, as shown in the following query:

```
SELECT ST_Union(the_geom) AS geom FROM (
    SELECT chp02.polygon_to_line(geom) AS geom FROM
      chp02.use_area
    ) AS unioned;
```

Now let's convert linestrings back to polygons, and for this we can polygonize the result using `ST_Polygonize`, as shown in the following query:

```
SELECT ST_Polygonize(geom) AS geom FROM (
  SELECT ST_Union(the_geom) AS geom FROM (
    SELECT chp02.polygon_to_line(geom) AS geom FROM
    chp02.use_area
  ) AS unioned
) as polygonized;
```

The `ST_Polygonize` function will create a single multi polygon, so we need to explode this into multiple single polygon geometries if we are to do anything useful with it. While we are at it, we might as well do the following within a `CREATE TABLE` statement:

```
CREATE TABLE chp02.use_area_alt AS (
  SELECT (ST_Dump(the_geom)).geom AS the_geom FROM (
    SELECT ST_Polygonize(the_geom) AS the_geom FROM (
      SELECT ST_Union(the_geom) AS the_geom FROM (
        SELECT chp02.polygon_to_line(the_geom) AS the_geom
        FROM chp02.use_area
      ) AS unioned
    ) as polygonized
  ) AS exploded
);
```

We will be performing spatial queries against this geometry, so we should create an index in order to ensure our query performs well, as shown in the following query:

```
CREATE INDEX chp02_use_area_alt_the_geom_gist
  ON chp02.use_area_alt
  USING gist(the_geom);
```

In order to find the appropriate table information from the original geometry and apply that back to our resultant geometries, we will perform a point-in-polygon query. For that, we first need to calculate centroids on the resultant geometry:

```
CREATE TABLE chp02.use_area_alt_p AS
  SELECT ST_SetSRID(ST_PointOnSurface(the_geom), 3734) AS
    the_geom FROM
    chp02.use_area_alt;
ALTER TABLE chp02.use_area_alt_p ADD COLUMN gid serial;
ALTER TABLE chp02.use_area_alt_p ADD PRIMARY KEY (gid);
```

And as always, create a spatial index using the following query:

```
CREATE INDEX chp02_use_area_alt_p_the_geom_gist
  ON chp02.use_area_alt_p
  USING gist(the_geom);
```

The centroids then structure our point-in-polygon (`ST_Intersects`) relationship between the original tabular information and resultant polygons, using the following query:

```
CREATE TABLE chp02.use_area_alt_relation AS
SELECT points.gid, cu.location FROM
  chp02.use_area_alt_p AS points,
  chp02.use_area AS cu
    WHERE ST_Intersects(points.the_geom, cu.the_geom);
```

If we view the first rows of the table, we can see it links the identifier of points to their respective locations:

gid integer	location character varying
147	The Chalet
148	The Chalet
149	The Chalet
162	Strongsville Wildlife Area
163	Strongsville Wildlife Area
165	Strongsville Wildlife Area
167	Strongsville Wildlife Area
169	Strongsville Wildlife Area
158	York Road Picnic Area
156	Squire Rich Museum
612	Red Oak Picnic Area
613	Red Oak Picnic Area
631	Short Line Railroad & Pipe...

How it works...

Our essential approach here is to look at the underlying topology of the geometry and reconstruct a topology that is non-overlapping, and then use the centroids of that new geometry to construct a query that establishes the relationship to the original data.

There's more...

At this stage, we can optionally establish a framework for referential integrity using a foreign key, as follows:

```
ALTER TABLE chp02.use_area_alt_relation ADD FOREIGN KEY (gid) REFERENCES
chp02.use_area_alt_p (gid);
```

Using polygon overlays for proportional census estimates

PostgreSQL functions abound for the aggregation of tabular data, including `sum`, `count`, `min`, `max`, and so on. PostGIS as a framework does not explicitly have spatial equivalents of these, but this does not prevent us from building functions using the aggregate functions from PostgreSQL in concert with PostGIS's spatial functionality.

In this recipe, we will explore spatial summarization with the United States census data. The US census data, by nature, is aggregated data. This is done intentionally to protect the privacy of citizens. But when it comes to doing analyses with this data, the aggregate nature of the data can become problematic. There are some tricks to disaggregate data. Amongst the simplest of these is the use of a proportional sum, which we will do in this exercise.

Getting ready

The problem at hand is that a proposed trail has been drawn in order to provide services for the public. This example could apply to road construction or even finding sites for commercial properties for the purpose of provisioning services.

First, unzip the `trail_census.zip` file, then perform a quick data load using the
following commands from the unzipped folder:

```
shp2pgsql -s 3734 -d -i -I -W LATIN1 -g the_geom census chp02.trail_census
| psql -U me -d postgis_cookbook
shp2pgsql -s 3734 -d -i -I -W LATIN1 -g the_geom
trail_alignment_proposed_buffer chp02.trail_buffer | psql -U me -d
postgis_cookbook
shp2pgsql -s 3734 -d -i -I -W LATIN1 -g the_geom trail_alignment_proposed
chp02.trail_alignment_prop | psql -U me -d postgis_cookbook
```

The preceding commands will produce the following outputs:

```
------------------------------------------------------------------
 chp02.trail_alignment_prop.the_geom SRID:3734 TYPE:MULTILINESTRING DIMS:2
(1 row)

INSERT 0 1
CREATE INDEX
COMMIT
ANALYZE
bash-3.2$
bash-3.2$
sed_buffer chp02.trail_buffer | psql -U may -d postgis_cookbookl_alignment_propo
Shapefile type: Polygon
Postgis type: MULTIPOLYGON[2]
SET
SET
                    dropgeometrycolumn
------------------------------------------------------------------
 chp02.trail_buffer.the_geom effectively removed.
(1 row)

DROP TABLE
BEGIN
CREATE TABLE
ALTER TABLE
                    addgeometrycolumn
------------------------------------------------------------------
 chp02.trail_buffer.the_geom SRID:3734 TYPE:MULTIPOLYGON DIMS:2
(1 row)

INSERT 0 1
CREATE INDEX
COMMIT
ANALYZE
bash-3.2$
```

If we view the proposed trail in our favorite desktop GIS, we have the following:

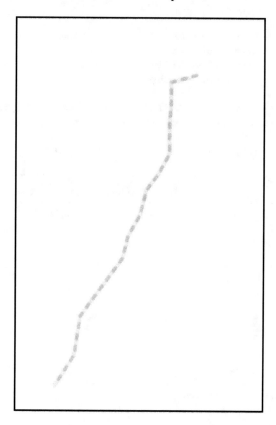

In our case, we want to know the population within 1 mile of the trail, assuming that persons living within 1 mile of the trail are the ones most likely to use it, and thus most likely to be served by it.

To find out the population near this proposed trail, we overlay census block group population density information. Illustrated in the next screenshot is a 1-mile buffer around the proposed trail:

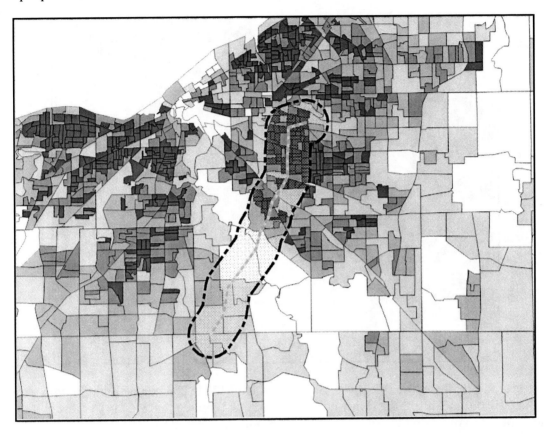

One of the things we might note about this census data is the wide range of census densities and census block group sizes. An approach to calculating the population would be to simply select all census blocks that intersect our area, as shown in the following screenshot:

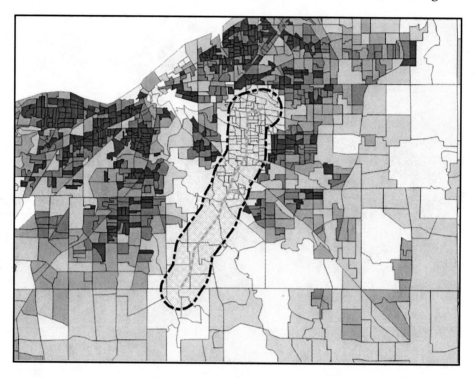

This is a simple procedure that gives us an estimate of 130 to 288 people living within 1 mile of the trail, but looking at the shape of the selection, we can see that we are overestimating the population by taking the complete blocks in our estimate.

Similarly, if we just used the block groups whose centroids lay within 1 mile of our proposed trail alignment, we would underestimate the population.

Instead, we will make some useful assumptions. Block groups are designed to be moderately homogeneous within the block group population distribution. Assuming that this holds true for our data, we can assume that for a given block group, if 50% of the block group is within our target area, we can attribute half of the population of that block group to our estimate. Apply this to all our block groups, sum them, and we have a refined estimate that is likely to be better than pure intersects or centroid queries. Thus, we employ a proportional sum.

How to do it...

As the problem of a proportional sum is a generic problem, it could apply to many problems. We will write the underlying proportioning as a function. A function takes inputs and returns a value. In our case, we want our proportioning function to take two geometries, that is, the geometry of our buffered trail and block groups as well as the value we want proportioned, and we want it to return the proportioned value:

```
CREATE OR REPLACE FUNCTION chp02.proportional_sum(geometry,    geometry,
numeric)
   RETURNS numeric AS
$BODY$
-- SQL here
$BODY$
   LANGUAGE sql VOLATILE;
```

Now, for the purpose of our calculation, for any given intersection of buffered area and block group, we want to find the proportion that the intersection is over the overall block group. Then this value should be multiplied by the value we want to scale.

In SQL, the function looks like the following query:

```
SELECT $3 * areacalc FROM
   (SELECT (ST_Area(ST_Intersection($1, $2)) / ST_Area($2)):: numeric AS
areacalc
   ) AS areac;
```

The preceding query in its full form looks as follows:

```
CREATE OR REPLACE FUNCTION chp02.proportional_sum(geometry,    geometry,
numeric)
   RETURNS numeric AS
$BODY$
    SELECT $3 * areacalc FROM
      (SELECT (ST_Area(ST_Intersection($1,
$2))/ST_Area($2))::numeric AS areacalc
        ) AS areac
 ;
$BODY$
   LANGUAGE sql VOLATILE;
```

How it works...

Since we have written the query as a function, the query uses the SELECT statement to loop through all available records and give us a proportioned population. Astute readers will note that we have not yet done any work on summarization; we have only worked on the proportionality portion of the problem. We can do the summarization upon calling the function using PostgreSQL's built-in aggregate functions. What is neat about this approach is that we need not just apply a sum, but we could also calculate other aggregates such as min or max. In the following example, we will just apply a sum:

```
SELECT ROUND(SUM(chp02.proportional_sum(a.the_geom, b.the_geom, b.pop)))
FROM
  chp02.trail_buffer AS a, chp02.trail_census as b
  WHERE ST_Intersects(a.the_geom, b.the_geom)
  GROUP BY a.gid;
```

The value returned is quite different (a population of 96,081), which is more likely to be accurate.

Working with Vector Data – The Basics

3

In this chapter, we will cover the following recipes:

- Working with GPS data
- Fixing invalid geometries
- GIS analysis with spatial joins
- Simplifying geometries
- Measuring distances
- Merging polygons using a common attribute
- Computing intersections
- Clipping geometries to deploy data
- Simplifying geometries with PostGIS topology

Introduction

In this chapter, you will work with a set of PostGIS functions and vector datasets. You will first take a look at how to use PostGIS with GPS data—you will import such datasets using `ogr2ogr` and then compose polylines from point geometries using the `ST_MakeLine` function.

Then, you will see how PostGIS helps you find and fix invalid geometries with functions such as `ST_MakeValid`, `ST_IsValid`, `ST_IsValidReason`, and `ST_IsValidDetails`.

You will then learn about one of the most powerful elements of a spatial database, spatial joins. PostGIS provides you with a rich set of operators, such as ST_Intersects, ST_Contains, ST_Covers, ST_Crosses, and ST_DWithin, for this purpose.

After that, you will use the ST_Simplify and ST_SimplifyPreverveTopology functions to simplify (generalize) geometries when you don't need too many details. While this function works well on linear geometries, topological anomalies may be introduced for polygonal ones. In such cases, you should consider using an external GIS tool such as GRASS.

You will then have a tour of PostGIS functions to make distance measurements—ST_Distance, ST_DistanceSphere, and ST_DistanceSpheroid are on the way.

One of the recipes explained in this chapter will guide you through the typical GIS workflow to merge polygons based on a common attribute; you will use the ST_Union function for this purpose.

You will then learn how to clip geometries using the ST_Intersection function, before deep diving into the **PostGIS topology** in the last recipe that was introduced in version 2.0.

Working with GPS data

In this recipe, you will work with GPS data. This kind of data is typically saved in a .gpx file. You will import a bunch of .gpx files to PostGIS from **RunKeeper**, a popular social network for runners.

If you have an account on RunKeeper, you can export your .gpx files and process them by following the instructions in this recipe. Otherwise, you can use the RunKeeper .gpx files included in the runkeeper-gpx.zip file located in the chp03 directory available in the code bundle for this book.

You will first create a bash script for importing the .gpx files to a PostGIS table, using ogr2ogr. After the import is completed, you will try to write a couple of SQL queries and test some very useful functions, such as ST_MakeLine to generate polylines from point geometries, ST_Length to compute distance, and ST_Intersects to perform a spatial join operation.

Getting ready

Extract the `data/chp03/runkeeper-gpx.zip` file to `working/chp03/runkeeper_gpx`.
In case you haven't been through `Chapter 1`, *Moving Data In and Out of PostGIS*, be sure to
have the `countries` dataset in the PostGIS database.

How to do it...

First, be sure of the format of the `.gpx` files that you need to import to PostGIS. Open one of
them and check the file structure—each file must be in the XML format composed of just
one `<trk>` element, which contains just one `<trkseg>` element, which contains many
`<trkpt>` elements (the points stored from the runner's GPS device). Import these points to
a PostGIS `Point` table:

1. Create a new schema named `chp03` to store the data for all the recipes in this
   chapter, using the following command:

   ```
   postgis_cookbook=# create schema chp03;
   ```

2. Create the `chp03.rk_track_points` table in PostgreSQL by executing the
   following command lines:

   ```
   postgis_cookbook=# CREATE TABLE chp03.rk_track_points
   (
       fid serial NOT NULL,
       the_geom geometry(Point,4326),
       ele double precision,
       "time" timestamp with time zone,
       CONSTRAINT activities_pk PRIMARY KEY (fid)
   );
   ```

3. Create the following script to import all of the `.gpx` files in the
   `chp03.rk_track_points` table using the GDAL `ogr2ogr` command.

   The following is the Linux version (name it `working/chp03/import_gpx.sh`):

   ```
   #!/bin/bash
   for f in `find runkeeper_gpx -name \*.gpx -printf "%f\n"`
   do
      echo "Importing gpx file $f to chp03.rk_track_points
           PostGIS table..." #, ${f%.*}"
      ogr2ogr -append -update  -f PostgreSQL
      PG:"dbname='postgis_cookbook' user='me'
   ```

```
    password='mypassword'" runkeeper_gpx/$f
    -nln chp03.rk_track_points
    -sql "SELECT ele, time FROM track_points"
done
```

The following is the command for macOS (name it
`working/chp03/import_gpx.sh`):

```
#!/bin/bash
for f in `find runkeeper_gpx -name \*.gpx `
do
  echo "Importing gpx file $f to chp03.rk_track_points
        PostGIS table..." #, ${f%.*}"
  ogr2ogr -append -update  -f PostgreSQL
  PG:"dbname='postgis_cookbook' user='me'
  password='mypassword'" $f
  -nln chp03.rk_track_points
  -sql "SELECT ele, time FROM track_points"
done
```

The following is the Windows version (name it
`working/chp03/import_gpx.bat`):

```
@echo off
for %%I in (runkeeper_gpx\*.gpx*) do (
  echo Importing gpx file %%~nxI to chp03.rk_track_points
      PostGIS table...
  ogr2ogr -append -update -f PostgreSQL
  PG:"dbname='postgis_cookbook' user='me'
  password='mypassword'" runkeeper_gpx/%%~nxI
  -nln chp03.rk_track_points
  -sql "SELECT ele, time FROM track_points"
)
```

4. In Linux and macOS, don't forget to assign execution permission to the script
   before running it. Then, run the following script:

```
$ chmod 775 import_gpx.sh
$ ./import_gpx.sh
Importing gpx file 2012-02-26-0930.gpx to chp03.rk_track_points
  PostGIS table...
Importing gpx file 2012-02-29-1235.gpx to chp03.rk_track_points
  PostGIS table...
...
Importing gpx file 2011-04-15-1906.gpx to chp03.rk_track_points
  PostGIS table...
```

In Windows, just double-click on the `.bat` file or run it from the command prompt using the following command:

```
> import_gpx.bat
```

5. Now, create a polyline table containing a single runner's track details using the `ST_MakeLine` function. Assume that on each distinct day, the runner had just one training session. In this table, you should include the start and end times of the track details as follows:

```
postgis_cookbook=# SELECT
ST_MakeLine(the_geom) AS the_geom,
run_date::date,
MIN(run_time) as start_time,
MAX(run_time) as end_time
INTO chp03.tracks
FROM (
  SELECT the_geom,
  "time"::date as run_date,
  "time" as run_time
  FROM chp03.rk_track_points
  ORDER BY run_time
) AS foo GROUP BY run_date;
```

6. Before querying the created tables, don't forget to add spatial indexes to both of the tables to improve their performance, as follows:

```
postgis_cookbook=# CREATE INDEX rk_track_points_geom_idx
ON chp03.rk_track_points USING gist(the_geom);
postgis_cookbook=# CREATE INDEX tracks_geom_idx
ON chp03.tracks USING gist(the_geom);
```

7. If you try to open both the spatial tables on a desktop GIS on any given day, you should see that the points from the rk_track_points table compose a single polyline geometry record in the tracks table, as shown in the following screenshot:

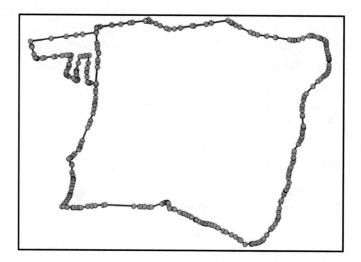

8. If you open all the tracks from a desktop GIS (such as QGIS), you will see the following:

9. Now, query the `tracks` table to get a report of the total distance run (in km) by the runner for each month. For this purpose, use the `ST_Length` function, as shown in the following query:

```
postgis_cookbook=# SELECT
   EXTRACT(year FROM run_date) AS run_year,
   EXTRACT(MONTH FROM run_date) as run_month,
   SUM(ST_Length(geography(the_geom)))/1000 AS distance
   FROM chp03.tracks
   GROUP BY run_year, run_month ORDER BY run_year, run_month;
```

run_year double pr...	run_month double pr...	distance double precision
2010	5	67.8069490339492
2010	6	81.18254818246
2010	7	139.380485552836
2010	8	92.5896428021623
2010	9	111.014558726927
2010	10	121.009036448297
2010	11	79.6208912564367
2010	12	91.7392081012794
2011	1	101.10522761749
2011	2	89.4396512604985
2011	3	96.0118360262582

(28 rows)

10. Using a spatial join between the `tracks` and `countries` tables, and again using the `ST_Length` function as follows, you will get a report of the distance run (in km) by the runner, per country:

```
postgis_cookbook=# SELECT
   c.country_name,
   SUM(ST_Length(geography(t.the_geom)))/1000 AS run_distance
FROM chp03.tracks AS t
JOIN chp01.countries AS c
ON ST_Intersects(t.the_geom, c.the_geom)
```

```
GROUP BY c.country_name
ORDER BY run_distance DESC;
```

name character...	run_distance double precision
Italy	2635.9526890749
Hungary	20.9972673975372
Switzerland	20.869686631018
Greece	18.1060004470219

(4 rows)

How it works...

The `.gpx` files store all the points' details in the WGS 84 spatial reference system; therefore, we created the `rk_track_points` table with SRID (4326).

After creating the `rk_track_points` table, we imported all of the `.gpx` files in the `runkeeper_gpx` directory using a bash script. The bash script iterates all of the files with the extension `*.gpx` in the `runkeeper_gpx` directory. For each of these files, the script runs the `ogr2ogr` command, importing the `.gpx` files to PostGIS using the GPX GDAL driver (for more details, go to `http://www.gdal.org/drv_gpx.html`).

In the GDAL's abstraction, a `.gpx` file is an OGR data source composed of several layers as follows:

```
Chapter 3 — bash — 76×26
bash-3.2$ ogrinfo -so 2012-08-29-1930.gpx
Had to open data source read-only.
INFO: Open of `2012-08-29-1930.gpx'
      using driver `GPX' successful.
1: waypoints (Point)
2: routes (Line String)
3: tracks (Multi Line String)
4: route_points (Point)
5: track_points (Point)
bash-3.2$
```

In the .gpx files (OGR data sources), you have just the tracks and track_points layers. As a shortcut, you could have imported just the tracks layer using ogr2ogr, but you would need to start from the track_points layer in order to generate the tracks layer itself, using some PostGIS functions. This is why in the ogr2ogr section in the bash script, we imported to the rk_track_points PostGIS table the point geometries from the track_points layer, plus a couple of useful attributes, such as elevation and timestamp.

Once the records were imported, we fed a new polylines table named tracks using a subquery and selected all of the point geometries and their dates and times from the rk_track_points table, grouped by date and with the geometries aggregated using the ST_MakeLine function. This function was able to create linestrings from point geometries (for more details, go to http://www.postgis.org/docs/ST_MakeLine.html).

You should not forget to sort the points in the subquery by datetime; otherwise, you will obtain an irregular linestring, jumping from one point to the other and not following the correct order.

After loading the tracks table, we tested the two spatial queries.

At first, you got a month-by-month report of the total distance run by the runner. For this purpose, you selected all of the track records grouped by date (year and month), with the total distance obtained by summing up the lengths of the single tracks (obtained with the ST_Length function). To get the year and the month from the run_date function, you used the PostgreSQL EXTRACT function. Be aware that if you measure the distance using geometries in the WGS 84 system, you will obtain it in degree units. For this reason, you have to project the geometries to a planar metric system designed for the specific region from which the data will be projected.

For large-scale areas, such as in our case where we have points that span all around Europe, as shown in the last query results, a good option is to use the geography data type introduced with PostGIS 1.5. The calculations may be slower, but are much more accurate than in other systems. This is the reason why you cast the geometries to the geography data type before making measurements.

The last spatial query used a spatial join with the ST_Intersects function to get the name of the country for each track the runner ran (with the assumption that the runner didn't run cross-border tracks). Getting the total distance run per country is just a matter of aggregating the selection on the country_name field and aggregating the track distances with the PostgreSQL SUM operator.

Fixing invalid geometries

You will often find invalid geometries in your PostGIS database. These invalid geometries could compromise the functioning of PostGIS itself and any external tool using it, such as QGIS and MapServer. PostGIS, being compliant with the OGC Simple Feature Specification, must manage and work with valid geometries.

Luckily, PostGIS 2.0 offers you the ST_MakeValid function, which together with the ST_IsValid, ST_IsValidReason, and ST_IsValidDetails functions, is the ideal toolkit for inspecting and fixing geometries within the database. In this recipe, you will learn how to fix a common case of invalid geometry.

Getting ready

Unzip the data/TM_WORLD_BORDERS-0.3.zip file into your working directory, working/chp3. Import the shapefile in PostGIS with the shp2pgsql command, as follows:

```
$ shp2pgsql -s 4326 -g the_geom -W LATIN1 -I TM_WORLD_BORDERS-0.3.shp
chp03.countries > countries.sql
$ psql -U me -d postgis_cookbook -f countries.sql
```

The file is also included with the name of wborders since for some operating systems, it does not work with the characters of TM_WORLD_BORDERS-0.3.shp.

How to do it...

The steps you need to perform to complete this recipe are as follows:

1. First, investigate whether or not any geometry is invalid in the imported table. As you can see in the following query, using the ST_IsValid and ST_IsValidReason functions, we find four invalid geometries that are all invalid for the same reason—ring self-intersection:

```
postgis_cookbook=# SELECT gid, name, ST_IsValidReason(the_geom)
   FROM chp03.countries
   WHERE ST_IsValid(the_geom)=false;
```

gid integer	name character...	st_isvalidreason text
24	Canada	Ring Self-intersection[-53.756367 48.50326200...
33	Chile	Ring Self-intersection[-70.917236 -54.708618]
155	Norway	Ring Self-intersection[5.33694400000002 61.5...
175	Russia	Ring Self-intersection[143.661926 49.31221]

(4 rows)

2. Now concentrate on just one of the invalid geometries, for example, in the multipolygon geometry representing Russia. Create a table containing just the ring generating the invalidity, selecting the table using the point coordinates given in the ST_IsValidReason response in the previous step:

```
postgis_cookbook=# SELECT * INTO chp03.invalid_geometries FROM (
    SELECT 'broken'::varchar(10) as status,
    ST_GeometryN(the_geom, generate_series(
        1, ST_NRings(the_geom)))::geometry(Polygon,4326)
    as the_geom FROM chp03.countries
    WHERE name = 'Russia') AS foo
    WHERE ST_Intersects(the_geom,
        ST_SetSRID(ST_Point(143.661926,49.31221), 4326));
```

ST_MakeValid requires GEOS 3.3.0 or higher; check whether or not your system supports it using the PostGIS_full_version function as follows:

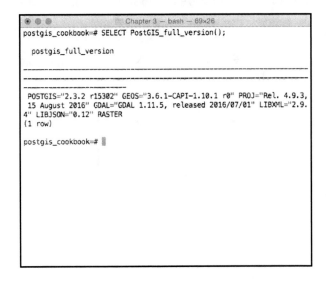

```
postgis_cookbook=# SELECT PostGIS_full_version();

 postgis_full_version

--------------------------------------------------------------
--------------------------------------------------------------
------------------------
 POSTGIS="2.3.2 r15302" GEOS="3.6.1-CAPI-1.10.1 r0" PROJ="Rel. 4.9.3,
 15 August 2016" GDAL="GDAL 1.11.5, released 2016/07/01" LIBXML="2.9.
4" LIBJSON="0.12" RASTER
(1 row)

postgis_cookbook=#
```

3. Now, using the `ST_MakeValid` function, add a new record in the previously created table with the valid version of the same geometry:

```
postgis_cookbook=# INSERT INTO chp03.invalid_geometries
VALUES ('repaired', (SELECT ST_MakeValid(the_geom)
FROM chp03.invalid_geometries));
```

4. Open this geometry on your desktop GIS; the invalid geometry has just one self-intersecting ring that produces a hole in its internal. While this is accepted in the ESRI shapefile format specification (that was the original dataset you imported), the OGC standard does not allow for the self-intersecting ring, so neither does PostGIS:

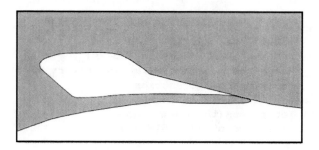

5. Now, in the `invalid_geometries` table, you have the invalid and valid versions of the polygon. It is easy to figure out that the self-intersecting ring was removed by `ST_MakeValid` adding one supplementary ring to the original polygon, which resulted in a valid geometry, according to the OGC standard:

```
postgis_cookbook=# SELECT status, ST_NRings(the_geom)
FROM chp03.invalid_geometries;
```

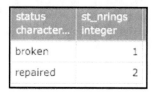

status character...	st_nrings integer
broken	1
repaired	2

(2 rows)

6. Now that you have identified the problem and its solution, don't forget to fix all the other invalid geometries in the `countries` table by executing the following code:

```
postgis_cookbook=# UPDATE chp03.countries
SET the_geom = ST_MakeValid(the_geom)
WHERE ST_IsValid(the_geom) = false;
```

A smart way to not have invalid geometries in the database at all is by adding a `CHECK` constraint on the table to check for validity. This will increase the computation time when updating or inserting new geometries, but will keep your dataset valid. For example, in the `countries` table, this can be implemented as follows:

```
ALTER TABLE chp03.countries
ADD CONSTRAINT geometry_valid_check
CHECK (ST_IsValid(the_geom));
```

Many times in real use cases, though, you will need to remove such a constraint in order to be able to import records from a different source. After making validations with the `ST_MakeValid` function, you can safely add the constraint again.

How it works...

There are a number of reasons why an invalid geometry could result in your database; for example, rings composed of polygons must be closed and cannot self-intersect or share more than one point with another ring.

After importing the `country` shapefile using the `ST_IsValid` and `ST_IsValidReason` functions, you will have figured out that four of the imported geometries are invalid, all because their polygons have self-intersecting rings.

At this point, a good way to investigate the invalid multipolygon geometry is by decomposing the polygon in to its component rings and checking out the invalid ones. For this purpose, we have exported the geometry of the ring causing the invalidity, using the `ST_GeometryN` function, which is able to extract the nth ring from the polygon. We coupled this function with the useful PostgreSQL `generate_series` function to iterate all of the rings composing the geometry, selecting the desired one using the `ST_Intersects` function.

As expected, the reason why this ring generates the invalidity is that it is self-intersecting and produces a hole in the polygon. While this adheres to the shapefile specification, it doesn't adhere to the OGC specification.

By running the `ST_MakeValid` function, PostGIS has been able to make the geometry valid, generating a second ring. Remember that the `ST_MakeValid` function is available only with the latest PostGIS compiled with the latest GEOS (3.3.0+). If that is not the setup for your working box and you cannot upgrade (upgrading is always recommended!), you can follow the techniques used in the past and discussed in a very popular, excellent presentation by *Paul Ramsey* at
`http://blog.opengeo.org/2010/09/08/tips-for-the-postgis-power-user/`.

GIS analysis with spatial joins

Joins for regular SQL tables have the real power in a relational database, and spatial joins are one of the most impressive features of a spatial database engine such as PostGIS.

Basically, it is possible to correlate information from different layers on the basis of the geometric relation of each feature from the input layers. In this recipe, we will take a tour of some common use cases of spatial joins.

Getting ready

1. First, import some data to be used as a test bed in PostGIS. Download the `.kmz` file containing information about 2012 global earthquakes from the USGS website at
   `http://earthquake.usgs.gov/earthquakes/eqarchives/epic/kml/2012_Earthq` `uakes_ALL.kmz`. Save it in the `working/chp03` directory (alternatively, you can use the copy of this file included in the code bundle provided with this book).

2. A `.kmz` file is a collection of `.kml` files packaged with the ZIP compressor. Therefore, after unzipping the file (you may need to change the `.kmz` file extension to `.zip`), you may notice that it is composed of just a single `.kml` file. This file, which is in the GDAL abstraction, constitutes an OGR KML data source composed of nine different layers and containing 3D point geometries. Each layer contains earthquake data for each distinct earthquake magnitude:

```
$ ogrinfo 2012_Earthquakes_ALL.kml
```

The output for this is as follows:

```
Chapter 3 — bash — 69×26
bash-3.2$ ogrinfo 2012_Earthquakes_ALL.kml
INFO: Open of `2012_Earthquakes_ALL.kml'
      using driver `LIBKML' successful.
1: Magnitude 8
2: Magnitude 7
3: Magnitude 6
4: Magnitude 5
5: Magnitude 4
6: Magnitude 3
7: Magnitude 2
8: Magnitude 1
9: Magnitude None
bash-3.2$
```

3. Import all of those layers in a PostGIS table named `chp03.earthquakes` simultaneously by executing one of the following scripts using the `ogr2ogr` command.

The following is the Linux version (name it `import_eq.sh`):

```
#!/bin/bash
for ((i = 1; i < 9 ; i++)) ; do
  echo "Importing earthquakes with magnitude $i
        to chp03.earthquakes PostGIS table..."
  ogr2ogr -append -f PostgreSQL -nln chp03.earthquakes
  PG:"dbname='postgis_cookbook' user='me'
  password='mypassword'" 2012_Earthquakes_ALL.kml
  -sql "SELECT name, description, CAST($i AS integer)
  AS magnitude FROM \"Magnitude $i\""
done
```

The following is the Windows version (name it `import_eq.bat`):

```
@echo off
for /l %%i in (1, 1, 9) do (
  echo "Importing earthquakes with magnitude %%i
        to chp03.earthquakes PostGIS table..."
  ogr2ogr -append -f PostgreSQL -nln chp03.earthquakes
  PG:"dbname='postgis_cookbook' user='me'
  password='mypassword'" 2012_Earthquakes_ALL.kml
  -sql "SELECT name, description, CAST(%%i AS integer)
  AS magnitude FROM \"Magnitude %%i\""
)
```

4. Execute the following script (for Linux, you need to add `execute` permissions to it):

```
$ chmod 775 import_eq.sh
$ ./import_eq.sh
Importing earthquakes with magnitude 1 to chp03.earthquakes
  PostGIS table...
Importing earthquakes with magnitude 2 to chp03.earthquakes
  PostGIS table...
...
```

5. To maintain consistency with the book's conventions, rename the geometric column `wkb_geometry` (the default geometry output name in `ogr2ogr`) to `the_geom`, as illustrated in the following command:

```
postgis_cookbook=# ALTER TABLE chp03.earthquakes
RENAME wkb_geometry  TO the_geom;
```

6. Download the `cities` shapefile for the USA from the `https://nationalmap.gov/` website at `http://dds.cr.usgs.gov/pub/data/nationalatlas/citiesx020_nt00007.tar.gz` (this archive is also included in the code bundle provided with this book) and import it in PostGIS by executing the following code:

```
$ ogr2ogr -f PostgreSQL -s_srs EPSG:4269 -t_srs EPSG:4326
-lco GEOMETRY_NAME=the_geom -nln chp03.cities
PG:"dbname='postgis_cookbook' user='me'
password='mypassword'" citiesx020.shp
```

7. Download the `states` shapefile for the USA from the `https://nationalmap.gov/` website at `http://dds.cr.usgs.gov/pub/data/nationalatlas/statesp020_nt00032.tar.gz` (this archive is also included in the code bundle provided with this book) and import it in PostGIS by executing the following code:

```
$ ogr2ogr -f PostgreSQL -s_srs EPSG:4269 -t_srs EPSG:4326
-lco GEOMETRY_NAME=the_geom -nln chp03.states -nlt MULTIPOLYGON
PG:"dbname='postgis_cookbook' user='me'
password='mypassword'" statesp020.shp
```

How to do it...

In this recipe, you will see for yourself the power of spatial SQL by solving a series of typical problems using spatial joins:

1. First, query PostGIS to get the number of registered earthquakes in 2012 by state:

```
postgis_cookbook=# SELECT s.state, COUNT(*) AS hq_count
FROM chp03.states AS s
  JOIN chp03.earthquakes AS e
  ON ST_Intersects(s.the_geom, e.the_geom)
  GROUP BY s.state
  ORDER BY hq_count DESC;
```

	state character varying (20)	hq_count bigint
1	Alaska	569
2	California	467
3	Hawaii	93
4	Oklahoma	69
5	Puerto Rico	50
6	Washington	45
7	Nevada	38
8	Texas	29
9	Utah	26
10	Montana	16
11	Virginia	15
12	Colorado	14
13	Wyoming	9
14	Missouri	8
15	South Carolina	7
16	Oregon	7
17	New Mexico	7
18	Arkansas	6

```
(33 rows)
```

2. Now, to make it just a bit more complex, query PostGIS to get the number of earthquakes, grouped per magnitude, that are no further than 200 km from the cities in the USA that have more than 1 million inhabitants; execute the following code:

```
postgis_cookbook=# SELECT c.name, e.magnitude, count(*) as hq_count
FROM chp03.cities AS c
  JOIN chp03.earthquakes AS e
  ON ST_DWithin(geography(c.the_geom), geography(e.the_geom), 200000)
  WHERE c.pop_2000 > 1000000
  GROUP BY c.name, e.magnitude
  ORDER BY c.name, e.magnitude, hq_count;
```

	name character varying (48)	magnitude integer	hq_count bigint
1	Chicago	2	1
2	Chicago	3	1
3	Dallas	2	12
4	Dallas	3	3
5	Los Angeles	1	6
6	Los Angeles	2	123
7	Los Angeles	3	42
8	Los Angeles	4	5
9	New York	2	1
10	Philadelphia	2	1
11	Phoenix	2	2
12	Phoenix	3	1
13	San Antonio	3	2
14	San Diego	1	5
15	San Diego	2	146
16	San Diego	3	115
17	San Diego	4	20
18	San Diego	5	2

(18 rows)

3. As a variant of the previous query, executing the following code gives you a complete list of earthquakes along with their distance from the city (in meters):

```
postgis_cookbook=# SELECT c.name, e.magnitude,
  ST_Distance(geography(c.the_geom), geography(e.the_geom))
AS distance FROM chp03.cities AS c
  JOIN chp03.earthquakes AS e
  ON ST_DWithin(geography(c.the_geom), geography(e.the_geom), 200000)
  WHERE c.pop_2000 > 1000000
  ORDER BY distance;
```

	name character varying (48)	magnitude integer	distance double precision
1	Dallas	2	10801.32538582
2	Los Angeles	3	13740.79435945
3	Los Angeles	2	14177.4254134
4	Los Angeles	3	14795.11395056
5	Los Angeles	2	16333.47874173
6	Los Angeles	2	16356.80430452
7	Los Angeles	2	17888.84269178
8	Los Angeles	3	17982.34713687
9	Los Angeles	2	18173.9790877
10	Los Angeles	1	18456.68842596
11	San Diego	2	20993.86018107
12	Los Angeles	2	21420.83066686
13	Los Angeles	2	21764.06476769
14	Los Angeles	2	25593.48907654
15	Los Angeles	2	29458.55628255
16	Los Angeles	2	30082.25041362

```
(488 rows)
```

4. Now, ask PostGIS for the city count and the total population in each state by executing the following code:

```
postgis_cookbook-# SELECT s.state, COUNT(*)
AS city_count, SUM(pop_2000) AS pop_2000
FROM chp03.states AS s
  JOIN chp03.cities AS c
  ON ST_Intersects(s.the_geom, c.the_geom)
  WHERE c.pop_2000 > 0 -- NULL values is -9999 on this field!
```

```
GROUP BY s.state
ORDER BY pop_2000 DESC;
```

	state character varying (20)	city_count bigint	pop_2000 numeric
1	California	470	27380349
2	Texas	1182	15738629
3	New York	613	12139544
4	Illinois	1273	10617791
5	Florida	389	7658770
6	Ohio	933	7448610
7	Pennsylvania	1008	5653936
8	Michigan	532	5433183
9	New Jersey	323	4088938
10	Arizona	87	4045436
11	North Carolina	536	4040565
12	Minnesota	849	3912592
13	Wisconsin	581	3679692
14	Missouri	937	3611495
15	Washington	275	3408303
16	Indiana	560	3099686
17	Colorado	269	3025069
18	Massachusetts	44	3011742

(51 rows)

5. As a final test, use a spatial join to update an existing table. You need to add the information in the `state_fips` field to the `earthquake` table from the `states` table. First, to host that kind of information, you need to create a column as shown in the following command:

```
postgis_cookbook-# ALTER TABLE chp03.earthquakes
ADD COLUMN state_fips character varying(2);
```

6. Then, you can update the new column using a spatial join, as follows:

```
postgis_cookbook-# UPDATE chp03.earthquakes AS e
   SET state_fips = s.state_fips
   FROM chp03.states AS s
   WHERE ST_Intersects(s.the_geom, e.the_geom);
```

How it works...

Spatial joins are one of the key features that unleash the spatial power of PostGIS. For a regular join, it is possible to relate entities from two distinct tables using a common field. For a spatial join, it is possible to relate features from two distinct spatial tables using any spatial relationship function, such as ST_Contains, ST_Covers, ST_Crosses, and ST_DWithin.

In the first query, we used the ST_Intersects function to join the earthquake points to their respective state. We grouped the query by the state column to obtain the number of earthquakes in the state.

In the second query, we used the ST_DWithin function to relate each city to the earthquake points within a 200 km distance of it. We filtered out the cities with a population of less than 1 million inhabitants and grouped them by city name and earthquake magnitude to get a report of the number of earthquakes per city and by magnitude.

The third query is similar to the second one, except it doesn't group per city and by magnitude. The distance is computed using the ST_Distance function. Note that as feature coordinates are stored in WGS 84, you need to cast the geometric column to a spheroid and use the spheroid to get the distance in meters. Alternatively, you could project the geometries to a planar system that is accurate for the area we are studying in this recipe (in this case, the *ESPG:2163, US National Atlas Equal Area* would be a good choice) using the ST_Transform function. However, in the case of large areas like the one we've dealt with in this recipe, casting to geography is generally the best option as it gives more accurate results.

The fourth query uses the ST_Intersects function. In this case, we grouped by the state column and used two aggregation SQL functions (SUM and COUNT) to get the desired results.

Finally, in the last query, you update a spatial table using the results of a spatial join. The concept behind this is like that of the previous query, except that it is in the context of an UPDATE SQL command.

Simplifying geometries

There will be many times when you will need to generate a less detailed and lighter version of a vector dataset, as you may not need very detailed features for several reasons. Think about a case where you are going to publish the dataset to a website and performance is a concern, or maybe you need to deploy the dataset to a colleague who does not need too much detail because they are using it for a large-area map. In all these cases, GIS tools include implementations of **simplification algorithms** that reduce unwanted details from a given dataset. Basically, these algorithms reduce the vertex numbers comprised in a certain tolerance, which is expressed in units measuring distance.

For this purpose, PostGIS provides you with the ST_Simplify and ST_SimplifyPreserveTopology functions. In many cases, they are the right solutions for simplification tasks, but in some cases, especially for polygonal features, they are not the best option out there and you will need a different GIS tool, such as GRASS or the new PostGIS topology support.

How to do it...

The steps you need to do to complete this recipe are as follows:

1. Set the PostgreSQL search_path variable such that all your newly created database objects will be stored in the chp03 schema, using the following code:

   ```
   postgis_cookbook=# SET search_path TO chp03,public;
   ```

2. Suppose you need a less-detailed version of the states layer for your mapping website or to deploy to a client; you could consider using the ST_SimplifyPreserveTopology function as follows:

   ```
   postgis_cookbook=# CREATE TABLE states_simplify_topology AS
     SELECT ST_SimplifyPreserveTopology(ST_Transform(
       the_geom, 2163), 500) FROM states;
   ```

3. The previous command works quickly, using a variant of the **Douglas-Peucker** algorithm, and effectively reduces the vertex number. But the resulting polygons, in some cases, are not adjacent any more. If you zoom in at any polygon border, you should notice something shown in the following screenshot: there are holes and overlaps along the shared border between two polygons. This is because PostGIS is using the OGC Simple Feature model, which doesn't implement topology, so the function just removes the redundant vertex without taking the adjacent polygons into consideration:

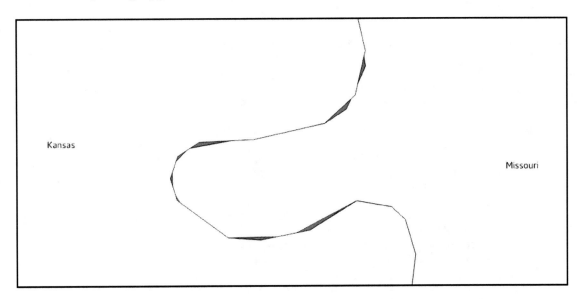

4. It looks like the ST_SimplifyPreserveTopology function, while working well with linear features, produces topological anomalies with polygons. In case you want topological simplification, another approach is the following code suggested by *Paul Ramsey* (http://gis.stackexchange.com/questions/178/simplifying-adjacent-polygons) and improved in a *Webspaces* blog post (http://webspaces.net.nz/page.php?view=polygon-dissolve-and-generalise):

```
SET search_path TO chp03, public;
-- first project the spatial table to a planar system
  (recommended for simplification operations)
CREATE TABLE states_2163 AS SELECT ST_Transform
  (the_geom, 2163)::geometry(MultiPolygon, 2163)
  AS the_geom, state FROM states;
```

```
-- now decompose the geometries from multipolygons to polygons (2895)
   using the ST_Dump function
CREATE TABLE polygons AS SELECT (ST_Dump(the_geom)).geom AS the_geom
   FROM states_2163;
-- now decompose from polygons (2895) to rings (3150)
   using the ST_DumpRings function
CREATE TABLE rings AS SELECT (ST_DumpRings(the_geom)).geom
   AS the_geom FROM polygons;
-- now decompose from rings (3150) to linestrings (3150)
   using the ST_Boundary function
CREATE TABLE ringlines AS SELECT(ST_boundary(the_geom))
   AS the_geom FROM rings;
-- now merge all linestrings (3150) in a single merged linestring
   (this way duplicate linestrings at polygon borders disappear)
CREATE TABLE mergedringlines AS SELECT ST_Union(the_geom)
   AS the_geom FROM ringlines;
-- finally simplify the linestring with a tolerance of 150 meters
CREATE TABLE simplified_ringlines AS SELECT
ST_SimplifyPreserveTopology(the_geom, 150)
AS the_geom FROM mergedringlines;
-- now compose a polygons collection from the linestring
using the ST_Polygonize function
CREATE TABLE simplified_polycollection AS SELECT
   ST_Polygonize(the_geom) AS the_geom FROM simplified_ringlines;
-- here you generate polygons (2895) from the polygons collection
   using ST_Dumps
CREATE TABLE simplified_polygons AS SELECT
   ST_Transform((ST_Dump(the_geom)).geom,
   4326)::geometry(Polygon,4326)
   AS the_geom FROM simplified_polycollection;
-- time to create an index, to make next operations faster
   CREATE INDEX simplified_polygons_gist ON simplified_polygons
   USING GIST (the_geom);
-- now copy the state name attribute from old layer with a spatial
   join using the ST_Intersects and ST_PointOnSurface function
CREATE TABLE simplified_polygonsattr AS SELECT new.the_geom,
   old.state FROM simplified_polygons new, states old
   WHERE ST_Intersects(new.the_geom, old.the_geom)
   AND ST_Intersects(ST_PointOnSurface(new.the_geom), old.the_geom);
-- now make the union of all polygons with a common name
CREATE TABLE states_simplified AS SELECT ST_Union(the_geom)
   AS the_geom, state FROM simplified_polygonsattr GROUP BY state;
```

5. This approach seems to work smoothly, but if you try to increment the simplifying tolerance from 150 to, let's say, 500 meters, you will again end up with topological anomalies (test this yourself). A better approach would be to use the PostGIS topology (you will do this in the *Simplifying geometries with PostGIS topology* recipe) or an external GIS tool that is able to manage topological operations the way GRASS can. For this recipe, you will use the GRASS approach.

6. Install GRASS on your system if you don't have it. Then, create a directory to contain the GRASS database (in GRASS jargon, a GISDBASE), as follows:

   ```
   $ mkdir grass_db
   ```

7. Now, start GRASS by typing grass in the Linux command prompt or by double-clicking on the **GRASS GUI** icon in Windows (**Start** | **All Programs** | **OSGeo4W** | **GRASS GIS 6.4.3** | **GRASS 6.4.3 GUI**) or on **Applications** in macOS. You will be prompted to select the grass_db database as the GIS data directory but should instead select the one you created in the previous step.

8. Using the **Location Wizard** button, create a location named postgis_cookbook with the title PostGIS Cookbook (GRASS uses subdirectories named locations, where all of the data is kept in the same coordinate system, map projection, and geographical boundaries).

9. When creating the new location, select the EPSG with SRID 2163 as the spatial reference system (you need to select the **Select EPSG code of spatial reference system** option under **Choose method for creating a new location**).

10. Now start GRASS by clicking on the **Start GRASS** button. The program's command line will start as shown in the following screenshot:

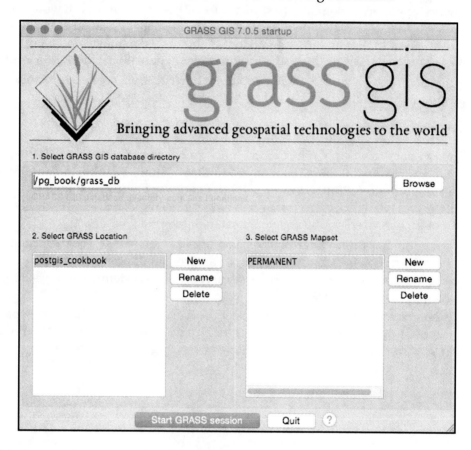

11. Import the states PostGIS spatial table to the GRASS location. To do so, use the v.in.ogr GRASS command, which will then use the OGR PostgreSQL driver (in fact, the PostGIS connection string syntax is the same):

```
GRASS 6.4.1 (postgis_cookbook):~ > v.in.ogr
input=PG:"dbname='postgis_cookbook' user='me'
password='mypassword'" layer=chp03.states_2163 out=states
```

12. GRASS will import the OGR PostGIS table and simultaneously build the topology for this layer, which is composed of points, lines, areas, and so on. The v.info command can be used in combination with the -c option to check the attributes table and get more information on the imported layer, as follows:

GRASS 6.4.1 (postgis_cookbook):~ > v.info states

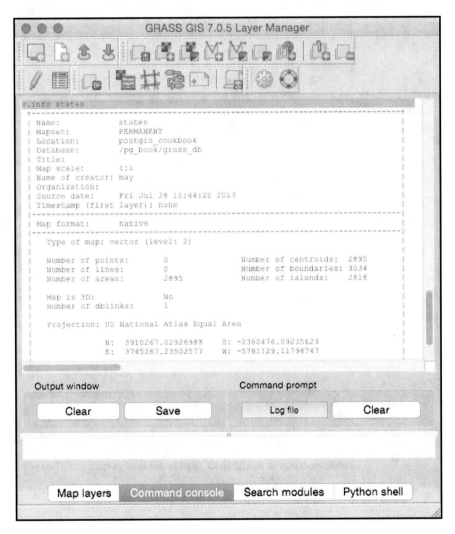

13. Now, you can simplify the polygon geometries using the
    v.generalizeGRASS command with a tolerance (threshold) of 500 meters. If you
    are using the same dataset used in this recipe, you will end up with 47,191
    vertices from the original 346,914 vertices, composing 1,919 polygons (areas) from
    the original 2,895 polygons:

    ```
    GRASS 6.4.1 (postgis_cookbook):~ > v.generalize input=states
    output=states_generalized_from_grass method=douglas threshold=500
    ```

14. Export the results back to PostGIS using the v.out.ogr command (the
    v.in.ogr counterpart) as follows:

    ```
    GRASS 6.4.1 (postgis_cookbook):~ > v.out.ogr
    input=states_generalized_from_grass
    type=area dsn=PG:"dbname='postgis_cookbook' user='me'
    password='mypassword'" olayer=chp03.states_simplified_from_grass
    format=PostgreSQL
    ```

15. Now, open a desktop GIS and check for differences between the geometry
    simplification performed by the ST_SimplifyPreserveTopology PostGIS
    function and GRASS. There should be no holes or overlaps at shared polygon
    borders. In the following screenshot, the original layer boundaries are in red, the
    boundaries built by ST_SimplifyPreserveTopology are in blue, and those
    built by GRASS are in green:

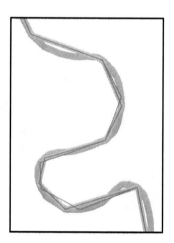

How it works...

The ST_Simplify PostGIS function is able to simplify and generalize either a (simple or multi) linear or polygonal geometry using the Douglas-Peucker algorithm (for more details, go to
http://en.wikipedia.org/wiki/Ramer%E2%80%93Douglas%E2%80%93Peucker_algorithm).
Since it can create invalid geometries in some cases, it is recommended that you use its evolved version—the ST_SimplifyPreserveTopology function—which will produce only valid geometries.

While the functions are working well with (multi) linear geometries, in the case of (multi) polygons, they will most likely create topological anomalies such as overlaps and holes at shared polygon borders.

To get a valid, topologically simplified dataset, there are the following two choices at the time of writing:

- Performing the simplified process on an external GIS tool such as GRASS
- Using the new PostGIS topological support

While you will see the new PostGIS topological features in the *Simplifying geometries with PostGIS topology* recipe, in this one you have been using GRASS to perform the simplification process.

We opened GRASS, created a GIS data directory and a project location, and then imported in the GRASS location, the polygonal PostGIS table using the v.ogr.in command, based on GDAL/OGR as the name suggests.

Until this point, you have been using the GRASS v.generalize command to perform the simplification of the dataset using a tolerance (threshold) expressed in meters.

After simplifying the dataset, you imported it back to PostGIS using the v.ogr.out GRASS command and then opened the derived spatial table in a desktop GIS to see whether or not the process was performed in a topologically correct way.

Measuring distances

In this recipe, we will check out the PostGIS functions needed for distance measurements (ST_Distance and its variants) and find out how considering the earth's curvature makes a big difference when measuring distances between distant points.

Getting ready

You should import the shapefile representing the cities from the USA that we generated in a previous recipe (the PostGIS table named chp03.cities). In case you haven't done so, download that shapefile from the https://nationalmap.gov/ website at http://dds.cr.usgs.gov/pub/data/nationalatlas/citiesx020_nt00007.tar.gz (this archive is also included in the code bundle available with this book) and import it to PostGIS:

```
$ ogr2ogr -f PostgreSQL -s_srs EPSG:4269 -t_srs EPSG:4326 -lco
GEOMETRY_NAME=the_geom -nln chp03.cities PG:"dbname='postgis_cookbook'
user='me' password='mypassword'" citiesx020.shp
```

How to do it...

The steps you need to perform to complete this recipe are as follows:

1. First, use the ST_Distance function to calculate the distances between cities in the USA that have more than 1 million inhabitants using the Spherical Mercator planar projection coordinate system (EPSG:900913, EPSG:3857, or EPSG:3785; all of these SRID representations are equivalent). Use the ST_Transform function as follows to convert the point coordinates from longitude latitude degrees (as the coordinates are originally in EPSG:4326) to a planar metric system if you want the results in meters:

```
postgis_cookbook=# SELECT c1.name, c2.name,
ST_Distance(ST_Transform(c1.the_geom, 900913),
ST_Transform(c2.the_geom, 900913))/1000 AS distance_900913
FROM chp03.cities AS c1
CROSS JOIN chp03.cities AS c2
WHERE c1.pop_2000 > 1000000 AND c2.pop_2000 > 1000000
```

```
AND c1.name < c2.name
ORDER BY distance_900913 DESC;
```

name character varying	name character...	distance_900913 double precision
Los Angeles	New York	5012.39789777705
New York	San Diego	4930.76973825481
Los Angeles	Philadelp...	4865.7736877805
Philadelphia	San Diego	4780.75534852016
New York	Phoenix	4357.65042348628
Philadelphia	Phoenix	4207.11144465307
Chicago	Los Angel...	3579.74499656761
Chicago	San Diego	3525.66220065254
New York	San Anto...	3131.1519653319
Chicago	Phoenix	2965.31085245556
Philadelphia	San Anto...	2964.38727187371
Houston	New York	2809.59489330785
Dallas	New York	2767.09085048549
Houston	Philadelp...	2641.3617700694
Houston	Los Angel...	2608.44376391324

(36 rows)

2. Now write the same query as we did in the previous recipe, but in a more compact expression using a PostgreSQL **Common Table Expression (CTE)**:

```
WITH cities AS (
  SELECT name, the_geom FROM chp03.cities
  WHERE pop_2000 > 1000000 )
SELECT c1.name, c2.name,
ST_Distance(ST_Transform(c1.the_geom, 900913),
ST_Transform(c2.the_geom, 900913))/1000 AS distance_900913
FROM cities c1 CROSS JOIN cities c2
where c1.name < c2.name
ORDER BY distance_900913 DESC;
```

3. For large distances such as in this case, it is not correct to use a planar spatial reference system, but you should make the calculations taking into consideration the earth's curvature. For example, the previously used Mercator planar system, while it is very good to use for map outputs, is very bad for measuring distances and areas as it assesses directions. For this purpose, it would be better to use a spatial reference system that is able to measure distance. You can also use the `ST_Distance_Sphere` or `ST_Distance_Spheroid` functions (the first being quicker, but less accurate, as it performs calculations on a sphere and not a spheroid). An even better option is converting the geometries to the geography data type, so you can use `ST_Distance` directly, as it will automatically make the calculations using the spheroid. Note that this is exactly equivalent to using `ST_DistanceSpheroid`. Try to check the difference between the various approaches, using the same query as before:

```
WITH cities AS (
    SELECT name, the_geom FROM chp03.cities
    WHERE pop_2000 > 1000000 )
SELECT c1.name, c2.name,
ST_Distance(ST_Transform(c1.the_geom, 900913),
ST_Transform(c2.the_geom, 900913))/1000 AS d_900913,
ST_Distance_Sphere(c1.the_geom, c2.the_geom)/1000 AS d_4326_sphere,
ST_Distance_Spheroid(c1.the_geom, c2.the_geom,
'SPHEROID["GRS_1980",6378137,298.257222101]')/1000
AS d_4326_spheroid, ST_Distance(geography(c1.the_geom),
geography(c2.the_geom))/1000 AS d_4326_geography
FROM cities c1 CROSS JOIN cities c2
where c1.name < c2.name
ORDER BY d_900913 DESC;
```

name character varying (48)	name character varying (48)	d_900913 double precision	d_4326_sphere double precision	d_4326_spheroid double precision	d_4326_geography double precision
1	Los Angeles	New York	5012.39789777705	3935.74115686369	3944.41160909487	3944.41160907395
2	New York	San Diego	4930.76973825481	3906.86148389954	3915.0331918683	3915.03319184967
3	Los Angeles	Philadelphia	4865.7736877805	3843.57873347389	3852.06330276004	3852.06330273953
4	Philadelphia	San Diego	4780.75534852016	3810.37613937718	3818.3784255823	3818.37842556397
5	New York	Phoenix	4357.65042348628	3443.7123168818	3450.94938077339	3450.9493807568
6	Philadelphia	Phoenix	4207.11144465307	3344.19956146655	3351.26898955653	3351.26898954022
7	Chicago	Los Angeles	3579.74499656761	2801.88019635806	2807.44581721511	2807.44581720319
8	Chicago	San Diego	3525.66220065253	2784.10287096005	2789.065461575	2789.06546156595
9	New York	San Antonio	3131.1519653319	2545.0828938848	2547.96583391574	2547.96583391556
10	Chicago	Phoenix	2965.31085245556	2333.8930279788	2337.84912942891	2337.84912942232
11	Philadelphia	San Antonio	2964.38727187371	2422.53245280971	2425.30930889039	2425.30930889006
12	Houston	New York	2809.59489330785	2280.7263645219	2282.91609704207	2282.91609704385
13	Dallas	New York	2767.09085048549	2205.66740133895	2209.26308349004	2209.26308348451
14	Houston	Philadelphia	2641.3617700694	2155.67372341016	2157.75876606099	2157.75876606259
15	Houston	Los Angeles	2608.44376391324	2206.76293230789	2210.80231596966	2210.80231596196
16	Dallas	Philadelphia	2605.01056974768	2088.00596040165	2091.47983940957	2091.47983940399
17	Houston	San Diego	2456.36247129124	2094.02398502667	2098.00430601384	2098.00430600582
18	Dallas	Los Angeles	2393.05949749462	1991.55671540954	1995.76534592514	1995.76534591543
19	Los Angeles	San Antonio	2280.57604848914	1933.76501677409	1937.0598836447	1937.05988363915
20	Dallas	San Diego	2266.14567028811	1900.84420484781	1904.83747081111	1904.83747080196

(36 rows)

4. You can easily verify from the output that there is a big difference with using the planar system (EPSG:900913, as in the `d_900913` column) instead of systems that take into consideration the curvature of the earth.

How it works...

If you need to compute the minimum Cartesian distance between two points, you can use the PostGIS `ST_Distance` function. This function accepts two-point geometries as input parameters and these geometries must be specified in the same **spatial reference system**.

If the two input geometries are using different spatial references, you can use the `ST_Transform` function on one or both of them to make them consistent with a single spatial reference system.

To get better results, you should consider the earth's curvature, which is mandatory when measuring large distances, and use the ST_Distance_Sphere or the ST_Distance_Spheroid functions. Alternatively, use ST_Distance, but cast the input geometries to the **geography spatial data type**, which is optimized for this kind of operation. The geography type stores the geometries in WGS 84 longitude latitude degrees, but it always returns the measurements in meters.

In this recipe, you have used a PostgreSQL CTE, which is a handy way to provide a subquery in the context of the main query. You can consider a CTE as a temporary table used only within the scope of the main query.

Merging polygons using a common attribute

There are many cases in GIS workflows where you need to merge a polygonal dataset based on a common attribute. A typical example is merging the European administrative areas (which you can see at
`http://en.wikipedia.org/wiki/Nomenclature_of_Territorial_Units_for_Statistics`),
starting from **Nomenclature des Units Territoriales Statistiques** (**NUTS**) level 4 to obtain the subsequent levels up to NUTS level 1, using the NUTS code or merging the USA counties layer using the state code to obtain the states layer.

PostGIS lets you perform this kind of processing operation with the ST_Union function.

Getting ready

Download the USA countries shapefile from the `https://nationalmap.gov/` website at
`http://dds.cr.usgs.gov/pub/data/nationalatlas/co2000p020_nt00157.tar.gz` (this archive is also included in the code bundle provided with this book) and import it in PostGIS as follows:

```
$ ogr2ogr -f PostgreSQL -s_srs EPSG:4269 -t_srs EPSG:4326 -lco
GEOMETRY_NAME=the_geom -nln chp03.counties -nlt MULTIPOLYGON
PG:"dbname='postgis_cookbook' user='me' password='mypassword'"
co2000p020.shp
```

How to do it...

The steps you need to perform to complete this recipe are as follows:

1. First, check the imported table by running the following commands:

   ```
   postgis_cookbook=# SELECT county, fips, state_fips
   FROM chp03.counties ORDER BY county;
   ```

county character varying	fips character...	state_fips character...
Abbeville County	45001	45
Acadia Parish	22001	22
Accomack County	51001	51
Accomack County	51001	51
Accomack County	51001	51
Accomack County	51001	51
Accomack County	51001	51
Accomack County	51001	51
Accomack County	51001	51
Accomack County	51001	51
Accomack County	51001	51
Accomack County	51001	51
Accomack County	51001	51
Accomack County	51001	51
Accomack County	51001	51
Accomack County	51001	51

   (6138 rows)

2. Now perform the merging operation based on the `state_fips` field, using the `ST_Union` PostGIS function:

   ```
   postgis_cookbook=# CREATE TABLE chp03.states_from_counties
   AS SELECT ST_Multi(ST_Union(the_geom)) as the_geom, state_fips
   FROM chp03.counties GROUP BY state_fips;
   ```

3. The following screenshot shows how the output PostGIS layer looks in a desktop GIS; the aggregate counties have successfully been composed by their respective state (indicated by the thick blue border):

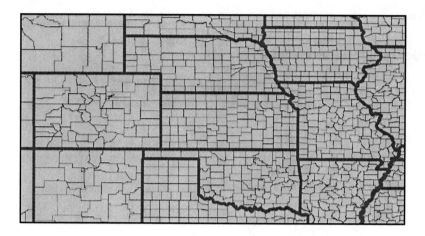

How it works...

You have been using the ST_Union PostGIS function to make a polygon merge on a common attribute. This function can be used as an aggregate PostgreSQL function (such as SUM, COUNT, MIN, and MAX) on the layer's geometric field, using the common attribute in the GROUP BY clause.

Note that ST_Union can also be used as a non-aggregate function to perform the union of two geometries (which are the two input parameters).

Computing intersections

One typical GIS geoprocessing workflow is to compute intersections generated by intersecting linear geometries.

PostGIS offers a rich set of functions for solving this particular type of problem and you will have a look at them in this recipe.

Getting ready

For this recipe, we will use the Rivers + lake centerlines dataset of North America and Europe with a scale 1:10m. Download the `rivers` dataset from the following `naturalearthdata.com` website (or use the ZIP file included in the code bundle provided with this book):

```
http://www.naturalearthdata.com/http//www.naturalearthdata.com/download/10m/phy
sical/ne_10m_rivers_lake_centerlines.zip
```

Or find it on the following website:

```
http://www.naturalearthdata.com/downloads/10m-physical-vectors/
```

Extract the shapefile to your working directory `chp03/working`. Import the shapefile in PostGIS using `shp2pgsql` as follows:

```
$ shp2pgsql -I -W LATIN1 -s 4326 -g the_geom
ne_10m_rivers_lake_centerlines.shp chp03.rivers > rivers.sql
$ psql -U me -d postgis_cookbook -f rivers.sql
```

How to do it...

The steps you need to perform to complete this recipe are as follows:

1. First, perform a self-spatial join between your `MultiLineString` dataset and the PostGIS `ST_Intersects` function and find intersections in the join context with the `ST_Intersection` PostGIS function. The following is the basic query, resulting in 1,448 records being selected:

```
postgis_cookbook=#  SELECT r1.gid AS gid1, r2.gid AS gid2,
ST_AsText(ST_Intersection(r1.the_geom, r2.the_geom)) AS the_geom
FROM chp03.rivers r1
JOIN chp03.rivers r2
ON ST_Intersects(r1.the_geom, r2.the_geom)
WHERE r1.gid != r2.gid;
```

2. You may hastily assume that all of the intersections are single points, but this is not the case; if you check the geometry type of the geometric intersections using the `ST_GeometryType` function, you have three different cases of intersection, resulting in the following geometries:

    - An `ST_POINT` geometry for a simple intersection between two linear geometries.

- An `ST_MultiPoint` geometry, if two linear geometries intersect each other at more points.
- An `ST_GeometryCollection` geometry in cases where the two `MultiLineString` objects intersect and share part of the line. In such a case, the geometry collection is composed of `ST_Point` and/or `ST_Line` geometries.

3. You can check the different cases with a query, shown as follows:

```
postgis_cookbook=# SELECT COUNT(*),
   ST_GeometryType(ST_Intersection(r1.the_geom, r2.the_geom))
     AS geometry_type
FROM chp03.rivers r1
JOIN chp03.rivers r2
ON ST_Intersects(r1.the_geom, r2.the_geom)
WHERE r1.gid != r2.gid
GROUP BY geometry_type;
```

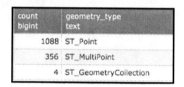

count bigint	geometry_type text
1088	ST_Point
356	ST_MultiPoint
4	ST_GeometryCollection

(3 rows)

4. First, try to compute the intersection for just the first two cases (intersections composed of the `ST_Point` and `ST_MultiPoint` geometries). Just generate a table with the `Point` and `MultiPoint` geometries, excluding the records that have an intersection composed of a geometric collection. By executing the following commands, 1,444 of the 1,448 records are imported (the four records with geometry collections are ignored using the `ST_GeometryType` function):

```
postgis_cookbook=# CREATE TABLE chp03.intersections_simple AS
   SELECT r1.gid AS gid1, r2.gid AS gid2,
     ST_Multi(ST_Intersection(r1.the_geom,
     r2.the_geom))::geometry(MultiPoint, 4326) AS the_geom
FROM chp03.rivers r1
JOIN chp03.rivers r2
ON ST_Intersects(r1.the_geom, r2.the_geom)
WHERE r1.gid != r2.gid
AND ST_GeometryType(ST_Intersection(r1.the_geom,
   r2.the_geom)) != 'ST_GeometryCollection';
```

5. In case you want to import the points from the geometry collection too (but just the points, ignoring the eventual linestrings), one way to go about it is by using the ST_CollectionExtract function in the context of a SELECTCASE PostgreSQL conditional statement; this way, you can import all the 1,448 intersections as follows:

```
postgis_cookbook=# CREATE TABLE chp03.intersections_all AS
SELECT gid1, gid2, the_geom::geometry(MultiPoint, 4326) FROM (
  SELECT r1.gid AS gid1, r2.gid AS gid2,
  CASE
    WHEN ST_GeometryType(ST_Intersection(r1.the_geom,
      r2.the_geom)) != 'ST_GeometryCollection' THEN
    ST_Multi(ST_Intersection(r1.the_geom,
      r2.the_geom))
    ELSE ST_CollectionExtract(ST_Intersection(r1.the_geom,
      r2.the_geom), 1)
  END AS the_geom
  FROM chp03.rivers r1
  JOIN chp03.rivers r2
  ON ST_Intersects(r1.the_geom, r2.the_geom)
  WHERE r1.gid != r2.gid
) AS only_multipoints_geometries;
```

6. You may see the difference between the two processes, counting the total number of points in each of the generated tables, as follows:

```
postgis_cookbook=# SELECT SUM(ST_NPoints(the_geom))
  FROM chp03.intersections_simple; --2268 points per 1444 records
postgis_cookbook=# SELECT SUM(ST_NPoints(the_geom))
  FROM chp03.intersections_all; --2282 points per 1448 records
```

7. In the following screenshot (taken from QGIS), you may notice the generated intersections generated by both approaches. In the case of the `intersection_all` layer, you will notice that some more intersections have been computed (in red):

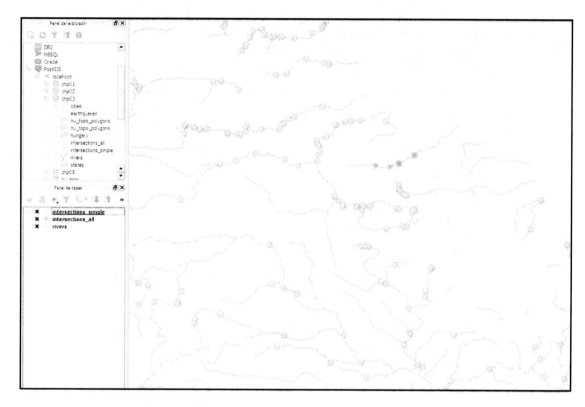

Layers of river intersections visualized in QGIS

How it works...

We have been using a self-spatial join of a linear PostGIS spatial layer to find intersections generated by the features of that layer.

To generate the self-spatial join, we used the `ST_Intersects` function. This way, we found that all of the features have at least an intersection in their respective geometries.

In the same self-spatial join context, we found out the intersections, using the `ST_Intersection` function.

The problem is that the computed intersections are not always single points. In fact, two intersecting lines can produce the origin for a single-point geometry (ST_Point) if the two lines just intersect once. But, the two intersecting lines can produce the origin for a point collection (ST_MultiPoint) or even a geometric collection if the two lines intersect at more points and/or share common parts.

As our target was to compute all the point intersections (ST_Point and ST_MultiPoint) using the ST_GeometryType function, we filtered out the values using a SQL SELECT CASE construct where the feature had a GeometryCollection geometry, for which we extracted just the points (and not the eventual linestrings) using the ST_CollectionExtract function (parameter type = 1) from the composing collections.

Finally, we compared the two result sets, both with plain SQL and a desktop GIS. The intersecting points computed filtered out the geometric collections from the output geometries and the intersecting points computed from all the geometries generated from the intersections, including the GeometryCollection features.

Clipping geometries to deploy data

A common GIS use case is clipping a big dataset into small portions (subsets), with each perhaps representing an area of interest. In this recipe, you will export from a PostGIS layer representing the rivers in the world, with one distinct shapefile composed of rivers for each country. For this purpose, you will use the ST_Intersection function.

Getting ready

Be sure that you have imported in PostGIS the same river dataset (a shapefile) that was used in the previous recipe.

How to do it...

The steps you need to take to complete this recipe are as follows:

1. First, you will create a view to clip the river geometries for each country using the `ST_Intersection` and `ST_Intersects` functions. Name the view `rivers_clipped_by_country`:

```
postgis_cookbook=> CREATE VIEW chp03.rivers_clipped_by_country AS
    SELECT r.name, c.iso2, ST_Intersection(r.the_geom,
      c.the_geom)::geometry(Geometry,4326) AS the_geom
    FROM chp03.countries AS c
    JOIN chp03.rivers AS r
    ON ST_Intersects(r.the_geom, c.the_geom);
```

2. Create a directory named `rivers` as follows:

```
mkdir working/chp03/rivers
```

3. Create the following scripts to export a `rivers` shapefile for each country.

   The following is the Linux version (name it `export_rivers.sh`):

```
#!/bin/bash
for f in `ogrinfo PG:"dbname='postgis_cookbook' user='me'
password='mypassword'" -sql "SELECT DISTINCT(iso2)
FROM chp03.countries ORDER BY iso2" | grep iso2 | awk '{print $4}'`
do
    echo "Exporting river shapefile for $f country..."
    ogr2ogr rivers/rivers_$f.shp PG:"dbname='postgis_cookbook'
    user='me' password='mypassword'"
    -sql "SELECT * FROM chp03.rivers_clipped_by_country
    WHERE iso2 = '$f'"
done
```

   The following is the Windows version (name it `export_rivers.bat`):

```
FOR /F "tokens=*" %%f IN ('ogrinfo
PG:"dbname=postgis_cookbook user=me password=password"
-sql "SELECT DISTINCT(iso2) FROM chp03.countries
 ORDER BY iso2" ^| grep iso2 ^| gawk "{print $4}"') DO (
    echo "Exporting river shapefile for %%f country..."
    ogr2ogr rivers/rivers_%%f.shp PG:"dbname='postgis_cookbook'
    user='me' password='password'"
```

```
-sql "SELECT * FROM chp03.rivers_clipped_by_country
WHERE iso2 = '%%f'"
)
```

For Windows users

The script uses the `grep` and `awk` Linux commands, so you will need to download their Windows versions from `http://unxutils.sourceforge.net/`. The script was tested with the `UnxUpdates.zip` file (which includes `gawk`, but not `awk`), but you are welcome to download the full version available at `https://sourceforge.net/projects/unxutils/`. Also remember to include the folder with the executable files on the Windows path. There's a chance that you already have them installed in your system if you have installed OSGeo4W, a binary distribution of a broad set of open source, geospatial software for win32 environments. You can find it at `http://trac.osgeo.org/osgeo4w/`.

4. In Windows, run the batch file:

   ```
   C:\export_rivers.bat
   ```

5. Now, run the following script (in Linux or macOS, you need to assign `execute` permissions to the script before running the shell file):

   ```
   $ chmod 775 export_rivers.sh
   $ ./export_rivers.sh
   Exporting river shapefile for AD country...
   Exporting river shapefile for AE country...
   ...
   Exporting river shapefile for ZM country...
   Exporting river shapefile for ZW country...
   ```

   You could eventually skip the creation of the `rivers_clipped_by_country` view by replacing the `ogr2ogr` statement in the previous script with the following command (`ogr2ogr` passes the content of the `-sql` option directly to PostGIS); use `%%f` for Windows:
   ```
   ogr2ogr rivers/rivers_$f.shp
   PG:"dbname='postgis_cookbook' user='me'
   password='mypassword'" -sql "SELECT r.name, c.iso2,
   ST_Intersection(r.the_geom, c.the_geom) AS the_geom FROM
   chp03.countries AS c JOIN chp03.rivers AS r ON
   ST_Intersects(r.the_geom, c.the_geom) WHERE c.iso2 =
   '$f'"
   ```

6. Check the output with `ogrinfo` or a desktop GIS. The following screenshot shows how the output looks in QGIS; we have added the original PostGIS `chp03.rivers` layer and a couple of the generated shapefiles:

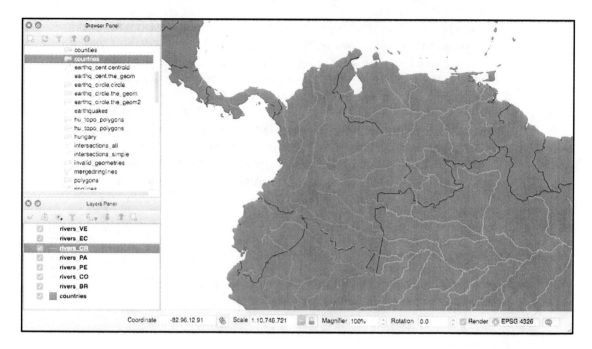

How it works...

You can use the `ST_Intersection` function to clip one dataset from another. In this recipe, you first created a view, where you performed a spatial join between a polygonal layer (countries) and a linear layer (rivers) using the `ST_Intersects` function. In the context of the spatial join, you have used the `ST_Intersection` function to generate a snapshot of the rivers in every country.

You have then created a bash script in which you iterated every single country and pulled out to a shapefile the clipped rivers for that country, using `ogr2ogr` and the previously created view as the input layer.

To iterate the countries in the script, you have been using `ogrinfo` with the `-sql` option, using a SQL `SELECT DISTINCT` statement. You have used a combination of the `grep` and `awk` Linux commands, piped together to get every single country code. The `grep` command is a utility for searching plaintext datasets for lines matching a regular expression, while `awk` is an interpreted programming language designed for text processing and typically used as a data extraction and reporting tool.

Simplifying geometries with PostGIS topology

In a previous recipe, we used the `ST_SimplifyPreserveTopology` function to try to generate a simplification of a polygonal PostGIS layer.

Unfortunately, while that function works well for linear layers, it produces topological anomalies (overlapping and holes) in shared polygon borders. You used an external toolset (`GRASS`) to generate a valid topological simplification.

In this recipe, you will use the PostGIS topology support to perform the same task within the spatial database, without needing to export the dataset to a different toolset.

Getting ready

To get started, perform the following steps:

1. Be sure that you have PostGIS topology support enabled in your database instance. This support is packaged as a separate extension and, if you are using PostgreSQL 9.1 or newer versions, you can install it using the following SQL `CREATE EXTENSION` command:

   `postgis_cookbook=# CREATE EXTENSION postgis_topology;`

2. Download the administrative area archive for Hungary from the `gadm.org` website at `http://gadm.org/country` (or use the copy included in the code bundle provided with this book).
3. Extract the `HUN_adm1.shp` shapefile from the archive to your working directory, `working/chp03`.

4. Import the shapefile to PostGIS using a tool such as `ogr2ogr` or `shp2pgsql`, as follows:

```
ogr2ogr -f PostgreSQL -t_srs EPSG:3857 -nlt MULTIPOLYGON
-lco GEOMETRY_NAME=the_geom -nln chp03.hungary
PG:"dbname='postgis_cookbook' user='me'
password='mypassword'" HUN_adm1.shp
```

5. After the import process is completed, you can check the count using the following command; note that this spatial table consists of 20 multipolygons, each representing one administrative area in Hungary:

```
postgis_cookbook=# SELECT COUNT(*) FROM chp03.hungary;
```

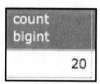

```
(1 row)
```

How to do it...

The steps you need to take to complete this recipe are as follows:

1. All functions and tables associated with the topology module are installed in a schema named `topology`, so let's add it to the search path to avoid prefixing it before every `topology` function or object:

```
postgis_cookbook=# SET search_path TO chp03, topology, public;
```

2. Now you will use the `CreateTopology` function to create a new `topology` schema named `hu_topo` in which you will import the 20 administrative areas from the `hungary` table. In PostGIS topology, all the topology entities and relations needed for one topology schema are stored in a single PostgreSQL schema using the same spatial reference system. You will name this schema `hu_topo` and use the EPSG:3857 spatial reference (the one used in the original shapefile):

```
postgis_cookbook=# SELECT CreateTopology('hu_topo', 3857);
```

3. Note how a record has been added to the `topology.topology` table in the following code:

```
postgis_cookbook=# SELECT * FROM topology.topology;
```

id integer	name character...	srid integer	precision double pr...	hasz boolean
1	hu_topo	3857	0	false

(1 rows)

4. Also note that four tables and one view, which are needed for storing and managing the topology, have been generated in the schema named `hu_topo`, created from the `CreateTopology` function:

```
postgis_cookbook=# \dtv hu_topo.*
```

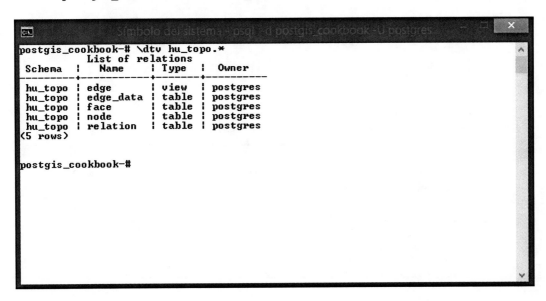

```
postgis_cookbook-# \dtv hu_topo.*
                List of relations
  Schema   |    Name    |  Type  |  Owner
-----------+------------+--------+----------
 hu_topo   | edge       | view   | postgres
 hu_topo   | edge_data  | table  | postgres
 hu_topo   | face       | table  | postgres
 hu_topo   | node       | table  | postgres
 hu_topo   | relation   | table  | postgres
(5 rows)

postgis_cookbook-#
```

(5 rows)

5. Check the initial information for the created topology using the `topologysummary` function, as follows; still, none of the topologic entities (nodes, edges, faces, and so on) are initialized:

```
postgis_cookbook=# SELECT topologysummary('hu_topo');
```

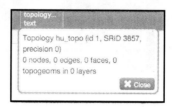

(1 row)

6. Create a new PostGIS table as follows for storing the topological administrative boundaries:

```
postgis_cookbook=# CREATE TABLE
   chp03.hu_topo_polygons(gid serial primary key, name_1 varchar(75));
```

7. Add a topological geometry column to this table as follows, using the `AddTopoGeometryColumn` function:

```
postgis_cookbook=# SELECT
   AddTopoGeometryColumn('hu_topo', 'chp03', 'hu_topo_polygons',
   'the_geom_topo', 'MULTIPOLYGON') As layer_id;
```

8. Insert the polygons from the non-topological `hungary` spatial table to the topological table, using the `toTopoGeom` function:

```
postgis_cookbook=> INSERT INTO
chp03.hu_topo_polygons(name_1, the_geom_topo)
   SELECT name_1, toTopoGeom(the_geom, 'hu_topo', 1)
   FROM chp03.hungary;
   Query returned successfully: 20 rows affected,
                               10598 ms execution time.
```

9. Now run the following code to check out how the content of the topology schema has been modified by the `toTopoGeom` function; you would expect to have 20 faces, one for each Hungarian administrative area, but instead there are 92:

```
postgis_cookbook=# SELECT topologysummary('hu_topo');
```

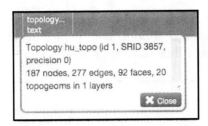

10. The problem is easily identifiable by analyzing the `hu_topo.face` table or using a desktop GIS. If you sort the polygons from this table by area, using the `ST_Area` function, you will notice after the details of the first polygon, which has 1 null area (used by the topology screenshot in the next step) and 20 large areas (each representing one administrative area), that there are 77 very small polygons generated by topological anomalies (polygon overlaps and holes):

```
postgis_cookbook=# SELECT row_number() OVER
(ORDER BY ST_Area(mbr) DESC) as rownum, ST_Area(mbr)/100000
AS area FROM hu_topo.face ORDER BY area DESC;
```

rownum bigint	area double precision
1	
2	366365.476705923
3	313236.739489459
4	290847.510314687
5	281960.845180014
6	266103.852066947
7	245731.431717149
8	235963.030648034
9	229519.671149496
10	207316.920420714
11	162677.435413211
12	158131.116221304
13	152034.757298787
14	148585.644854029
15	148471.930523326

(93 rows)

11. You can eventually look at the built topology elements (nodes, edges, faces, and topological geometries, or topogeoms) using a desktop GIS. The following screenshot shows how they look in QGIS:

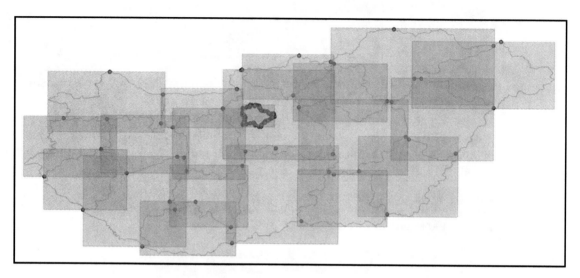

12. Now you will rebuild the topology using a small tolerance value—1 meter—as an additional parameter to the CreateTopology function, in order to get rid of the unnecessary faces (the tolerance will collapse the vertex together, eliminating the small polygons). First, drop your topology schema with the DropTopology function and the topological table with the DROP TABLE command, and rebuild both of them using a topology tolerance of 1 meter, as follows:

```
postgis_cookbook=# SELECT DropTopology('hu_topo');
postgis_cookbook=# DROP TABLE chp03.hu_topo_polygons;
postgis_cookbook=# SELECT CreateTopology('hu_topo', 3857, 1);
postgis_cookbook=# CREATE TABLE chp03.hu_topo_polygons(
   gid serial primary key, name_1 varchar(75));
postgis_cookbook=# SELECT AddTopoGeometryColumn('hu_topo',
   'chp03', 'hu_topo_polygons', 'the_geom_topo',
   'MULTIPOLYGON') As layer_id;
postgis_cookbook=# INSERT INTO
chp03.hu_topo_polygons(name_1, the_geom_topo)
   SELECT name_1, toTopoGeom(the_geom, 'hu_topo', 1)
   FROM chp03.hungary;
```

13. Now, if you check the information related to the topology using the `topologysummary` function as follows, you can see that there is one face per administrative boundary and the previous 72 faces generated by topological anomalies have been eliminated, leaving only 20:

```
postgis_cookbook=# SELECT topologysummary('hu_topo');
```

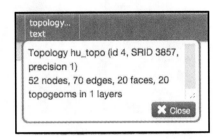

Topology... text

Topology hu_topo (id 4, SRID 3857, precision 1)
52 nodes, 70 edges, 20 faces, 20 topogeoms in 1 layers

✖ Close

(1 row)

14. Finally, simplify the polygons of the `topo_polygons` table using a tolerance of 500 meters, as follows:

```
postgis_cookbook=# SELECT ST_ChangeEdgeGeom('hu_topo',
   edge_id, ST_SimplifyPreserveTopology(geom, 500))
   FROM hu_topo.edge;
```

15. Now it's time to update the original `hungary` table using a join with the `hu_topo_polygons` table by running the following commands:

```
postgis_cookbook=# UPDATE chp03.hungary hu
   SET the_geom = hut.the_geom_topo
   FROM chp03.hu_topo_polygons hut
   WHERE hu.name_1 = hut.name_1;
```

16. The simplification process should have worked smoothly and produced a valid topological dataset. The following screenshot shows how the reduced topology looks (in red) compared to the original one (in black):

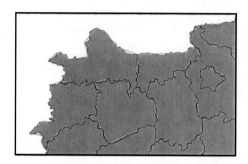

How it works...

We created a new PostGIS topology schema using the `CreateTopology` function. This function creates a new PostgreSQL schema where all the topological entities are stored.

We can have more topological schemas within the same spatial database, each being contained in a different PostgreSQL schema. The PostGIS `topology.topology` table manages all the metadata for all the topological schemas.

Each topological schema is composed of a series of tables and views to manage the topological entities (such as edge, edge data, face, node, and topogeoms) and their relations.

We can have a quick look at the description of a single topological schema using the `topologysummary` function, which summarizes the main metadata information-name, SRID, and precision; the number of nodes, edges, faces, topogeoms, and topological layers; and, for each topological layer, the geometry type, and the number of topogeoms.

After creating the topology schema, we created a new PostGIS table and added to it a topological geometry column (`topogeom` in PostGIS topology jargon) using the `AddTopoGeometryColumn` function.

We then used the `ST_ChangeEdgeGeom` function to alter the geometries for the topological edges, using the `ST_SimplifyPreserveTopology` function, with a tolerance of 500 meters, and checked that this function, used in the context of a topological schema, produces topologically correct results for polygons too.

Working with Vector Data – Advanced Recipes

In this chapter, we will cover:

- Improving proximity filtering with KNN
- Improving proximity filtering with KNN – advanced
- Rotating geometries
- Improving ST_Polygonize
- Translating, scaling, and rotating geometries – advanced
- Detailed building footprints from LiDAR
- Creating a fixed number of clusters from a set of points
- Calculating a Voronoi diagrams

Introduction

Beyond being a spatial database with the capacity to store and query spatial data, PostGIS is a very powerful analytical tool. What this means to the user is a tremendous capacity to expose and encapsulate deep spatial analyses right within a PostgreSQL database.

The recipes in this chapter can roughly be divided into four main sections:

- Highly optimized queries:
    - Improving proximity filtering with KNN
    - Improving proximity filtering with KNN – advanced

- Using the database to create and modify geometries:
    - Rotating geometries
    - Improving ST_Polygonize
    - Translating, scaling, and rotating geometries – advanced
    - Getting detailed building footprints from LiDAR
- Creating a fixed number of clusters from a set of points:
    - Using the PostGIS function, `ST_ClusterKMeans`, to create K clusters from a set of points
    - Using a minimum bounding circle to visually represent the clusters with the `ST_ MinimumBoundingCircle` function
- Calculating a Voronoi diagram:
    - Using the `ST_VoronoiPolygon` function in order to calculate Voronoi diagrams

Improving proximity filtering with KNN

The basic question that we seek to answer in this recipe is the fundamental distance question, *which are the five coffee shops closest to me?* It turns out that while it is a fundamental question, it's not always easy to answer, though we will make this possible in this recipe. We will approach this in two steps. The first step with which we'll approach this is in a simple heuristic way, which will allow us to come to a solution quickly. Then, we'll take advantage of the deeper PostGIS functionality to make the solution faster and more general with a **k-Nearest Neighbor (KNN)** approach.

A concept that we need to understand from the outset is that of a spatial index. A spatial index, like other database indexes, functions like a book index. It is a special construct to make looking for things inside our table easier, much in the way a book index helps us find content in a book faster. In the case of a spatial index, it helps us find faster ways, when things are in space. Therefore, by using a spatial index in our geographic searches, we can speed up our searches by orders of magnitude.

To learn more about spatial indexes,
see http://en.wikipedia.org/wiki/Spatial_index#Spatial_index.

Getting ready

We will start by loading our data. Our data is the address records from Cuyahoga County, Ohio, USA:

```
shp2pgsql -s 3734 -d -i -I -W LATIN1 -g the_geom CUY_ADDRESS_POINTS
chp04.knn_addresses | psql -U me -d postgis_cookbook
```

As this dataset may take a while to load, you can alternatively load a subset:

```
shp2pgsql -s 3734 -d -i -I -W LATIN1 -g the_geom CUY_ADDRESS_POINTS_subset
chp04.knn_addresses | psql -U me -d postgis_cookbook
```

We specified the -I flag in order to request that a spatial index be created upon the import of this data.

Let us start by seeing how many records we are dealing with:

```
SELECT COUNT(*) FROM chp04.knn_addresses;
--484958
```

We have, in this address table, almost half a million address records, which is not an insubstantial number to perform a query.

How to do it...

KNN is an approach of searching for an arbitrary number of points closest to a given point. Without the right tools, this can be a very slow process that requires testing the distance between the point of interest and all the possible neighbors. The problem with this approach is that the search becomes exponentially slower with a greater number of points. Let's start with this naive approach and then improve on it.

Suppose we were interested in finding the 10 records closest to the geographic location -81.738624, 41.396679. The naive approach would be to transform this value into our local coordinate system and compare the distance to each point in the database from the search point, order those values by distance, and limit the search to the first 10 closest records (it is not recommended that you run the following query as it could run indefinitely):

```
SELECT ST_Distance(searchpoint.the_geom, addr.the_geom) AS dist, * FROM
  chp04.knn_addresses addr,
  (SELECT ST_Transform(ST_SetSRID(ST_MakePoint(-81.738624, 41.396679),
    4326), 3734) AS the_geom) searchpoint
  ORDER BY ST_Distance(searchpoint.the_geom, addr.the_geom)
  LIMIT 10;
```

This is a fine approach for smaller datasets. This is a logical, simple, fast approach for a relatively small numbers of records; however, this approach scales very poorly, getting exponentially slower with the addition of records (with 500,000 points, this would take a very long time).

An alternative is to only compare the point of interest to the ones known to be close by setting a search distance. So, for example, in the following diagram, we have a star that represents the current location, and we want to know the 10 closest addresses. The grid in the diagram is 100 feet long, so we can search for the points within 200 feet, then measure the distance to each of these points, and return the closest 10 points:

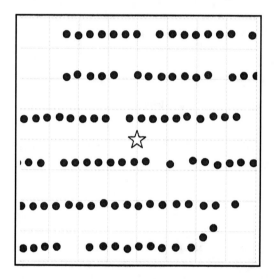

Thus, our approach to answer this question is to limit the search using the ST_DWithin operator to only search for records within a certain distance. ST_DWithin uses our spatial index, so the initial distance search is fast and the list of returned records should be short enough to do the same pair-wise distance comparison we did earlier in this section. In our case here, we could limit the search to within 200 feet:

```
SELECT ST_Distance(searchpoint.the_geom, addr.the_geom) AS dist, * FROM
    chp04.knn_addresses addr,
    (SELECT ST_Transform(ST_SetSRID(ST_MakePoint(-81.738624, 41.396679),
        4326), 3734) AS the_geom) searchpoint
    WHERE ST_DWithin(searchpoint.the_geom, addr.the_geom, 200)
    ORDER BY ST_Distance(searchpoint.the_geom, addr.the_geom)
    LIMIT 10;
```

The output for the previous query is as follows:

dist double precision	gid integer	addr_id numeric	str_id numeric	addr_num character var	pre_dir character va	pre_type character v	str_name character varying (30)	str_type character va
72.0240864930752	22220	i2.0000000	i7.0000000	07810	[null]	[null]	LANYARD	DR
73.8171473817856	6776	i1.0000000	i0.0000000	07811	[null]	[null]	DEERFIELD	DR
76.0214998230187	28202	i1.0000000	i7.0000000	07808	[null]	[null]	LANYARD	DR
76.3407822341641	22215	i0.0000000	i0.0000000	07815	[null]	[null]	DEERFIELD	DR
88.3623418476741	6782	i3.0000000	i7.0000000	07902	[null]	[null]	LANYARD	DR
88.9067246262422	22216	i2.0000000	i0.0000000	07807	[null]	[null]	DEERFIELD	DR
100.849524292145	441562	i9.0000000	i0.0000000	07903	[null]	[null]	DEERFIELD	DR
115.121788763982	22221	i4.0000000	i7.0000000	07906	[null]	[null]	LANYARD	DR
117.703864029602	6777	i3.0000000	i0.0000000	07803	[null]	[null]	DEERFIELD	DR
128.249088418467	22214	i8.0000000	i0.0000000	07907	[null]	[null]	DEERFIELD	DR

This approach performs well so long as our search window, ST_DWithin, is the right size for the data. The problem with this approach is that, in order to optimize it, we need to know how to set a search window that is about the right size. Any larger than the right size and the query will run more slowly than we'd like. Any smaller than the right size and we might not get all the points back that we need. Inherently, we don't know this ahead of time, so we can only hope for the best guess.

In this same dataset, if we apply the same query in another location, the output will return no points because the 10 closest points are further than 200 feet away. We can see this in the following diagram:

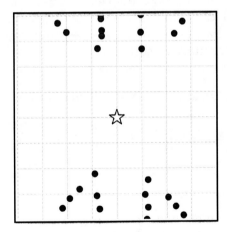

Fortunately, for PostGIS 2.0+ we can leverage the distance operators (<-> and <#>) to do indexed nearest neighbor searches. This makes for very fast KNN searches that don't require us to guess ahead of time how far away we need to search. Why are the searches fast? The spatial index helps of course, but in the case of the distance operator, we are using the structure of the index itself, which is hierarchical, to very quickly sort our neighbors.

When used in an `ORDER BY` clause, the distance operator uses the index:

```
SELECT ST_Distance(searchpoint.the_geom, addr.the_geom) AS dist, * FROM
    chp04.knn_addresses addr,
    (SELECT ST_Transform(ST_SetSRID(ST_MakePoint(-81.738624, 41.396679),
        4326), 3734) AS the_geom) searchpoint
    ORDER BY addr.the_geom <-> searchpoint.the_geom
    LIMIT 10;
```

This approach requires no prior knowledge of how far the nearest neighbors might be. It also scales very well, returning thousands of records in not more than the time it takes to return a few records. It is sometimes slower than using `ST_DWithin`, depending on how small our search distance is and how large the dataset we are dealing with is. But the trade-off is that we don't need to make a guess of our search distance and for large queries, it can be much faster than the naive approach.

How it works...

What makes this magic possible is that PostGIS uses an R-tree index. This means that the index itself is sorted hierarchically based on spatial information. As demonstrated, we can leverage the structure of the index in sorting distances from a given arbitrary location, and thus use the index to directly return the sorted records. This means that the structure of the spatial index itself helps us answer such fundamental questions quickly and inexpensively.

More information about KNN and R-tree can be found at
`http://workshops.boundlessgeo.com/postgis-intro/knn.html` and
`https://en.wikipedia.org/wiki/R-tree`.

See also

- The *Improving proximity filtering with KNN – advanced* recipe

Improving proximity filtering with KNN – advanced

In the preceding recipe, we wanted to answer the simple question of which are the nearest 10 locations to a given point. There is another simple question with a surprisingly sophisticated answer. The question is how do we approach this problem when we want to traverse an entire dataset and test each record for its nearest neighbors?

Our problem is as follows: for each point in our table, we are interested in the angle to the nearest object in another table. A case demonstrating this scenario is if we want to represent address points as building-like squares rotated to align with an adjacent road, similar to the historic **United States Geological Survey (USGS)** quadrangle maps, as shown in the following screenshot:

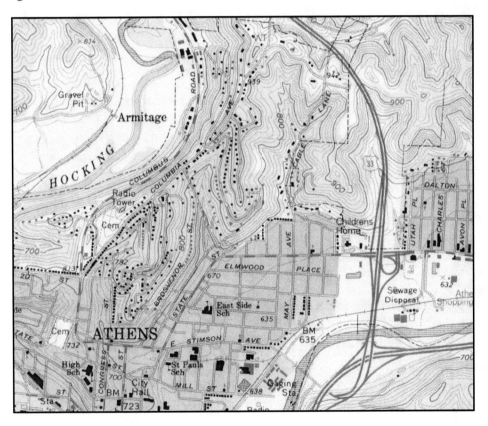

For larger buildings, USGS quads show the buildings' footprints, but for residential buildings below their minimum threshold, the points are just rotated squares—a nice cartographic effect that could easily be replicated with address points.

Getting ready

As in the previous recipe, we will start off by loading our data. Our data is the address records from Cuyahoga County, Ohio, USA. If you loaded this in the previous recipe, there is no need to reload the data. If you have not loaded the data yet, run the following command:

```
shp2pgsql -s 3734 -d -i -I -W LATIN1 -g the_geom CUY_ADDRESS_POINTS
chp04.knn_addresses | psql -U me -d postgis_cookbook
```

As this dataset may take a while to load, you can alternatively load a subset using the following command:

```
shp2pgsql -s 3734 -d -i -I -W LATIN1 -g the_geom CUY_ADDRESS_POINTS_subset
chp04.knn_addresses | psql -U me -d postgis_cookbook
```

The address points will serve as a proxy for our building structures. However, to align our structure to the nearby streets, we will need a `streets` layer. We will use Cuyahoga County's street centerline data for this:

```
shp2pgsql -s 3734 -d -i -I -W LATIN1 -g the_geom CUY_STREETS
chp04.knn_streets | psql -U me -d postgis_cookbook
```

Before we commence, we have to consider another aspect of using indexes, which we didn't need to consider in our previous KNN recipe. When our KNN approach used only points, our indexing was exact—the bounding box of a point is effectively a point. As bounding boxes are what indexes are built around, our indexing estimates of distance perfectly reflected the actual distances between our points. In the case of non-point geometries, as is our example here, the bounding box is an approximation of the lines to which we will be comparing our points. Put another way, what this means is that our nearest neighbor may not be our very nearest neighbor, but is likely our approximate nearest neighbor, or one of our nearest neighbors.

In practice, we apply a heuristic approach: we simply gather slightly more than the number of nearest neighbors we are interested in and then sort them based on the actual distance in order to gather only the number we are interested in. In this way, we only need to sort a small number of records.

How to do it...

Insofar as KNN is a nuanced approach to these problems, forcing KNN to run on all the records in a dataset takes what I like to call a venerable and age-old approach. In other words, it requires a bit of a hack.

 More on the general solution to using KNN within a function can be found in Alexandre Neto's post on the PostGIS users list at the following link: `http://lists.osgeo.org/pipermail/postgis-users/2012-May/034017.html`

In SQL, the typical way to loop is to use a `SELECT` statement. For our case, we don't have a function that does KNN looping through the records in a table to use; we simply have an operator that allows us to efficiently order our returning records by distance from a given record. The workaround is to write a temporary function and thus be able to use `SELECT` to loop through the records for us. The cost is the creation and deletion of the function, plus the work done by the query, and the combination of costs is well worth the *hackiness* of the approach.

First, consider the following function:

```
CREATE OR REPLACE FUNCTION chp04.angle_to_street (geometry) RETURNS double
precision AS $$

WITH index_query as (SELECT ST_Distance($1,road.the_geom) as dist,
degrees(ST_Azimuth($1, ST_ClosestPoint(road.the_geom, $1))) as azimuth FROM
chp04.knn_streets As road ORDER BY $1 <#> road.the_geom limit 5)

SELECT azimuth FROM index_query ORDER BY dist
LIMIT 1;

$$ LANGUAGE SQL;
```

Now, we can use this function quite easily:

```
CREATE TABLE chp04.knn_address_points_rot AS SELECT addr.*,
chp04.angle_to_street(addr.the_geom) FROM chp04.knn_addresses  addr;
```

If you have loaded the whole address dataset, this will take a while.

If we choose to, we can optionally drop the function so that extra functions are not left in our database:

```
DROP FUNCTION chp04.angle_to_street (geometry);
```

In the next recipe, *Rotating geometries*, the calculated angle will be used to build new geometries.

How it works...

Our function is simple, KNN magic aside. As an input to the function, we allow geometry, as shown in the following query:

```
CREATE OR REPLACE FUNCTION chp04.angle_to_street (geometry) RETURNS double
precision AS $$
```

The preceding function returns a floating-point value.

We then use a WITH statement to create a temporary table, which returns the five closest lines to our point of interest. Remember, as the index uses bounding boxes, we don't really know which line is the closest, so we gather a few extra points and then filter them based on distance. This idea is implemented in the following query:

```
WITH index_query as (SELECT ST_Distance($1,road.geom) as dist,
degrees(ST_Azimuth($1, ST_ClosestPoint(road.geom, $1))) as azimuth
FROM street_centerlines As road
ORDER BY $1 <#> road.geom LIMIT 5)
```

Note that we are actually returning to columns. The first column is dist, in which we calculate the distance to the nearest five road lines. Note that this operation is performed after the ORDER BY and LIMIT functions have been used as filters, so this does not take much computation. Then, we use ST_Azimuth to calculate the angle from our point to the closest points (ST_ClosestPoint) on each of our nearest five lines. In summary, what returns with our temporary index_query table is the distance to the nearest five lines and the respective rotation angles to the nearest five lines.

If we recall, however, we were not looking for the angle to the nearest five but to the true nearest road line. For this, we order the results by distance and further use LIMIT 1:

```
SELECT azimuth FROM index_query ORDER BY dist
LIMIT 1;
```

See also

- The *Improving proximity filtering with KNN* recipe

Rotating geometries

Among the many functions that PostGIS provides, geometry manipulation is a very powerful addition. In this recipe, we will explore a simple example of using the `ST_Rotate` function to rotate geometries. We will use a function from the *Improving proximity filtering with KNN – advanced* recipe to calculate our rotation values.

Getting ready

`ST_Rotate` has a few variants: `ST_RotateX`, `ST_RotateY`, and `ST_RotateZ`, with the `ST_Rotate` function serving as an alias for `ST_RotateZ`. Thus, for two-dimensional cases, `ST_Rotate` is a typical use case.

In the *Improving proximity filtering with KNN – advanced* recipe, our function calculated the angle to the nearest road from a building's centroid or address point. We can symbolize that building's point according to that rotation factor as a square symbol, but more interestingly, we can explicitly build the area of that footprint in real space and rotate it to match our calculated rotation angle.

How to do it...

Recall our function from the *Improving proximity filtering with KNN – advanced* recipe:

```
CREATE OR REPLACE FUNCTION chp04.angle_to_street (geometry) RETURNS double
precision AS $$

WITH index_query as (SELECT ST_Distance($1,road.the_geom) as dist,
degrees(ST_Azimuth($1, ST_ClosestPoint(road.the_geom, $1))) as azimuth
FROM  chp04.knn_streets As road
ORDER BY $1 <#> road.the_geom limit 5)

SELECT azimuth FROM index_query ORDER BY dist
LIMIT 1;

$$ LANGUAGE SQL;
```

This function will calculate the geometry's angle to the nearest road line. Now, to construct geometries using this calculation, run the following function:

```
CREATE TABLE chp04.tsr_building AS

SELECT ST_Rotate(ST_Envelope(ST_Buffer(the_geom, 20)), radians(90 -
chp04.angle_to_street(addr.the_geom)), addr.the_geom)
  AS the_geom FROM chp04.knn_addresses addr
LIMIT 500;
```

How it works...

In the first step, we are taking each of the points and first applying a buffer of 20 feet to them:

```
ST_Buffer(the_geom, 20)
```

Then, we calculate the envelope of the buffer, providing us with a square around that buffered area. This is a quick and easy way to create a square geometry of a specified size from a point:

```
ST_Envelope(ST_Buffer(the_geom, 20))
```

Finally, we use ST_Rotate to rotate the geometry to the appropriate angle. Here is where the query becomes harder to read. The ST_Rotate function takes two arguments:

```
ST_Rotate(geometry to rotate, angle, origin around which to rotate)
```

The geometry we are using is the newly calculated geometry from the buffering and envelope creation. The angle is the one we calculate using our chp04.angle_to_street function. Finally, the origin around which we rotate is the input point itself, resulting in the following portion of our query:

```
ST_Rotate(ST_Envelope(ST_Buffer(the_geom, 20)), radians(90 -
chp04.angle_to_street(addr.the_geom)), addr.the_geom);
```

This gives us some really nice cartography, as shown in the following diagram:

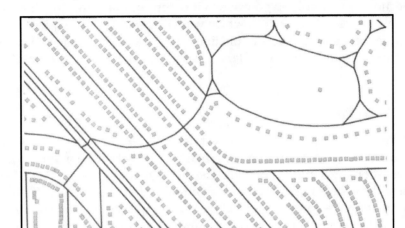

See also

- The *Improving proximity filtering with KNN – advanced* recipe
- The *Translating, scaling, and rotating geometries – advanced* recipe

Improving ST_Polygonize

In this short recipe, we will be using a common coding pattern in use when geometries are being constructed with ST_Polygonize and formalizing it into a function for reuse.

ST_Polygonize is a very useful function. You can pass a set of *unioned* lines or an array of lines to ST_Polygonize, and the function will construct polygons from the input. ST_Polygonize does so aggressively insofar as it will construct all possible polygons from the inputs. One frustrating aspect of the function is that it does not return a multi-polygon, but instead returns a geometry collection. Geometry collections can be problematic in third-party tools for interacting with PostGIS as so many third party tools don't have mechanisms in place for recognizing and displaying geometry collections.

The pattern we will formalize here is the commonly recommended approach for changing geometry collections into mutlipolygons when it is appropriate to do so. This approach will be useful not only for ST_Polygonize, which we will use in the subsequent recipe, but can also be adapted for other cases where a function returns geometry collections, which are, for all practical purposes, multi-polygons. Hence, this is why it merits its own dedicated recipe.

Getting ready

The basic pattern for handling geometry collections is to use ST_Dump to convert them to a dump type, extract the geometry portion of the dump, collect the geometry, and then convert this collection into a multi-polygon. The dump type is a special PostGIS type that is a combination of the geometries and an index number for the geometries. It's typical to use ST_Dump to convert from a geometry collection to a dump type and then do further processing on the data from there. Rarely is a dump object used directly, but it is typically an intermediate type of data.

How to do it...

We expect this function to take a geometry and return a multi-polygon geometry:

```
CREATE OR REPLACE FUNCTION chp04.polygonize_to_multi (geometry) RETURNS
geometry AS $$
```

For readability, we will use a WITH statement to construct the series of transformations in geometry. First, we will polygonize:

```
WITH polygonized AS (
  SELECT ST_Polygonize($1) AS the_geom
),
```

Then, we will dump:

```
dumped AS (
  SELECT (ST_Dump(the_geom)).geom AS the_geom FROM polygonized
)
```

Now, we can collect and construct a multi-polygon from our result:

```
SELECT ST_Multi(ST_Collect(the_geom)) FROM dumped;
```

Put this together into a single function:

```
CREATE OR REPLACE FUNCTION chp04.polygonize_to_multi (geometry) RETURNS
geometry AS $$

WITH polygonized AS (
  SELECT ST_Polygonize($1) AS the_geom
),
dumped AS (
  SELECT (ST_Dump(the_geom)).geom AS the_geom FROM polygonized
)
SELECT ST_Multi(ST_Collect(the_geom)) FROM dumped;
$$ LANGUAGE SQL;
```

Now, we can polygonize directly from a set of closed lines and skip the typical intermediate step when we use the ST_Polygonize function of having to handle a geometry collection.

See also

- The *Translating, scaling, and rotating geometries – advanced* recipe

Translating, scaling, and rotating geometries – advanced

Often, in a spatial database, we are interested in making explicit the representation of geometries that are implicit in the data. In the example that we will use here, the explicit portion of the geometry is a single point coordinate where a field survey plot has taken place. In the following screenshot, this explicit location is the dot. The implicit geometry is the actual extent of the field survey, which includes 10 subplots arranged in a 5 x 2 array and rotated according to a bearing.

These subplots are the purple squares in the following diagram:

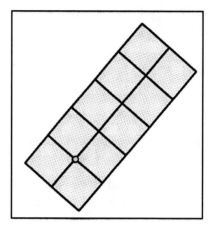

Getting ready

There are a number of ways for us to approach this problem. In the interest of simplicity, we will first construct our grid and then rotate it in place. Also, we could in principle use a ST_Buffer function in combination with ST_Extent to construct the squares in our resultant geometry, but, as ST_Extent uses floating-point approximations of the geometry for the sake of efficiency, this could result in some mismatches at the edges of our subplots.

The approach we will use for the construction of the subplots is to construct the grid with a series of ST_MakeLine and use ST_Node to *flatten* or node the results. This ensures that we have all of our lines properly intersecting each other. ST_Polygonize will then construct our multi-polygon geometry for us. We will leverage this function through our wrapper function from the *Improving ST_Polygonize* recipe.

Our plots are 10 units on a side, in a 5 x 2 array. As such, we can imagine a function to which we pass our plot origin, and the function returns a multi-polygon of all the subplot geometries. One additional element to consider is that the orientation of the layout of our plots is rotated to a bearing. We expect the function to actually use two inputs, so origin and rotation will be the variables that we will pass to our function.

How to do it...

We can consider geometry and a float value as the inputs, and we want the function to return geometry:

```
CREATE OR REPLACE FUNCTION chp04.create_grid (geometry, float) RETURNS
geometry AS $$
```

In order to construct the subplots, we will require three lines running parallel to the X axis:

```
WITH middleline AS (
  SELECT ST_MakeLine(ST_Translate($1, -10, 0),
    ST_Translate($1, 40.0, 0)) AS the_geom
),
topline AS (
  SELECT ST_MakeLine(ST_Translate($1, -10, 10.0),
    ST_Translate($1, 40.0, 10)) AS the_geom
),
bottomline AS (
  SELECT ST_MakeLine(ST_Translate($1, -10, -10.0),
    ST_Translate($1, 40.0, -10)) AS the_geom
),
```

And we will require six lines running parallel to the Y axis:

```
oneline AS (
  SELECT ST_MakeLine(ST_Translate($1, -10, 10.0),
    ST_Translate($1, -10, -10)) AS the_geom
),
twoline AS (
  SELECT ST_MakeLine(ST_Translate($1, 0, 10.0),
    ST_Translate($1, 0, -10)) AS the_geom
),
threeline AS (
  SELECT ST_MakeLine(ST_Translate($1, 10, 10.0),
    ST_Translate($1, 10, -10)) AS the_geom
),
fourline AS (
  SELECT ST_MakeLine(ST_Translate($1, 20, 10.0),
    ST_Translate($1, 20, -10)) AS the_geom
),
fiveline AS (
  SELECT ST_MakeLine(ST_Translate($1, 30, 10.0),
    ST_Translate($1, 30, -10)) AS the_geom
),
sixline AS (
  SELECT ST_MakeLine(ST_Translate($1, 40, 10.0),
```

```
    ST_Translate($1, 40, -10)) AS the_geom
),
```

To use these for polygon construction, we will require them to have nodes where they cross and touch. A `UNION ALL` function will combine these lines in a single record; `ST_Union` will provide the geometric processing necessary to construct the nodes of interest and will combine our lines into a single entity ready for `chp04.polygonize_to_multi`:

```
combined AS (
  SELECT ST_Union(the_geom) AS the_geom FROM
  (
    SELECT the_geom FROM middleline
      UNION ALL
    SELECT the_geom FROM topline
      UNION ALL
    SELECT the_geom FROM bottomline
      UNION ALL
    SELECT the_geom FROM oneline
      UNION ALL
    SELECT the_geom FROM twoline
      UNION ALL
    SELECT the_geom FROM threeline
      UNION ALL
    SELECT the_geom FROM fourline
      UNION ALL
    SELECT the_geom FROM fiveline
      UNION ALL
    SELECT the_geom FROM sixline
  ) AS alllines
)
```

But we have not created polygons yet, just lines. The final step, using our `polygonize_to_multi` function, finishes the work for us:

```
SELECT chp04.polygonize_to_multi(ST_Rotate(the_geom, $2, $1)) AS the_geom
FROM combined;
```

The combined query is as follows:

```
CREATE OR REPLACE FUNCTION chp04.create_grid (geometry, float) RETURNS
geometry AS $$

WITH middleline AS (
  SELECT ST_MakeLine(ST_Translate($1, -10, 0),
    ST_Translate($1, 40.0, 0)) AS the_geom
),
topline AS (
```

```
    SELECT ST_MakeLine(ST_Translate($1, -10, 10.0),
      ST_Translate($1, 40.0, 10)) AS the_geom
),
bottomline AS (
  SELECT ST_MakeLine(ST_Translate($1, -10, -10.0),
    ST_Translate($1, 40.0, -10)) AS the_geom
),
oneline AS (
  SELECT ST_MakeLine(ST_Translate($1, -10, 10.0),
    ST_Translate($1, -10, -10)) AS the_geom
),
twoline AS (
  SELECT ST_MakeLine(ST_Translate($1, 0, 10.0),
    ST_Translate($1, 0, -10)) AS the_geom
),
threeline AS (
  SELECT ST_MakeLine(ST_Translate($1, 10, 10.0),
    ST_Translate($1, 10, -10)) AS the_geom
),
fourline AS (
  SELECT ST_MakeLine(ST_Translate($1, 20, 10.0),
    ST_Translate($1, 20, -10)) AS the_geom
),
fiveline AS (
  SELECT ST_MakeLine(ST_Translate($1, 30, 10.0),
    ST_Translate($1, 30, -10)) AS the_geom
),
sixline AS (
  SELECT ST_MakeLine(ST_Translate($1, 40, 10.0),
    ST_Translate($1, 40, -10)) AS the_geom
),
combined AS (
  SELECT ST_Union(the_geom) AS the_geom FROM
  (
    SELECT the_geom FROM middleline
      UNION ALL
    SELECT the_geom FROM topline
      UNION ALL
    SELECT the_geom FROM bottomline
      UNION ALL
    SELECT the_geom FROM oneline
      UNION ALL
    SELECT the_geom FROM twoline
      UNION ALL
    SELECT the_geom FROM threeline
      UNION ALL
    SELECT the_geom FROM fourline
      UNION ALL
```

```
    SELECT the_geom FROM fiveline
      UNION ALL
    SELECT the_geom FROM sixline
  ) AS alllines
)
SELECT chp04.polygonize_to_multi(ST_Rotate(the_geom, $2, $1)) AS the_geom
FROM combined;
$$ LANGUAGE SQL;
```

How it works...

This function, shown in the preceding section, essentially draws the geometry from a single input point and rotation value. It does so by using nine instances of ST_MakeLine. Typically, one might use ST_MakeLine in combination with ST_MakePoint to accomplish this. We bypass this need by having the function consume a point geometry as an input. We can, therefore, use ST_Translate to move this point geometry to the endpoints of the lines of interest in order to construct our lines with ST_MakeLine.

One final step, of course, is to test the use of our new geometry constructing function:

```
CREATE TABLE chp04.tsr_grid AS

-- embed inside the function
  SELECT chp04.create_grid(ST_SetSRID(ST_MakePoint(0,0),
  3734), 0) AS the_geom
    UNION ALL
  SELECT chp04.create_grid(ST_SetSRID(ST_MakePoint(0,100),
  3734), 0.274352 * pi()) AS the_geom
    UNION ALL
  SELECT chp04.create_grid(ST_SetSRID(ST_MakePoint(100,0),
  3734), 0.824378 * pi()) AS the_geom
    UNION ALL
  SELECT chp04.create_grid(ST_SetSRID(ST_MakePoint(0,-100), 3734),
  0.43587 * pi()) AS the_geom
    UNION ALL
  SELECT chp04.create_grid(ST_SetSRID(ST_MakePoint(-100,0), 3734),
  1 * pi()) AS the_geom;
```

The different grids generated by the previous functions are the following:

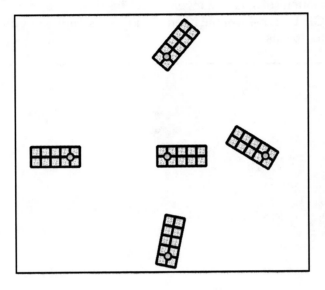

See also

- The *Improving ST_Polygonize* recipe
- The *Improving proximity filtering with KNN – advanced* recipe

Detailed building footprints from LiDAR

Frequently, with spatial analyses, we receive data in one form that seems quite promising but we need it in another more extensive form. LiDAR is an excellent solution for such problems; LiDAR data is laser scanned either from an airborne platform, such as a fixed-wing plane or helicopter, or from a ground unit. LiDAR devices typically return a cloud of points referencing absolute or relative positions in space. As a raw dataset, they are often not as useful as they are once they have been processed. Many LiDAR datasets are classified into land cover types, so a LiDAR dataset, in addition to having data that contains x, y, and z values for all the points sampled across a space, will often contain LiDAR points that are classified as ground, vegetation, tall vegetation, buildings, and so on.

As useful as this is, the data is intensive, that is, it has discreet points, rather than extensive, as polygon representations of such data would be. This recipe was developed as a simple method to use PostGIS to transform the intensive LiDAR samples of buildings into extensive building footprints:

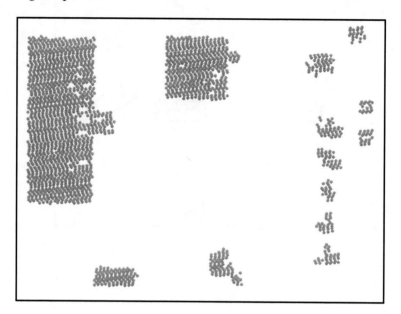

Getting ready

The LiDAR dataset we will use is a 2006 collection, which was classified into ground, tall vegetation (> 20 feet), buildings, and so on. One characteristic of the analysis that follows is that we assume the classification to be correct, and so we are not revisiting the quality of the classification or attempting to improve it within PostGIS.

A characteristic of the LiDAR dataset is that a sample point exists for relatively flat surfaces at approximately no fewer than 1 for every 5 feet. This will inform you about how we manipulate the data.

First, let's load our dataset using the following command:

```
shp2pgsql -s 3734 -d -i -I -W LATIN1 -g the_geom lidar_buildings
chp04.lidar_buildings | psql -U me -d postgis_cookbook
```

How to do it...

The simplest way to convert point data to polygon data would be to buffer the points by their known separation:

```
ST_Buffer(the_geom, 5)
```

We can imagine, however, that such a simplistic approach might look strange:

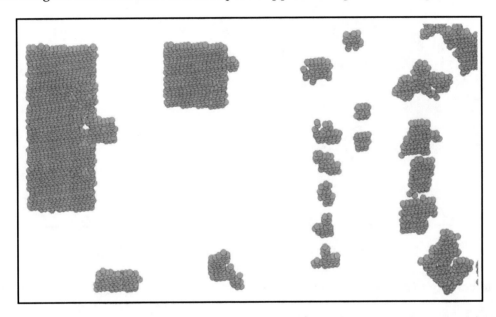

As such, it would be good to perform a union of these geometries in order to dissolve the internal boundaries:

```
ST_Union(ST_Buffer(the_geom, 5))
```

Now, we can see the start of some simple building footprints:

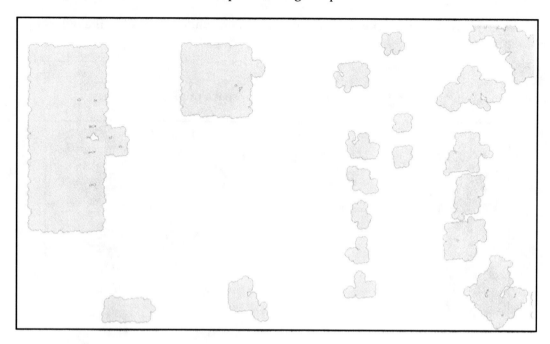

While this is marginally better, the result is quite lumpy. We will use the ST_Simplify_PreserveTopology function to simplify the polygons and then grab just the external ring to remove the internal holes:

```
CREATE TABLE chp04.lidar_buildings_buffer AS

WITH lidar_query AS
(SELECT ST_ExteriorRing(ST_SimplifyPreserveTopology(
  (ST_Dump(ST_Union(ST_Buffer(the_geom, 5)))).geom, 10
)) AS the_geom FROM chp04.lidar_buildings)

SELECT chp04.polygonize_to_multi(the_geom) AS the_geom from lidar_query;
```

Now, we have simplified versions of our buffered geometries:

There are two things to note here. The larger the building, relative to the density of the sampling, the better it looks. We might query to eliminate smaller buildings, which are likely to degenerate when this approach is used, depending on the density of our LiDAR data.

How it works...

To put it informally, our buffering technique effectively lumps together or clusters adjacent samples. This is possible only because we have regularly sampled data, but that is OK. The density and scan patterns for the LiDAR data are typical of such datasets, so we can expect this approach to be applicable to other datasets.

The ST_Union function converts these discreet buffered points into a single record with dissolved internal boundaries. To complete the clustering, we simply need to use ST_Dump to convert these boundaries back to discreet polygons so that we can utilize individual building footprints. Finally, we simplify the pattern with ST_SimplifyPreserveTopology and extract the external ring, or use ST_ExteriorRing outside these polygons, which removes the holes inside the building footprints. Since ST_ExteriorRing returns a line, we have to reconstruct our polygon. We use chp04.polygonize_to_multi, a function we wrote in the *Improving ST_Polygonize* recipe, to handle just such occasions. In addition, you can check the *Normalizing internal overlays* recipe in Chapter 2, *Structures That Work*, in order to learn how to correct polygons with possible geographical errors.

Creating a fixed number of clusters from a set of points

In PostGIS version 2.3, some cluster functionalities were introduced. In this recipe, we will explore `ST_ClusterKMeans`, a function that aggregates geometries into *k* clusters and retrieves the *id* of the assigned cluster for each geometry in the input. The general syntax for the function is as follows:

```
ST_ClusterKMeans(geometry winset geom, integer number_of_clusters);
```

Getting ready

In this recipe, we will use the earthquake dataset included in the source from `Chapter 3`, *Working with Vector Data – The Basics*, as our input geometries for the function. We also need to define the number of clusters that the function will output; the value of *k* for this example will be 10. You could play with this value and see the different cluster arrangements the function outputs; the greater the value for *k*, the smaller the number of geometries each cluster will contain.

If you have not previously imported the earthquake data into the `Chapter 3`, *Working with Vector Data – The Basics*, schema, refer to the *Getting ready* section of the *GIS analysis with spatial joins* recipe.

Once we have created the `chp03.earthquake` table, we will need two tables. The first one will contain the centroid geometries of the clusters and their respective IDs, which the `ST_ClusterKMeans` function retrieves. The second table will have the geometries for the minimum bounding circle for each cluster. To do so, run the following SQL commands:

```
CREATE TABLE chp04.earthq_cent (
  cid integer PRIMARY KEY, the_geom geometry('POINT',4326)
);

CREATE TABLE chp04.earthq_circ (
  cid integer PRIMARY KEY, the_geom geometry('POLYGON',4326)
);
```

How to do it...

We will then populate the centroid table by generating the cluster ID for each geometry in chp03.earthquakes using the ST_ClusterKMeans function, and then we will use the ST_Centroid function to calculate the 10 centroids for each cluster:

```
INSERT INTO chp04.earthq_cent (the_geom, cid) (
  SELECT DISTINCT ST_SetSRID(ST_Centroid(tab2.ge2), 4326) as centroid,
  tab2.cid FROM(
    SELECT ST_UNION(tab.ge) OVER (partition by tab.cid ORDER BY tab.cid)
    as ge2, tab.cid as cid FROM(
      SELECT ST_ClusterKMeans(e.the_geom, 10) OVER() AS cid, e.the_geom
      as ge FROM chp03.earthquakes as e) as tab
  )as tab2
);
```

If we check the inserted rows with the following command:

```
SELECT * FROM chp04.earthq_cent;
```

The output will be as follows:

	cid integer	the_geom geometry
1	0	0101000020E6100000902728...
2	1	0101000020E6100000C626E4...
3	2	0101000020E61000004AC41D...
4	3	0101000020E6100000F5D636...
5	4	0101000020E6100000EA1BAD...
6	6	0101000020E6100000D6202E...
7	5	0101000020E6100000FD315E...
8	7	0101000020E61000001A534F...
9	9	0101000020E6100000E0B808...
10	8	0101000020E6100000743518...

Then, insert the corresponding minimum bounding circles for the clusters in the chp04.earthq_circ table. Execute the following SQL command:

```
# INSERT INTO chp04.earthq_circ (the_geom, cid) (
  SELECT DISTINCT ST_SetSRID(
    ST_MinimumBoundingCircle(tab2.ge2), 4326) as circle, tab2.cid
    FROM(
      SELECT ST_UNION(tab.ge) OVER (partition by tab.cid ORDER BY tab.cid)
```

```
    as ge2, tab.cid as cid
    FROM(
      SELECT ST_ClusterKMeans(e.the_geom, 10) OVER() as cid, e.the_geom
      as ge FROM chp03.earthquakes AS e
    ) as tab
  )as tab2
);
```

In a desktop GIS, import all three tables as layers (`chp03.earthquakes`, `chp04.earthq_cent`, and `chp04.earthq_circ`) in order to visualize them and understand the clustering. Note that circles may overlap; however, this does not mean that clusters do as well, since each point belongs to one and only one cluster, but the minimum bounding circle for a cluster may overlap with another minimum bounding circle for another cluster:

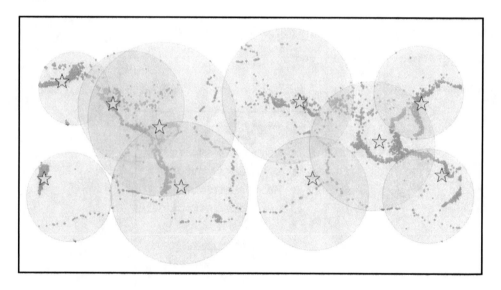

Calculating Voronoi diagrams

In the 2.3 version, PostGIS provides a way to create Voronoi diagrams from the vertices of a geometry; this will work only with versions of GEOS greater than or equal to 3.5.0.

The following is a Voronoi diagram generated from a set of address points. Note how the points from which the diagram was generated are equidistant to the lines that divide them. Packed soap bubbles viewed from above form a similar network of shapes:

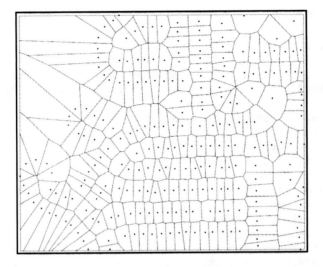

Voronoi diagrams are a space-filling approach that are useful for a variety of spatial analysis problems. We can use these to create space filling polygons around points, the edges of which are equidistant from all the surrounding points.

> More information about Voronoi diagrams can be found at the following link:
> http://en.wikipedia.org/wiki/Voronoi_diagram

The PostGIS function ST_VoronoiPolygons(), receives the following parameters: a geometry from which to build the Voronoi diagram, a tolerance, which is a float that will tell the function the distance within which vertices will be treated as equivalent for the output, and an extent_to geometry that will tell the extend of the diagram if this geometry is bigger than the calculated output from the input vertices. For this recipe, we will not use tolerance, which defaults to 0.0 units, nor extend_to, which is set to NULL by default.

Getting ready

We will create a small arbitrary point dataset to feed into our function around which we will calculate the Voronoi diagram:

```
DROP TABLE IF EXISTS chp04.voronoi_test_points;
CREATE TABLE chp04.voronoi_test_points
(
  x numeric,
```

```
      y numeric
)
WITH (OIDS=FALSE);

ALTER TABLE chp04.voronoi_test_points ADD COLUMN gid serial;
ALTER TABLE chp04.voronoi_test_points ADD PRIMARY KEY (gid);

INSERT INTO chp04.voronoi_test_points (x, y)
  VALUES (random() * 5, random() * 7);
INSERT INTO chp04.voronoi_test_points (x, y)
  VALUES (random() * 2, random() * 8);
INSERT INTO chp04.voronoi_test_points (x, y)
  VALUES (random() * 10, random() * 4);
INSERT INTO chp04.voronoi_test_points (x, y)
  VALUES (random() * 1, random() * 15);
INSERT INTO chp04.voronoi_test_points (x, y)
  VALUES (random() * 4, random() * 9);
INSERT INTO chp04.voronoi_test_points (x, y)
  VALUES (random() * 8, random() * 3);
INSERT INTO chp04.voronoi_test_points (x, y)
  VALUES (random() * 5, random() * 3);
INSERT INTO chp04.voronoi_test_points (x, y)
  VALUES (random() * 20, random() * 0.1);
INSERT INTO chp04.voronoi_test_points (x, y)
  VALUES (random() * 5, random() * 7);

SELECT AddGeometryColumn
('chp04','voronoi_test_points','the_geom',3734,'POINT',2);

UPDATE chp04.voronoi_test_points
  SET the_geom = ST_SetSRID(ST_MakePoint(x,y), 3734)
  WHERE the_geom IS NULL
;
```

How to do it...

With preparations in place, now we are ready to create the Voronoi diagram. First, we will create the table that will contain the MultiPolygon:

```
DROP TABLE IF EXISTS chp04.voronoi_diagram;
CREATE TABLE chp04.voronoi_diagram(
  gid serial PRIMARY KEY,
  the_geom geometry(MultiPolygon, 3734)
);
```

Now, to calculate the Voronoi diagram, we use ST_Collect in order to provide a MultiPoint object for the ST_VoronoiPolygons function. The output of this alone would be a GeometryCollection; however, we are interested in getting a MultiPolygon instead, so we need to use the ST_CollectionExtract function, which when given the number 3 as the second parameter, extracts all polygons from a GeometryCollection:

```
INSERT INTO chp04.voronoi_diagram(the_geom) (
  SELECT ST_CollectionExtract(
    ST_SetSRID(
      ST_VoronoiPolygons(points.the_geom),
    3734),
  3)
  FROM (
    SELECT
    ST_Collect(the_geom) as the_geom
    FROM chp04.voronoi_test_points
  )
as points);
```

If we import the layers for voronoi_test_points and voronoi_diagram into a desktop GIS, we get the following Voronoi diagram of the randomly generated points:

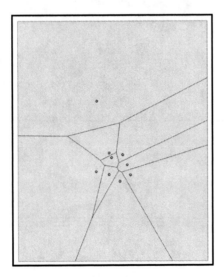

Now we can process much larger datasets. The following is a Voronoi diagram derived from the address points from the *Improving proximity filtering with KNN – advanced* recipe, with the coloration based on the azimuth to the nearest street, also calculated in that recipe:

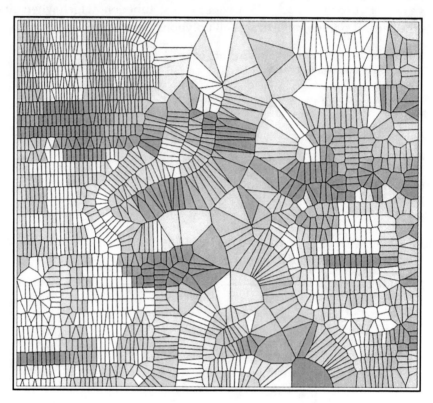

5
Working with Raster Data

In this chapter, we will cover the following:

- Getting and loading rasters
- Working with basic raster information and analysis
- Performing simple map-algebra operations
- Combining geometries with rasters for analysis
- Converting between rasters and geometries
- Processing and loading rasters with GDAL VRT
- Warping and resampling rasters
- Performing advanced map-algebra operations
- Executing DEM operations
- Sharing and visualizing rasters through SQL

Introduction

In this chapter, the recipes are presented in a step-by-step workflow that you may apply while working with a raster. This entails loading the raster, getting a basic understanding of the raster, processing and analyzing it, and delivering it to consumers. We intentionally add some detours to the workflow to reflect the reality that the raster, in its original form, may be confusing and not suitable for analysis. At the end of this chapter, you should be able to take the lessons learned from the recipes and confidently apply them to solve your raster problems.

Before going further, we should describe what a raster is, and what a raster is used for. At the simplest level, a raster is a photo or image with information describing where to place the raster on the Earth's surface. A photograph typically has three sets of values: one set for each primary color (red, green, and blue). A raster also has sets of values, often more than those found in a photograph. Each set of values is known as a **band**. So, a photograph typically has three bands, while a raster has at least one band. Like digital photographs, rasters come in a variety of file formats. Common raster formats you may come across include PNG, JPEG, GeoTIFF, HDF5, and NetCDF. Since rasters can have many bands and even more values, they can be used to store large quantities of data in an efficient manner. Due to their efficiency, rasters are used for satellite and aerial sensors and modeled surfaces, such as weather forecasts.

There are a few keywords used in this chapter and in the PostGIS ecosystem that need to be defined:

- **Raster**: This is the PostGIS data type for storing raster files in PostgreSQL.
- **Tile**: This is a small chunk of the original raster file to be stored in one column of a table's row. Each tile has its own set of spatial information, and thus is independent of all the other tiles in the same column of the same table, even if the other tiles are from the same original raster file.
- **Coverage**: This consists of all the tiles of a single raster column from one table.

We make heavy use of GDAL in this chapter. GDAL is generally considered the de facto Swiss Army knife for working with rasters. GDAL is not a single application, but is a raster-abstraction library with many useful utilities. Through GDAL, you can get the metadata of a raster, convert that raster to a different format, and warp that raster among many other capabilities. For our needs in this chapter, we will use three GDAL utilities: `gdalinfo`, `gdalbuildvrt`, and `gdal_translate`.

Getting and loading rasters

In this recipe, we load most of the rasters used in this chapter. These rasters are examples of satellite imagery and model-generated surfaces, two of the most common raster sources.

Getting ready

If you have not done so already, create a directory and copy the chapter's datasets; for Windows, use the following commands:

```
> mkdir C:\postgis_cookbook\data\chap05
> cp -r /path/to/book_dataset/chap05 C:\postgis_cookbook\data\chap05
```

For Linux or macOS, go into the folder you wish to use and run the following commands, where /path/to/book_dataset/chap05 is the path where you originally stored the book source code:

```
> mkdir -p data/chap05
> cd data/chap05
> cp -r /path/to/book_dataset/chap05
```

You should also create a new schema for this chapter in the database:

```
> psql -d postgis_cookbook -c "CREATE SCHEMA chp05"
```

How to do it...

We will start with the PRISM average monthly minimum-temperature raster dataset for 2016 with coverage for the continental United States. The raster is provided by the PRISM Climate Group at Oregon State University, with additional rasters available at http://www.prism.oregonstate.edu/mtd/.

On the command line, navigate to the PRISM directory as follows:

```
> cd C:\postgis_cookbook\data\chap05\PRISM
```

Let us spot check one of the PRISM rasters with the GDAL utility gdalinfo. It is always a good practice to inspect at least one raster to get an idea of the metadata and ensure that the raster does not have any issues. This can be done using the following command:

```
> gdalinfo PRISM_tmin_provisional_4kmM2_201703_asc.asc
```

The `gdalinfo` output is as follows:

```
Driver: AAIGrid/Arc/Info ASCII Grid
Files: PRISM_tmin_provisional_4kmM2_201703_asc.asc
       PRISM_tmin_provisional_4kmM2_201703_asc.asc.aux.xml
       PRISM_tmin_provisional_4kmM2_201703_asc.prj
Size is 1405, 621
Coordinate System is:
GEOGCS["GCS_North_American_1983",
    DATUM["North_American_Datum_1983",
        SPHEROID["GRS_1980",6378137.0,298.257222101]],
    PRIMEM["Greenwich",0.0],
    UNIT["Degree",0.0174532925199432951]]
Origin = (-125.020833333333002,49.937499999999702)
Pixel Size = (0.041666666666700,-0.041666666666700)
Corner Coordinates:
Upper Left   (-125.0208333,   49.9375000) (125d 1'15.00"W, 49d56'15.00"N)
Lower Left   (-125.0208333,   24.0625000) (125d 1'15.00"W, 24d 3'45.00"N)
Upper Right  ( -66.4791667,   49.9375000) ( 66d28'45.00"W, 49d56'15.00"N)
Lower Right  ( -66.4791667,   24.0625000) ( 66d28'45.00"W, 24d 3'45.00"N)
Center       ( -95.7500000,   37.0000000) ( 95d45' 0.00"W, 37d 0' 0.00"N)
Band 1 Block=1405x1 Type=Float32, ColorInterp=Undefined
  Min=-16.169 Max=20.986
  Minimum=-16.169, Maximum=20.986, Mean=0.657, StdDev=6.186
  NoData Value=-9999
  Metadata:
    STATISTICS_MAXIMUM=20.986000061035
    STATISTICS_MEAN=0.65659218990218
    STATISTICS_MINIMUM=-16.16900062561
    STATISTICS_STDDEV=6.1857249305236
```

The `gdalinfo` output reveals that the raster has no issues, as evidenced by the `Corner Coordinates`, `Pixel Size`, `Band`, and `Coordinate System` being unempty.

Looking through the metadata, we find that the metadata about the spatial reference system indicates that raster uses the NAD83 coordinate system. We can double-check this by searching for the details of NAD83 in the `spatial_ref_sys` table:

```
SELECT srid, auth_name, auth_srid, srtext, proj4text
FROM spatial_ref_sys WHERE proj4text LIKE '%NAD83%'
```

Comparing the text of `srtext` to the PRISM raster's metadata spatial attributes, we find that the raster is in EPSG (SRID 4269).

You can load the PRISM rasters into the `chp05.prism` table with `raster2pgsql`, which will import the raster files to the database in a similar manner as the `shp2pgsql` command:

```
> raster2pgsql -s 4269 -t 100x100 -F -I -C -Y
.\PRISM_tmin_provisional_4kmM2_*_asc.asc
chp05.prism | psql -d postgis_cookbook -U me
```

The `raster2pgsql` command is called with the following flags:

- `-s`: This flag assigns SRID `4269` to the imported rasters.
- `-t`: This flag denotes the tile size. It chunks the imported rasters into smaller and more manageable pieces; each record added to the table will be, at most, 100 x 100 pixels.
- `-F`: This flag adds a column to the table and fills it with the raster's filename.
- `-I`: This flag creates a GIST spatial index on the table's raster column.
- `-C`: This flag applies the standard set of constraints on the table. The standard set of constraints includes checks for dimension, scale, skew, upper-left coordinate, and SRID.
- `-Y`: This flag instructs `raster2pgsql` to use `COPY` statements instead of `INSERT` statements. `COPY` is typically faster than `INSERT`.

There is a reason why we passed `-F` to `raster2pgsql`. If you look at the filenames of the PRISM rasters, you'll note the year and month. So, let's convert the value in the `filename` column to a date in the table:

```
ALTER TABLE chp05.prism ADD COLUMN month_year DATE;
UPDATE chp05.prism SET  month_year = ( SUBSTRING(split_part(filename, '_',
5), 0, 5) || '-' || SUBSTRING(split_part(filename, '_', 5), 5, 4) || '-01'
) :: DATE;
```

This is all that needs to be done with the PRISM rasters for now.

Now, let's import a **Shuttle Radar Topography Mission (SRTM)** raster. The SRTM raster is from the SRTM that was conducted by the NASA Jet Propulsion Laboratory in February, 2000. This raster and others like it are available at: http://dds.cr.usgs.gov/srtm/version2_1/SRTM1/.

Change the current directory to the SRTM directory:

```
> cd C:\postgis_cookbook\data\chap05\SRTM
```

Make sure you spot check the SRTM raster with `gdalinfo` to ensure that it is valid and has a value for `Coordinate System`. Once checked, import the SRTM raster into the `chp05.srtm` table:

```
> raster2pgsql -s 4326 -t 100x100 -F -I -C -Y N37W123.hgt chp05.srtm | psql
-d postgis_cookbook
```

We use the same `raster2pgsql` flags for the SRTM raster as those for the PRISM rasters.

We also need to import a `shapefile` of San Francisco provided by the City and County of San Francisco, available with the book's dataset files, or the one found on the following link, after exporting the data to a shapefile:

```
https://data.sfgov.org/Geographic-Locations-and-Boundaries/SF-Shoreline-and-
Islands/rgcx-5tix
```

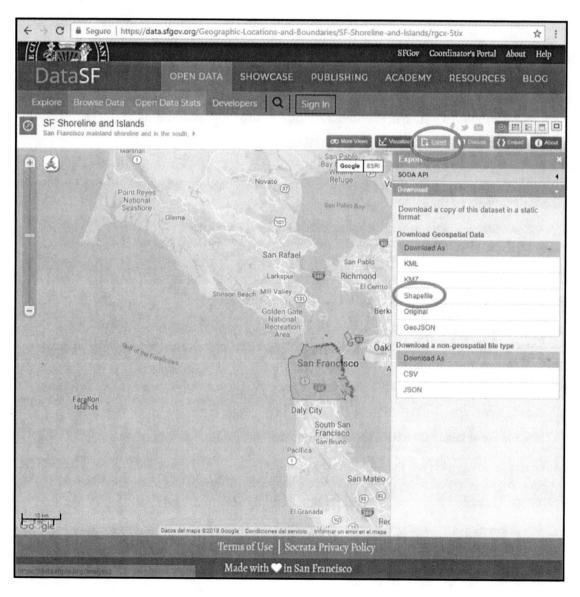

The San Francisco's boundaries from the book's files will be used in many of the follow-up recipes, and it must be loaded to the database as follows:

```
> cd C:\postgis_cookbook\data\chap05\SFPoly
> shp2pgsql -s 4326 -I sfpoly.shp chp05.sfpoly | psql -d postgis_cookbook -
U me
```

How it works...

In this recipe, we imported the required PRISM and SRTM rasters needed for the rest of the recipes. We also imported a `shapefile` containing San Francisco's boundaries to be used in the various raster analyses. Now, on to the fun!

Working with basic raster information and analysis

So far, we've checked and imported the PRISM and SRTM rasters into the `chp05` schema of the `postgis_cookbook` database. We will now proceed to work with the rasters within the database.

Getting ready

In this recipe, we explore functions that provide insight into the raster attributes and characteristics found in the `postgis_cookbook` database. In doing so, we can see if what is found in the database matches the information provided by accessing `gdalinfo`.

How to do it...

PostGIS includes the `raster_columns` view to provide a high-level summary of all the raster columns found in the database. This view is similar to the `geometry_columns` and `geography_columns` views in function and form.

Let's run the following SQL query in the `raster_columns` view to see what information is available in the `prism` table:

```sql
SELECT
  r_table_name,
  r_raster_column,
  srid,
  scale_x,
  scale_y,
  blocksize_x,
  blocksize_y,
  same_alignment,
  regular_blocking,
  num_bands,
  pixel_types,
  nodata_values,
  out_db,
  ST_AsText(extent) AS extent FROM raster_columns WHERE r_table_name =
'prism';
```

The SQL query returns a record similar to the following:

	r_table_name name	r_raster_column name	srid integer	scale_x double precision	scale_y double precision	blocksize_x integer	blocksize_y integer
1	prism	rast	4269	0.0416666667	-0.0416666667	100	100

same_alignment boolean	regular_blocking boolean	num_bands integer	pixel_types text[]	nodata_values double precision[]	out_db boolean[]	extent text
true	false	2	32BF,32BF	{-9999,-9999}	false,false	POLYG...

(1 row)

If you look back at the `gdalinfo` output for one of the PRISM rasters, you'll see that the values for the scales (the pixel size) match. The flags passed to `raster2pgsql`, specifying tile size and SRID, worked.

Let's see what the metadata of a single raster tile looks like. We will use the `ST_Metadata()` function:

```sql
SELECT  rid,  (ST_Metadata(rast)).*
FROM chp05.prism
WHERE month_year = '2017-03-01'::date
LIMIT 1;
```

The output will look similar to the following:

rid	upperleftx	upperlefty	width	height	scalex	scaley	skewx	skewy	srid	numbands
integer	double precision	double precision	integer	integer	double precision	double precision	double pre	double pri	integer	integer
1	1 -125.020833333333	49.9374999999997	100	100	0.0416666666667	-0.0416666666667	0	0	4269	2

Use `ST_BandMetadata()` to examine the first and only band of raster tiles at the record ID 54:

```
SELECT  rid,  (ST_BandMetadata(rast, 1)).*
FROM chp05.prism
WHERE rid = 54;
```

The results indicate that the band is of pixel type 32BF, and has a NODATA value of -9999. The NODATA value is the value assigned to an empty pixel:

	rid	pixeltype	nodatavalue	isoutdb	path
	integer	text	double precision	boolean	text
1	54	32BF	-9999	false	[null]

Now, to do something a bit more useful, run some basic statistic functions on this raster tile.

First, let's compute the summary statistics (count, mean, standard deviation, min, and max) with `ST_SummaryStats() for an specific raster, in this case, number 54`:

```
WITH stats AS (SELECT (ST_SummaryStats(rast, 1)).*  FROM prism  WHERE rid =
54)
SELECT  count,  sum,  round(mean::numeric, 2) AS mean,
round(stddev::numeric, 2) AS stddev,  min,  max
FROM stats;
```

The output of the preceding code will be as follows:

	count	sum	mean	stddev	min	max
	bigint	double precision	numeric	numeric	double precision	double precision
1	10000	60549.6879644394	6.05	1.70	2.08899998664856	10.0200004577637

In the summary statistics, if the count indicates less than *10,000 (100²)*, it means that the raster is 10,000-count/100. In this case, the raster tile is about 0% NODATA.

Let's see how the values of the raster tile are distributed with ST_Histogram():

```
WITH hist AS (
   SELECT (ST_Histogram(rast, 1)).* FROM chp05.prism WHERE rid = 54
)
SELECT round(min::numeric, 2) AS min, round(max::numeric, 2) AS max, count,
round(percent::numeric, 2) AS percent FROM hist
ORDER BY min;
```

The output will look as follows:

	min numeric	max numeric	count bigint	percent numeric
1	2.09	2.62	85	0.01
2	2.62	3.15	211	0.02
3	3.15	3.68	354	0.04
4	3.68	4.20	622	0.06
5	4.20	4.73	1359	0.14
6	4.73	5.26	997	0.10
7	5.26	5.79	1270	0.13
8	5.79	6.32	984	0.10
9	6.32	6.85	803	0.08
10	6.85	7.38	890	0.09
11	7.38	7.91	833	0.08
12	7.91	8.43	547	0.05
13	8.43	8.96	378	0.04
14	8.96	9.49	533	0.05
15	9.49	10.02	134	0.01

It looks like about 78% of all of the values are at or below 1370.50. Another way to see how the pixel values are distributed is to use ST_Quantile():

```
SELECT (ST_Quantile(rast, 1)).*
FROM chp05.prism
WHERE rid = 54;
```

The output of the preceding code is as follows:

	quantile double precision	value double precision
1	0	2.08899998664856
2	0.25	4.68800020217896
3	0.5	5.84000015258789
4	0.75	7.3254998922348
5	1	10.0200004577637

Let's see what the top 10 occurring values are in the raster tile with `ST_ValueCount()`:

```
SELECT (ST_ValueCount(rast, 1)).*
FROM chp05.prism WHERE rid = 54
ORDER BY count DESC, value
LIMIT 10;
```

The output of the code is as follows:

	value double precision	count integer
1	5.61299991607666	10
2	4.17600011825562	9
3	4.6230001449585	9
4	5.53999996185303	9
5	4.59700012207031	8
6	5.45100021362305	8
7	5.67999982833862	8
8	6.02799987792969	8
9	7.13800001144409	8
10	4.51700019836426	7

The ST_ValueCount allows other combinations of parameters that will allow rounding up of the values in order to aggregate some of the results, but a previous subset of values to look for must be defined; for example, the following code will count the appearance of values 2, 3, 2.5, 5.612999 and 4.176 rounded to the fifth decimal point 0.00001:

```
SELECT (ST_ValueCount(rast, 1, true, ARRAY[2,3,2.5,5.612999,4.176]::double
precision[] ,0.0001)).*
FROM chp05.prism
WHERE rid = 54
ORDER BY count DESC, value
LIMIT 10;
```

The results show the number of elements that appear similar to the rounded-up values in the array. The two values borrowed from the results on the previous figure, confirm the counting:

	value double precision	count integer
1	5.613	10
2	4.176	9
3	3	1
4	2	0
5	2.5	0

How it works...

In the first part of this recipe, we looked at the metadata of the prism raster table and a single raster tile. We focused on that single raster tile to run a variety of statistics. The statistics provided some idea of what the data looks like.

We mentioned that the pixel values looked wrong when we looked at the output from ST_SummaryStats(). This same issue continued in the output from subsequent statistics functions. We also found that the values were in Celsius degrees. In the next recipe, we will recompute all the pixel values to their true values with a map-algebra operation.

Performing simple map-algebra operations

In the previous recipe, we saw that the values in the PRISM rasters did not look correct for temperature values. After looking at the PRISM metadata, we learned that the values were scaled by 100.

In this recipe, we will process the scaled values to get the true values. Doing this will prevent future end-user confusion, which is always a good thing.

Getting ready

PostGIS provides two types of map-algebra functions, both of which return a new raster with one band. The type you use depends on the problem being solved and the number of raster bands involved.

The first map-algebra function (ST_MapAlgebra() or ST_MapAlgebraExpr()) depends on a valid, user-provided PostgreSQL algebraic expression that is called for every pixel. The expression can be as simple as an equation, or as complex as a logic-heavy SQL expression. If the map-algebra operation only requires at most two raster bands, and the expression is not complicated, you should have no problems using the expression-based map-algebra function.

The second map-algebra function (ST_MapAlgebra(), ST_MapAlgebraFct(), or ST_MapAlgebraFctNgb()) requires the user to provide an appropriate PostgreSQL function to be called for each pixel. The function being called can be written in any of the PostgreSQL PL languages (for example, PL/pgSQL, PL/R, PL/Perl), and be as complex as needed. This type is more challenging to use than the expression map-algebra function type, but it has the flexibility to work on any number of raster bands.

For this recipe, we use only the expression-based map-algebra function, ST_MapAlgebra(), to create a new band with the temperature values in Fahrenheit, and then append this band to the processed raster. If you are not using PostGIS 2.1 or a later version, use the equivalent ST_MapAlgebraExpr() function.

How to do it...

With any operation that is going to take a while and/or modify a stored raster, it is best to test that operation to ensure there are no mistakes and the output looks correct.

Let's run `ST_MapAlgebra()` on one raster tile, and compare the summary statistics before and after the map-algebra operation:

```
WITH stats AS (
  SELECT
    'before' AS state,
    (ST_SummaryStats(rast, 1)).*
  FROM chp05.prism
  WHERE rid = 54
  UNION ALL
  SELECT
    'after' AS state, (ST_SummaryStats(ST_MapAlgebra(rast, 1, '32BF',
'([rast]*9/5)+32', -9999), 1 )).*
  FROM chp05.prism
  WHERE rid = 54
)
SELECT
  state,
  count,
  round(sum::numeric, 2) AS sum,
  round(mean::numeric, 2) AS mean,
  round(stddev::numeric, 2) AS stddev,
  round(min::numeric, 2) AS min,
  round(max::numeric, 2) AS max
FROM stats ORDER BY state DESC;
```

The output looks as follows:

	state text	count bigint	sum numeric	mean numeric	stddev numeric	min numeric	max numeric
1	before	10000	60549.69	6.05	1.70	2.09	10.02
2	after	10000	428989.44	42.90	3.06	35.76	50.04

In the `ST_MapAlgebra()` function, we indicate that the output raster's band will have a pixel type of `32BF` and a `NODATA` value of `-9999`. We use the expression `'([rast]*9/5)+32'` to convert each pixel value to its new value in Fahrenheit. Before `ST_MapAlgebra()` evaluates the expression, the pixel value replaces the placeholder `'[rast]'`. There are several other placeholders available, and they can be found in the `ST_MapAlgebra()` documentation.

Looking at the summary statistics and comparing the before and after processing, we see that the map-algebra operation works correctly. So, let's correct the entire table. We will append the band created from `ST_MapAlgebra()` to the existing raster:

```
UPDATE chp05.prism SET  rast = ST_AddBand(rast, ST_MapAlgebra(rast, 1,
'32BF', '([rast]*9/5)+32', -999), 1   );
ERROR:  new row for relation "prism" violates check constraint "
enforce_nodata_values_rast"
```

The SQL query will not work. Why? If you remember, when we loaded the PRISM rasters, we instructed `raster2pgsql` to add the standard constraints with the `-c` flag. It looks like we violated at least one of those constraints.

When installed, the standard constraints enforce a set of rules on each value of a raster column in the table. These rules guarantee that each raster column value has the same (or appropriate) attributes. The standard constraints comprise the following rules:

- **Width and height**: This rule states that all the rasters must have the same width and height
- **Scale X and Y**: This rule states that all the rasters must have the same scale X and Y
- **SRID**: This rule states that all rasters must have the same SRID
- **Same alignment**: This rule states that all rasters must be aligned to one another
- **Maximum extent**: This rule states that all rasters must be within the table's maximum extent
- **Number of bands**: This rule states that all rasters must have the same number of bands
- **NODATA values**: This rule states that all raster bands at a specific index must have the same NODATA value
- **Out-db**: This rule states that all raster bands at a specific index must be `in-db` or `out-db`, not both
- **Pixel type**: This rule states that all raster bands at a specific index must be of the same pixel type

The error message indicates that we violated the `out-db` constraint. But we can't accept the error message as it is, because we are not doing anything related to `out-db`. All we are doing is adding a second band to the raster. Adding the second band violates the `out-db` constraint, because the constraint is prepared only for one band in the raster, not a raster with two bands.

We will have to drop the constraints, make our changes, and reapply the constraints:

```
SELECT DropRasterConstraints('chp05', 'prism', 'rast'::name);
```

After this command, we will have the following output showing the constraints were dropped:

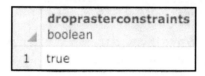

```
UPDATE chp05.prism SET rast = ST_AddBand(rast, ST_MapAlgebra(rast, 1,
'32BF', ' ([rast]*9/5)+32', -9999), 1);
SELECT AddRasterConstraints('chp05', 'prism', 'rast'::name);
```

The UPDATE will take some time, and the output will look as follows, showing that the constraints were added again:

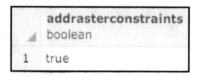

There is not much information provided in the output, so we will inspect the rasters. We will look at one raster tile:

```
SELECT (ST_Metadata(rast)).numbands
FROM chp05.prism
WHERE rid = 54;
```

The output is as follows:

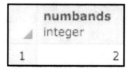

The raster has two bands. The following are the details of these two bands:

```
SELECT 1 AS bandnum, (ST_BandMetadata(rast, 1)).*
FROM chp05.prism
WHERE rid = 54
UNION ALL
SELECT 2 AS bandnum, (ST_BandMetadata(rast, 2)).*
FROM chp05.prism
WHERE rid = 54
ORDER BY bandnum;
```

The output looks as follows:

	bandnum integer	pixeltype text	nodatavalue double precision	isoutdb boolean	path text
1	1	32BF	-9999	false	[null]
2	2	32BF	-9999	false	[null]

The first band is the same as the new second band with the correct attributes (the 32BF pixel type, and the NODATA value of -9999) that we specified in the call to ST_MapAlgebra().The real test, though, is to look at the summary statistics:

```
WITH stats AS (
  SELECT
    1 AS bandnum,
    (ST_SummaryStats(rast, 1)).*
  FROM chp05.prism
  WHERE rid = 54
  UNION ALL
  SELECT
    2 AS bandnum,
    (ST_SummaryStats(rast, 2)).*
  FROM chp05.prism
  WHERE rid = 54
)
SELECT
  bandnum,
  count,
  round(sum::numeric, 2) AS sum,
  round(mean::numeric, 2) AS mean,
  round(stddev::numeric, 2) AS stddev,
  round(min::numeric, 2) AS min,
  round(max::numeric, 2) AS max
FROM stats ORDER BY bandnum;
```

The output is as follows:

	bandnum integer	count bigint	sum numeric	mean numeric	stddev numeric	min numeric	max numeric
1	1	10000	60549.69	6.05	1.70	2.09	10.02
2	2	10000	428989.44	42.90	3.06	35.76	50.04

The summary statistics show that band 2 is correct after the values from band 1 were transformed into Fahrenheit; that is, the mean temperature is 6.05 of band 1 in degrees Celsius, and 42.90 in degrees Fahrenheit in band 2).

How it works...

In this recipe, we applied a simple map-algebra operation with ST_MapAlgebra() to correct the pixel values. In a later recipe, we will present an advanced map-algebra operation to demonstrate the power of ST_MapAlgebra().

Combining geometries with rasters for analysis

In the previous two recipes, we ran basic statistics only on one raster tile. Though running operations on a specific raster is great, it is not very helpful for answering real questions. In this recipe, we will use geometries to filter, clip, and unite raster tiles so that we can answer questions for a specific area.

Getting ready

We will use the San Francisco boundaries geometry previously imported into the sfpoly table. If you have not imported the boundaries, refer to the first recipe of this chapter for instructions.

How to do it...

Since we are to look at rasters in the context of San Francisco, an easy question to ask is: what was the average temperature for March, 2017 in San Francisco? Have a look at the following code:

```
SELECT (ST_SummaryStats(ST_Union(ST_Clip(prism.rast, 1,
ST_Transform(sf.geom, 4269), TRUE)), 1)).mean
FROM chp05.prism
JOIN chp05.sfpoly sf ON ST_Intersects(prism.rast, ST_Transform(sf.geom,
4269))
WHERE prism.month_year = '2017-03-01'::date;
```

In the preceding SQL query, there are four items to pay attention to, which are as follows:

- `ST_Transform()`: This method converts the geometry's coordinates from one spatial reference system to another. Transforming a geometry is typically faster than transforming a raster. Transforming a raster requires the pixel values to be resampled, a compute-intensive process, and one that could introduce undesirable results. If possible, always transform a geometry before transforming a raster, because spatial joins need to use the same SRID.

- `ST_Intersects()`: The `ST_Intersects()` method found in the `JOIN ON` clause tests if the raster tile and the geometry spatially intersect. It will use any available spatial indexes. Depending on the installed version of PostGIS, `ST_Intersects()` will implicitly convert the input geometry to a raster (PostGIS 2.0), or the input raster to a geometry (PostGIS 2.1), before comparing the two inputs.

- `ST_Clip()`: This method trims each intersecting raster tile only to the area that intersects the geometry. It eliminates the pixels that are not spatially part of the geometry. Like `ST_Intersects()`, the geometry is implicitly converted to a raster before clipping.

- `ST_Union()`: This method aggregates and merges the clipped raster tiles into one raster for further processing.

The following output shows the average minimum temperature for San Francisco:

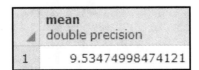

	mean double precision
1	9.53474998474121

San Francisco was really cold in March, 2017. So, how does the rest of 2017 look? Is San Francisco always cold?

```
SELECT prism.month_year, (ST_SummaryStats(ST_Union(ST_Clip(prism.rast, 1,
ST_Transform(sf.geom, 4269), TRUE)), 1)).mean
FROM chp05.prism
JOIN chp05.sfpoly sf ON ST_Intersects(prism.rast, ST_Transform(sf.geom,
4269))
GROUP BY prism.month_year
ORDER BY prism.month_year;
```

The only change from the prior SQL query is the removal of the WHERE clause and the addition of a GROUP BY clause. Since ST_Union() is an aggregate function, we need to group the clipped rasters by month_year.

The output is as follows:

	month_year date	mean double precision
1	2017-03-01	9.53474998474121
2	2017-04-01	10.1283749341965
3	2017-05-01	10.4667500257492
4	2017-06-01	11.6341251134872
5	2017-07-01	12.1107499599457
6	2017-08-01	13.8238750696182

Based on the results, the late summer months of 2017 were the warmest, though not by a huge margin.

How it works...

By using a geometry to filter the rasters in the prism table, only a small set of rasters needed clipping with the geometry and unionizing to compute the mean. This maximized the query performance, and more importantly, provided the answer to our question.

Converting between rasters and geometries

In the last recipe, we used the geometries to filter and clip rasters only to the areas of interest. The ST_Clip() and ST_Intersects() functions implicitly converted the geometry before relating it to the raster.

PostGIS provides several functions for converting rasters to geometries. Depending on the function, a pixel can be returned as an area or a point.

PostGIS provides one function for converting geometries to rasters.

Getting ready

In this recipe, we will convert rasters to geometries, and geometries to rasters. We will use the ST_DumpAsPolygons() and ST_PixelsAsPolygons() functions to convert rasters to geometries. We will then convert geometries to rasters using ST_AsRaster().

How to do it...

Let's adapt part of the query used in the last recipe to find out the average minimum temperature in San Francisco. We replace ST_SummaryStats() with ST_DumpAsPolygons(), and then return the geometries as WKT:

```
WITH geoms AS (SELECT ST_DumpAsPolygons(ST_Union(ST_Clip(prism.rast, 1,
ST_Transform(sf.geom, 4269), TRUE)), 1 ) AS gv
FROM chp05.prism
JOIN chp05.sfpoly sf ON ST_Intersects(prism.rast, ST_Transform(sf.geom,
4269))
WHERE prism.month_year = '2017-03-01'::date )
SELECT (gv).val, ST_AsText((gv).geom) AS geom
FROM geoms;
```

The output is as follows:

	val double precision	geom text
1	9.70699977874756	POLYGON((-122.479166666664 37.812499...
2	9.99499988555908	POLYGON((-122.437499999998 37.812499...
3	9.54199981689453	POLYGON((-122.520833333331 37.770833...
4	9.08399963378906	POLYGON((-122.479166666664 37.770833...
5	9.97900009155273	POLYGON((-122.437499999998 37.770833...
6	9.40200042724609	POLYGON((-122.520833333331 37.729166...
7	8.97700023651123	POLYGON((-122.479166666664 37.729166...
8	9.59200000762939	POLYGON((-122.437499999998 37.729166...

Now, replace the `ST_DumpAsPolygons()` function with `ST_PixelsAsPolyons()`:

```
WITH geoms AS (SELECT (ST_PixelAsPolygons(ST_Union(ST_Clip(prism.rast, 1,
ST_Transform(sf.geom, 4269), TRUE)), 1 )) AS gv
FROM chp05.prism
JOIN chp05.sfpoly sf ON ST_Intersects(prism.rast, ST_Transform(sf.geom,
4269))
WHERE prism.month_year = '2017-03-01'::date)
SELECT (gv).val, ST_AsText((gv).geom) AS geom
FROM geoms;
```

The output is as follows:

	val double precision	geom text
1	9.70699977874756	POLYGON((-122.479...
2	9.99499988555908	POLYGON((-122.437...
3	9.54199981689453	POLYGON((-122.520...
4	9.08399963378906	POLYGON((-122.479...
5	9.97900009155273	POLYGON((-122.437...
6	9.40200042724609	POLYGON((-122.520...
7	8.97700023651123	POLYGON((-122.479...
8	9.59200000762939	POLYGON((-122.437...

Again, the query results have been trimmed. What is important is the number of rows returned. `ST_PixelsAsPolygons()` returns significantly more geometries than `ST_DumpAsPolygons()`. This is due to the different mechanism used in each function.

The following images show the difference between `ST_DumpAsPolygons()` and `ST_PixelsAsPolygons()`. The `ST_DumpAsPolygons()` function only dumps pixels with a value and unites these pixels with the same value. The `ST_PixelsAsPolygons()` function does not merge pixels and dumps all of them, as shown in the following diagrams:

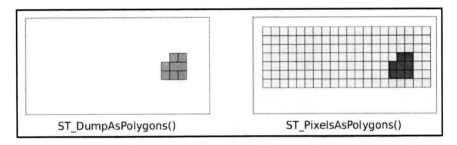

ST_DumpAsPolygons()   ST_PixelsAsPolygons()

The `ST_PixelsAsPolygons()` function returns one geometry for each pixel. If there are 100 pixels, there will be 100 geometries. Each geometry of `ST_DumpAsPolygons()` is the union of all of the pixels in an area with the same value. If there are 100 pixels, there may be up to 100 geometries.

There is one other significant difference between `ST_PixelAsPolygons()` and `ST_DumpAsPolygons()`. Unlike `ST_DumpAsPolygons()`, `ST_PixelAsPolygons()` returns a geometry for pixels with the NODATA value, and has an empty value for the `val` column.

Let's convert a geometry to a raster with `ST_AsRaster()`. We insert `ST_AsRaster()` to return a raster with a pixel size of 100 by –100 meters containing four bands of the pixel type 8BUI. Each of these bands will have a pixel NODATA value of 0, and a specific pixel value (29, 194, 178, and 255 for each band respectively). The units for the pixel size are determined by the geometry's projection, which is also the projection of the created raster:

```
SELECT ST_AsRaster(
  sf.geom,
  100., -100.,
  ARRAY['8BUI', '8BUI', '8BUI', '8BUI']::text[],
  ARRAY[29, 194, 178, 255]::double precision[],
  ARRAY[0, 0, 0, 0]::double precision[]
)
FROM sfpoly sf;
```

If we visualize the generated raster of San Francisco's boundaries and overlay the source geometry, we get the following result, which is a zoomed-in view of the San Francisco boundary's geometry converted to a raster with `ST_AsRaster()`:

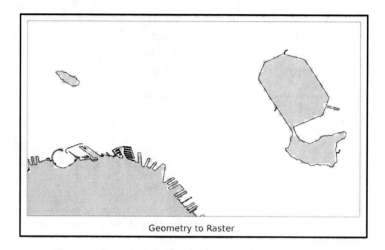

Geometry to Raster

Though it is great that the geometry is now a raster, relating the generated raster to other rasters requires additional processing. This is because the generated raster and the other raster will most likely not be aligned. If the two rasters are not aligned, most PostGIS raster functions do not work. The following figure shows two non-aligned rasters (simplified to pixel grids):

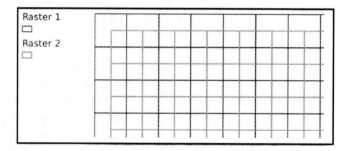

The pixel grids of **Raster 1** and **Raster 2** are not aligned. If the rasters are aligned, the edges of one grid's cell will be on top of one of the other grid's cell's edges.

When a geometry needs to be converted to a raster so as to relate to an existing raster, use that existing raster as a reference when calling ST_AsRaster():

```
SELECT ST_AsRaster(
    sf.geom, prism.rast,
    ARRAY['8BUI', '8BUI', '8BUI', '8BUI']::text[],
    ARRAY[29, 194, 178, 255]::double precision[],
    ARRAY[0, 0, 0, 0]::double precision[]
)
FROM chp05.sfpoly sf
CROSS JOIN chp05.prism
WHERE prism.rid = 1;
```

In the preceding query, we use the raster tile at rid = 1 as our reference raster. The ST_AsRaster() function uses the reference raster's metadata to create the geometry's raster. If the geometry and reference raster have different SRIDs, the geometry is transformed to the same SRID before creating the raster.

How it works...

In this recipe, we converted rasters to geometries. We also created new rasters from geometries. The ability to convert between rasters and geometries allows the use of functions that would otherwise not be possible.

Processing and loading rasters with GDAL VRT

Though PostGIS has plenty of functions for working with rasters, it is sometimes more convenient and more efficient to work on the source rasters before importing them into the database. One of the times when working with rasters outside the database is more efficient is when the raster contains subdatasets, typically found in HDF4, HDF5, and NetCDF files.

Getting ready

In this recipe, we will preprocess a MODIS raster with the **GDAL VRT** format to filter and rearrange the subdatasets. Internally, a VRT file is comprised of XML tags. This means we can create a VRT file with any text editor. But since creating a VRT file manually can be tedious, we will use the gdalbuildvrt utility.

The MODIS raster we use is provided by NASA, and is available in the source package.

You will need GDAL built with HDF4 support to continue with this recipe, as MODIS rasters are usually in the HDF4-EOS format.

The following screenshot shows the MODIS raster used in this recipe and the next two recipes. In the following image, we see parts of California, Nevada, Arizona, and Baja California:

To allow PostGIS to properly support MODIS rasters, we will also need to add the MODIS Sinusoidal projection to the `spatial_ref_sys` table.

How to do it...

On the command line, navigate to the `MODIS` directory:

```
> cd C:\postgis_cookbook\data\chap05\MODIS
```

In the `MODIS` directory, there should be several files. One of these files has the name `srs.sql` and contains the `INSERT` statement needed for the MODIS Sinusoidal projection. Run the `INSERT` statement:

```
> psql -d postgis_cookbook -f srs.sql
```

The main file has the extension HDF. Let's check the metadata of that HDF file:

```
> gdalinfo MYD09A1.A2012161.h08v05.005.2012170065756.hdf
```

When run, `gdalinfo` outputs a lot of information. We are looking for the list of subdatasets found in the `Subdatasets` section:

Subdatasets:

```
   SUBDATASET_1_DESC=[2400x2400] sur_refl_b01 MOD_Grid_500m_Surface_Reflectance (
16-bit integer)
   SUBDATASET_2_NAME=HDF4_EOS:EOS_GRID:"MYD09A1.A2012161.h08v05.005.2012170065756
.hdf":MOD_Grid_500m_Surface_Reflectance:sur_refl_b02
   SUBDATASET_2_DESC=[2400x2400] sur_refl_b02 MOD_Grid_500m_Surface_Reflectance (
16-bit integer)
   SUBDATASET_3_NAME=HDF4_EOS:EOS_GRID:"MYD09A1.A2012161.h08v05.005.2012170065756
.hdf":MOD_Grid_500m_Surface_Reflectance:sur_refl_b03
   SUBDATASET_3_DESC=[2400x2400] sur_refl_b03 MOD_Grid_500m_Surface_Reflectance (
16-bit integer)
   SUBDATASET_4_NAME=HDF4_EOS:EOS_GRID:"MYD09A1.A2012161.h08v05.005.2012170065756
.hdf":MOD_Grid_500m_Surface_Reflectance:sur_refl_b04
   SUBDATASET_4_DESC=[2400x2400] sur_refl_b04 MOD_Grid_500m_Surface_Reflectance (
16-bit integer)
   SUBDATASET_5_NAME=HDF4_EOS:EOS_GRID:"MYD09A1.A2012161.h08v05.005.2012170065756
.hdf":MOD_Grid_500m_Surface_Reflectance:sur_refl_b05
   SUBDATASET_5_DESC=[2400x2400] sur_refl_b05 MOD_Grid_500m_Surface_Reflectance (
16-bit integer)
   SUBDATASET_6_NAME=HDF4_EOS:EOS_GRID:"MYD09A1.A2012161.h08v05.005.2012170065756
.hdf":MOD_Grid_500m_Surface_Reflectance:sur_refl_b06
   SUBDATASET_6_DESC=[2400x2400] sur_refl_b06 MOD_Grid_500m_Surface_Reflectance (
16-bit integer)
   SUBDATASET_7_NAME=HDF4_EOS:EOS_GRID:"MYD09A1.A2012161.h08v05.005.2012170065756
.hdf":MOD_Grid_500m_Surface_Reflectance:sur_refl_b07
   SUBDATASET_7_DESC=[2400x2400] sur_refl_b07 MOD_Grid_500m_Surface_Reflectance (
16-bit integer)
   SUBDATASET_8_NAME=HDF4_EOS:EOS_GRID:"MYD09A1.A2012161.h08v05.005.2012170065756
.hdf":MOD_Grid_500m_Surface_Reflectance:sur_refl_qc_500m
   SUBDATASET_8_DESC=[2400x2400] sur_refl_qc_500m MOD_Grid_500m_Surface_Reflectan
ce (32-bit unsigned integer)
   SUBDATASET_9_NAME=HDF4_EOS:EOS_GRID:"MYD09A1.A2012161.h08v05.005.2012170065756
.hdf":MOD_Grid_500m_Surface_Reflectance:sur_refl_szen
   SUBDATASET_9_DESC=[2400x2400] sur_refl_szen MOD_Grid_500m_Surface_Reflectance
(16-bit integer)
   SUBDATASET_10_NAME=HDF4_EOS:EOS_GRID:"MYD09A1.A2012161.h08v05.005.201217006575
6.hdf":MOD_Grid_500m_Surface_Reflectance:sur_refl_vzen
   SUBDATASET_10_DESC=[2400x2400] sur_refl_vzen MOD_Grid_500m_Surface_Reflectance
(16-bit integer)
   SUBDATASET_11_NAME=HDF4_EOS:EOS_GRID:"MYD09A1.A2012161.h08v05.005.201217006575
6.hdf":MOD_Grid_500m_Surface_Reflectance:sur_refl_raz
   SUBDATASET_11_DESC=[2400x2400] sur_refl_raz MOD_Grid_500m_Surface_Reflectance
(16-bit integer)
   SUBDATASET_12_NAME=HDF4_EOS:EOS_GRID:"MYD09A1.A2012161.h08v05.005.201217006575
6.hdf":MOD_Grid_500m_Surface_Reflectance:sur_refl_state_500m
   SUBDATASET_12_DESC=[2400x2400] sur_refl_state_500m MOD_Grid_500m_Surface_Refle
ctance (16-bit unsigned integer)
   SUBDATASET_13_NAME=HDF4_EOS:EOS_GRID:"MYD09A1.A2012161.h08v05.005.201217006575
6.hdf":MOD_Grid_500m_Surface_Reflectance:sur_refl_day_of_year
```

Each subdataset is one variable of the MODIS raster included in the source code for this chapter. For our purposes, we only need the first four subdatasets, which are as follows:

- Subdataset 1: 620 - 670 nm (red)
- Subdataset 2: 841 - 876 nm (near infrared or NIR)
- Subdataset 3: 459 - 479 nm (blue)
- Subdataset 4: 545 - 565 nm (green)

The VRT format allows us to select the subdatasets to be included in the VRT raster as well as change the order of the subdatasets. We want to rearrange the subdatasets so that they are in the RGB order.

Let's call gdalbuildvrt to create a VRT file for our MODIS raster. Do not run the following!

```
> gdalbuildvrt -separate  modis.vrt
HDF4_EOS:EOS_GRID:"MYD09A1.A2012161.h08v05.005.2012170065756.hdf":MOD_Grid_
500m_Surface_Reflectance:sur_refl_b01
HDF4_EOS:EOS_GRID:"MYD09A1.A2012161.h08v05.005.2012170065756.hdf":MOD_Grid_
500m_Surface_Reflectance:sur_refl_b04
HDF4_EOS:EOS_GRID:"MYD09A1.A2012161.h08v05.005.2012170065756.hdf":MOD_Grid_
500m_Surface_Reflectance:sur_refl_b03
HDF4_EOS:EOS_GRID:"MYD09A1.A2012161.h08v05.005.2012170065756.hdf":MOD_Grid_
500m_Surface_Reflectance:sur_refl_b02
```

We really hope you did not run the preceding code. The command does work but is too long and cumbersome. It would be better if we can pass a file indicating the subdatasets to include and their order in the VRT. Thankfully, gdalbuildvrt provides such an option with the -input_file_list flag.

In the MODIS directory, the modis.txt file can be passed to gdalbuildvrt with the -input_file_list flag. Each line of the modis.txt file is the name of a subdataset. The order of the subdatasets in the text file dictates the placement of each subdataset in the VRT:

```
HDF4_EOS:EOS_GRID:"MYD09A1.A2012161.h08v05.005.2012170065756.hdf":MOD_Grid_
500m_Surface_Reflectance:sur_refl_b01
HDF4_EOS:EOS_GRID:"MYD09A1.A2012161.h08v05.005.2012170065756.hdf":MOD_Grid_
500m_Surface_Reflectance:sur_refl_b04
HDF4_EOS:EOS_GRID:"MYD09A1.A2012161.h08v05.005.2012170065756.hdf":MOD_Grid_
500m_Surface_Reflectance:sur_refl_b03
HDF4_EOS:EOS_GRID:"MYD09A1.A2012161.h08v05.005.2012170065756.hdf":MOD_Grid_
500m_Surface_Reflectance:sur_refl_b02
```

Now, call `gdalbuildvrt` with `modis.txt` in the following manner:

```
> gdalbuildvrt -separate -input_file_list modis.txt modis.vrt
```

Feel free to inspect the generated `modis.vrt` VRT file in your favorite text editor. Since the contents of the VRT file are just XML tags, it is easy to make additions, changes, and deletions.

We will do one last thing before importing our processed MODIS raster into PostGIS. We will convert the VRT file to a GeoTIFF file with the `gdal_translate` utility, because not all applications have built-in support for HDF4, HDF5, NetCDF, or VRT, and the superior portability of GeoTIFF:

```
> gdal_translate -of GTiff modis.vrt modis.tif
```

Finally, import `modis.tif` with `raster2pgsql`:

```
> raster2pgsql -s 96974 -F -I -C -Y modis.tif chp05.modis | psql -d
postgis_cookbook
```

The `raster2pgsql` supports a long list of input formats. You can call the command with the option -G to see the complete list.

How it works...

This recipe was all about processing a MODIS raster into a form suitable for use in PostGIS. We used the `gdalbuildvrt` utility to create our VRT. As a bonus, we used `gdal_translate` to convert between raster formats; in this case, from VRT to GeoTIFF.

If you're feeling particularly adventurous, try using `gdalbuildvrt` to create a VRT of the 12 PRISM rasters with each raster as a separate band.

Warping and resampling rasters

In the previous recipe, we processed a MODIS raster to extract only those subdatasets that are of interest, in a more suitable order. Once done with the extraction, we imported the MODIS raster into its own table.

Here, we make use of the warping capabilities provided in PostGIS. This ranges from simply transforming the MODIS raster to a more suitable projection, to creating an overview by resampling the pixel size.

Getting ready

We will use several PostGIS warping functions, specifically ST_Transform() and ST_Rescale(). The ST_Transform() function reprojects a raster to a new spatial reference system (for example, from WGS84 to NAD83). The ST_Rescale() function shrinks or grows the pixel size of a raster.

How to do it...

The first thing we will do is transform our raster, since the MODIS rasters have their own unique spatial-reference system. We will convert the raster from **MODIS Sinusoidal projection** to **US National Atlas Equal Area (SRID 2163)**.

Before we transform the raster, we will clip the MODIS raster with our San Francisco boundaries geometry. By clipping our raster before transformation, the operation takes less time than it does to transform and then clip the raster:

```
SELECT  ST_Transform(ST_Clip(m.rast, ST_Transform(sf.geom, 96974)), 2163)
FROM chp05.modis m
CROSS JOIN chp05.sfpoly sf;
```

The following image shows the clipped MODIS raster with the San Francisco boundaries on top for comparison:

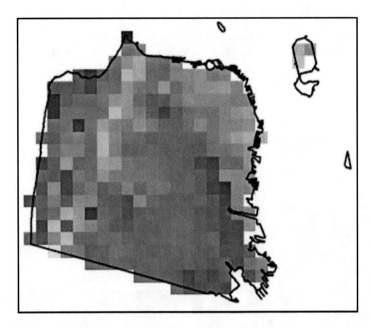

When we call ST_Transform() on the MODIS raster, we only pass the destination SRID 2163. We could specify other parameters, such as the **resampling algorithm** and **error tolerance**. The default resampling algorithm and error tolerance are set to NearestNeighbor and 0.125. Using a different algorithm and/or lowering the error tolerance may improve the quality of the resampled raster at the cost of more processing time.

Let's transform the MODIS raster again, this time specifying the resampling algorithm and error tolerance as Cubic and 0.05, respectively. We also indicate that the transformed raster must be aligned to a reference raster:

```
SELECT  ST_Transform(ST_Clip(m.rast, ST_Transform(sf.geom, 96974)),
  prism.rast, 'cubic', 0.05)
FROM chp05.modis m
CROSS JOIN chp05.prism
CROSS JOIN chp05.sfpoly sf
WHERE prism.rid = 1;
```

Unlike the prior queries where we transform the MODIS raster, let's create an **overview**. An overview is a lower-resolution version of the source raster. If you are familiar with pyramids, an overview is level one of a pyramid, while the source raster is the base level:

```
WITH meta AS (SELECT (ST_Metadata(rast)).* FROM chp05.modis)
SELECT ST_Rescale(modis.rast, meta.scalex * 4., meta.scaley * 4., 'cubic')
AS rast
FROM chp05.modis
CROSS JOIN meta;
```

The overview is 25% of the resolution of the original MODIS raster. This means four times the scale, and one quarter the width and height. To prevent hardcoding the desired scale X and scale Y, we use the MODIS raster's scale X and scale Y returned by ST_Metadata(). As you can see in the following image, the overview has a coarser resolution:

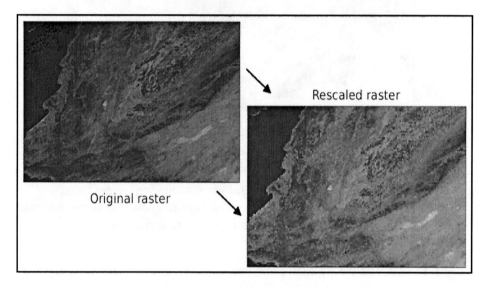

 The rescaled raster is more pixelated due to the reduction of resolution.

How it works...

Using some of PostGIS's resampling capabilities, we projected the MODIS raster to a different spatial reference with `ST_Transform()` as well as controlled the quality of the projected raster. We also created an overview with `ST_Rescale()`.

Using these functions and other PostGIS resampling functions, you should be able to manipulate all the rasters.

Performing advanced map-algebra operations

In a prior recipe, we used the expression-based map-algebra function `ST_MapAlgebra()` to convert the PRISM pixel values to their true values. The expression-based `ST_MapAlgebra()` method is easy to use, but limited to operating on at most two raster bands. This restricts the `ST_MapAlgebra()` function's usefulness for processes that require more than two input raster bands, such as the **Normalized Difference Vegetation Index (NDVI)** and the **Enhanced Vegetation Index (EVI)**.

There is a variant of `ST_MapAlgebra()` designed to support an unlimited number of input raster bands. Instead of taking an expression, this `ST_MapAlgebra()` variant requires a callback function. This callback function is run for each set of input pixel values, and returns either a new pixel value, or `NULL` for the output pixel. Additionally, this variant of `ST_MapAlgebra()` permits operations on neighborhoods (sets of pixels around a center pixel).

PostGIS comes with a set of ready-to-use `ST_MapAlgebra()` callback functions. All of these functions are intended for neighborhood calculations, such as computing the average value of a neighborhood, or interpolating empty pixel values.

Getting ready

We will use the MODIS raster to compute the EVI. EVI is a three-band operation consisting of the red, blue, and near-infrared bands. To do an `ST_MapAlgebra()` operation on three bands, PostGIS 2.1 or a higher version is required.

How to do it...

To use `ST_MapAlgebra()` on more than two bands, we must use the callback function variant. This means we need to create a callback function. Callback functions can be written in any PostgreSQL PL language, such as PL/pgSQL or PL/R. Our callback functions are all written in PL/pgSQL, as this language is always included with a base PostgreSQL installation.

Our callback function uses the following equation to compute the three-band EVI:

$$EVI = G \times \frac{(NIR - RED)}{(NIR + C1 \times RED - C2 \times BLUE + L)}$$

The following code implements the MODIS EVI function in SQL:

```
CREATE OR REPLACE FUNCTION chp05.modis_evi(value double precision[][][],
"position" int[][], VARIADIC userargs text[])
RETURNS double precision
AS $$
DECLARE
  L double precision;
  C1 double precision;
  C2 double precision;
  G double precision;
  _value double precision[3];
  _n double precision;
  _d double precision;
BEGIN
  -- userargs provides coefficients
  L := userargs[1]::double precision;
  C1 := userargs[2]::double precision;
  C2 := userargs[3]::double precision;
  G := userargs[4]::double precision;
  -- rescale values, optional
  _value[1] := value[1][1][1] * 0.0001;
  _value[2] := value[2][1][1] * 0.0001;
  _value[3] := value[3][1][1] * 0.0001;
  -- value can't be NULL
  IF
    _value[1] IS NULL OR
    _value[2] IS NULL OR
    _value[3] IS NULL
  THEN
      RETURN NULL;
  END IF;
  -- compute numerator and denominator
  _n := (_value[3] - _value[1]);
```

```
  _d := (_value[3] + (C1 * _value[1]) - (C2 * _value[2]) + L);
  -- prevent division by zero
  IF _d::numeric(16, 10) = 0.::numeric(16, 10) THEN
    RETURN NULL;
  END IF;
  RETURN G * (_n / _d);
END;
$$ LANGUAGE plpgsql IMMUTABLE;
```

If you can't create the function, you probably do not have the necessary privileges in the database.

There are several characteristics required for all of the callback functions. These are as follows:

- All ST_MapAlgebra() callback functions must have three input parameters, namely, double precision[], integer[], and variadic text[]. The value parameter is a 3D array where the first dimension denotes the raster index, the second dimension the Y axis, and the third dimension the X axis. The position parameter is an array of two dimensions, with the first dimension indicating the raster index, and the second dimension consisting of the X, Y coordinates of the center pixel. The last parameter, userargs, is a 1D array of zero or more elements containing values that a user wants to pass to the callback function. If visualized, the parameters look like the following:

```
value = ARRAY[ 1 =>
  [ -- raster 1
    [pixval, pixval, pixval], -- row of raster 1
    [pixval, pixval, pixval],
    [pixval, pixval, pixval]
  ],
  2 => [ -- raster 2
    [pixval, pixval, pixval], -- row of raster 2
    [pixval, pixval, pixval],
    [pixval, pixval, pixval]
  ],
  ...
  N => [ -- raster N
    [pixval, pixval, pixval], -- row of raster
    [pixval, pixval, pixval],
    [pixval, pixval, pixval]
  ]
];
pos := ARRAY[
  0 => [x-coordinate, y-coordinate], -- center pixel o f output
raster
```

```
    1 => [x-coordinate, y-coordinate], -- center pixel o f raster 1
    2 => [x-coordinate, y-coordinate], -- center pixel o f raster 2
    ...
    N => [x-coordinate, y-coordinate], -- center pixel o f raster N
];
userargs := ARRAY[
  'arg1',
  'arg2',
  ...
  'argN'
];
```

- All ST_MapAlgebra() callback functions must return a double-precision value.

If the callback functions are not correctly structured, the ST_MapAlgebra() function will fail or behave incorrectly.

In the function body, we convert the user arguments to their correct datatypes, rescale the pixel values, check that no pixel values are NULL (arithmetic operations with NULL values always result in NULL), compute the numerator and denominator components of EVI, check that the denominator is not zero (prevent division by zero), and then finish the computation of EVI.

Now we call our callback function, modis_evi(), with ST_MapAlgebra():

```
SELECT ST_MapAlgebra(rast, ARRAY[1, 3, 4]::int[], -- only use the red, blue
a
nd near infrared bands 'chp05.modis_evi(
  double precision[], int[], text[])'::regprocedure,
  -- signature for callback function '32BF',
  -- output pixel type 'FIRST',
  NULL, 0, 0, '1.', -- L '6.', -- C1 '7.5', -- C2 '2.5' -- G
) AS rast
FROM modis m;
```

In our call to ST_MapAlgebra(), there are three criteria to take note of, which are as follows:

- The signature for the modis_evi() callback function. When passing the callback function to ST_MapAlgebra(), it must be written as a string containing the function name and the input-parameter types.

- The last four function parameters (`'1.'`, `'6.'`, `'7.5'`, `'2.5'`) are user-defined arguments that are passed for processing by the `callback` function.
- The order of the band numbers affects the order of the pixel values passed to the callback function.

The following images show the MODIS raster before and after running the EVI operation. The EVI raster has a pale white to dark green colormap applied for highlighting areas of high vegetation:

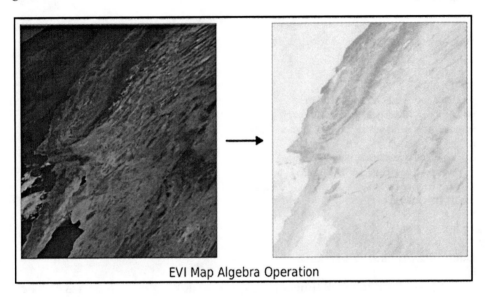

EVI Map Algebra Operation

If you are unable to run the standard EVI operation, or want more practice, we will now compute a two-band EVI. We will use the `ST_MapAlgebraFct()` function. Please note that `ST_MapAlgebraFct()` is deprecated in PostGIS 2.1, and may be removed in the future versions.

For the two-band EVI, we will use the following `callback` function. The two-band EVI equation is computed with the following code:

```
CREATE OR REPLACE FUNCTION chp05.modis_evi2(value1 double precision, value2
double precision, pos int[], VARIADIC userargs text[])
RETURNS double precision
AS $$
DECLARE
  L double precision;
  C double precision;
  G double precision;
```

```
      _value1 double precision;
      _value2 double precision;
      _n double precision;
      _d double precision;
   BEGIN
      -- userargs provides coefficients
      L := userargs[1]::double precision;
      C := userargs[2]::double precision;
      G := userargs[3]::double precision;
      -- value can't be NULL
      IF
        value1 IS NULL OR
        value2 IS NULL
        THEN
           RETURN NULL;
      END IF;
      _value1 := value1 * 0.0001;
      _value2 := value2 * 0.0001;
      -- compute numerator and denominator
      _n := (_value2 - _value1);
      _d := (L + _value2 + (C * _value1));
      -- prevent division by zero
      IF _d::numeric(16, 10) = 0.::numeric(16, 10) THEN
        RETURN NULL;
      END IF;
      RETURN G * (_n / _d);
   END;
   $$ LANGUAGE plpgsql IMMUTABLE;
```

Like ST_MapAlgebra() callback functions, ST_MapAlgebraFct() requires callback functions to be structured in a specific manner. There is a difference between the callback function for ST_MapAlgebraFct() and the prior one for ST_MapAlgebra(). This function has two simple pixel-value parameters instead of an array for all pixel values:

```
SELECT ST_MapAlgebraFct(
    rast, 1, -- red band
    rast, 4, -- NIR band
    'modis_evi2(double precision, double precision, int[],
text[])'::regprocedure,
    -- signature for callback function '32BF', -- output pixel type 'FIRST',
    '1.', -- L '2.4', -- C '2.5' -- G) AS rast
FROM chp05.modis m;
```

Besides the difference in function names, ST_MapAlgebraFct() is called differently than ST_MapAlgebra(). The same raster is passed to ST_MapAlgebraFct() twice. The other difference is that there is one less user-defined argument being passed to the callback function, as the two-band EVI has one less coefficient.

How it works...

We demonstrated some of the advanced uses of PostGIS's map-algebra functions by computing the three-band and two-band EVIs from our MODIS raster. This was achieved using ST_MapAlgebra() and ST_MapAlgebraFct(), respectively. With some planning, PostGIS's map-algebra functions can be applied to other uses, such as edge detection and contrast stretching.

For additional practice, write your own callback function to generate an *NDVI* raster from the MODIS raster. The equation for NDVI is: $NDVI = ((IR - R)/(IR + R))$ where IR is the pixel value on the infrared band, and R is the pixel value on the red band. This index generates values between -1.0 and 1.0, in which negative values usually represent non-green elements (water, snow, clouds), and values close to zero represent rocks and deserted land.

Executing DEM operations

PostGIS comes with several functions for use on digital elevation model (DEM) rasters to solve terrain-related problems. Though these problems have historically been in the hydrology domain, they can now be found elsewhere; for example, finding the most fuel-efficient route from point A to point B or determining the best location on a roof for a solar panel. PostGIS 2.0 introduced ST_Slope(), ST_Aspect(), and ST_HillShade() while PostGIS 2.1 added the new functions ST_TRI(), ST_TPI(), and ST_Roughness(), and new variants of existing elevation functions.

Getting ready

We will use the SRTM raster, loaded as 100 x 100 tiles, in this chapter's first recipe. With it, we will generate slope and hillshade rasters using San Francisco as our area of interest.

The next two queries in the How to do it section use variants of ST_Slope() and ST_HillShade() that are only available in PostGIS 2.1 or higher versions. The new variants permit the specification of a custom extent to constrain the processing area of the input raster.

How to do it...

Let's generate a slope raster from a subset of our SRTM raster tiles using `ST_Slope()`. A slope raster computes the rate of elevation change from one pixel to a neighboring pixel:

```
WITH r AS ( -- union of filtered tiles
  SELECT ST_Transform(ST_Union(srtm.rast), 3310) AS rast
  FROM chp05.srtm
  JOIN chp05.sfpoly sf ON ST_DWithin(ST_Transform(srtm.rast::geometry,
    3310), ST_Transform(sf.geom, 3310), 1000)),
  cx AS ( -- custom extent
    SELECT ST_AsRaster(ST_Transform(sf.geom, 3310), r.rast) AS rast
    FROM chp05.sfpoly sf CROSS JOIN r
  )
  SELECT ST_Clip(ST_Slope(r.rast, 1, cx.rast), ST_Transform(sf.geom, 3310))
AS rast FROM r
CROSS JOIN cx
CROSS JOIN chp05.sfpoly sf;
```

All spatial objects in this query are projected to **California Albers (SRID 3310)**, a projection with units in meters. This projection eases the use of `ST_DWithin()` to broaden our area of interest to include the tiles within 1,000 meters of San Francisco's boundaries, which improves the computed slope values for the pixels at the edges of the San Francisco boundaries. We also use a rasterized version of our San Francisco boundaries as the custom extent for restricting the computed area. After running `ST_Slope()`, we clip the slope raster just to San Francisco.

We can reuse the `ST_Slope()` query and substitute `ST_HillShade()` for `ST_Slope()` to create a hillshade raster, showing how the sun would illuminate the terrain of the SRTM raster:

```
WITH r AS ( -- union of filtered tiles
  SELECT ST_Transform(ST_Union(srtm.rast), 3310) AS rast
  FROM chp05.srtm
  JOIN chp05.sfpoly sf ON ST_DWithin(ST_Transform(srtm.rast::geometry,
    3310), ST_Transform(sf.geom, 3310), 1000)),
  cx AS ( -- custom extent
    SELECT ST_AsRaster(ST_Transform(sf.geom, 3310), r.rast) AS rast FROM
chp05.sfpoly sf CROSS JOIN r)
SELECT ST_Clip(ST_HillShade(r.rast, 1, cx.rast),ST_Transform(sf.geom,
3310)) AS rast FROM r
CROSS JOIN cx
CROSS JOIN chp05.sfpoly sf;
```

In this case, ST_HillShade() is a drop-in replacement for ST_Slope() because we do not specify any special input parameters for either function. If we need to specify additional arguments for ST_Slope() or ST_HillShade(), all changes are confined to just one line.

The following images show the SRTM raster before and after processing it with ST_Slope() and ST_HillShade():

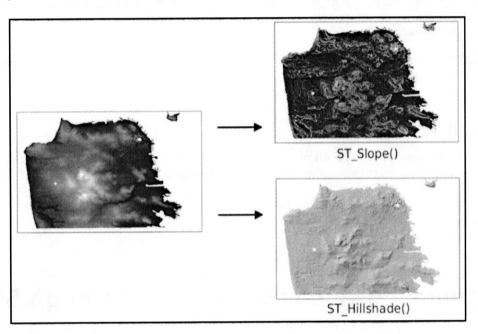

As you can see in the screenshot, the slope and hillshade rasters help us better understand the terrain of San Francisco.

If PostGIS 2.0 is available, we can still use 2.0's ST_Slope() and ST_HillShade() to create slope and hillshade rasters. But there are several differences you need to be aware of, which are as follows:

- ST_Slope() and ST_Aspect() return a raster with values in radians instead of degrees
- Some input parameters of ST_HillShade() are expressed in radians instead of degrees
- The computed raster from ST_Slope(), ST_Aspect(), or ST_HillShade() has an empty 1-pixel border on all four sides

We can adapt our ST_Slope() query from the beginning of this recipe by removing the creation and application of the custom extent. Since the custom extent constrained the computation to just a specific area, the inability to specify such a constraint means PostGIS 2.0's ST_Slope() will perform slower:

```
WITH r AS ( -- union of filtered tiles
  SELECT ST_Transform(ST_Union(srtm.rast), 3310) AS rast FROM srtm
    JOIN sfpoly sf ON ST_DWithin(ST_Transform(srtm.rast::geometry, 3310),
      ST_Transform(sf.geom, 3310), 1000)
)
SELECT ST_Clip(ST_Slope(r.rast, 1), ST_Transform(sf.geom, 3310)) AS rast
FROM r CROSS JOIN sfpoly sf;
```

How it works...

The DEM functions in PostGIS allowed us to quickly analyze our SRTM raster. In the basic use cases, we were able to swap one function for another without any issues.

What is impressive about these DEM functions is that they are all wrappers around ST_MapAlgebra(). The power of ST_MapAlgebra() is in its adaptability to different problems.

Sharing and visualizing rasters through SQL

In Chapter 4, *Working with Vector Data – Advanced Recipes*, we used gdal_translate to export PostGIS rasters to a file. This provides a method for transferring files from one user to another, or from one location to another. The only problem with this method is that you may not have access to the gdal_translate utility.

A different but equally functional approach is to use the ST_AsGDALRaster() family of functions available in PostGIS. In addition to ST_AsGDALRaster(), PostGIS provides ST_AsTIFF(), ST_AsPNG(), and ST_AsJPEG() to support the most common raster file formats.

To easily visualize raster files without the need for a GIS application, PostGIS 2.1 and later versions provide ST_ColorMap(). This function applies a built-in or user-specified color palette to a raster, that upon exporting with ST_AsGDALRaster(), can be viewed with any image viewer, such as a web browser.

Getting ready

In this recipe, we will use `ST_AsTIFF()` and `ST_AsPNG()` to export rasters to GeoTIFF and PNG file formats, respectively. We will also apply the `ST_ColorMap()` so that we can see them in any image viewer.

To enable GDAL drivers in PostGIS, you should run the following command in `pgAdmin`:

```
SET postgis.gdal_enabled_drivers = 'ENABLE_ALL';
SELECT short_name
FROM ST_GDALDrivers();
```

The following queries can be run in a standard SQL client, such as **psql** or **pgAdminIII**; however, we can't use the returned output because the output has escaped, and these clients do not undo the escaping. Applications with lower-level API functions can unescape the query output. Examples of this would be a PHP script, a pass-a-record element to `pg_unescape_bytea()`, or a Python script using Psycopg2's implicit decoding while fetching a record. A sample PHP script (`save_raster_to_file.php`) can be found in this chapter's `data` directory.

How to do it...

Let us say that a colleague asks for the monthly minimum temperature data for San Francisco during the summer months as a single raster file. This entails restricting our PRISM rasters to June, July, and August, clipping each monthly raster to San Francisco's boundaries, creating one raster with each monthly raster as a band, and then outputting the combined raster to a portable raster format. We will convert the combined raster to the GeoTIFF format:

```
WITH months AS ( -- extract monthly rasters clipped to San Francisco
    SELECT prism.month_year, ST_Union(ST_Clip(prism.rast, 2,
ST_Transform(sf.geom, 4269), TRUE)) AS rast
  FROM chp05.prism
  JOIN chp05.sfpoly sf ON ST_Intersects(prism.rast, ST_Transform(sf.geom,
4269))
  WHERE prism.month_year BETWEEN '2017-06-01'::date AND '2017-08-01'::date
  GROUP BY prism.month_year
  ORDER BY prism.month_year
), summer AS ( -- new raster with each monthly raster as a band
  SELECT ST_AddBand(NULL::raster, array_agg(rast)) AS rast FROM months)
SELECT -- export as GeoTIFF ST_AsTIFF(rast) AS content FROM summer;
```

To filter our PRISM rasters, we use `ST_Intersects()` to keep only those raster tiles that spatially intersect San Francisco's boundaries. We also remove all rasters whose relevant month is not June, July, or August. We then use `ST_AddBand()` to create a new raster with each summer month's new raster band. Finally, we pass the combined raster to `ST_AsTIFF()` to generate a GeoTIFF.

If you output the returned value from `ST_AsTIFF()` to a file, run `gdalinfo` on that file. The `gdalinfo` output shows that the GeoTIFF file has three bands, and the coordinate system of SRID 4322:

```
Driver: GTiff/GeoTIFF
Files: surface.tif
Size is 20, 7
Coordinate System is:
GEOGCS["WGS 72",
  DATUM["WGS_1972",
  SPHEROID["WGS 72",6378135,298.2600000000045, AUTHORITY["EPSG","7043"]],
        TOWGS84[0,0,4.5,0,0,0.554,0.2263], AUTHORITY["EPSG","6322"]],
      PRIMEM["Greenwich",0], UNIT["degree",0.0174532925199433],
      AUTHORITY["EPSG","4322"]]
  Origin = (-123.145833333333314,37.937500000000114)
  Pixel Size = (0.041666666666667,-0.041666666666667)
  Metadata:
    AREA_OR_POINT=Area
  Image Structure Metadata:
    INTERLEAVE=PIXEL
Corner Coordinates:
  Upper Left  (-123.1458333,  37.9375000) (123d 8'45.00"W, 37d56'15.00"N)
  Lower Left  (-123.1458333,  37.6458333) (123d 8'45.00"W, 37d38'45.00"N)
  Upper Right (-122.3125000,  37.9375000) (122d18'45.00"W, 37d56'15.00"N)
  Lower Right (-122.3125000,  37.6458333) (122d18'45.00"W, 37d38'45.00"N)
  Center      (-122.7291667,  37.7916667) (122d43'45.00"W, 37d47'30.00"N)
Band 1 Block=20x7 Type=Float32, ColorInterp=Gray
  NoData Value=-9999
Band 2 Block=20x7 Type=Float32, ColorInterp=Undefined
  NoData Value=-9999
Band 3 Block=20x7 Type=Float32, ColorInterp=Undefined
  NoData Value=-9999
```

The problem with the GeoTIFF raster is that we generally can't view it in a standard image viewer. If we use ST_AsPNG() or ST_AsJPEG(), the image generated is much more readily viewable. But PNG and JPEG images are limited by the supported pixel types 8BUI and 16BUI (PNG only). Both formats are also limited to, at the most, three bands (four, if there is an alpha band).

To help get around various file format limitations, we can use ST_MapAlgebra(), ST_Reclass() , or ST_ColorMap(), for this recipe. The ST_ColorMap() function converts a raster band of any pixel type to a set of up to four 8BUI bands. This facilitates creating a grayscale, RGB, or RGBA image that is then passed to ST_AsPNG(), or ST_AsJPEG().

Taking our query for computing a slope raster of San Francisco from our SRTM raster in a prior recipe, we can apply one of ST_ColorMap() function's built-in colormaps, and then pass the resulting raster to ST_AsPNG() to create a PNG image:

```
WITH r AS (SELECT ST_Transform(ST_Union(srtm.rast), 3310) AS rast
  FROM chp05.srtm
  JOIN chp05.sfpoly sf ON ST_DWithin(ST_Transform(srtm.rast::geometry,
3310),
  ST_Transform(sf.geom, 3310), 1000)
), cx AS (
  SELECT ST_AsRaster(ST_Transform(sf.geom, 3310), r.rast) AS rast
  FROM sfpoly sf CROSS JOIN r
)
SELECT ST_AsPNG(ST_ColorMap(ST_Clip(ST_Slope(r.rast, 1, cx.rast),
ST_Transform(sf.geom, 3310) ), 'bluered')) AS rast
FROM r
CROSS JOIN cx
CROSS JOIN chp05.sfpoly sf;
```

The bluered colormap sets the minimum, median, and maximum pixel values to dark blue, pale white, and bright red, respectively. Pixel values between the minimum, median, and maximum values are assigned colors that are linearly interpolated from the minimum to median or median to maximum range. The resulting image readily shows where the steepest slopes in San Francisco are.

The following is a PNG image generated by applying the bluered colormap with ST_ColorMap() and ST_AsPNG(). The pixels in red represent the steepest slopes:

In our use of ST_AsTIFF() and ST_AsPNG(), we passed the raster to be converted as the sole argument. Both of these functions have additional parameters to customize the output TIFF or PNG file. These additional parameters include various compression and data organization settings.

How it works...

Using ST_AsTIFF() and ST_AsPNG(), we exported rasters from PostGIS to GeoTIFF and PNG. The ST_ColorMap() function helped generate images that can be opened in any image viewer. If we needed to export these images to a different format supported by GDAL, we would use ST_AsGDALRaster().

6
Working with pgRouting

In this chapter, we will cover the following topics:

- Startup – Dijkstra routing
- Loading data from OpenStreetMap and finding the shortest path using A*
- Calculating the driving distance/service area
- Calculating the driving distance with demographics
- Extracting the centerlines of polygons

Introduction

So far, we have used PostGIS as a vector and raster tool, using relatively simple relationships between objects and simple structures. In this chapter, we review an additional PostGIS-related extension: **pgRouting**. pgRouting allows us to interrogate graph structures in order to answer questions such as "What is the shortest route from where I am to where I am going?" This is an area that is heavily occupied by the existing web APIs (such as Google, Bing, MapQuest, and others) and services, but it can be better served by *rolling our own* services for many use cases. Which cases? It might be a good idea to create our own services in situations where we are trying to answer questions that aren't answered by the existing services; where the data available to us is better or more applicable; or where we need or want to avoid the terms of service conditions for these APIs.

Startup – Dijkstra routing

pgRouting is a separate extension used in addition to PostGIS, which is now available in the PostGIS bundle on the Application Stack Builder (recommended for Windows). It can also be downloaded and installed by DEB, RPM, and macOS X packages and Windows binaries available at `http://pgrouting.org/download.html`.

For macOS users, it is recommended that you use the source packages available on Git (`https://github.com/pgRouting/pgrouting/releases`), and use CMake, available at `https://cmake.org/download/`, to make the installation build.

Packages for Linux Ubuntu users can be found at `http://trac.osgeo.org/postgis/wiki/UsersWikiPostGIS22UbuntuPGSQL95Apt`.

Getting ready

pgRouting doesn't deal well with nondefault schemas, so before we begin, we will set the schema in our user preferences using the following command:

```
ALTER ROLE me SET search_path TO chp06,public;
```

Next, we need to add the `pgrouting` extension to our database. If PostGIS is not already installed on the database, we'll need to add it as an extension as well:

```
CREATE EXTENSION postgis;
CREATE EXTENSION pgrouting;
```

We will start by loading a test dataset. You can get some really basic sample data from `http://docs.pgrouting.org/latest/en/sampledata.html`.

This sample data consists of a small grid of streets in which any functions can be run.

Then, run the create table and data insert scripts available at the dataset website. You should make adjustments to preserve the schema structure for chp06—for example:

```
CREATE TABLE chp06.edge_table (
    id BIGSERIAL,
    dir character varying,
    source BIGINT,
    target BIGINT,
    cost FLOAT,
    reverse_cost FLOAT,
    capacity BIGINT,
    reverse_capacity BIGINT,
```

```
    category_id INTEGER,
    reverse_category_id INTEGER,
    x1 FLOAT,
    y1 FLOAT,
    x2 FLOAT,
    y2 FLOAT,
    the_geom geometry
);
```

Now that the data is loaded, let's build topology on the table (if you haven't already done this during the data-load process):

```
SELECT pgr_createTopology('chp06.edge_table',0.001);
```

Building a topology creates a new node table—chp06.edge_table_vertices_pgr—for us to view. This table will aid us in developing queries.

How to do it...

Now that the data is loaded, we can run a quick test. We'll use a simple algorithm called Dijkstra to calculate the shortest path from node 5 to node 12.

Dijkstra's algorithm is an effective and simple routing algorithm that runs a search on all available paths from point A to point B in a network, also known as the **graph structure**. It is not the most efficient routing algorithm, but will always find the best route. For more information on Dijkstra's algorithm, refer to Wikipedia, which has a good explanation, with illustrations, at
http://en.wikipedia.org/wiki/Dijkstra%27s_algorithm. The animation at http://en.wikipedia.org/wiki/File:Dijkstras_progress_animation.gif is particularly helpful.

An important point to note is that the nodes created in pgRouting during the topology creation process are created unintentionally for some versions. This has been patched in future versions, but for some versions of pgRouting, this means that your node numbers will not be the same as those we use here in the book. View your data in an application to determine which nodes to use or whether you should use a k-nearest neighbors search for the node nearest to a static geographic point. See Chapter 11, *Using Desktop Clients*, for more information on viewing PostGIS data and Chapter 4, *Working with Vector Data – Advanced Recipes*, for approaches to finding the nearest node automatically:

```
SELECT * FROM pgr_dijkstra(
  'SELECT id, source, target, cost
  FROM chp06.edge_table_vertices_pgr', 2, 9,
);
```

The preceding query will result in the following:

	seq integer	path_seq integer	node bigint	edge bigint	cost double precision	agg_cost double precision
1	1	1	2	4	1	0
2	2	2	5	8	1	1
3	3	3	6	9	1	2
4	4	4	9	-1	0	3

When we ask for a route using Dijkstra and other routing algorithms, the result often comes in the following form:

- seq: This returns the sequence number so we can maintain the order of the output
- node: This is the node ID
- edge: This is the edge ID
- cost: This is the cost for the route traversal (often, the distance)
- agg_cost: This is the aggregated cost for the route from the starting node

For example, to get the geometry back, we need to rejoin the edge IDs with the original table. To make this approach work transparently, we will use the WITH common table expression to create a temporary table to which we will join our geometry:

```
WITH dijkstra AS (
  SELECT pgr_dijkstra(
    'SELECT id, source, target, cost, x1, x2, y1, y2
```

```
        FROM chp06.edge_table', 2, 9
    )
)
SELECT id, ST_AsText(the_geom)
FROM chp06.edge_table et, dijkstra d
WHERE et.id = (d.pgr_dijkstra).edge;
```

The preceding code will give the following output:

id bigint	st_astext text
4	LINESTRING(2 1,2 2)
8	LINESTRING(2 2,3 2)
9	LINESTRING(3 2,4 2)

Congratulations! You have just completed a route in pgRouting. The following diagram illustrates this scenario:

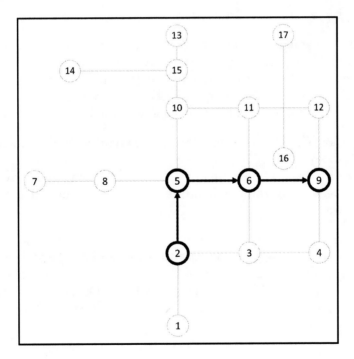

Loading data from OpenStreetMap and finding the shortest path using A*

Test data is great for understanding how algorithms work, but the real data is often more interesting. A good source for real data worldwide is **OpenStreetMap (OSM)**, a worldwide, accessible, wiki-style, geospatial dataset. What is wonderful about using OSM in conjunction with pgRouting is that it is inherently a topological model, meaning that it follows the same kinds of rules in its construction as we do in graph traversal within pgRouting. Because of the way editing and community participation works in OSM, it is often an equally good or better data source than commercial ones and is, of course, quite compatible with our open source model.

Another great feature is that there is free and open source software to ingest OSM data and import it into a routing database—osm2pgrouting.

Getting ready

It is recommended that you get the downloadable files from the example dataset that we have provided, available at http://www.packtpub.com/support. You will be using the XML OSM data. You can also get custom extracts directly from the web interface at http://www.openstreetmap.org/or by using the overpass turbo interface to access OSM data (https://overpass-turbo.eu/), but this could limit the area we would be able to extract.

Once we have the data, we need to unzip it using our favorite compression utility. Double-clicking on the file to unzip it will typically work on Windows and macOS machines. Two good utilities for unzipping on Linux are bunzip2 and zip. What will remain is an XML extract of the data we want for routing. In our use case, we are downloading the data for the greater Cleveland area.

Now we need a utility for placing this data into a routable database. An example of one such tool is osm2pgrouting, which can be downloaded and compiled using the instructions at http://github.com/pgRouting/osm2pgrouting. Use CMake from https://cmake.org/download/ to make the installation build in macOS. For Linux Ubuntu users there is an available package at https://packages.ubuntu.com/artful/osm2pgrouting.

How to do it...

When `osm2pgrouting` is run without anything set, the output shows us the options that are required and available to use with `osm2pgrouting`:

```
● ● ●                          build — bash — 87×32
bash-3.2$ osm2pgrouting
the option '--dbname' is required but missing
Allowed options:

Help:
  --help                              Produce help message for this version.
  -v [ --version ]                    Print version string

General:
  -f [ --file ] arg                   REQUIRED: Name of the osm file.
  -c [ --conf ] arg (=/usr/share/osm2pgrouting/mapconfig.xml)
                                      Name of the configuration xml file.
  --schema arg                        Database schema to put tables.
                                         blank: defaults to default schema
                                                dictated by PostgreSQL
                                                search_path.
  --prefix arg                        Prefix added at the beginning of the
                                      table names.
  --suffix arg                        Suffix added at the end of the table
                                      names.
  --addnodes                          Import the osm_nodes table.
  --clean                             Drop previously created tables.

Database options:
  -d [ --dbname ] arg                 Name of your database (Required).
  -U [ --username ] arg (=postgres)   Name of the user, which have write
                                      access to the database.
  -h [ --host ] arg (=localhost)      Host of your postgresql database.
  -p [ --port ] arg (=5432)           db_port of your database.
  -W [ --password ] arg               Password for database access.

bash-3.2$ █
```

To run the `osm2pgrouting` command, we have a small number of required parameters. Double-check the paths pointing to `mapconfig.xml` and `cleveland.osm` before running the following command:

```
osm2pgrouting --file cleveland.osm --conf
/usr/share/osm2pgrouting/mapconfig.xml --dbname postgis_cookbook --user me
--schema chp06 --host localhost --prefix cleveland_ --clean
```

Our dataset may be quite large, and could take some time to process and import—be patient. The end of the output should say something like the following:

```
● ● ●                         build — bash — 87×32
Export Types ...
    Processing 4 way types:     Inserted: 4 in osm_way_types

Export Classes ...
    Processing way's classes:   Inserted: 36 in osm_way_classes

Export Relations ...
    Processing 0 relations:     Inserted: 0 in osm_relations

Export RelationsWays ...
    Processing way's relations:        Inserted: 0 in cleveland_relations_ways

Export Ways ...
    Processing 104065 ways:
[*********|                                 ] (19%)    Ways Processed: 20000
    Split Ways generated: 45305  Vertices inserted 41827 Inserted 45305 split ways
[******************|                         ] (38%)    Ways Processed: 40000
    Split Ways generated: 43276  Vertices inserted 39811 Inserted 43276 split ways
[***************************|                ] (57%)    Ways Processed: 60000
    Split Ways generated: 51371  Vertices inserted 41485 Inserted 51371 split ways
[**************************************|      ] (76%)    Ways Processed: 80000
    Split Ways generated: 48504  Vertices inserted 36168 Inserted 48504 split ways
[************************************************| ] (99%)    Ways Processed: 104065
    Split Ways generated: 37114  Vertices inserted 14381 Inserted 37111 split ways
Creating Foreign Keys ...
Foreign keys for osm_way_classes table created
Foreign keys for cleveland_relations_ways table created
Foreign keys for Ways table created
#########################
size of streets: 104065
#########################
bash-3.2$ █
```

Our new vector table, by default, is named `cleveland_ways`. If no `-prefix` flag was used, the table name would just be `ways`.

You should have the created following tables:

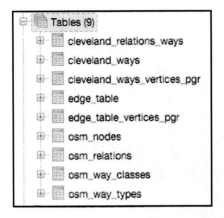

How it works...

`osm2pgrouting` is a powerful tool that handles a lot of the translation of OSM data into a format that can be used in pgRouting. In this case, it creates eight tables from our input file. Of those eight, we'll address the two primary tables: the `ways` table and the `nodes` table.

Our `ways` table is a table of the lines that represent all our streets, roads, and trails that are in OSM. The nodes table contains all the intersections. This helps us identify the beginning and end points for routing.

Let's apply an *A* ("A star")* routing approach to this problem.

A* is an extension of Dijkstra's algorithm which uses a heuristic to speed up the search for the shortest path, at the cost of occasionally not finding the optimum route. See `http://en.wikipedia.org/wiki/A*` and `http://en.wikipedia.org/wiki/File:Astar_progress_animation.gif` for more information.

You will recognize the following syntax from Dijkstra:

```
WITH astar AS (
  SELECT * FROM pgr_astar(
    'SELECT gid AS id, source, target,
    length AS cost, x1, y1, x2, y2
    FROM chp06.cleveland_ways', 89475, 14584, false
  )
```

```
)

SELECT gid, the_geom
FROM chp06.cleveland_ways w, astar a
WHERE w.gid = a.edge;
```

The following screenshot shows the results displayed on a map (map tiles by *Stamen Design, under CC BY 3.0*; data by *OpenStreetMap, under CC BY SA*):

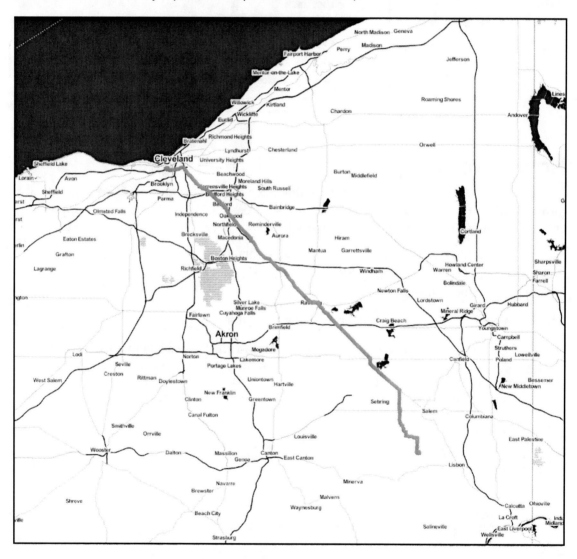

Sample calculated route with pgRouting visualized in QGIS

Calculating the driving distance/service area

Driving distance (`pgr_drivingDistance`) is a query that calculates all nodes within the specified driving distance of a starting node. This is an optional function compiled with pgRouting; so if you compile pgRouting yourself, make sure that you enable it and include the CGAL library, an optional dependency for `pgr_drivingDistance`.

Driving distance is useful when *user sheds* are needed that give realistic driving distance estimates, for example, for all customers with five miles driving, biking, or walking distance. These estimates can be contrasted with buffering techniques, which assume no barrier to travelling and are useful for revealing the underlying structures of our transportation networks relative to individual locations.

Getting ready

We will load the same dataset that we used in the *Startup – Dijkstra routing* recipe. Refer to this recipe to import data.

How to do it...

In the following example, we will look at all users within a distance of three units from our starting point—that is, a proposed bike shop at node 2:

```
SELECT * FROM pgr_drivingDistance(
  'SELECT id, source, target, cost FROM chp06.edge_table',
  2, 3
);
```

The preceding command gives the following output:

	seq integer	node bigint	edge bigint	cost double precision	agg_cost double precision
1	1	2	-1	0	0
2	2	5	4	1	1
3	3	6	8	1	2
4	4	10	10	1	2
5	5	9	9	1	3
6	6	11	11	1	3
7	7	13	14	1	3

As usual, we just get a list from the `pgr_drivingDistance` table that, in this case, comprises sequence, node, edge cost, and aggregate cost. PgRouting, like PostGIS, gives us low-level functionality; we need to reconstruct what geometries we need from that low-level functionality. We can use that node ID to extract the geometries of all of our nodes by executing the following script:

```
WITH DD AS (
  SELECT * FROM pgr_drivingDistance(
    'SELECT id, source, target, cost
    FROM chp06.edge_table', 2, 3
  )
)
SELECT ST_AsText(the_geom)
FROM chp06.edge_table_vertices_pgr w, DD d
WHERE w.id = d.node;
```

The preceding command gives the following output:

	st_astext text
1	POINT(2 1)
2	POINT(2 2)
3	POINT(3 2)
4	POINT(2 3)
5	POINT(4 2)
6	POINT(3 3)
7	POINT(2 4)

But the output seen is just a cluster of points. Normally, when we think of driving distance, we visualize a polygon. Fortunately, we have the `pgr_alphaShape` function that provides us that functionality. This function expects id, x, and y values for input, so we will first change our previous query to convert to x and y from the geometries in `edge_table_vertices_pgr`:

```
WITH DD AS (
  SELECT * FROM pgr_drivingDistance(
    'SELECT id, source, target, cost FROM chp06.edge_table',
    2, 3
  )
)
SELECT id::integer,  ST_X(the_geom)::float AS x, ST_Y(the_geom)::float AS y
FROM chp06.edge_table_vertices_pgr w, DD d
WHERE w.id = d.node;
```

The output is as follows:

	id integer	x double precision	y double precision
1	2	2	1
2	5	2	2
3	6	3	2
4	10	2	3
5	9	4	2
6	11	3	3
7	13	2	4

Now we can wrap the preceding script up in the `alphashape` function:

```
WITH alphashape AS (
  SELECT pgr_alphaShape('
    WITH DD AS (
      SELECT * FROM pgr_drivingDistance(
        ''SELECT id, source, target, cost
        FROM chp06.edge_table'', 2, 3
      )
    ),
    dd_points AS(
      SELECT id::integer, ST_X(the_geom)::float AS x,
      ST_Y(the_geom)::float AS y
      FROM chp06.edge_table_vertices_pgr w, DD d
      WHERE w.id = d.node
    )
    SELECT * FROM dd_points
  ')
),
```

So first, we will get our cluster of points. As we did earlier, we will explicitly convert the text to geometric points:

```
alphapoints AS (
  SELECT ST_MakePoint((pgr_alphashape).x, (pgr_alphashape).y) FROM
alphashape
),
```

Now that we have points, we can create a line by connecting them:

```
alphaline AS (
  SELECT ST_Makeline(ST_MakePoint) FROM alphapoints
)
SELECT ST_MakePolygon(ST_AddPoint(ST_Makeline, ST_StartPoint(ST_Makeline)))
FROM alphaline;
```

Finally, we construct the line as a polygon using `ST_MakePolygon`. This requires adding the start point by executing `ST_StartPoint` in order to properly close the polygon. The complete code is as follows:

```
WITH alphashape AS (
  SELECT pgr_alphaShape('
    WITH DD AS (
      SELECT * FROM pgr_drivingDistance(
        ''SELECT id, source, target, cost
        FROM chp06.edge_table'', 2, 3
      )
    ),
    dd_points AS(
      SELECT id::integer, ST_X(the_geom)::float AS x,
      ST_Y(the_geom)::float AS y
      FROM chp06.edge_table_vertices_pgr w, DD d
      WHERE w.id = d.node
    )
    SELECT * FROM dd_points
  ')
),
alphapoints AS (
  SELECT ST_MakePoint((pgr_alphashape).x,
  (pgr_alphashape).y)
  FROM alphashape
),
alphaline AS (
  SELECT ST_Makeline(ST_MakePoint) FROM alphapoints
)
SELECT ST_MakePolygon(
  ST_AddPoint(ST_Makeline, ST_StartPoint(ST_Makeline))
)
FROM alphaline;
```

Our first driving distance calculation can be better understood in the context of the following diagram, where we can reach nodes 9, 11, 13 from node 2 with a driving distance of 3:

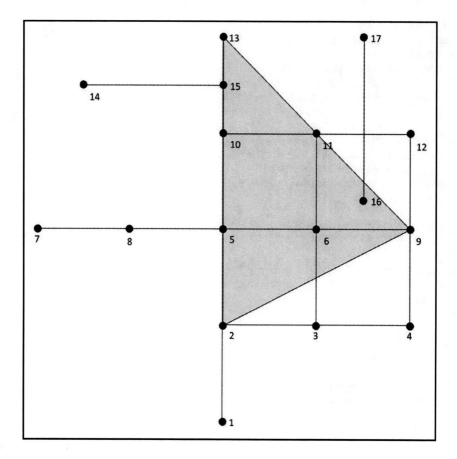

See also

- The *Calculating the driving distance with demographics* recipe

Calculating the driving distance with demographics

In the *Using polygon overlays for proportional census estimates* recipe in Chapter 2, *Structures That Work,* we employed a simple buffer around a trail alignment in conjunction with the census data to get estimates of what the demographics were of the people within walking distance of the trail, estimated as a mile long. The problem with this approach, of course, is that it assumes that it is an "as the crow flies" estimate. In reality, rivers, large roads, and roadless stretches serve as real barriers to people's movement through space. Using pgRouting's pgr_drivingDistance function, we can realistically simulate people's movement on the routable networks and get better estimates. For our use case, we'll keep the simulation a bit simpler than a trail alignment—we'll consider the demographics of a park facility, say, the Cleveland Metroparks Zoo, and potential bike users within 4 miles of it, which adds up approximately to a 15-minute bike ride.

Getting ready

For our analysis, we will use the proportional_sum function from Chapter 2, *Structures That Work,* so if you have not added this to your PostGIS tool belt, run the following commands:

```
CREATE OR REPLACE FUNCTION chp02.proportional_sum(geometry, geometry,
numeric)
RETURNS numeric AS
$BODY$
SELECT $3 * areacalc FROM
(
  SELECT (ST_Area(ST_Intersection($1, $2))/ST_Area($2))::numeric AS
areacalc
) AS areac
;
$BODY$
LANGUAGE sql VOLATILE;
```

The `proportional_sum` function will take our input geometry into account and the `count` value of the population and return an estimate of the proportional population.

Now we need to load our census data. Use the following command:

```
shp2pgsql -s 3734 -d -i -I -W LATIN1 -g the_geom census chp06.census | psql
-U me -d postgis_cookbook -h localhost
```

Also, if you have not yet loaded the data mentioned in the *Loading data from OpenStreetMap and finding the shortest path A** recipe, take the time to do so now.

Once all the data is entered, we can proceed with the analysis.

How to do it...

The `pgr_drivingdistance` polygon we created is the first step in the demographic analysis. Refer to the *Driving distance/service area calculation* recipe if you need to familiarize yourself with its use. In this case, we'll consider the cycling distance. The nearest node to the Cleveland Metroparks Zoo is 24746, according to our loaded dataset; so we'll use that as the center point for our `pgr_drivingdistance` calculation and we'll use approximately 6 kilometers as our distance, as we want to know the number of zoo visitors within this distance of the Cleveland Metroparks Zoo. However, since our data is using 4326 EPSG, the distance we will give the function will be in degrees, so 0.05 will give us an approximate distance of 6 km that will work with the `pgr_drivingDistance` function:

```
CREATE TABLE chp06.zoo_bikezone AS (
  WITH alphashape AS (
    SELECT pgr_alphaShape('
      WITH DD AS (
        SELECT * FROM pgr_drivingDistance(
          ''SELECT gid AS id, source, target, reverse_cost
          AS cost FROM chp06.cleveland_ways'',
          24746, 0.05, false
        )
      ),
      dd_points AS(
        SELECT id::int4, ST_X(the_geom)::float8 as x,
          ST_Y(the_geom)::float8 AS y
        FROM chp06.cleveland_ways_vertices_pgr w, DD d
        WHERE w.id = d.node
      )
      SELECT * FROM dd_points
    ')
  ),
```

```
alphapoints AS (
  SELECT ST_MakePoint((pgr_alphashape).x, (pgr_alphashape).y)
  FROM alphashape
),
alphaline AS (
  SELECT ST_Makeline(ST_MakePoint) FROM alphapoints
)
  SELECT 1 as id, ST_SetSRID(ST_MakePolygon(ST_AddPoint(ST_Makeline,
ST_StartPoint(ST_Makeline))), 4326) AS the_geom FROM alphaline
);
```

The preceding script gives us a very interesting shape (map tiles by *Stamen Design, under CC BY 3.0*; data by *OpenStreetMap, under CC BY SA*). See the following screenshot:

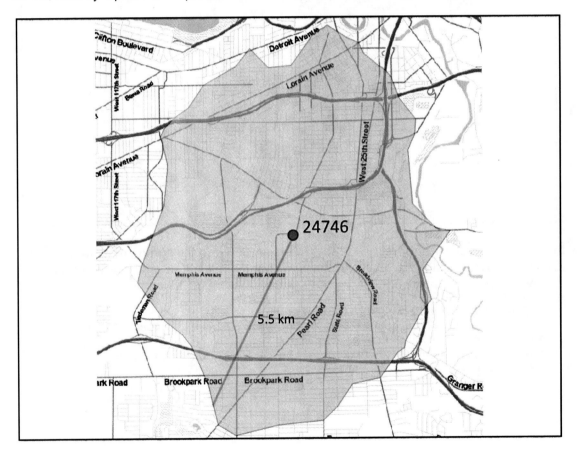

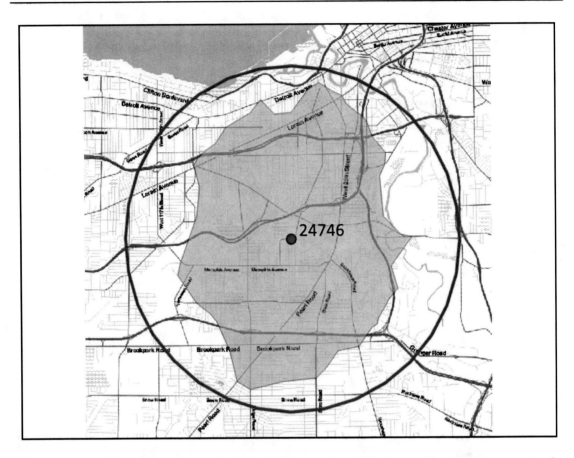

In the previous screenshot, we can see the difference between the cycling distance across the real road network, shaded in blue, and the equivalent 4-mile buffer or as-the-crow-flies distance. Let's apply this to our demographic analysis using the following script:

```
SELECT ROUND(SUM(chp02.proportional_sum(
    ST_Transform(a.the_geom,3734), b.the_geom, b.pop))) AS population
FROM Chp06.zoo_bikezone AS a, chp06.census as b
WHERE ST_Intersects(ST_Transform(a.the_geom, 3734), b.the_geom)
GROUP BY a.id;
```

The output is as follows:

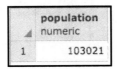

(1 row)

So, how does the preceding output compare to what we would get if we look at the buffered distance?

```
SELECT ROUND(SUM(chp02.proportional_sum(
  ST_Transform(a.the_geom,3734), b.the_geom, b.pop))) AS population
    FROM (SELECT 1 AS id, ST_Buffer(ST_Transform(the_geom, 3734), 17000)
      AS the_geom
    FROM chp06.cleveland_ways_vertices_pgr WHERE id = 24746
) AS a,   chp06.census as b
WHERE ST_Intersects(ST_Transform(a.the_geom, 3734), b.the_geom)
GROUP BY a.id;
```

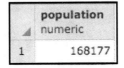

(1 row)

The preceding output shows a difference of more than 60,000 people. In other words, using a buffer overestimates the population compared to using `pgr_drivingdistance`.

Extracting the centerlines of polygons

In several recipes in Chapter 4, *Working with Vector Data – Advanced Recipes*, we explored extracting Voronoi polygons from sets of points. In this recipe, we'll use the Voronoi function employed in the *Using external scripts to embed new functionality to calculate Voronoi polygons* section to serve as the first step in extracting the centerline of a polygon. One could also use the *Using external scripts to embed new functionality to calculate Voronoi polygons—advanced* recipe, which would run faster on large datasets. For this recipe, we will use the simpler but slower approach.

One additional dependency is that we will be using the
chp02.polygon_to_line(geometry) function from the *Normalizing internal overlays*
recipe in Chapter 2, *Structures That Work*.

What do we mean by the centerline of a polygon? Imagine a digitized stream flowing
between its pair of banks, as shown in the following screenshot:

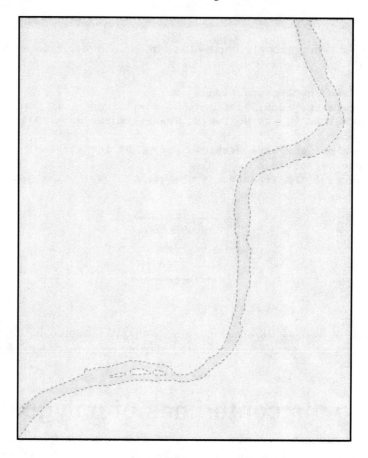

If we wanted to find the center of this in order to model the water flow, we could extract it using a skeletonization approach, as shown in the following screenshot:

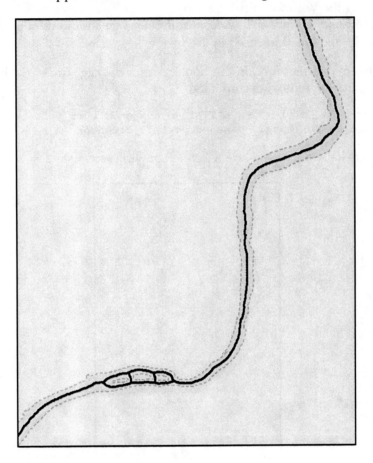

The difficulty with skeletonization approaches, as we'll soon see, is that they are often subject to noise, which is something that natural features such as our stream make plenty of. This means that typical skeletonization, which could be done simply with a Voronoi approach, is therefore inherently inadequate for our purposes.

This brings us to the reason why skeletonization is included in this chapter. Routing is a way for us to simplify skeletons derived from the Voronoi method. It allows us to trace from one end of a major feature to the other and skip all the noise in between.

Getting ready

As we will be using the Voronoi calculations from the *Calculating Voronoi Diagram* recipe in Chapter 4, *Working with Vector Data – Advanced Recipes,* you should refer to that recipe to prepare yourself for the functions used in this recipe.

We will use a stream dataset found in this book's source package under the hydrology folder. To load it, use the following command:

```
shp2pgsql -s 3734 -d -i -I -W LATIN1 -g the_geom ebrr_polygon
chp06.voronoi_hydro | psql -U me -d postgis_cookbook
```

The streams we create will look as shown in the following screenshot:

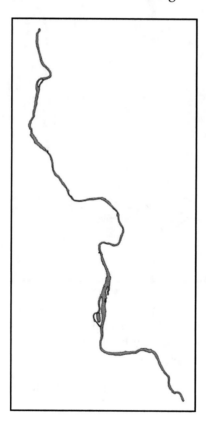

How to do it...

In order to perform the basic skeletonization, we'll calculate the Voronoi polygons on the nodes that make up the original stream polygon. By default, the edges of the Voronoi polygons find the line that demarcates the midpoint between points. We will leverage this tendency by treating our lines like points—adding extra points to the lines and then converting the lines to a point set. This approach, in combination with the Voronoi approach, will provide an initial estimate of the polygon's centerline.

We will add extra points to our input geometries using the ST_Segmentize function and then convert the geometries to points using ST_DumpPoints:

```
CREATE TABLE chp06.voronoi_points AS(
  SELECT (ST_DumpPoints(ST_Segmentize(the_geom, 5))).geom AS the_geom
    FROM chp06.voronoi_hydro
  UNION ALL
  SELECT (ST_DumpPoints(ST_Extent(the_geom))).geom AS the_geom
    FROM chp06.voronoi_hydro
)
```

The following screenshot shows our polygons as a set of points if we view it on a desktop GIS:

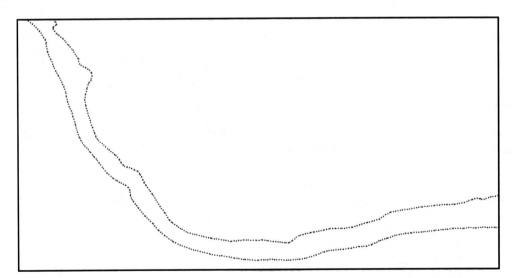

The set of points in the preceding screenshot is what we feed into our Voronoi calculation:

```
CREATE TABLE chp06.voronoi AS(
  SELECT (ST_Dump(
    ST_SetSRID(
      ST_VoronoiPolygons(points.the_geom),
      3734))).geom as the_geom
FROM (SELECT ST_Collect(ST_SetSRID(the_geom, 3734)) as the_geom FROM
chp06.voronoi_points) as points);
```

The following screenshot shows a Voronoi diagram derived from our points:

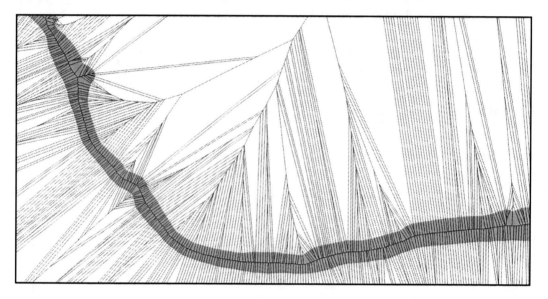

If you look closely at the preceding screenshot, you will see the basic centerline displayed in our new data. Now we will take the first step toward extracting it. We should index our inputs and then intersect the Voronoi output with the original stream polygon in order to clean the data back to something reasonable. In the extraction process, we'll also extract the edges from the polygons and remove the edges along the original polygon in order to remove any excess lines before our routing step. This is implemented in the following script:

```
CREATE INDEX chp06_voronoi_geom_gist
ON chp06.voronoi
USING gist(the_geom);
DROP TABLE IF EXISTS voronoi_intersect;
CREATE TABLE chp06.voronoi_intersect AS WITH vintersect AS (
  SELECT ST_Intersection(ST_SetSRID(ST_MakeValid(a.the_geom), 3734),
```

```
    ST_MakeValid(b.the_geom)) AS the_geom
    FROM Chp06.voronoi a, chp06.voronoi_hydro b
    WHERE ST_Intersects(ST_SetSRID(a.the_geom, 3734), b.the_geom)
),
linework AS (
    SELECT chp02.polygon_to_line(the_geom) AS the_geom
    FROM vintersect
),
polylines AS (
    SELECT ((ST_Dump(ST_Union(lw.the_geom))).geom)
      ::geometry(linestring, 3734) AS the_geom
    FROM linework AS lw
),
externalbounds AS (
    SELECT chp02.polygon_to_line(the_geom) AS the_geom
    FROM voronoi_hydro
)
SELECT (ST_Dump(ST_Union(p.the_geom))).geom
    FROM polylines p, externalbounds b
    WHERE NOT ST_DWithin(p.the_geom, b.the_geom, 5);
```

Now we have a second-level approximatio of the skeleton (shown in the following screenshot). It is messy, but it starts to highlight the centerline that we seek:

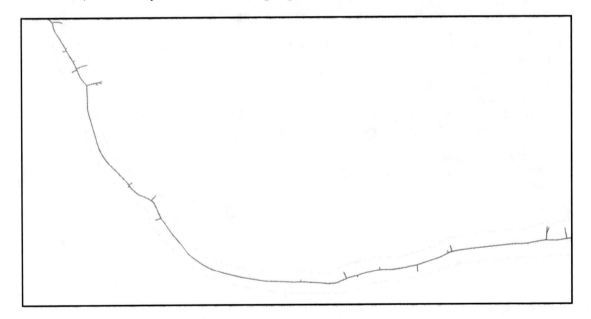

There's more...

Now we are nearly ready for routing. The centerline calculation we have is a good approximation of a straight skeleton, but is still subject to the noisiness of the natural world. We'd like to eliminate that noisiness by choosing our features and emphasizing them through routing. First, we need to prepare the table to allow for routing calculations, as shown in the following commands:

```
ALTER TABLE chp06.voronoi_intersect ADD COLUMN gid serial;
ALTER TABLE chp06.voronoi_intersect ADD PRIMARY KEY (gid);
ALTER TABLE chp06.voronoi_intersect ADD COLUMN source integer;
ALTER TABLE chp06.voronoi_intersect ADD COLUMN target integer;
```

Then, to create a routable network from our skeleton, enter the following commands:

```
SELECT pgr_createTopology('voronoi_intersect', 0.001, 'the_geom', 'gid',
'source', 'target', 'true');
CREATE INDEX source_idx ON chp06.voronoi_intersect("source");
CREATE INDEX target_idx ON chp06.voronoi_intersect("target");
ALTER TABLE chp06.voronoi_intersect ADD COLUMN length double precision;
UPDATE chp06.voronoi_intersect SET length = ST_Length(the_geom);
ALTER TABLE chp06.voronoi_intersect ADD COLUMN reverse_cost double
precision;
UPDATE chp06.voronoi_intersect SET reverse_cost = length;
```

Now we can route along the primary centerline of our polygon using the following commands:

```
CREATE TABLE chp06.voronoi_route AS
WITH dijkstra AS (
  SELECT * FROM pgr_dijkstra('SELECT gid AS id, source, target, length
    AS cost FROM chp06.voronoi_intersect', 10851, 3, false)
)
SELECT gid, geom
FROM voronoi_intersect et, dijkstra d
WHERE et.gid = d.edge;
```

If we look at the detail of this routing, we see the following:

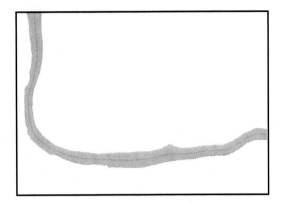

Now we can compare the original polygon with the trace of its centerline:

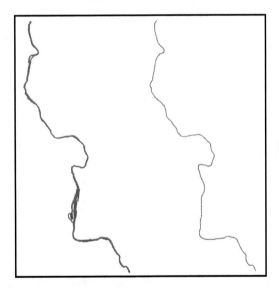

The preceding screenshot shows the original geometry of the stream in contrast to our centerline or skeleton. It is an excellent output that vastly simplifies our input geometry while retaining its relevant features.

7

Into the Nth Dimension

In this chapter, we will cover:

- Importing LiDAR data
- Performing 3D queries on a LiDAR point cloud
- Constructing and serving buildings 2.5D
- Using ST_Extrude to extrude building footprints
- Creating arbitrary 3D objects for PostGIS
- Exporting models as X3D for the web
- Reconstructing Unmanned Aerial Vehicle (UAV) image footprints with PostGIS 3D
- UAV photogrammetry in PostGIS – point cloud
- UAV photogrammetry in PostGIS – DSM creation

Introduction

In this chapter, we will explore the 3D capabilities of PostGIS. We will focus on three main categories: how to insert 3D data into PostGIS, how to analyze and perform queries using 3D data, and how to dump 3D data out of PostGIS. This chapter will use 3D point clouds as 3D data, including LiDAR data and those derived from **Structure from Motion (SfM)** techniques. Additionally, we will build a function that extrudes building footprints to 3D.

It is important to note that for this chapter, we will address the postgreSQL-pointcloud extension; point clouds are usually large data sets of a three dimensional representation of point coordinates in a coordinate system. Point clouds are used to represent surfaces of sensed objects with great accuracy, such as by using geographic LiDAR data. The pointcloud extension will help us store LiDAR data into point cloud objects in our database. Also, this extension adds functions that allow you to transform point cloud objects into geometries and do spatial filtering using point cloud data. For more information about this extension, you can visit the official GitHub repository at `https://github.com/pgpointcloud/pointcloud`. In addition, you can check out Paul Ramsey's tutorial at `http://workshops.boundlessgeo.com/tutorial-lidar/`.

Download the example datasets we have for your use, available at `http://www.packtpub.com/support`.

Importing LiDAR data

Light Detection And Ranging (LiDAR) is one of the most common devices for generating point cloud data. The system captures 3D location and other properties of objects or surfaces in a given space. This approach is very similar to radar in that it uses electromagnetic waves to measure distance and brightness, among other things. However, one main difference between LIDAR and radar is that the first one uses laser beam technology, instead of microwaves or radio waves. Another distinction is that LiDAR generally sends out a single focused pulse and measures the time of the returned pulse, calculating distance and depth. Radar, by contrast, will send out multiple pulses before receiving return pulses and thus, requires additional processing to determine the source of each pulse.

LiDAR data has become quite common in conjunction with both ground and airborne applications, aiding in ground surveys, enhancing and substantially automating aspects of photogrammetric engineering. There are many data sources with plenty of LiDAR data.

LiDAR data is typically distributed in the **LAS** or **LASer format.** The **American Society for Photogrammetry and Remote Sensing (ASPRS)** established the LAS standard. LAS is a binary format, so reading it to push into a PostGIS database is non-trivial. Fortunately, we can make use of the open source tool PDAL.

Getting ready

Our source data will be in the LAS format, which we will insert into our database using the PDAL library, available at `https://www.pdal.io/`. This tool is available for Linux/UNIX and Mac users; for Windows, it is available with the OSGeo4W package (`https://www.pdal.io/workshop/osgeo4w.html`).

LAS data can contain a lot of interesting data, not just *X*, *Y*, and *Z* values. It can include the intensity of the return from the object sensed and the classification of the object (ground versus vegetation versus buildings). When we place our LAS file in our PostGIS database, we can optionally collect any of this information. Furthermore, PDAL internally constructs a pipeline to translate data for reading, processing, and writing.

In preparation for this, we need to create a JSON file that represents the PDAL processing pipeline. For each LAS file, we create a JSON file to configure the reader and the writer to use the postgres-pointcloud option. We also need to write the database connection parameters. For the test file `test_1.las`, the code is as follows:

```
 1 {
 2     "pipeline": [{
 3         "type": "readers.las",
 4         "filename": "/data/test_1.las"
 5     }, {
 6         "type": "writers.pgpointcloud",
 7         "connection": "host='localhost' dbname='postgis-cookbook' user='me' password='me' port='5432'",
 8         "table": "test_1",
 9         "srid": "3734",
10         "schema": "chp07"
11     }]
12 }
13
```

Now, we can download our data. It is recommended to either download it from `http://gis5.oit.ohio.gov/geodatadownload/` or to download the sample dataset we have for your use, available at `http://www.packtpub.com/support`.

How to do it...

First, we need to convert our LAS file to a format that can be used by PDAL. We created a Python script, which reads from a directory of LAS files and generates its corresponding JSON. With this script, we can automate the generation if we have a large directory of files. Also, we chose Python for its simplicity and because you can execute the script regardless of the operating system you are using. To execute the script, run the following in the console (for Windows users, make sure you have the Python interpreter included in the PATH variable):

```
$ python insert_files.py -f <lasfiles_path>
```

This script will read each LAS file, and will store within a folder called `pipelines` all the metadata related to the LAS file that will be inserted into the database.

Now, using PDAL, we execute a `for` loop to insert LAS files into Postgres:

```
$ for file in `ls pipelines/*.json`;
  do
    pdal pipeline $file;
  done
```

This point cloud data is split into three different tables. If we want to merge them, we need to execute the following SQL command:

```
DROP TABLE IF EXISTS chp07.lidar;
CREATE TABLE chp07.lidar AS WITH patches AS
(
  SELECT
    pa
  FROM "chp07"."N2210595"
  UNION ALL
  SELECT
    pa
  FROM "chp07"."N2215595"
  UNION ALL
  SELECT
    pa
  FROM "chp07"."N2220595"
)
SELECT
  2 AS id,
PC_Union(pa) AS pa
FROM patches;
```

The postgres-pointcloud extension uses two main point cloud objects as variables: the *PcPoint* object, which is a point that can have many dimensions, but a minimum of X and Y values that are placed in a space; and the *PcPatch* object, which is a collection of multiple PcPoints that are close together. According to the documentation of the plugin, it becomes inefficient to store large amounts of points as individual records in a table.

Now that we have all of our data into our database within a single table, if we want to visualize our point cloud data, we need to create a spatial table to be understood by our layer viewer; for instance, QGIS. The point cloud plugin for Postgres has PostGIS integration, so we can transform our *PcPatch* and *PcPoint* objects into geometries and use PostGIS functions for analyzing the data:

```
CREATE TABLE chp07.lidar_patches AS WITH pts AS
(
  SELECT
    PC_Explode(pa) AS pt
```

```
   FROM chp07.lidar
)
SELECT
   pt::geometry AS the_geom
FROM pts;
ALTER TABLE chp07.lidar_patches ADD COLUMN gid serial;
ALTER TABLE chp07.lidar_patches ADD PRIMARY KEY (gid);
```

This SQL script performs an inner query, which initially returns a set of *PcPoints* from the *PcPatch* using the `PC_Explode` function. Then, for each point returned, we cast from *PcPoint* object to a PostGIS geometry object. Finally, we create the `gid` column and add it to the table as a primary key.

Now, we can view our data using our favorite desktop GIS, as shown in the following image:

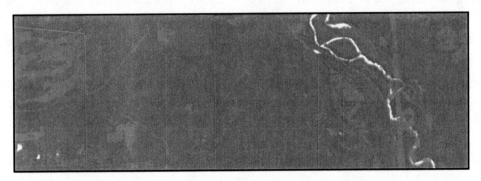

See also

- The *Performing 3D queries on a LiDAR point cloud* recipe

Performing 3D queries on a LiDAR point cloud

In the previous recipe, *Importing LiDAR data*, we brought a LiDAR 3D point cloud into PostGIS, creating an explicit 3D dataset from the input. With the data in 3D form, we have the ability to perform spatial queries against it. In this recipe, we will leverage 3D indexes so that our nearest-neighbor search works in all the dimensions our data are in.

How to do it...

We will use the LiDAR data imported in the previous recipe as our dataset of choice. We named that table `chp07.lidar`. To perform a nearest-neighbor search, we will require an index created on the dataset. Spatial indexes, much like ordinary database table indexes, are similar to book indexes insofar as they help us find what we are looking for faster. Ordinarily, such an index-creation step would look like the following (which we won't run this time):

```
CREATE INDEX chp07_lidar_the_geom_idx
ON chp07.lidar USING gist(the_geom);
```

A 3D index does not perform as quickly as a 2D index for 2D queries, so a `CREATE INDEX` query defaults to creating a 2D index. In our case, we want to force the gist to apply to all three dimensions, so we will explicitly tell PostgreSQL to use the n-dimensional version of the index:

```
CREATE INDEX chp07_lidar_the_geom_3dx
ON chp07.lidar USING gist(the_geom gist_geometry_ops_nd);
```

Note that the approach depicted in the previous code would also work if we had a time dimension or a 3D plus time. Let's load a second 3D dataset and the stream centerlines that we will use in our query:

```
$ shp2pgsql -s 3734 -d -i -I -W LATIN1 -t 3DZ -g the_geom hydro_line
chp07.hydro | PGPASSWORD=me psql -U me -d "postgis-cookbook" -h localhost
```

This data, as shown in the following image, overlays nicely with our LiDAR point cloud:

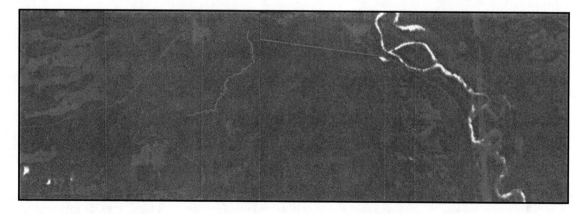

Now, we can build a simple query to retrieve all the LiDAR points within one foot of our stream centerline:

```
DROP TABLE IF EXISTS chp07.lidar_patches_within;
CREATE TABLE chp07.lidar_patches_within AS
SELECT chp07.lidar_patches.gid, chp07.lidar_patches.the_geom
FROM chp07.lidar_patches, chp07.hydro
WHERE ST_3DDWithin(chp07.hydro.the_geom, chp07.lidar_patches.the_geom, 5);
```

But, this is a little bit of a sloppy approach; we could end up with duplicate LiDAR points, so we will refine our query with LEFT JOIN and SELECT DISTINCT instead, but continue using ST_DWithin as our limiting condition:

```
DROP TABLE IF EXISTS chp07.lidar_patches_within_distinct;
CREATE TABLE chp07.lidar_patches_within_distinct AS
SELECT DISTINCT (chp07.lidar_patches.the_geom), chp07.lidar_patches.gid
FROM chp07.lidar_patches, chp07.hydro
WHERE ST_3DDWithin(chp07.hydro.the_geom, chp07.lidar_patches.the_geom, 5);
```

Now we can visualize our returned points, as shown in the following image:

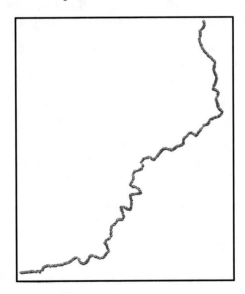

Try this query using ST_DWithin instead of ST_3DDWithin. You'll find an interesting difference in the number of points returned, since ST_DWithin will collect LiDAR points that may be close to our streamline in the XY plane, but not as close when looking at a 3D distance.

You can imagine `ST_3DWithin` querying within a tunnel around our line. `ST_DWithin`, by contrast, is going to query a vertical wall of LiDAR points, as it is only searching for adjacent points based on XY distance, ignoring height altogether, and thus gathering up all the points within a narrow wall above and below our points.

Constructing and serving buildings 2.5D

In the *Detailed building footprints from LiDAR* recipe in `Chapter 4`, *Working with Vector Data - Advanced Recipes*, we explored the automatic generation of building footprints using LiDAR data. What we were attempting to do was create 2D data from 3D data. In this recipe, we attempt the opposite, in a sense. We start with 2D polygons of building footprints and feed them into a function that extrudes them as 3D polygons.

Getting ready

For this recipe, we will extrude a building footprint of our own making. Let us quickly create a table with a single building footprint, for testing purposes, as follows:

```
DROP TABLE IF EXISTS chp07.simple_building;
CREATE TABLE chp07.simple_building AS
SELECT 1 AS gid, ST_MakePolygon(
  ST_GeomFromText(
    'LINESTRING(0 0,2 0, 2 1, 1 1, 1 2, 0 2, 0 0)'
  )
) AS the_geom;
```

It would be beneficial to keep the creation of 3D buildings encapsulated as simply as possible in a function:

```
CREATE OR REPLACE FUNCTION chp07.threedbuilding(footprint geometry, height
numeric)
RETURNS geometry AS
$BODY$
```

Our function takes two inputs: the building footprint and a height to extrude to. We can also imagine a function that takes in a third parameter: the height of the base of the building.

To construct the building walls, we will need to first convert our polygons into linestrings and then further separate the linestrings into their individual, two-point segments:

```
WITH simple_lines AS
```

```
(
  SELECT
    1 AS gid,
    ST_MakeLine(ST_PointN(the_geom,pointn),
    ST_PointN(the_geom,pointn+1)) AS the_geom
  FROM (
    SELECT 1 AS gid,
    polygon_to_line($1) AS the_geom
  ) AS a
  LEFT JOIN(
    SELECT
      1 AS gid,
      generate_series(1,
        ST_NumPoints(polygon_to_line($1))-1
      ) AS pointn
  ) AS b
  ON a.gid = b.gid
),
```

The preceding code returns each of the two-point segments of our original shape. For example, for simple_building, the output is as follows:

```
st_astext
--------------------------------------------------
MULTILINESTRING((2 0,2 1),(1 2,0 2),(2 1,1 1),
  (0 0,2 0),(1 1,1 2),(0 2,0 0))
(1 row)
```

Now that we have a series of individual lines, we can use those to construct the walls of the building. First, we need to recast our 2D lines as 3D using ST_Force3DZ:

```
threeDlines AS
(
  SELECT ST_Force3DZ(the_geom) AS the_geom FROM simple_lines
),
```

The output is as follows:

```
MULTILINESTRING Z ((2 0 0,2 1 0),(1 2 0,0 2 0),
  (2 1 0,1 1 0),(0 0 0,2 0 0),(1 1 0,1 2 0),
  (0 2 0,0 0 0))
```

The next step is to break each of those lines from `MULTILINESTRING` into many `LINESTRINGS`:

```
exploreLine AS
(
   SELECT (ST_Dump(the_geom)).geom AS the_geom FROM threeDLines
),
```

The output for this is as follows:

```
LINESTRING Z (2 0 0,2 1 0)
LINESTRING Z (1 2 0,0 2 0)
LINESTRING Z (2 1 0,1 1 0)
LINESTRING Z (0 0 0,2 0 0)
LINESTRING Z (1 1 0,1 2 0)
LINESTRING Z (0 2 0,0 0 0)
```

The next step is to construct a line representing the boundary of the extruded wall:

```
threeDline AS
(
   SELECT ST_MakeLine(
      ARRAY[
         ST_StartPoint(the_geom),
         ST_EndPoint(the_geom),
         ST_Translate(ST_EndPoint(the_geom), 0, 0, $2),
         ST_Translate(ST_StartPoint(the_geom), 0, 0, $2),
         ST_StartPoint(the_geom)
      ]
   )
   AS the_geom FROM explodedLine
),
```

Now, we need to convert each linestring to `polygon.threeDwall`:

```
threeDwall AS
(
   SELECT ST_MakePolygon(the_geom) as the_geom FROM threeDline
),
```

Finally, put in the roof and floor on our building, using the original geometry for the floor (forced to 3D) and a copy of the original geometry translated to our input height:

```
buildingTop AS
(
```

```
    SELECT ST_Translate(ST_Force3DZ($1), 0, 0, $2) AS the_geom
),
-- and a floor
buildingBottom AS
(
    SELECT ST_Translate(ST_Force3DZ($1), 0, 0, 0) AS the_geom
),
```

We put the walls, roof, and floor together and, during the process, convert this to a 3D MULTIPOLYGON:

```
wholeBuilding AS
(
    SELECT the_geom FROM buildingBottom
        UNION ALL
    SELECT the_geom FROM threeDwall
        UNION ALL
    SELECT the_geom FROM buildingTop
),
-- then convert this collecion to a multipolygon
multiBuilding AS
(
    SELECT ST_Multi(ST_Collect(the_geom)) AS the_geom FROM
        wholeBuilding
),
```

While we could leave our geometry as a MULTIPOLYGON, we'll do things properly and munge an informal cast to POLYHEDRALSURFACE. In our case, we are already effectively formatted as a POLYHEDRALSURFACE, so we'll just convert our geometry to text with ST_AsText, replace the word with POLYHEDRALSURFACE, and then convert our text back to geometry with ST_GeomFromText:

```
textBuilding AS
(
    SELECT ST_AsText(the_geom) textbuilding FROM multiBuilding
),
textBuildSurface AS
(
    SELECT ST_GeomFromText(replace(textbuilding, 'MULTIPOLYGON',
            'POLYHEDRALSURFACE')) AS the_geom FROM textBuilding
)
SELECT the_geom FROM textBuildSurface
```

Finally, the entire function is:

```
CREATE OR REPLACE FUNCTION chp07.threedbuilding(footprint geometry,
    height numeric)
```

```
RETURNS geometry AS
$BODY$

-- make our polygons into lines, and then chop up into individual line
segments
WITH simple_lines AS
(
  SELECT 1 AS gid, ST_MakeLine(ST_PointN(the_geom,pointn),
    ST_PointN(the_geom,pointn+1)) AS the_geom
  FROM (SELECT 1 AS gid, polygon_to_line($1) AS the_geom ) AS a
  LEFT JOIN
  (SELECT 1 AS gid, generate_series(1,
    ST_NumPoints(polygon_to_line($1))-1) AS pointn
  ) AS b
  ON a.gid = b.gid
),
-- convert our lines into 3D lines, which will set our third  coordinate to
0 by default
threeDlines AS
(
  SELECT ST_Force3DZ(the_geom) AS the_geom FROM simple_lines
),
-- now we need our lines as individual records, so we dump them out using
ST_Dump, and then just grab the geometry portion of the dump
explodedLine AS
(
  SELECT (ST_Dump(the_geom)).geom AS the_geom FROM threeDLines
),
-- Next step is to construct a line representing the boundary of the
extruded "wall"
threeDline AS
(
  SELECT ST_MakeLine(
    ARRAY[
    ST_StartPoint(the_geom),
    ST_EndPoint(the_geom),
    ST_Translate(ST_EndPoint(the_geom), 0, 0, $2),
    ST_Translate(ST_StartPoint(the_geom), 0, 0, $2),
    ST_StartPoint(the_geom)
    ]
  )
AS the_geom FROM explodedLine
),
-- we convert this line into a polygon
threeDwall AS
(
  SELECT ST_MakePolygon(the_geom) as the_geom FROM threeDline
),
```

```
-- add a top to the building
buildingTop AS
(
   SELECT ST_Translate(ST_Force3DZ($1), 0, 0, $2) AS the_geom
),
-- and a floor
buildingBottom AS
(
   SELECT ST_Translate(ST_Force3DZ($1), 0, 0, 0) AS the_geom
),
-- now we put the walls, roof, and floor together
wholeBuilding AS
(
   SELECT the_geom FROM buildingBottom
     UNION ALL
   SELECT the_geom FROM threeDwall
     UNION ALL
   SELECT the_geom FROM buildingTop
),
-- then convert this collecion to a multipolygon
multiBuilding AS
(
   SELECT ST_Multi(ST_Collect(the_geom)) AS the_geom FROM wholeBuilding
),
-- While we could leave this as a multipolygon, we'll do things properly
and munge an informal cast
-- to polyhedralsurfacem which is more widely recognized as the appropriate
format for a geometry like
-- this. In our case, we are already formatted as a polyhedralsurface,
minus the official designation,
-- so we'll just convert to text, replace the word MULTIPOLYGON with
POLYHEDRALSURFACE and then convert
-- back to geometry with ST_GeomFromText

textBuilding AS
(
   SELECT ST_AsText(the_geom) textbuilding FROM multiBuilding
),
textBuildSurface AS
(
   SELECT ST_GeomFromText(replace(textbuilding, 'MULTIPOLYGON',
     'POLYHEDRALSURFACE')) AS the_geom FROM textBuilding
)
SELECT the_geom FROM textBuildSurface
;
$BODY$
   LANGUAGE sql VOLATILE
   COST 100;
```

```
ALTER FUNCTION chp07.threedbuilding(geometry, numeric)
  OWNER TO me;
```

How to do it...

Now that we have a 3D-building extrusion function, we can easily extrude our building footprint with our nicely encapsulated function:

```
DROP TABLE IF EXISTS chp07.threed_building;
CREATE TABLE chp07.threed_building AS
SELECT chp07.threeDbuilding(the_geom, 10) AS the_geom
FROM chp07.simple_building;
```

We can apply this function to a real building footprint dataset (available in our data directory), in which case, if we have a height field, we can extrude according to it:

```
shp2pgsql -s 3734 -d -i -I -W LATIN1 -g the_geom
building_footprints\chp07.building_footprints | psql -U me -d postgis-
cookbook \
-h <HOST> -p <PORT>

DROP TABLE IF EXISTS chp07.build_footprints_threed;
CREATE TABLE chp07.build_footprints_threed AS
SELECT gid, height, chp07.threeDbuilding(the_geom, height) AS the_geom
FROM chp07.building_footprints;
```

The resulting output gives us a nice, extruded set of building footprints, as shown in the following image:

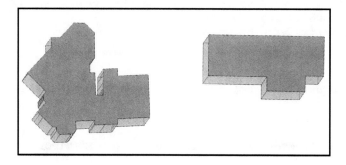

The *Detailed building footprints from LiDAR* recipe in `Chapter 4`, *Working with Vector Data - Advanced Recipes*, explores the extraction of building footprints from LiDAR. A complete workflow could be envisioned, which extracts building footprints from LiDAR and then reconstructs polygon geometries using the current recipe, thus converting point clouds to surfaces, combining the current recipe with the one referenced previously.

Using ST_Extrude to extrude building footprints

PostGIS 2.1 brought a lot of really cool additional functionality to PostGIS. Operations on PostGIS raster types are among the more important improvements that come with PostGIS 2.1. A quieter and equally potent game changer was the addition of the SFCGAL library as an optional extension to PostGIS. According to the website `http://sfcgal.org/`, SFCGAL is a C++ wrapper library around CGAL with the aim of supporting ISO 19107:2013 and OGC Simple Features Access 1.2 for 3D operations.

From a practical standpoint, what does this mean? It means that PostGIS is moving toward a fully functional 3D environment, from representation of the geometries themselves and the operations on those 3D geometries. More information is available at `http://postgis.net/docs/reference.html#reference_sfcgal`.

This and several other recipes will assume that you have a version of PostGIS installed with SFCGAL compiled and enabled. Doing so enables the following functions:

- `ST_Extrude`: This extrudes a surface to a related volume
- `ST_StraightSkeleton`: This computes a straight skeleton from a geometry
- `ST_IsPlanar`: This checks whether a surface is a planar or not
- `ST_Orientation`: This determines the surface orientation
- `ST_ForceLHR`: This forces LHR orientation
- `ST_MinkowskiSum`: This computes the Minkowski sum
- `ST_Tesselate`: This performs surface Tessellation

How to do it...

For this recipe, we'll use `ST_Extrude` in much the same way we used our own custom-built function in the previous recipe, *Constructing and serving buildings 2.5D*. The advantage over the previous recipe is that we are not required to have the SFCGAL library compiled in PostGIS. The advantage to this recipe is that we have more control over the extrusion process; that is, we can extrude in all three dimensions.

`ST_Extrude` returns a geometry, specifically a polyhedral surface. It requires four parameters: an input geometry and the extrusion amount along the *X*, *Y*, and *Z* axes:

```
DROP TABLE IF EXISTS chp07.buildings_extruded;
CREATE TABLE chp07.buildings_extruded AS
SELECT gid, ST_CollectionExtract(ST_Extrude(the_geom, 20, 20, 40), 3) as
the_geom
FROM chp07.building_footprints
```

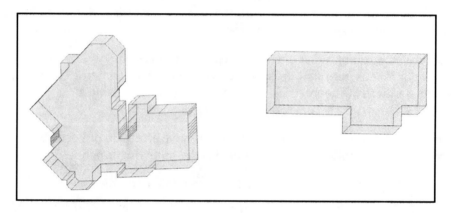

And so, with the help of the *Constructing and serving buildings 2.5D* recipe, we get our extruded buildings, but with some additional flexibility.

Creating arbitrary 3D objects for PostGIS

Sources of 3D information are not only generated from LiDAR, nor are they purely synthesized from 2D geometries and associated attributes as in the *Constructing and serving buildings 2.5D* and *Using ST_Extrude to extrude building footprints* recipes, but they can also be created from the principles of computer vision as well. The process of calculating 3D information from the association of related keypoints between images is known as SfM.

As a computer vision concept, we can leverage SfM to generate 3D information in ways similar to how the human mind perceives the world in 3D, and further store and process that information in a PostGIS database.

 Computer vision is a discipline within computer science focused on automated analysis and inference from images and video. It is considered a research area that develops algorithms that interpret the world in a way that is similar to human vision. An excellent summary can be found at `http://en.wikipedia.org/wiki/Computer_vision`.

A number of open source projects have matured to deal with solving SfM problems. Popular among these are Bundler, which can be found at `http://phototour.cs.washington.edu/bundler/`, and **VisualSFM** at `http://ccwu.me/vsfm/`. Binaries exist for multiple platforms for these tools, including versions. The nice thing about such projects is that a simple set of photos can be used to reconstruct 3D scenes.

For our purposes, we will use VisualSFM and skip the installation and configuration of this software. The reason for this is that SfM is beyond the scope of a PostGIS book to cover in detail, and we will focus on how we can use the data in PostGIS.

Getting ready

It is important to understand that SfM techniques, while highly effective, have certain limitations in the kinds of imagery that can be effectively processed into point clouds. The techniques are dependent upon finding matches between subsequent images and thus can have trouble processing images that are smooth, are missing the camera's embedded **Exchangeable Image File Format (EXIF)** information, or are from cell phone cameras.

 EXIF tags are a metadata format for images. Stored in these tags are often the camera settings, camera type, lens type, and other information relevant to SfM extraction.

We will start processing an image series into a point cloud with a photo series that we know largely works, but as you experiment with SfM, you can feed in your own photo series. Good tips on how to create a photo series that will result in a 3D model can be found at `https://www.youtube.com/watch?v=IStU-WP2XKs&t=348s` and `http://www.cubify.com/products/capture/photography_tips.aspx`.

How to do it...

Download VisualSFM from `http://ccwu.me/vsfm/`. In a console terminal, execute the following:

```
Visualsfm <IMAGES_FOLDER>
```

VisualSFM will start rendering the 3D, model using as input a folder with images. It will take a couple of hours to process. Then, when it finishes, it will return a point cloud file.

We can view this data in a program such as **MeshLab** at `http://meshlab.sourceforge.net/`. A good tutorial on using MeshLab to view point clouds can be found at `http://www.cse.iitd.ac.in/~mcs112609/Meshlab%20Tutorial.pdf`.

The following image shows what our point cloud looks like when viewed in MeshLab:

In the VisualSFM output, there is a file with the extension `.ply`, for example, `giraffe.ply` (included in the source code for this chapter). If you open this file in a text editor, it will look something like the following:

```
ply
format ascii 1.0
element vertex 276539
property float x
property float y
property float z
property float nx
property float ny
property float nz
property uchar red
property uchar green
property uchar blue
end_header
0.58174 -0.0940152 -8.62386 0.0897906 0.0893454 0.991945 185 185 179
0.663161 0.850887 -7.57239 -0.635235 0.475179 0.608836 144 117 85
0.660386 0.849393 -7.57599 -0.838368 0.530371 -0.125881 127 99 65
0.664645 0.849737 -7.56985 -0.736177 0.618385 0.275033 126 98 69
0.653817 0.84765 -7.58713 -0.955944 0.282847 -0.0785467 162 135 100
0.652211 0.845895 -7.58218 -0.678657 0.356864 0.641929 134 106 79
0.662668 0.848185 -7.57326 -0.785914 0.61084 0.0959887 143 116 84
0.660412 0.846526 -7.57264 -0.699131 0.700875 0.141383 144 114 84
```

This is the header portion of our file. It specifies the .ply format, the encoding format
ascii 1.0, the number of vertices, and then the column names for all the data returned: x,
y, z, nx, ny, nz, red, green, and blue.

For importing into PostGIS, we will import all the fields, but will focus on x, y, and z for
our point cloud, as well as look at color. For our purposes, this file specifies relative x, y,
and z coordinates, and the color of each of those points in channels red, green, and blue.
These colors are 24-bit colors—and thus they can have integer values between 0 and 255.

For the remainder of the recipe, we will create a PDAL pipeline, modifying the JSON
structure reader to be a .ply file. Check the recipe for *Importing LiDAR data* in this chapter
to see how to create a PDAL pipeline:

```
{
  "pipeline": [{
    "type": "readers.ply",
    "filename": "/data/giraffe/giraffe.ply"
  }, {
    "type": "writers.pgpointcloud",
    "connection": "host='localhost' dbname='postgis-cookbook' user='me'
    password='me' port='5432'",
    "table": "giraffe",
    "srid": "3734",
    "schema": "chp07"
  }]
}
```

Then we execute in the Terminal:

```
$ pdal pipeline giraffe.json"
```

This output will serve us for input in the next recipe.

Exporting models as X3D for the web

Entering 3D data in a PostGIS database is not nearly as interesting if we have no capacity for extracting the data back out in some useable form. One way to approach this problem is to leverage the PostGIS ability to write 3D tables to the X3D format.

X3D is an XML standard for displaying 3D data and works well via the web. For those familiar with **Virtual Reality Modeling Language (VRML)**, X3D is the next generation of that.

To view X3D in the browser, a user has the choice of a variety of plugins, or they can leverage JavaScript APIs to enable viewing. We will perform the latter, as it requires no user configuration to work. We will use X3DOM's JavaScript framework to accomplish this. X3DOM is a demonstration of the integration of HTML5 and 3D and uses **Web Graphics Library (WebGL)**; (https://en.wikipedia.org/wiki/WebGL) to allow rendering and interaction with 3D content in the browser. This means that our data will not get displayed in browsers that are not WebGL compatible.

Getting ready

We will be using the point cloud from the previous example to serve in X3D format. PostGIS documentation on X3D includes an example of using the ST_AsX3D function to output the formatted X3D code:

```
COPY(WITH pts AS (SELECT PC_Explode(pa) AS pt FROM chp07.giraffe) SELECT '
<X3D xmlns="http://www.web3d.org/specifications/x3d-namespace"
 showStat="false" showLog="false" x="0px" y="0px" width="800px"
 height="600px">
 <Scene>
   <Transform>
     <Shape>' ||  ST_AsX3D(ST_Union(pt::geometry))  ||'</Shape>
   </Transform>
 </Scene>
</X3D>' FROM pts)
TO STDOUT WITH CSV;
```

We included the copy to STDOUT WITH CSV to make a dump in raw code. The user is able to save this query as an SQL script file and execute it from the console in order to dump the result into a file. For instance:

```
$ psql -U me -d postgis-cookbook -h localhost -f "x3d_query.sql" >
result.html
```

How to do it...

This example, while complete in serving the pure X3D, needs additional code to allow in-browser viewing. We do so by including style sheets, and the appropriate X3DOM includes the headers of an XHTML document:

```
<link rel="stylesheet" type="text/css"
href="http://x3dom.org/x3dom/example/x3dom.css" />
<script type="text/javascript"
src="http://x3dom.org/x3dom/example/x3dom.js"></script>
```

The full query to generate the XHTML of X3D data is as follows:

```
COPY(WITH pts AS (
  SELECT PC_Explode(pa) AS pt FROM chp07.giraffe
)
SELECT regexp_replace('
  <!DOCTYPE html PUBLIC "-//W3C//DTD XHTML 1.0 Strict//EN"
"http://www.w3.org/TR/xhtml1/DTD/xhtml1-strict.dtd">
  <html xmlns="http://www.w3.org/1999/xhtml">
    <head>
      <meta http-equiv="X-UA-Compatible" content="chrome=1" />
      <meta http-equiv="Content-Type" content="text/html;charset=utf-8"/>
      <title>Point Cloud in a Browser</title>
      <link rel="stylesheet" type="text/css"
       href="http://x3dom.org/x3dom/example/x3dom.css" />
      <script type="text/javascript"
       src="http://x3dom.org/x3dom/example/x3dom.js">
      </script>
    </head>
    <body>
      <h1>Point Cloud in the Browser</h1>
      <p>
        Use mouse to rotate, scroll wheel to zoom, and control
        (or command) click to pan.
      </p>
      <X3D xmlns="http://www.web3d.org/specifications/x3d-namespace
       showStat="false" showLog="false" x="0px" y="0px" width="800px"
```

```
              height="600px">
                <Scene>
                  <Transform>
                    <Shape>' ||  ST_AsX3D(ST_Union(pt::geometry)) || '</Shape>
                  </Transform>
                </Scene>
            </X3D>
          </body>
        </html>', E'[\\n\\r]+','', 'g')
    FROM pts)TO STDOUT;
```

If we open the `.html` file in our favorite browser, we will get the following:

There's more...

One might want to use this X3D conversion as a function, feeding geometry into a function and getting a page in return. In this way, we can reuse the code easily for other tables. Embodied in a function, X3D conversion is as follows:

```
CREATE OR REPLACE FUNCTION AsX3D_XHTML(geometry)
RETURNS character varying AS
$BODY$
SELECT regexp_replace(
  '
    <!DOCTYPE html PUBLIC "-//W3C//DTD XHTML 1.0 Strict//EN"
     "http://www.w3.org/TR/xhtml1/DTD/xhtml1-strict.dtd">
    <html xmlns= "http://www.w3.org/1999/xhtml">
      <head>
        <meta http-equiv="X-UA-Compatible" content="chrome=1"/>
        <meta http-equiv="Content-Type" content="text/html;charset=utf-8"/>
        <title>Point Cloud in a Browser</title>
        <link rel="stylesheet" type="text/css"
         href="http://x3dom.org/x3dom/example/x3dom.css"/>
        <script type="text/javascript"
         src="http://x3dom.org/x3dom/example/x3dom.js">
        </script>
      </head>
      <body>
        <h1>Point Cloud in the Browser</h1>
        <p>
          Use mouse to rotate, scroll wheel to zoom, and control
          (or command) click to pan.
        </p>
        <X3D xmlns="http://www.web3d.org/specifications/x3d-namespace"
         showStat="false" showLog="false"  x="0px" y="0px" width="800px"
         height="600px">
          <Scene>
            <Transform>
              <Shape>'||  ST_AsX3D($1)  || '</Shape>
            </Transform>
          </Scene>
        </X3D>
      </body>
    </html>
  ', E'[\\n\\r]+' , '' , 'g' ) As x3dXHTML;
$BODY$
LANGUAGE sql VOLATILE
COST 100;
```

In order for the function to work, we need to first use `ST_UNION` on the geometry parameter to pass to the `AsX3D_XHTML` function:

```
copy(
  WITH pts AS (
    SELECT
      PC_Explode(pa) AS pt
    FROM giraffe
  )
  SELECT AsX3D_XHTML(ST_UNION(pt::geometry)) FROM pts) to stdout;
```

We can now very simply generate the appropriate XHTML directly from the command line or a web framework.

Reconstructing Unmanned Aerial Vehicle (UAV) image footprints with PostGIS 3D

The rapid development of **Unmanned Aerial Systems (UAS)**, also known as **Unmanned Aerial Vehicles (UAVs)**, as data collectors is revolutionizing remote data collection in all sectors. Barriers to wider adoption outside military sectors include regulatory frameworks preventing their flight in some nations, such as, the United States, and the lack of open source implementations of post-processing software. In the next four recipes, we'll attempt preliminary solutions to the latter of these two barriers.

For this recipe, we will be using the metadata from a UAV flight in Seneca County, Ohio, by the Ohio Department of Transportation to map the coverage of the flight. This is included in the code folder for this chapter.

The basic idea for this recipe is to estimate the field of view of the UAV camera, generate a 3D pyramid that represents that field of view, and use the flight ephemeris (bearing, pitch, and roll) to estimate ground coverage.

Getting started

The metadata or ephemeris we have for the flight includes the bearing, pitch, and roll of the UAS, in addition to its elevation and location:

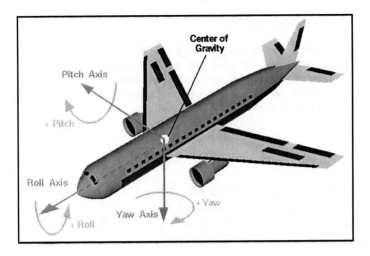

To translate these ephemeris into PostGIS terms, we'll assume the following:

- 90 degrees minus the pitch is equivalent to `ST_RotateX`
- The negative roll is equivalent to `ST_RotateY`
- 90 degrees minus the bearing is equivalent to `ST_RotateZ`

In order to perform our analysis, we require external functions. These functions can be downloaded from `https://github.com/smathermather/postgis-etc/tree/master/3D`.

We will use patched versions of `ST_RotateX`, `ST_RotateY` (`ST_RotateX.sql`, and `ST_RotateY.sql`), which allow us to rotate geometries around an input point, as well as a function for calculating our field of view, `pyramidMaker.sql`. Future versions of PostGIS will include these versions of `ST_RotateX` and `ST_RotateY` built in. We have another function, `ST_RotateXYZ`, which is built upon these and will also simplify our code by allowing us to specify three axes at the same time for rotation.

For the final step, we'll need the capacity to perform volumetric intersection (the 3D equivalent of intersection). For this, we'll use `volumetricIntersection.sql`, which allows us to just return the volumetric portion of the intersection as a **triangular irregular network (TIN)**.

A TIN is a 3D surface model for representing surfaces and volumes as a mesh of triangles.

We will install the functions as follows:

```
psql -U me -d postgis_cookbook -f ST_RotateX.sql
psql -U me -d postgis_cookbook -f ST_RotateY.sql
psql -U me -d postgis_cookbook -f ST_RotateXYZ.sql
psql -U me -d postgis_cookbook -f pyramidMaker.sql
psql -U me -d postgis_cookbook -f volumetricIntersection.sql
```

How to do it...

In order to calculate the viewing footprint, we will calculate a rectangular pyramid descending from the viewpoint to the ground. This pyramid will need to point to the left and right of the nadir according to the UAS's roll, forward or backward from the craft according to its pitch, and be oriented relative to the direction of movement of the craft according to its bearing.

The `pyramidMaker` function will construct our pyramid for us and `ST_RotateXYZ` will rotate the pyramid in the direction we need to compensate for roll, pitch, and bearing.

The following image is an example map of such a calculated footprint for a single image. Note the slight roll to the left for this example, resulting in an asymmetric-looking pyramid when viewed from above:

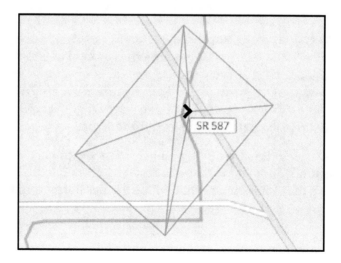

The total track for the UAS flight overlayed on a contour map is shown in the following image:

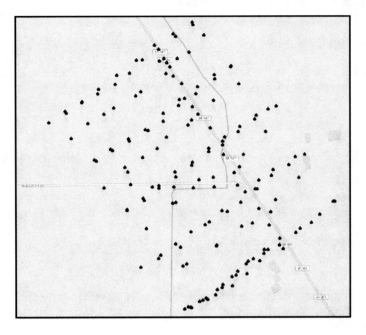

Total track for the flight viewed with QGIS

We will write a function to calculate our footprint pyramid. To input to the function, we'll need the position of the UAS as geometry (origin), the pitch, bearing, and roll, as well as the field of view angle in x and y for the camera. Finally, we'll need the relative height of the craft above ground:

```
CREATE OR REPLACE FUNCTION chp07.pbr(origin geometry, pitch numeric,
    bearing numeric, roll numeric, anglex numeric, angley numeric,
    height numeric)
    RETURNS geometry AS
$BODY$
```

Our pyramid function assumes that we know what the base size of our pyramid is. We don't know this initially, so we'll calculate its size based on the field of view angle of the camera and the height of the craft:

```
WITH widthx AS
(
    SELECT height / tan(anglex) AS basex
),
```

```
widthy AS
(
  SELECT height / tan(angley) AS basey
),
```

Now, we have enough information to construct our pyramid:

```
iViewCone AS (
  SELECT pyramidMaker(origin, basex::numeric, basey::numeric, height)
    AS the_geom
    FROM widthx, widthy
),
```

We will require the following code to rotate our view relative to pitch, roll, and bearing:

```
iViewRotated AS (
  SELECT ST_RotateXYZ(the_geom, pi() - pitch, 0 - roll, pi() -
    bearing, origin) AS the_geom FROM iViewCone
)
SELECT the_geom FROM iViewRotated
```

The whole function is as follows:

```
CREATE OR REPLACE FUNCTION chp07.pbr(origin geometry, pitch numeric,
  bearing numeric, roll numeric, anglex numeric, angley numeric,
  height numeric)
  RETURNS geometry AS
$BODY$

WITH widthx AS
(
  SELECT height / tan(anglex) AS basex
),
widthy AS
(
  SELECT height / tan(angley) AS basey
),
iViewCone AS (
  SELECT pyramidMaker(origin, basex::numeric, basey::numeric, height)
    AS the_geom
    FROM widthx, widthy
),
iViewRotated AS (
  SELECT ST_RotateXYZ(the_geom, pi() - pitch, 0 - roll, pi() -
    bearing, origin) AS the_geom FROM iViewCone
)
SELECT the_geom FROM iViewRotated
;
```

```
$BODY$
  LANGUAGE sql VOLATILE
  COST 100;
```

Now, to use our function, let us import the UAS positions from the `uas_locations` shapefile included in the source for this chapter:

```
shp2pgsql -s 3734 -W LATIN1 uas_locations_altitude_hpr_3734 uas_locations |
\PGPASSWORD=me psql -U me -d postgis-cookbook -h localhost
```

Now, it is possible to calculate an estimated footprint for each UAS position:

```
DROP TABLE IF EXISTS chp07.viewshed;
CREATE TABLE chp07.viewshed AS
SELECT 1 AS gid, roll, pitch, heading, fileName,
chp07.pbr(ST_Force3D(geom),
  radians(0)::numeric, radians(heading)::numeric, radians(roll)::numeric,
  radians(40)::numeric, radians(50)::numeric,
  ( (3.2808399 * altitude_a) - 838)::numeric)
AS the_geom FROM uas_locations;
```

If you import this with your favorite desktop GIS, such as QGIS, you will be able to see the following:

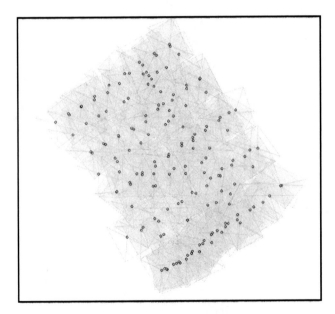

With a terrain model, we can go a step deeper in this analysis. Since our UAS footprints are volumetric, we will first load the terrain model. We will load this from a `.backup` file included in the source code for this chapter:

```
pg_restore -h localhost -p 8000 -U me -d "postgis-cookbook" \ --schema
chp07 --verbose "lidar_tin.backup"
```

Next, we will create a smaller version of our `viewshed` table:

```
DROP TABLE IF EXISTS chp07.viewshed;
CREATE TABLE chp07.viewshed AS
SELECT 1 AS gid, roll, pitch, heading, fileName,
chp07.pbr(ST_Force3D(geom), radians(0)::numeric, radians(heading)::numeric,
radians(roll) ::numeric, radians(40)::numeric, radians(50)::numeric,
1000::numeric) AS the_geom
FROM uas_locations
WHERE fileName = 'IMG_0512.JPG';
```

If you import this with your favorite desktop GIS, such as QGIS, you will be able to see the following:

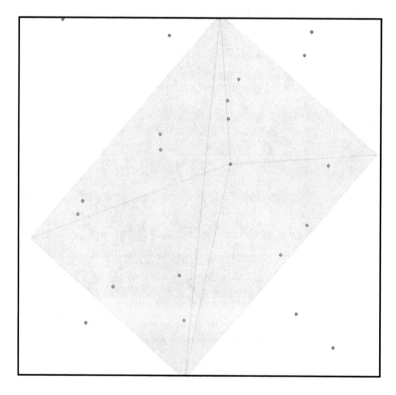

UAV photogrammetry in PostGIS – point cloud

We will use the techniques we've used in the previous recipe named *Creating arbitrary 3D objects for PostGIS* learn how to create and import a UAV-derived point cloud in PostGIS.

One caveat before we begin is that while we will be working with geospatial data, we will be doing so in relative space, rather than a known coordinate system. In other words, this approach will calculate our dataset in an arbitrary coordinate system. ST_Affine could be used in combination with the field measurements of locations to transform our data into a known coordinate system, but this is beyond the scope of this book.

Getting ready

Much like with the *Creating arbitrary 3D objects for PostGIS* recipe, we will be taking an image series and converting it into a point cloud. In this case, however, our image series will be from UAV imagery. Download the image series included in the code folder for this chapter, uas_flight, and feed it into VisualSFM (check http://ccwu.me/vsfm/for more information on how to use this tool); in order to retrieve a point cloud, name it uas_points.ply (this file is also included in this folder in case you would rather use it).

The input for PostGIS is the same as before. Create a JSON file and use PDAL store it into the database:

```
{
  "pipeline": [{
    "type": "readers.ply",
    "filename": "/data/uas_flight/uas_points.ply"
  }, {
    "type": "writers.pgpointcloud",
    "connection": "host='localhost' dbname='postgis-cookbook' user='me'
                 password='me' port='5432'",
    "table": "uas",
    "schema": "chp07"
  }]
}
```

How to do it...

Now, we copy data from the point cloud into our table. Refer to the *Importing LiDAR data recipe* in this chapter to verify the pointcloud extension object representation:

```
$ pdal pipeline uas_points.json
```

This data, as viewed in MeshLab (http://www.meshlab.net/) from the .ply file, is pretty interesting:

The original data is color infrared imagery, so vegetation shows up red, and farm fields and roads as gray. Note the bright colors in the sky; those are camera position points that we'll need to filter out.

The next step is to generate orthographic imagery from this data.

UAV photogrammetry in PostGIS – DSM creation

The photogrammetry example would be incomplete if we did not produce a digital terrain model from our inputs. A fully rigorous solution where the input point cloud would be classified into ground points, building points, and vegetation points is not feasible here, but this recipe will provide the basic framework for accomplishing such a solution.

In this recipe, we will create a 3D TIN, which will represent the surface of the point cloud.

Getting ready

Before we start, ST_DelaunayTriangles is available only in PostGIS 2.1 using GEOS 3.4. This is one of the few recipes in this book to require such advanced versions of PostGIS and GEOS.

How to do it...

ST_DelaunayTriangles will calculate a 3D TIN with the correct flag: geometry ST_DelaunayTriangles (geometry g1, float tolerance, int4 flags):

```
DROP TABLE IF EXISTS chp07.uas_tin;
CREATE TABLE chp07.uas_tin AS WITH pts AS
(
    SELECT PC_Explode(pa) AS pt
    FROM chp07.uas_flights
)
SELECT ST_DelaunayTriangles(ST_Union(pt::geometry), 0.0, 2) AS the_geom
FROM pts;
```

Now, we have a full TIN of a digital surface model at our disposal:

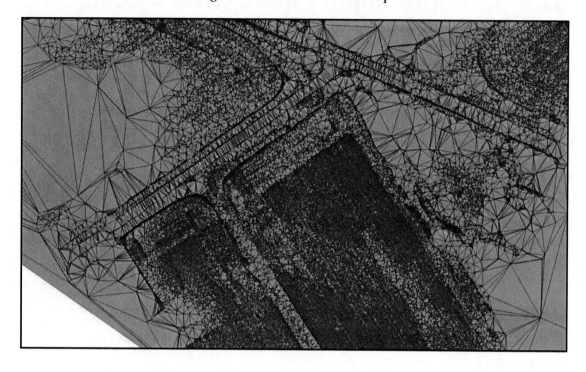

8
PostGIS Programming

In this chapter, we will cover the following topics:

- Writing PostGIS vector data with Psycopg
- Writing PostGIS vector data with OGR Python bindings
- Writing PostGIS functions with PL/Python
- Geocoding and reverse geocoding using the GeoNames datasets
- Geocoding using the OSM datasets with trigrams
- Geocoding with geopy and PL/Python
- Importing NetCDF datasets with Python and GDAL

Introduction

There are several ways to write PostGIS programs, and in this chapter we will see a few of them. You will mainly use the Python language throughout this chapter. Python is a fantastic language with a plethora of GIS and scientific libraries that can be combined with PostGIS to write awesome geospatial applications.

If you are new to Python, you can quickly get productive with these excellent web resources:

- The official Python tutorial at `http://docs.python.org/2/tutorial/`
- The popular *Dive into Python* book at `http://www.diveintopython.net/`

You can combine Python with some excellent and popular libraries, such as:

- **Psycopg**: This is the most complete and popular Python DB API implementation for PostgreSQL; see `http://initd.org/psycopg/`
- **GDAL**: Used to unchain the powerful GDAL library in your Python scripts; see `http://www.gdal.org/gdal_tutorial.html`
- **requests**: This is a handy Python standard library to manage HTTP stuff, such as opening URLs
- **simplejson**: This is a simple and fast JSON encoder/decoder

The recipes in this chapter will cover some other useful geospatial Python libraries that are worthy of being looked at if you are developing a geospatial application. Under these Python libraries, the following libraries are included:

- **Shapely**: This is a Python interface to the GEOS library for the manipulation and analysis of planar geometric objects: `http://toblerity.github.io/shapely/`
- **Fiona**: This is a very light OGR Python API, which can be used as an alternative to the OGR bindings used in this chapter to manage vector datasets: `https://github.com/Toblerity/Fiona`
- **Rasterio**: This a Pythonic GDAL Python API, which can be used as an alternative to the GDAL bindings used in this chapter in order to manage raster datasets: `https://github.com/mapbox/rasterio`
- **pyproj**: This is the Python interface to the PROJ.4 library: `https://pypi.python.org/pypi/pyproj`
- **Rtree**: This is a `ctype` Python wrapper to the `libspatialindex` library, providing several spatial indexing features that can be extremely useful for some kinds of geospatial development: `http://toblerity.github.io/rtree/`

In the first recipe, you will write a program that uses Python and its utilities such as `psycopg`, `requests`, and `simplejson` to fetch weather data from the web and import it in PostGIS.

In the second recipe, we will drive you to use Python and the GDAL OGR Python bindings library to create a script for geocoding a list of place names using one of the GeoNames web services.

You will then write a Python function for PostGIS using the PL/Python language to query the `http://openweathermap.org/` web services, already used in the first recipe, to calculate the weather for a PostGIS geometry from within a PostgreSQL function.

In the fourth recipe, you will create two PL/pgSQL PostGIS functions that will let you perform geocoding and reverse geocoding using the GeoNames datasets.

After this, there is a recipe in which you will use the `OpenStreetMap` street datasets imported in PostGIS to implement a very basic Python class in order to provide a geocode implementation to the class's consumer using PostGIS trigram support.

The sixth recipe will show you how to create a PL/Python function using the geopy library to geocode addresses using a web geocoding API such as Google Maps, Yahoo! Maps, Geocoder, GeoNames, and others.

In the last recipe of this chapter, you will create a Python script to import data from the `netCDF` format to PostGIS using the GDAL Python bindings.

Let's see some notes before starting with the recipes in this chapter.

If you are using Linux or macOS, follow these steps:

1. Create a Python `virtualenv` (http://www.virtualenv.org/en/latest/) to keep a Python-isolated environment to be used for all the Python recipes in this book and activate it. Create it in a central directory, as you will need to use it for most of the Python recipes in this book:

```
$ cd ~/virtualenvs
$ virtualenv --no-site-packages postgis-cb-env
$ source postgis-cb-env/bin/activate
```

2. Once activated, you can install the Python libraries you will need for the recipes in this chapter:

```
$ pip install simplejson
$ pip install psycopg2
$ pip install numpy
$ pip install requests
$ pip install gdal
$ pip install geopy
```

3. If you are new to the virtual environment and you are wondering where the libraries have been installed, you should find everything in the `virtualenv` directory in our development box. You can find the libraries using the following command:

```
$ ls /home/capooti/virtualenv/postgis-cb-env/lib/
    python2.7/site-packages
```

If you are wondering what is going on with the previous command lines, then `virtualenv` is a tool that will be used to create isolated Python environments, and you can find more information about this tool at `http://www.virtualenv.org`, while `pip` (`http://www.pip-installer.org`) is a package management system used to install and manage software packages written in Python.

If you are using Windows, follow these steps:

1. The easiest way to get Python and all the libraries needed for the recipes in this chapter is to use **OSGeo4W**, a popular binary distribution of open source geospatial software for Windows. You can download it from `http://trac.osgeo.org/osgeo4w/`.

2. In our Windows box the OSGeo4W shell, at the time of writing this book comes with Python 2.7, GDAL 2.2 Python bindings, simplejson, psycopg2, and numpy. You will only need to install geopy.

3. The easiest way to install geopy and to eventually add more Python libraries to the OSGeo4W shell is to install `setuptools` and `pip` by following the instructions found at `http://www.pip-installer.org/en/latest/installing.html`. Open the OSGeo4W shell and just enter the following commands:

```
> python ez_setup.py
> python get-pip.py
> pip install requests
> pip install geopy
```

Writing PostGIS vector data with Psycopg

In this recipe, you will use Python combined with Psycopg, the most popular PostgreSQL database library for Python, in order to write some data to PostGIS using the SQL language.

You will write a procedure to import weather data for the most populated US cities. You will import such weather data from `http://www.openweatherdata.org/`, which is a web service that provides free weather data and a forecast API. The procedure you are going to write will iterate each major USA city and get the actual temperature for it from the closest weather stations using the `http://www.openweatherdata.org/` web service API, getting the output in JSON format. (In case you are new to the JSON format, you can find details about it at `http://www.json.org/`.)

You will also generate a new PostGIS layer with the 10 closest weather stations to each city.

Getting ready

1. Create a database schema for the recipes in this chapter using the following command:

   ```
   postgis_cookbook=# CREATE SCHEMA chp08;
   ```

2. Download the USA cities' shapefile from the `https://nationalmap.gov/` website at `http://dds.cr.usgs.gov/pub/data/nationalatlas/citiesx020_nt00007.tar.gz` (this archive is also included in the book's dataset that is available with the code bundle), extract it to `working/chp08`, and import it in PostGIS, filtering out cities with less than 100,000 inhabitants:

   ```
   $ ogr2ogr -f PostgreSQL -s_srs EPSG:4269 -t_srs EPSG:4326
   -lco GEOMETRY_NAME=the_geom -nln chp08.cities
   PG:"dbname='postgis_cookbook' user='me'
   password='mypassword'" -where "POP_2000 $ 100000" citiesx020.shp
   ```

3. Add a `real` field to store the temperature for each city using the following command:

   ```
   postgis_cookbook=# ALTER TABLE chp08.cities
   ADD COLUMN temperature real;
   ```

4. If you are on Linux, ensure that you follow the initial instructions in this chapter and create a Python virtual environment in order to keep a Python-isolated environment to be used for all the Python recipes in this book. Then, activate it:

   ```
   $ source postgis-cb-env/bin/activate
   ```

How to do it...

Carry out the following steps:

1. Create the following table to host weather stations' data:

   ```
   CREATE TABLE chp08.wstations
   (
     id bigint NOT NULL,
   ```

```
    the_geom geometry(Point,4326),
    name character varying(48),
    temperature real,
    CONSTRAINT wstations_pk PRIMARY KEY (id )
);
```

2. Create an account at `https://openweathermap.org` to get an API key. Then, check the JSON response for the web service you are going to use. If you want the 10 closest weather stations from a point (the city centroid), the request you need to run is as follows (test it in a browser): `http://api.openweathermap.org/data/2.5/find?lat=55&lon=37&cnt=10&appid=YOURKEY`

3. You should get the following JSON response (the closest 10 stations and their relative data are ordered by their distance from the point coordinates, which in this case are `lon=37` and `lat=55`):

```
{
    "message": "accurate",
    "cod": "200",
    "count": 10,
    "list": [
        {
            "id": 529315,
            "name": "Marinki",
            "coord": {
            "lat": 55.0944,
            "lon": 37.03
        },
        "main": {
            "temp": 272.15,
            "pressure": 1011,
            "humidity": 80,
            "temp_min": 272.15,
            "temp_max": 272.15
        },          "dt": 1515114000,
        "wind": {
            "speed": 3,
            "deg": 140
        },
        "sys": {
            "country": ""
        },
        "rain": null,
        "snow": null,
        "clouds": {
            "all": 90
```

```
      },
      "weather": [
        {
          "id": 804,
          "main": "Clouds",
          "description": "overcast clouds",
          "icon": "04n"
        }
      ]
    },
```

4. Now, create the Python program that will provide the desired output and name it `get_weather_data.py`:

```python
import sys
import requests
import simplejson as json
import psycopg2

def GetWeatherData(lon, lat, key):
    """
    Get the 10 closest weather stations data for a given point.
    """
    # uri to access the JSON openweathermap web service
    uri = (
        'https://api.openweathermap.org/data/2.5/find?
         lat=%s&lon=%s&cnt=10&appid=%s'
        % (lat, lon, key))
    print 'Fetching weather data: %s' % uri
    try:
        data = requests.get(uri)
        print 'request status: %s' % data.status_code
        js_data = json.loads(data.text)
        return js_data['list']
    except:
        print 'There was an error getting the weather data.'
        print sys.exc_info()[0]
        return []

def AddWeatherStation(station_id, lon, lat, name, temperature):
    """
    Add a weather station to the database, but only if it does
    not already exists.
    """
    curws = conn.cursor()
    curws.execute('SELECT * FROM chp08.wstations WHERE id=%s',
                  (station_id,))
```

```
          count = curws.rowcount
          if count==0: # we need to add the weather station
              curws.execute(
            """INSERT INTO chp08.wstations (id, the_geom, name,
                temperature) VALUES (%s, ST_GeomFromText('POINT(%s %s)',
                4326), %s, %s)""",
              (station_id, lon, lat, name, temperature)
          )
          curws.close()
          print 'Added the %s weather station to the database.' % name
          return True
        else: # weather station already in database
          print 'The %s weather station is already in the database.' % name
          return False

    # program starts here
    # get a connection to the database
    conn = psycopg2.connect('dbname=postgis_cookbook user=me
                             password=password')
    # we do not need transaction here, so set the connection
    # to autocommit mode
    conn.set_isolation_level(0)

    # open a cursor to update the table with weather data
    cur = conn.cursor()

    # iterate all of the cities in the cities PostGIS layer,
    # and for each of them grap the actual temperature from the
    # closest weather station, and add the 10
    # closest stations to the city to the wstation PostGIS layer
    cur.execute("""SELECT ogc_fid, name,
        ST_X(the_geom) AS long, ST_Y(the_geom) AS lat
        FROM chp08.cities;""")
    for record in cur:
        ogc_fid = record[0]
        city_name = record[1]
        lon = record[2]
        lat = record[3]
        stations = GetWeatherData(lon, lat, 'YOURKEY')
        print stations
        for station in stations:
          print station
          station_id = station['id']
          name = station['name']
          # for weather data we need to access the 'main' section in the
          # json 'main': {'pressure': 990, 'temp': 272.15, 'humidity':
54}
          if 'main' in station:
```

```
      if 'temp' in station['main']:
        temperature = station['main']['temp']
    else:
      temperature = -9999
      # in some case the temperature is not available
    # "coord":{"lat":55.8622,"lon":37.395}
    station_lat = station['coord']['lat']
    station_lon = station['coord']['lon']
    # add the weather station to the database
    AddWeatherStation(station_id, station_lon, station_lat,
                    name, temperature)
    # first weather station from the json API response is always
    # the closest to the city, so we are grabbing this temperature
    # and store in the temperature field in cities PostGIS layer
    if station_id == stations[0]['id']:
      print 'Setting temperature to %s for city %s'
            % (temperature, city_name)
      cur2 = conn.cursor()
      cur2.execute(
        'UPDATE chp08.cities SET temperature=%s WHERE ogc_fid=%s',
        (temperature, ogc_fid))
      cur2.close()

  # close cursor, commit and close connection to database
  cur.close()
  conn.close()
```

5. Run the Python program:

```
(postgis-cb-env)$ python get_weather_data.py
Added the PAMR weather station to the database.
Setting temperature to 268.15 for city Anchorage
Added the PAED weather station to the database.
Added the PANC weather station to the database.
...
The KMFE weather station is already in the database.
Added the KOPM weather station to the database.
The KBKS weather station is already in the database.
```

6. Check the output of the Python program you just wrote. Open the two PostGIS layers, `cities` and `wstations`, with your favorite GIS desktop tool and investigate the results. The following screenshot shows how it looks in QGIS:

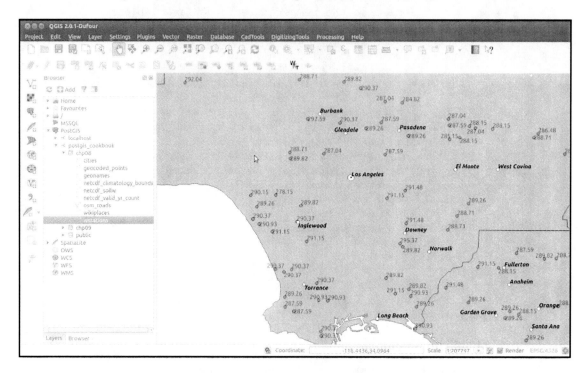

How it works...

Psycopg is the most popular PostgreSQL adapter for Python, and it can be used to create Python scripts that send SQL commands to PostGIS. In this recipe, you created a Python script that queries weather data from the https://openweathermap.org/ web server using the popular **JSON** format to get the output data and then used that data to update two PostGIS layers.

For one of the layers, `cities`, the weather data is used to update the `temperature` field using the temperature data of the weather station closest to the city. For this purpose, you used an `UPDATE` SQL command. The other layer, `wstations`, is updated every time a new weather station is identified from the weather data and inserted in the layer. In this case, you used an `INSERT` SQL statement.

This is a quick overview of the script's behavior (you can find more details in the comments within the Python code). In the beginning, a PostgreSQL connection is created using the Psycopg `connection` object. The `connection` object is created using the main connection parameters (`dbname`, `user`, and `password`, while default values for `server name` and `port` are not specified; instead, `localhost` and `5432` are used). The connection behavior is set to `auto commit` so that any SQL performed by Psycopg will be run immediately and will not be embedded in a transaction.

Using a cursor, you first iterate all of the records in the `cities` PostGIS layer; for each of the cities, you need to get the temperature from the `https://openweathermap.org/` web server. For this purpose, for each city you make a call to the `GetWeatherData` method, passing the coordinates of the city to it. The method queries the server using the `requests` library and parses the JSON response using the `simplejson` Python library.

You should send the URL request to a `try...catch` block. This way, if there is any issue with the web service (internet connection not available, or any HTTP status codes different from 200, or whatever else), the process can safely continue with the data of the next city (iteration).

The JSON response contains, as per the request, the information about the 10 weather stations closest to the city. You will use the information of the first weather station, the closest one to the city, to set the `temperature` field for the city.

You then iterate all of the `station` JSON objects, and by using the `AddWeatherStation` method, you create a weather station in the `wstation` PostGIS layer, but only if a weather station with the same `id` does not exist.

Writing PostGIS vector data with OGR Python bindings

In this recipe, you will use Python and the Python bindings of the GDAL/OGR library to create a script for geocoding a list of the names of places using one of the GeoNames web services (`http://www.geonames.org/export/ws-overview.html`). You will use the **Wikipedia Fulltext Search** web service (`http://www.geonames.org/export/wikipedia-webservice.html#wikipediaSearch`), which for a given search string returns the coordinates of the places matching that search string as the output, and some other useful attributes from Wikipedia, including the Wikipedia `page title` and `url`.

The script should first create a PostGIS point layer named `wikiplaces` in which all of the locations and their attributes returned by the web service will be stored.

This recipe should give you the basis to use other similar web services, such as Google Maps, Yahoo! BOSS Geo Services, and so on, to get results in a similar way.

Before you start, please note the terms of use of GeoNames: `http://www.geonames.org/export/`. In a few words, at the time of writing, you have a 30,000 credits' daily limit per application (identified by the `username` parameter); the hourly limit is 2,000 credits. A credit is a web service request hit for most services.

You will generate the PostGIS table containing the geocoded place names using the GDAL/OGR Python bindings (`http://trac.osgeo.org/gdal/wiki/GdalOgrInPython`).

Getting ready

1. To access GeoNames web services, you need to create a user at `http://www.geonames.org/login`. The user we created for this recipe is `postgis`; you will need to change it with your username whenever you query the GeoNames web service URL.
2. If you are using Windows, be sure to have OSGeo4W installed as suggested in the initial instructions of this chapter.
3. If you are using Linux, follow the initial instructions for this chapter, create a Python `virtualenv` in order to keep a Python-isolated environment to be used for all the Python recipes in this book, and activate it:

```
$ source postgis-cb-env/bin/activate
```

4. Once activated, if you still haven't done so, you have to install the `gdal` and `simplejson` Python packages needed for this recipe:

```
(postgis-cb-env)$ pip install gdal
(postgis-cb-env)$ pip install simplejson
```

How to do it...

Carry out the following steps:

1. First, test the web services and their JSON output yourself with the following request (change the `q` and `username` parameters as you wish): `http://api.geonames.org/wikipediaSearchJSON?formatted=trueq=londonmaxRows=10 username=postgisstyle=full.`

   You should get the following JSON output:

```
{
  "geonames": [
    {
      "summary": "London is the capital and most populous city of
          England and United Kingdom. Standing on the River Thames,
          London has been a major settlement for two millennia,
          its history going back to its founding by the Romans,
          who named it Londinium (...)",
      "elevation": 8,
      "geoNameId": 2643743,
      "feature": "city",
      "lng": -0.11832,
      "countryCode": "GB",
      "rank": 100,
      "thumbnailImg": "http://www.geonames.org/img/wikipedia/
                      43000/thumb-42715-100.jpg",
      "lang": "en",
      "title": "London",
      "lat": 51.50939,
      "wikipediaUrl": "en.wikipedia.org/wiki/London"
    },
    {
      "summary": "New London is a city and a port of entry on the
          northeast coast of the United States. It is located at
          the mouth of the Thames River in New London County,
          southeastern Connecticut. New London is located about from
          the state capital of Hartford,
          from Boston, Massachusetts, from Providence, Rhode (...)",
      "elevation": 27,
      "feature": "landmark",
      "lng": -72.10083333333333,
      "countryCode": "US",
      "rank": 100,
      "thumbnailImg": "http://www.geonames.org/img/wikipedia/
                      160000/thumb-159123-100.jpg",
      "lang": "en",
```

```
            "title": "New London, Connecticut",
            "lat": 41.355555555555554,
            "wikipediaUrl": "en.wikipedia.org/wiki/
                            New_London%2C_Connecticut"
        }, ...
    ]
}
```

2. As you can see from the JSON output for the GeoNames web service, for a given query string (a location name), you get a list of Wikipedia pages related to that location in JSON format. For each JSON object representing a Wikipedia page, you can get access to the attributes, such as the page `title`, `summary`, `url`, and the `coordinates` of the location.

3. Now, create a text file named `working/chp08/names.txt` with the names of places you would like to geocode from the **Wikipedia Fulltext Search** web services. Add some place names, for example (in Windows, use a text editor such as Notepad):

```
$ vi names.txt
London
Rome
Boston
Chicago
Madrid
Paris
...
```

4. Now, create a file named `import_places.py` under `working/chp08/` and add to it the Python script for this recipe. The following is how the script should look (you should be able to follow it by reading the inline comments and the *How it works...* section):

```
import sys
import requests
import simplejson as json
from osgeo import ogr, osr

MAXROWS = 10
USERNAME = 'postgis' #enter your username here
def CreatePGLayer():
    """
    Create the PostGIS table.
    """
    driver = ogr.GetDriverByName('PostgreSQL')
    srs = osr.SpatialReference()
```

```
srs.ImportFromEPSG(4326)
ogr.UseExceptions()
pg_ds = ogr.Open("PG:dbname='postgis_cookbook' host='localhost'
    port='5432' user='me' password='password'", update = 1)
pg_layer = pg_ds.CreateLayer('wikiplaces', srs = srs,
        geom_type=ogr.wkbPoint, options = [
    'DIM=3',
    # we want to store the elevation value in point z coordinate
    'GEOMETRY_NAME=the_geom',
    'OVERWRITE=YES',
    # this will drop and recreate the table every time
    'SCHEMA=chp08',
])
# add the fields
fd_title = ogr.FieldDefn('title', ogr.OFTString)
pg_layer.CreateField(fd_title)
fd_countrycode = ogr.FieldDefn('countrycode', ogr.OFTString)
pg_layer.CreateField(fd_countrycode)
fd_feature = ogr.FieldDefn('feature', ogr.OFTString)
pg_layer.CreateField(fd_feature)
fd_thumbnail = ogr.FieldDefn('thumbnail', ogr.OFTString)
pg_layer.CreateField(fd_thumbnail)
fd_wikipediaurl = ogr.FieldDefn('wikipediaurl', ogr.OFTString)
pg_layer.CreateField(fd_wikipediaurl)
return pg_ds, pg_layer

def AddPlacesToLayer(places):
"""
  Read the places dictionary list and add features in the
  PostGIS table for each place.
"""
# iterate every place dictionary in the list
print "places: ", places
for place in places:
    lng = place['lng']
    lat = place['lat']
    z = place.get('elevation') if 'elevation' in place else 0
    # we generate a point representation in wkt,
    # and create an ogr geometry
    point_wkt = 'POINT(%s %s %s)' % (lng, lat, z)
    point = ogr.CreateGeometryFromWkt(point_wkt)
    # we create a LayerDefn for the feature using the one
    # from the layer
    featureDefn = pg_layer.GetLayerDefn()
    feature = ogr.Feature(featureDefn)
    # now time to assign the geometry and all the
    # other feature's fields, if the keys are contained
    # in the dictionary (not always the GeoNames
```

```
      # Wikipedia Fulltext Search contains all of the information)
      feature.SetGeometry(point)
      feature.SetField('title',
        place['title'].encode("utf-8") if 'title' in place else '')
      feature.SetField('countrycode',
        place['countryCode'] if 'countryCode' in place else '')
      feature.SetField('feature',
        place['feature'] if 'feature' in place else '')
      feature.SetField('thumbnail',
        place['thumbnailImg'] if 'thumbnailImg' in place else '')
      feature.SetField('wikipediaurl',
        place['wikipediaUrl'] if 'wikipediaUrl' in place else '')
      # here we create the feature (the INSERT SQL is issued here)
      pg_layer.CreateFeature(feature)
      print 'Created a places titled %s.' % place['title']

  def GetPlaces(placename):
      """
        Get the places list for a given placename.
      """
      # uri to access the JSON GeoNames Wikipedia Fulltext Search
      # web service
      uri = ('http://api.geonames.org/wikipediaSearchJSON?
          formatted=true&q=%s&maxRows=%s&username=%s&style=full'
          % (placename, MAXROWS, USERNAME))
      data = requests.get(uri)
      js_data = json.loads(data.text)
      return js_data['geonames']

  def GetNamesList(filepath):
      """
        Open a file with a given filepath containing place names
        and return a list.
      """
      f = open(filepath, 'r')
      return f.read().splitlines()

# first we need to create a PostGIS table to contains the places
# we must keep the PostGIS OGR dataset and layer global,
# for the reasons
# described here: http://trac.osgeo.org/gdal/wiki/PythonGotchas
from osgeo import gdal
gdal.UseExceptions()
pg_ds, pg_layer = CreatePGLayer()
```

```
try:
    # query geonames for each name and store found
    # places in the table
    names = GetNamesList('names.txt')
    print names
        for name in names:
        AddPlacesToLayer(GetPlaces(name))
except Exception as e:
    print(e)
    print sys.exc_info()[0]
```

5. Now, execute the Python script:

```
(postgis-cb-env)$ python import_places.py
```

```
Chapter 8 — bash — 70×25

: u'http://www.geonames.org/img/wikipedia/77000/thumb-76073-100.jpg'},
{u'lang': u'en', u'elevation': 35, u'countryCode': u'fr', u'title': u
'La Courneuve', u'geoNameId': 3009824, u'feature': u'city', u'rank': 1
00, u'summary': u'La Courneuve is a commune in Seine-Saint-Denis, Fran
ce. It is located from the center of Paris.  (...)', u'wikipediaUrl':
u'en.wikipedia.org/wiki/La_Courneuve', u'lat': 48.9322, u'lng': 2.3967
, u'thumbnailImg': u'http://www.geonames.org/img/wikipedia/87000/thumb
-86056-100.jpg'}, {u'lang': u'en', u'elevation': 49, u'countryCode': u
'fr', u'title': u'Charenton-le-Pont', u'geoNameId': 3026637, u'feature
': u'city', u'rank': 100, u'summary': u'Charenton-le-Pont is a commune
 in the southeastern suburbs of Paris, France. It is located from the
centre of Paris. It is one of the most densely populated municipalitie
s in Europe. The Charenton Psychiatric Hospital is located in the neig
hbouring commune Charenton-Saint-Maurice, which changed its (...)', u'
wikipediaUrl': u'en.wikipedia.org/wiki/Charenton-le-Pont', u'lat': 48.
821389, u'lng': 2.411944, u'thumbnailImg': u'http://www.geonames.org/i
mg/wikipedia/47000/thumb-46131-100.jpg'}]
Created a places titled Gare de Paris-Est.
Created a places titled Paris.
Created a places titled Paris-Gare de Lyon.
Created a places titled Gare Montparnasse.
Created a places titled Sorbonne.
Created a places titled University of Paris.
Created a places titled Gennevilliers.
Created a places titled Notre Dame de Paris.
```

6. Test whether the table was correctly created and populated using SQL and use your favorite GIS desktop tool to display the layer:

```
postgis_cookbook=# select ST_AsText(the_geom), title,
    countrycode, feature from chp08.wikiplaces;
```

	st_astext text	title character varying	countrycode character varying	feature character varying
1	POINT Z (-0.11832 51.50...	London	GB	city
2	POINT Z (-72.100833333...	New London, Con...	US	landmark
3	POINT Z (-81.2497 42.98...	London, Ontario	CA	city
4	POINT Z (27.9036078333...	East London, East...	ZA	city
5	POINT Z (-0.086 51.4965...	London Borough o...	GB	adm1st
6	POINT Z (-0.087778 51.5...	London Bridge	GB	landmark
7	POINT Z (-0.1004 51.372...	London Borough o...	GB	adm1st
8	POINT Z (-0.119722 51.5...	London Eye	GB	landmark
9	POINT Z (-0.333333 51.4...	London Borough o...	GB	adm1st
10	POINT Z (-0.1448 51.496...	London Victoria st...	GB	landmark
11	POINT Z (12.501944 41.9...	Roma Termini rail...	AT	landmark
12	POINT Z (-85.170833 34....	Rome, Georgia	US	city
13	POINT Z (12.71667 41.81...	Monte Porzio Cato...	IT	adm3rd
14	POINT Z (12.2775 42.088...	Anguillara Sabazia	IT	adm3rd
15	POINT Z (12.476816 41.8...	Pantheon, Rome		landmark
16	POINT Z (12.452 41.903 ...	Vatican City		city

```
(60 rows)
```

How it works...

This Python script uses the `requests` and `simplejson` libraries to fetch data from the GeoNames `wikipediaSearchJSON` web service, and the GDAL/OGR library to store geographic information inside the PostGIS database.

First, you create a PostGIS point table to store the geographic data. This is made using the GDAL/OGR bindings. You need to instantiate an OGR PostGIS driver (http://www.gdal.org/drv_pg.html) from where it is possible to instantiate a dataset to connect to your `postgis_cookbook` database using a specified connection string.

The `update` parameter in the connection string specifies to the GDAL driver that you will open the dataset for updating.

From the PostGIS dataset, we created a PostGIS layer named `wikiplaces` that will store points (`geom_type=ogr.wkbPoint`) using the *WGS 84* spatial reference system (`srs.ImportFromEPSG(4326)`). When creating the layer, we specified other parameters as well, such as `dimension` (3, as you want to store the z values), `GEOMETRY_NAME` (name of the geometric field), and `schema`. After creating the layer, you can use the `CreateField` layer method to create all the fields that are needed to store the information. Each field will have a specific `name` and `datatype` (all of them are `ogr.OFTString` in this case).

After the layer has been created (note that we need to have the `pg_ds` and `pg_layer` objects always in context for the whole script, as noted at `http://trac.osgeo.org/gdal/wiki/PythonGotchas`), you can query the GeoNames web services for each place name in the `names.txt` file using the `urllib2` library.

We parsed the JSON response using the `simplejson` library, then iterated the JSON objects list and added a feature to the PostGIS layer for each of the objects in the JSON output. For each element, we created a feature with a point `wkt` geometry (using the `lng`, `lat`, and `elevation` object attributes) using the `ogr.CreateGeometryFromWkt` method, and updated the other fields using the other object attributes returned by GeoNames, using the feature `setField` method (`title`, `countryCode`, and so on).

You can get more information on programming with GDAL Python bindings by using the following great resource by *Chris Garrard*:

`https://www.manning.com/books/geoprocessing-with-python`

Writing PostGIS functions with PL/Python

In this recipe, you will write a Python function for PostGIS using the PL/Python language. The PL/Python procedural language allows you to write PostgreSQL functions with the Python language.

You will use Python to query the `http://openweathermap.org/` web services, already used in a previous recipe, to get the weather for a PostGIS geometry from within a PostgreSQL function.

Getting ready

1. Verify your PostgreSQL server installation has PL/Python support. In Windows, this should be already included, but this is not the default if you are using, for example, Ubuntu 16.04 LTS, so you will most likely need to install it:

   ```
   $ sudo apt-get install postgresql-plpython-9.1
   ```

2. Install PL/Python on the database (you could consider installing it in your `template1` database; in this way, every newly created database will have PL/Python support by default):

   You could alternatively add PL/Python support to your database, using the `createlang` shell command (this is the only way if you are using PostgreSQL version 9.1 or lower):
   ```
   $ createlang plpythonu postgis_cookbook
   $ psql -U me postgis_cookbook
   postgis_cookbook=# CREATE EXTENSION plpythonu;
   ```

How to do it...

Carry out the following steps:

1. In this recipe, as with the previous one, you will use a `http://openweathermap.org/` web service to get the temperature for a point from the closest weather station. The request you need to run (test it in a browser) is
   `http://api.openweathermap.org/data/2.5/find?lat=55&lon=37&cnt=10&appid=YOURKEY`.

2. You should get the following JSON output (the closest weather station's data from which you will read the temperature to the point, with the coordinates of the given longitude and latitude):

   ```
   {
     message: "",
     cod: "200",
     calctime: "",
     cnt: 1,
     list: [
       {
         id: 9191,
         dt: 1369343192,
   ```

```
name: "100704-1",
type: 2,
coord: {
    lat: 13.7408,
    lon: 100.5478
},
distance: 6.244,
main: {
    temp: 300.37
},
wind: {
    speed: 0,
    deg: 141
},
rang: 30,
rain: {
    1h: 0,
    24h: 3.302,
    today: 0
}
}
]
}
```

3. Create the following PostgreSQL function in Python, using the PL/Python language:

```
CREATE OR REPLACE FUNCTION chp08.GetWeather(lon float, lat float)
  RETURNS float AS $$
  import urllib2
  import simplejson as json
  data = urllib2.urlopen(
    'http://api.openweathermap.org/data/
    2.1/find/station?lat=%s&lon=%s&cnt=1'
    % (lat, lon))
  js_data = json.load(data)
  if js_data['cod'] == '200':
  # only if cod is 200 we got some effective results
    if int(js_data['cnt'])>0:
    # check if we have at least a weather station
      station = js_data['list'][0]
      print 'Data from weather station %s' % station['name']
      if 'main' in station:
        if 'temp' in station['main']:
          temperature = station['main']['temp'] - 273.15
          # we want the temperature in Celsius
        else:
```

```
            temperature = None
    else:
        temperature = None
    return temperature
$$ LANGUAGE plpythonu;
```

4. Now, test your function; for example, get the temperature from the weather station closest to Wat Pho Templum in Bangkok:

```
postgis_cookbook=# SELECT chp08.GetWeather(100.49, 13.74);
getweather
------------
27.22
(1 row)
```

5. If you want to get the temperature for the point features in a PostGIS table, you can use the coordinates of each feature's geometry:

```
postgis_cookbook=# SELECT name, temperature,
chp08.GetWeather(ST_X(the_geom), ST_Y(the_geom))
AS temperature2 FROM chp08.cities LIMIT 5;
name        | temperature | temperature2
------------+-------------+--------------
Minneapolis |     275.15  |        15
Saint Paul  |     274.15  |        16
Buffalo     |     274.15  |     19.44
New York    |     280.93  |     19.44
Jersey City |     282.15  |     21.67
(5 rows)
```

6. Now it would be nice if our function could accept not only the coordinates of a point, but also a true PostGIS geometry as well as an input parameter. For the temperature of a feature, you could return the temperature of the weather station closest to the centroid of the feature geometry. You can easily get this behavior using function overloading. Add a new function, with the same name, supporting a PostGIS geometry directly as an input parameter. In the body of the function, call the previous function, passing the coordinates of the centroid of the geometry. Note that in this case, you can write the function without using Python, with the PL/PostgreSQL language:

```
CREATE OR REPLACE FUNCTION chp08.GetWeather(geom geometry)
RETURNS float AS $$
BEGIN
   RETURN chp08.GetWeather(ST_X(ST_Centroid(geom)),
          ST_Y(ST_Centroid(geom)));
```

```
END;
$$ LANGUAGE plpgsql;
```

7. Now, test the function, passing a PostGIS geometry to the function:

```
postgis_cookbook=# SELECT chp08.GetWeather(
  ST_GeomFromText('POINT(-71.064544 42.28787)'));
  getweather
------------
23.89
(1 row)
```

8. If you use the function on a PostGIS layer, you can pass the feature's geometries to the function directly, using the overloaded function written in the PL/PostgreSQL language:

```
postgis_cookbook=# SELECT name, temperature,
chp08.GetWeather(the_geom) AS temperature2
FROM chp08.cities LIMIT 5;
 name        | temperature | temperature2
-------------+-------------+--------------
 Minneapolis |     275.15 |     17.22
 Saint Paul  |     274.15 |        16
 Buffalo     |     274.15 |     18.89
 New York    |     280.93 |     19.44
 Jersey City |     282.15 |     21.67
(5 rows)
```

How it works...

In this recipe, you wrote a Python function in PostGIS, using the PL/Python language. Using Python inside PostgreSQL and PostGIS functions gives you the great advantage of being able to use any Python library you wish. Therefore, you will be able to write much more powerful functions compared to those written using the standard PL/PostgreSQL language.

In fact, in this case, you used the urllib2 and simplejson Python libraries to query a web service from within a PostgreSQL function—this would be an impossible operation to do using plain PL/PostgreSQL. You have also seen how to overload functions in order to provide the function's user a different way to access the function, using input parameters in a different way.

Geocoding and reverse geocoding using the GeoNames datasets

In this recipe, you will write two PL/PostgreSQL PostGIS functions that will let you perform geocoding and reverse geocoding using the GeoNames datasets.

GeoNames is a database of place names in the world, containing over 8 million records that are available for download free of charge. For the purpose of this recipe, you will download a part of the database, load it in PostGIS, and then use it within two functions to perform geocoding and reverse geocoding. **Geocoding** is the process of finding coordinates from geographical data, such as an address or a place name, while **reverse geocoding** is the process of finding geographical data, such as an address or place name, from its coordinates.

You are going to write the two functions using PL/pgSQL, which adds on top of the PostgreSQL SQL commands the ability to tie more commands and queries together, a bunch of control structures, cursors, error management, and other goodness.

Getting ready

Download a GeoNames dataset. At the time of writing, you can find some of the datasets ready to be downloaded from `http://download.geonames.org/export/dump/`. You may decide which dataset you want to use; if you want to follow this recipe, it will be enough to download the Italian dataset, `IT.zip` (included in the book's dataset, in the `chp08` directory).

If you want to download the full GeoNames dataset, you need to download the `allCountries.zip` file; it will take longer as it is about 250 MB.

How to do it...

Carry out the following steps:

1. Unzip the `IT.zip` file to the `working/chp08` directory. Two files will be extracted: the `readme.txt` file that contains information on the GeoNames database structure—you can read it to get some more information—and the `IT.txt` file, which is a `.csv` file containing all the GeoNames entities for Italy. As suggested in the `readme.txt` file, the content of the CSV file is composed of records with the following attributes:

```
geonameid          : integer id of record in geonames  database
name               : name of geographical point (utf8) varchar(200)
asciiname          : name of geographical point in  plain
                     ascii characters, varchar(200)
alternatenames     : alternatenames, comma separated varchar(5000)
latitude           : latitude in decimal degrees (wgs84)
longitude          : longitude in decimal degrees (wgs84)
...
```

2. Get an overview of this CSV dataset, using `ogrinfo`:

```
$ ogrinfo CSV:IT.txt IT -al -so
```

```
● ● ●                     IT — bash — 70×27
          using driver `CSV' successful.

Layer name: IT
Geometry: Point
Feature Count: 49700
Extent: (1.200000, 35.483330) - (27.766670, 48.966670)
Layer SRS WKT:
(unknown)
GEONAMEID: String (0.0)
NAME: String (0.0)
ASCIINAME: String (0.0)
ALTNAMES: String (0.0)
LATITUDE: Real (0.0)
LONGITUDE: Real (0.0)
FEATCLASS: String (0.0)
FEATCODE: String (0.0)
COUNTRY: String (0.0)
CC2: String (0.0)
ADMIN1: String (0.0)
ADMIN2: String (0.0)
ADMIN3: String (0.0)
ADMIN4: String (0.0)
POPULATION: Real (0.0)
ELEVATION: Integer (0.0)
GTOPO30: Integer (0.0)
TIMEZONE: String (0.0)
MODDATE: String (0.0)
```

3. You could query the `IT.txt` file as an OGR entity. For example, analyze one of the dataset features, as shown in the following code:

```
$ ogrinfo CSV:IT.txt IT -where "NAME = 'San Gimignano'"
```

```
 ● ● ●                    IT — bash — 80×29
  ELEVATION (Integer) = (null)
  GTOP030 (Integer) = 312
  TIMEZONE (String) = Europe/Rome
  MODDATE (String) = 2012-02-15
  POINT (11.04272 43.46924)

OGRFeature(IT):37204
  GEONAMEID (String) = 6539741
  NAME (String) = San Gimignano
  ASCIINAME (String) = San Gimignano
  ALTNAMES (String) = Comune di San Gimignano,San Gimignano
  LATITUDE (Real) = 43.46924
  LONGITUDE (Real) = 11.04272
  FEATCLASS (String) = A
  FEATCODE (String) = ADM3
  COUNTRY (String) = IT
  CC2 (String) =
  ADMIN1 (String) = 16
  ADMIN2 (String) = SI
  ADMIN3 (String) = 052028
  ADMIN4 (String) =
  POPULATION (Real) = 7770
  ELEVATION (Integer) = (null)
  GTOP030 (Integer) = 312
  TIMEZONE (String) = Europe/Rome
  MODDATE (String) = 2011-02-25
  POINT (11.04272 43.46924)

Nina:IT may$
```

4. For your purpose, you just need the `name`, `asciiname`, `latitude`, and `longitude` attributes. You will import the file to PostGIS using the CSV OGR driver (`http://www.gdal.org/drv_csv.html`). Use the `ogr2ogr` command to import this GeoNames dataset in PostGIS:

```
$ ogr2ogr -f PostgreSQL -s_srs EPSG:4326 -t_srs EPSG:4326
-lco GEOMETRY_NAME=the_geom -nln chp08.geonames
PG:"dbname='postgis_cookbook' user='me' password='mypassword'"
CSV:IT.txt -sql "SELECT NAME, ASCIINAME FROM IT"
```

5. Try to query the new `geonames` table in PostGIS to see if the process works correctly:

```
postgis_cookbook=# SELECT ST_AsText(the_geom), name
FROM chp08.geonames LIMIT 10;
```

6. Now, create a PL/PostgreSQL function that will return the five place names closest to the given point and their coordinates (reverse geocoding):

```
CREATE OR REPLACE FUNCTION chp08.Get_Closest_PlaceNames(
    in_geom geometry, num_results int DEFAULT 5,
    OUT geom geometry, OUT place_name character varying)
RETURNS SETOF RECORD AS $$
BEGIN
  RETURN QUERY
  SELECT the_geom as geom, name as place_name
  FROM chp08.geonames
  ORDER BY the_geom <-> ST_Centroid(in_geom) LIMIT num_results;
END;
$$ LANGUAGE plpgsql;
```

7. Query the new function. You can specify the number of results you want by passing the optional `num_results` input parameter:

```
postgis_cookbook=# SELECT * FROM chp08.Get_Closest_PlaceNames(
  ST_PointFromText('POINT(13.5 42.19)', 4326), 10);
```

The following is the output for this query:

	geom geometry	place_name character varying
1	01010000...	Monte Rotondo
2	01010000...	Monte Canelle
3	01010000...	Rocca di Mezzo
4	01010000...	Rocca di Mezzo
5	01010000...	Monte Selva Canuta
6	01010000...	Rovere
7	01010000...	Rocca di Cambio
8	01010000...	Rocca di Cambio
9	01010000...	Monte della Cerreta
10	01010000...	Terranera

8. If you don't specify the `num_results` optional parameter, it will default to five results:

```
postgis_cookbook=# SELECT * FROM chp08.Get_Closest_PlaceNames(
ST_PointFromText('POINT(13.5 42.19)', 4326));
```

And you will get the following rows:

	geom geometry	place_name character varying
1	01010000...	Monte Rotondo
2	01010000...	Monte Canelle
3	01010000...	Rocca di Mezzo
4	01010000...	Rocca di Mezzo
5	01010000...	Monte Selva Canuta

9. Now, create a PL/pgSQL function that will return a list of place names and geometries containing a text search in their name field (geocoding):

```
CREATE OR REPLACE FUNCTION chp08.Find_PlaceNames(search_string text,
    num_results int DEFAULT 5,
    OUT geom geometry,
    OUT place_name character varying)
RETURNS SETOF RECORD AS $$
BEGIN
    RETURN QUERY
    SELECT the_geom as geom, name as place_name
    FROM chp08.geonames
    WHERE name @@ to_tsquery(search_string)
    LIMIT num_results;
END;
$$ LANGUAGE plpgsql;
```

10. Query this second function to check if it is working properly:

```
postgis_cookbook=# SELECT * FROM chp08.Find_PlaceNames('Rocca', 10);
```

	geom geometry	place_name character varying
1	01010000...	Rocca di Neto
2	01010000...	Rocca
3	01010000...	Rocca Pignatello
4	01010000...	Rocca Mollachella
5	01010000...	La Rocca
6	01010000...	Casa la Rocca
7	01010000...	Rocca Busambra
8	01010000...	Alessandria della ...
9	01010000...	Santa Maria Rocca
10	01010000...	Torre di Rocca Ve...

How it works...

In this recipe, you wrote two PostgreSQL functions to perform geocoding and reverse geocoding. For both the functions, you defined a set of input and output parameters, and after some PL/PostgreSQL processing, you returned a set of records to the function client, given by executing a query.

As the input parameters, the Get_Closest_PlaceNames function accepts a PostGIS geometry and an optional num_results parameter that is set to a default of 5 in case the function caller does not provide it. The output of this function is SETOF RECORD, which is returned after running a query in the function body (defined by the $$ notation). Here, the query finds the places closest to the centroid of the input geometry. This is done using an indexed nearest neighbor search (KNN index), a new feature available in PostGIS 2.

The Find_PlaceNames function accepts as the input parameters a search string to look for and an optional num_results parameter, which in this case is also set to a default of 5 if not provided by the function caller. The output is a SETOF RECORD, which is returned after running a query that uses the to_tsquery PostgreSQL text search function. The results of the query are the places from the database that contain the search_string value in the name field.

Geocoding using the OSM datasets with trigrams

In this recipe, you will use **OpenStreetMap** streets' datasets imported in PostGIS to implement a very basic Python class in order to provide geocoding features to the class' consumer. The geocode engine will be based on the implementation of the PostgreSQL trigrams provided by the `contrib` module of PostgreSQL: `pg_trgm`.

A trigram is a group of three consecutive characters contained in a string, and it is a very effective way to measure the similarity of two strings by counting the number of trigrams they have in common.

This recipe aims to be a very basic sample to implement some kinds of geocoding functionalities (it will just return one or more points from a street name), but it could be extended to support more advanced features.

Getting ready

1. For this recipe, make sure you have the latest GDAL, at least version 1.10, as you will use it with the `ogr2ogr` the OGR OSM driver (`http://www.gdal.org/drv_osm.html`):

   ```
   $ ogrinfo --version GDAL 2.1.2, released 2016/10/24
   $ ogrinfo --formats | grep -i osm
   -> "OSM -vector- (rov): OpenStreetMap XML and PBF"
   ```

2. As you will use PostgreSQL trigrams, install the PostgreSQL `contrib` package (which includes `pg_trgm`). The Windows EDB installer should already include this. In an Ubuntu 12.4 box, the following command will help you to do it:

   ```
   $ sudo apt-get install postgresql-contrib-9.1
   ```

3. Make sure to add the `pg_trgm` extension to the database:

   ```
   postgis_cookbook=# CREATE EXTENSION pg_trgm;
   CREATE EXTENSION
   ```

You will need to use some OSM datasets included in the source for this chapter. (in the `data/chp08` book's dataset directory). If you are using Windows, be sure to have installed the OSGeo4W suite, as suggested in the initial instructions for this chapter.

4. If you are using Linux, follow the initial instructions for this chapter and create a Python virtual environment in order to keep a Python-isolated environment to be used for all the Python recipes of this book. Then, activate it as follows:

```
$ source postgis-cb-env/bin/activate
```

5. Once the environment has been activated, if you still haven't done so, you can install the Python packages needed for this recipe:

```
(postgis-cb-env)$ pip install pygdal
(postgis-cb-env)$ pip install psycopg2
```

How to do it...

Carry out the following steps:

1. First, check out how the OSM `.pbf` file is built using `ogrinfo`. PBF is a binary format intended as an alternative to the OSM XML format, mainly because it is much smaller. As you must have noticed, it is composed of several layers—you will export the `lines` layer to PostGIS as that layer contains the street names that you will use for the overall geocoding process:

```
$ ogrinfo lazio.pbf
  Had to open data source read-only.
  INFO: Open of `lazio.pbf'
    using driver `OSM' successful.
1: points (Point)
2: lines (Line String)
3: multilinestrings (Multi Line String)
4: multipolygons (Multi Polygon)
5: other_relations (Geometry Collection)
```

2. Export the lines' OSM features to a PostGIS table, using `ogr2ogr` (ogr2ogr, as always, will implicitly create the GiST index that is needed by the `pg_trgm` module to run):

```
$ ogr2ogr -f PostgreSQL -lco GEOMETRY_NAME=the_geom
-nln chp08.osm_roads
PG:"dbname='postgis_cookbook' user='me'
password='mypassword'" lazio.pbf lines
```

3. Now try a trigram matching to identify the road names similar to a given search text, using a query such as the following. Note that the `similarity` function returns a value that decreases from 1 to 0 as the similarity of the word decreases (with 1, the strings are identical; with 0, they are totally different):

```
postgis_cookbook=# SELECT name,
    similarity(name, 'via benedetto croce') AS sml,
    ST_AsText(ST_Centroid(the_geom)) AS the_geom
FROM chp08.osm_roads
WHERE name % 'via benedetto croce'
ORDER BY sml DESC, name;
```

	name character varying	sml real	the_geom text
1	Via Benedetto Cro...	1	POINT(12....
2	Via Benedetto Cro...	1	POINT(13....
3	Via Benedetto Cro...	1	POINT(12....
4	Via Benedetto Cro...	1	POINT(13....
5	Via Benedetto Cro...	1	POINT(13....
6	Via Benedetto Cro...	1	POINT(12....
7	Via Benedetto Cro...	1	POINT(14....
8	Via Benedetto Cro...	1	POINT(12....
9	Via Benedetto XV	0.608696	POINT(12....
10	Piazza Benedetto ...	0.592593	POINT(12....
11	Via Benedetto XIV	0.583333	POINT(12....
12	Via Benedetto XIV	0.583333	POINT(12....
13	Via San Benedetto	0.583333	POINT(13....
14	Via San Benedetto	0.583333	POINT(13....
15	Via Benedetto Stay	0.56	POINT(12....
16	Via Benedetto Stay	0.56	POINT(12....

4. As a variant, you will use the following query to complete the recipe (in this case, when the weight is 0, the strings are identical):

```
postgis_cookbook=# SELECT name,
  name <-> 'via benedetto croce' AS weight
FROM chp08.osm_roads
ORDER BY weight LIMIT 10;
```

	name character varying	weight real
1	Via Benedetto Cro...	0
2	Via Benedetto Cro...	0
3	Via Benedetto Cro...	0
4	Via Benedetto Cro...	0
5	Via Benedetto Cro...	0
6	Via Benedetto Cro...	0
7	Via Benedetto Cro...	0
8	Via Benedetto Cro...	0
9	Via Benedetto XV	0.391304
10	Piazza Benedetto ...	0.407407

5. We will use the last query as the SQL core of a Python class, which will provide geocoding features to the consumer, using the layer we just imported in PostGIS (chp08.osm_roads). First, create a file named osmgeocoder.py and add the following class to it:

```python
import sys
import psycopg2

class OSMGeocoder(object):
    """
    A class to provide geocoding features using an OSM
    dataset in PostGIS.
    """

    def __init__(self, db_connectionstring):
        # initialize db connection parameters
        self.db_connectionstring = db_connectionstring

    def geocode(self, placename):
        """
        Geocode a given place name.
```

```
"""
# here we create the connection object
conn = psycopg2.connect(self.db_connectionstring)
cur = conn.cursor()
# this is the core sql query, using trigrams to detect
# streets similar to a given placename
sql = """
  SELECT name, name <-> '%s' AS weight,
  ST_AsText(ST_Centroid(the_geom)) as  point
  FROM chp08.osm_roads
  ORDER BY weight LIMIT 10;
""" % placename
# here we execute the sql and return all of the results
cur.execute(sql)
rows = cur.fetchall()
cur.close()
conn.close()
return rows
```

6. Now, add the __main__ check to provide the class user a method to directly use the geocoder from the command line:

```
if __name__ == '__main__':
  # the user must provide at least two parameters, the place name
  # and the connection string to PostGIS
  if len(sys.argv) < 3 or len(sys.argv) > 3:
    print "usage: <placename> <connection string>"
    raise SystemExit
  placename = sys.argv[1]
  db_connectionstring = sys.argv[2]
  # here we instantiate the geocoder, providing the needed
  # PostGIS connection parameters
  geocoder = OSMGeocoder(db_connectionstring)
  # here we query the geocode method, for getting the
  # geocoded points for the given placename
  results = geocoder.geocode(placename)
  print results
```

7. Now you can test the class by calling the script, as shown here:

```
(postgis-cb-env)$ python osmgeocoder.py "Via Benedetto Croce"
  "dbname=postgis_cookbook user=me password=mypassword"
[('Via Benedetto Croce', 0.0, 'POINT(12.6999095325807
                                  42.058016054317)'),...
```

8. So, now that you wrote a class that can be used to geocode street names, let's suppose that another user wants to use it to geocode a file with a list of street names in order to import it in a new PostGIS layer. Here is how the user could do this (try this as well). First, create a `streets.txt` file with a list of street names; for example:

```
Via Delle Sette Chiese
Via Benedetto Croce
Lungotevere Degli Inventori
Viale Marco Polo
Via Cavour
```

9. Now, create a file named `geocode_streets.py` and add this Python code to it (you are going to use the `OSMGeocoder` class to geocode the street name list, and GDAL/OGR to create a new PostGIS layer for storing the geocoded points for the street names):

```python
from osmgeocoder import OSMGeocoder
from osgeo import ogr, osr

# here we read the file
f = open('streets.txt')
streets = f.read().splitlines()
f.close()

# here we create the PostGIS layer using gdal/ogr
driver = ogr.GetDriverByName('PostgreSQL')
srs = osr.SpatialReference()
srs.ImportFromEPSG(4326)
pg_ds = ogr.Open(
  "PG:dbname='postgis_cookbook' host='localhost' port='5432'
     user='me' password='mypassword'", update = 1 )
  pg_layer = pg_ds.CreateLayer('geocoded_points', srs = srs,
        geom_type=ogr.wkbPoint, options = [
     'GEOMETRY_NAME=the_geom',
     'OVERWRITE=YES',
       # this will drop and recreate the table every time
     'SCHEMA=chp08',
  ])
# here we add the field to the PostGIS layer
fd_name = ogr.FieldDefn('name', ogr.OFTString)
pg_layer.CreateField(fd_name)
print 'Table created.'

# now we geocode all of the streets in the file
# using the osmgeocoder class
```

```
geocoder = OSMGeocoder('dbname=postgis_cookbook user=me
                        password=mypassword')
for street in streets:
  print street
  geocoded_street = geocoder.geocode(street)[0]
  print geocoded_street
  # format is
  # ('Via delle Sette Chiese', 0.0,
  #  'POINT(12.5002166330412 41.859774874774)')
  point_wkt = geocoded_street[2]
  point = ogr.CreateGeometryFromWkt(point_wkt)
  # we create a LayerDefn for the feature using the
  # one from the layer
  featureDefn = pg_layer.GetLayerDefn()
  feature = ogr.Feature(featureDefn)
  # now we store the feature geometry and
  # the value for the name field
  feature.SetGeometry(point)
  feature.SetField('name', geocoded_street[0])
  # finally we create the feature
  # (an INSERT command is issued only here)
  pg_layer.CreateFeature(feature)
```

10. Run the preceding script, and then check with your favorite PostgreSQL client or with a GIS desktop tool if the points for the street names were correctly geocoded:

```
(postgis-cb-env)capooti@ubuntu:~/postgis_cookbook/working/chp08$
python geocode_streets.py
Table created.
Via Delle Sette Chiese
('Via delle Sette Chiese', 0.0,
 'POINT(12.5002166330412 41.859774874774)')
...
Via Cavour
('Via Cavour', 0.0, 'POINT(12.7519263341222 41.9631244835521)')
```

How it works...

For this recipe, you first imported an OSM dataset to PostGIS with `ogr2ogr`, using the GDAL OSM driver.

Then, you created a Python class, `OSMGeocoder`, to provide very basic support to the class consumer for geocoding street names, using the OSM data imported in PostGIS. For this purpose, you used the trigram support included in PostgreSQL with the `pg_trgm contrib` module.

The class that you have written is mainly composed of two methods: the `__init__` method, where the connection parameters must be passed in order to instantiate an `OSMGeocoder` object, and the `geocode` method. The `geocode` method accepts an input parameter, `placename`, and creates a connection to the PostGIS database using the Psycopg2 library in order to execute a query to find the streets in the database with a name similar to the `placename` parameter.

The class can be consumed both from the command line, using the `__name__` == `'__main__'` code block, or from an external Python code. You tried both approaches. In the latter, you created another Python script, where you imported the `OSMGeocoder` class combined with the GDAL/OGR Python bindings to generate a new PostGIS point layer with features resulted from a list of geocoded street names.

Geocoding with geopy and PL/Python

In this recipe, you will geocode addresses using web geocoding APIs, such as Google Maps, Yahoo! Maps, Geocoder, GeoNames, and so on. Be sure to read the terms of service of these APIs carefully before using them in production.

The `geopy` Python library (`https://github.com/geopy/geopy`) offers convenient uniform access to all of these web services. Therefore, you will use it to create a PL/Python PostgreSQL function that can be used in your SQL commands to query all of these engines.

Getting ready

1. Install `geopy` globally. (You cannot use a virtual environment in this case, as the user running the PostgreSQL service needs to access it on its Python path.)

   In a Debian/Ubuntu box, it is as easy as typing the following:

   ```
   $ sudo pip install geopy
   ```

In Windows, you can use the following command:

```
> pip install geopy
```

2. If you still have not used PL/Python, verify whether your PostgreSQL server installation supports it. The Windows EDB installer should already include support, but this is not the default if you are using, for example, Ubuntu 16.04 LTS, so you most likely need to install it:

```
$ sudo apt-get install postgresql-plpython-9.1
```

3. Install PL/Python in the database (you could consider installing it in the `template1` database; this way, every newly created database will have PL/Python support by default):

```
$ psql -U me postgis_cookbook
psql (9.1.6, server 9.1.8)
Type "help" for help.
postgis_cookbook=# CREATE EXTENSION plpythonu;
```

Alternatively, you could add PL/Python support to your database, using the `createlang` shell command (this is the only way if you are using PostgreSQL Version 9.1 and lower):
```
$ createlang plpythonu postgis_cookbook
```

How to do it...

Carry out the following steps:

1. As the first test, open your favorite SQL client (`psql` or `pgAdmin`), and write a very basic PL/Python function, just using the GoogleV3 geocoding API with `geopy`. The function will accept the address string as an input parameter and, after importing `geopy`, it will instantiate a `geopy` Google Geocoder, run the geocode process, and then return the point geometry, using the `ST_GeomFromText` function and the `geopy` output:

```
CREATE OR REPLACE FUNCTION chp08.Geocode(address text)
  RETURNS geometry(Point,4326) AS $$
  from geopy import geocoders
  g = geocoders.GoogleV3()
  place, (lat, lng) = g.geocode(address)
  plpy.info('Geocoded %s for the address: %s' % (place, address))
  plpy.info('Longitude is %s, Latitude is %s.' % (lng, lat))
  plpy.info("SELECT ST_GeomFromText('POINT(%s %s)', 4326)"
```

```
                % (lng, lat))
     result = plpy.execute("SELECT ST_GeomFromText('POINT(%s %s)',
                           4326) AS point_geocoded" % (lng, lat))
     geometry = result[0]["point_geocoded"]
     return geometry
  $$ LANGUAGE plpythonu;
```

2. After creating the function, try to test it:

```
postgis_cookbook=# SELECT chp08.Geocode('Viale Ostiense 36, Rome');
INFO:   Geocoded Via Ostiense, 36, 00154 Rome,
Italy for the address: Viale Ostiense 36, Rome
CONTEXT:   PL/Python function "geocode"
INFO:   Longitude is 12.480457, Latitude is 41.874345.
CONTEXT:   PL/Python function "geocode"
INFO:   SELECT ST_GeomFromText('POINT(12.480457 41.874345)', 4326)
CONTEXT:   PL/Python function "geocode"
                   geocode
--------------------------------------------------------
0101000020E6100000BF44BC75FEF52840E7357689EAEF4440
(1 row)
```

3. Now, you will make the function a little bit more sophisticated. First, you will add another input parameter to let the user specify the geocode API engine (defaulting to GoogleV3). Then, using the Python try...except block, you will try to add some kind of error management in case the geopy Geocoder cannot manage to return valid results for any reason:

```
CREATE OR REPLACE FUNCTION chp08.Geocode(address text,
                                     api text DEFAULT 'google')
RETURNS geometry(Point,4326) AS $$
from geopy import geocoders
plpy.info('Geocoing the given address using the %s api' % (api))
if api.lower() == 'geonames':
  g = geocoders.GeoNames()
elif api.lower() == 'geocoderdotus':
  g = geocoders.GeocoderDotUS()
else: # in all other cases, we use google
  g = geocoders.GoogleV3()
try:
  place, (lat, lng) = g.geocode(address)
  plpy.info('Geocoded %s for the address: %s' % (place, address))
   plpy.info('Longitude is %s, Latitude is %s.' % (lng, lat))
  result = plpy.execute("SELECT ST_GeomFromText('POINT(%s %s)',
                        4326) AS point_geocoded" % (lng, lat))
  geometry = result[0]["point_geocoded"]
  return geometry
```

```
except:
  plpy.warning('There was an error in the geocoding process,
               setting geometry to Null.')
  return None
$$ LANGUAGE plpythonu;
```

4. Test the new version of your function without specifying the parameter for the API. In such a case, it should default to the Google API:

```
postgis_cookbook=# SELECT chp08.Geocode('161 Court Street,
                  Brooklyn, NY');
INFO:  Geocoing the given address using the google api
CONTEXT:  PL/Python function "geocode2"
INFO:  Geocoded 161 Court Street, Brooklyn, NY 11201,
       USA for the address: 161 Court Street, Brooklyn, NY
CONTEXT:  PL/Python function "geocode2"
INFO:  Longitude is -73.9924659, Latitude is 40.688665.
CONTEXT:  PL/Python function "geocode2"
INFO:  SELECT ST_GeomFromText('POINT(-73.9924659 40.688665)', 4326)
CONTEXT:  PL/Python function "geocode2"
                geocode2
--------------------------------------------------------
0101000020E61000004BB9B18F847F52C02E73BA2C26584440
(1 row)
```

5. If you test it by specifying a different API, it should return the result processed for the given API. For example:

```
postgis_cookbook=# SELECT chp08.Geocode('161 Court Street,
                  Brooklyn, NY', 'GeocoderDotUS');
INFO:  Geocoing the given address using the GeocoderDotUS api
CONTEXT:  PL/Python function "geocode2"
INFO:  Geocoded 161 Court St, New York, NY 11201 for the address: 161
       Court Street, Brooklyn, NY
CONTEXT:  PL/Python function "geocode2"
INFO:  Longitude is -73.992809, Latitude is 40.688774.
CONTEXT:  PL/Python function "geocode2"
INFO:  SELECT ST_GeomFromText('POINT(-73.992809 40.688774)', 4326)
CONTEXT:  PL/Python function "geocode2"
                geocode2
--------------------------------------------------------
0101000020E61000002A8BC22E8A7F52C0E52A16BF29584440
(1 row)
```

6. As a bonus step, create a table in PostgreSQL with street addresses, and generate a new point PostGIS layer storing the geocoded points returned by the Geocode function.

How it works...

You wrote a PL/Python function to geocode an address. For this purpose, you used the `geopy` Python library, which lets you query several geocoding APIs in the same manner.

Using geopy, you need to instantiate a `geocoder` object with a given API and query it to get the results, such as a place name and a couple of coordinates. You can use the `plpy` module utilities to run a query on the database using the PostGIS `ST_GeomFromText` function, and log informative messages and warnings for the user.

If the geocoding process fails, you return a `NULL` geometry to the user with a warning message, using a `try..except` Python block.

Importing NetCDF datasets with Python and GDAL

In this recipe, you will write a Python script to import data from the NetCDF format to PostGIS.

NetCDF is an open standard format, widely used for scientific applications, and can contain multiple raster datasets, each composed of a spectrum of bands. For this purpose, you will use the GDAL Python bindings and the popular NumPy (`http://www.numpy.org/`) scientific library.

Getting ready

1. If you are using Windows, be sure to install OSGeo4W, as suggested in the initial instructions for this chapter. This will include Python and GDAL Python bindings with NumPy support.

   For Linux users, in case you did not do it yet, follow the initial instructions for this chapter and create a Python virtual environment in order to keep a Python-isolated environment to be used for all the Python recipes in this book. Then, activate it:

   ```
   $ source postgis-cb-env/bin/activate
   ```

2. For this recipe, you need the GDAL Python bindings and NumPy, the latter being needed by a GDAL method (ReadAsArray) for arrays. In the most likely case, you have already installed GDAL in your virtual environment as you have been using it for other recipes, so be sure to remove it and reinstall it after installing NumPy. In fact, GDAL needs to be compiled with NumPy support if you want to use its array's features:

   ```
   (postgis-cb-env)$ pip uninstall gdal
   (postgis-cb-env)$ pip install numpy
   (postgis-cb-env)$ pip install gdal
   ```

3. For the purpose of this recipe, you will use a sample dataset from NOAA **Earth System Research Laboratory (ESRL)**. The excellent ESRL web portal offers a plethora of data in the NetCDF format to be freely downloaded. For example, download the following dataset from the ESRL CPC Soil Moisture data repository (you can find, as usual, a copy of this dataset in the book's dataset directory for this chapter): https://www.esrl.noaa.gov/psd/data/gridded/data.cpcsoil.html.

How to do it...

Carry out the following steps:

1. As the first step, investigate the NetCDF format of the dataset you downloaded using `gdalinfo`. This kind of dataset is composed of several subdatasets, as you may have realized by looking at the `gdalinfo` output:

   $ gdalinfo NETCDF:"soilw.mon.ltm.v2.nc"

```
Driver: netCDF/Network Common Data Format
Files: none associated
Size is 512, 512
Coordinate System is `'
Metadata:
  NC_GLOBAL#Conventions=CF-1.0
  NC_GLOBAL#history=Created 2011/08/31 by doMonthLTM
  NC_GLOBAL#institution=NOAA/ESRL PSD
  NC_GLOBAL#not_missing_threshold_percent=minimum 3% values input to have non-missing output value
  NC_GLOBAL#references=http://www.cpc.ncep.noaa.gov/soilmst/index.htm
http://www.esrl.noaa.gov/psd/data/gridded/data.cpcsoil.html
  NC_GLOBAL#title=CPC Soil Moisture
Subdatasets:
  SUBDATASET_1_NAME=NETCDF:"soilw.mon.ltm.v2.nc":climatology_bounds
  SUBDATASET_1_DESC=[12x2] climatology_bounds (64-bit floating-point)
  SUBDATASET_2_NAME=NETCDF:"soilw.mon.ltm.v2.nc":soilw
  SUBDATASET_2_DESC=[12x360x720] lwe_thickness_of_soil_moisture_content (32-bit floating-point)
  SUBDATASET_3_NAME=NETCDF:"soilw.mon.ltm.v2.nc":valid_yr_count
  SUBDATASET_3_DESC=[12x360x720] valid_yr_count (16-bit integer)
Corner Coordinates:
Upper Left  (    0.0,    0.0)
Lower Left  (    0.0,  512.0)
Upper Right (  512.0,    0.0)
Lower Right (  512.0,  512.0)
Center      (  256.0,  256.0)
```

2. Use `gdalinfo` to investigate one of the file's subdatasets. The syntax that the NetCDF GDAL driver (http://www.gdal.org/frmt_netcdf.html) uses is to append a colon followed by the variable name at the end of the filename. For example, try to figure out how many bands the `soilw` subdataset is composed of. This subdataset, representing `lwe_thickness_of_soil_moisture_content`, is composed of 12 bands. Each band, according to the information derived by its metadata, represents the CPC Monthly Soil Moisture for a given month. The month is identified by the `NETCDF_DIM_time` metadata value, which is the number of days from the beginning of the year (`0` for January, `31` for February, `59` for March, and so on):

```
$  gdalinfo NETCDF:"soilw.mon.ltm.v2.nc":soilw
```

```
● ● ●                          Chapter 8 — bash — 102×30
Driver: netCDF/Network Common Data Format
Files: none associated
Size is 512, 512
Coordinate System is ``
Metadata:
  NC_GLOBAL#Conventions=CF-1.0
  NC_GLOBAL#history=Created 2011/08/31 by doMonthLTM
  NC_GLOBAL#institution=NOAA/ESRL PSD
  NC_GLOBAL#not_missing_threshold_percent=minimum 3% values input to have non-missing output value
  NC_GLOBAL#references=http://www.cpc.ncep.noaa.gov/soilmst/index.htm
http://www.esrl.noaa.gov/psd/data/gridded/data.cpcsoil.html
  NC_GLOBAL#title=CPC Soil Moisture
Subdatasets:
  SUBDATASET_1_NAME=NETCDF:"soilw.mon.ltm.v2.nc":climatology_bounds
  SUBDATASET_1_DESC=[12x2] climatology_bounds (64-bit floating-point)
  SUBDATASET_2_NAME=NETCDF:"soilw.mon.ltm.v2.nc":soilw
  SUBDATASET_2_DESC=[12x360x720] lwe_thickness_of_soil_moisture_content (32-bit floating-point)
  SUBDATASET_3_NAME=NETCDF:"soilw.mon.ltm.v2.nc":valid_yr_count
  SUBDATASET_3_DESC=[12x360x720] valid_yr_count (16-bit integer)
Corner Coordinates:
Upper Left  (    0.0,    0.0)
Lower Left  (    0.0,  512.0)
Upper Right (  512.0,    0.0)
Lower Right (  512.0,  512.0)
Center      (  256.0,  256.0)
Nina:Chapter 8 may$
Nina:Chapter 8 may$
Nina:Chapter 8 may$
Nina:Chapter 8 may$ gdalinfo NETCDF:"soilw.mon.ltm.v2.nc":soilw
Driver: netCDF/Network Common Data Format
```

```
...(12 bands)...
```

3. What you are going to do is create a Python script using GDAL and NumPy. You will read a given NetCDF dataset, iterate its subdatasets, and then iterate each subdataset's bands. For each subdataset, you will create a point PostGIS layer, and you will add a field for each band in order to store the band values in the layer table. Then, you will iterate the band's cells, and for each cell, you will add a point in the layer with the corresponding band's values. Therefore, create a `netcdf2postgis.py` file and add the following Python code to it:

```python
import sys
from osgeo import gdal, ogr, osr
from osgeo.gdalconst import GA_ReadOnly, GA_Update

def netcdf2postgis(file_nc, pg_connection_string,
                   postgis_table_prefix):
  # register gdal drivers
  gdal.AllRegister()
  # postgis driver, needed to create the tables
  driver = ogr.GetDriverByName('PostgreSQL')
  srs = osr.SpatialReference()
  # for simplicity we will assume all of the bands in the datasets
  # are in the same spatial reference, wgs 84
  srs.ImportFromEPSG(4326)

  # first, check if dataset exists
  ds = gdal.Open(file_nc, GA_ReadOnly)
  if ds is None:
    print 'Cannot open ' + file_nc
    sys.exit(1)

  # 1. iterate subdatasets
  for sds in ds.GetSubDatasets():
    dataset_name = sds[0]
    variable = sds[0].split(':')[-1]
    print 'Importing from %s the variable %s...' %
          (dataset_name, variable)
    # open subdataset and read its properties
    sds = gdal.Open(dataset_name, GA_ReadOnly)
    cols = sds.RasterXSize
    rows = sds.RasterYSize
    bands = sds.RasterCount

    # create a PostGIS table for the subdataset variable
    table_name = '%s_%s' % (postgis_table_prefix, variable)
    pg_ds = ogr.Open(pg_connection_string, GA_Update )
    pg_layer = pg_ds.CreateLayer(table_name, srs = srs,
    geom_type=ogr.wkbPoint, options = [
```

```
    'GEOMETRY_NAME=the_geom',
    'OVERWRITE=YES',
      # this will drop and recreate the table every time
    'SCHEMA=chp08',
  ])
print 'Table %s created.' % table_name

# get georeference transformation information
transform = sds.GetGeoTransform()
pixelWidth = transform[1]
pixelHeight = transform[5]
xOrigin = transform[0] + (pixelWidth/2)
yOrigin = transform[3] - (pixelWidth/2)

# 2. iterate subdataset bands and append them to data
data = []
for b in range(1, bands+1):
  band = sds.GetRasterBand(b)
  band_data = band.ReadAsArray(0, 0, cols, rows)
  data.append(band_data)
  # here we add the fields to the table, a field for each band
  # check datatype (Float32, 'Float64', ...)
  datatype = gdal.GetDataTypeName(band.DataType)
  ogr_ft = ogr.OFTString # default for a field is string
  if datatype in ('Float32', 'Float64'):
    ogr_ft = ogr.OFTReal
  elif datatype in ('Int16', 'Int32'):
    ogr_ft = ogr.OFTInteger
  # here we add the field to the PostGIS layer
  fd_band = ogr.FieldDefn('band_%s' % b, ogr_ft)
  pg_layer.CreateField(fd_band)
  print 'Field band_%s created.' % b

# 3. iterate rows and cols
for r in range(0, rows):
  y = yOrigin + (r * pixelHeight)
  for c in range(0, cols):
    x = xOrigin + (c * pixelWidth)
    # for each cell, let's add a point feature
    # in the PostGIS table
    point_wkt = 'POINT(%s %s)' % (x, y)
    point = ogr.CreateGeometryFromWkt(point_wkt)
    featureDefn = pg_layer.GetLayerDefn()
    feature = ogr.Feature(featureDefn)
    # now iterate bands, and add a value for each table's field
    for b in range(1, bands+1):
      band = sds.GetRasterBand(1)
      datatype = gdal.GetDataTypeName(band.DataType)
```

```
value = data[b-1][r,c]
print 'Storing a value for variable %s in point x: %s,
 y: %s, band: %s, value: %s' % (variable, x, y, b, value)
if datatype in ('Float32', 'Float64'):
  value = float(data[b-1][r,c])
elif datatype in ('Int16', 'Int32'):
  value = int(data[b-1][r,c])
else:
  value = data[r,c]
feature.SetField('band_%s' % b, value)
# set the feature's geometry and finalize its creation
feature.SetGeometry(point)
pg_layer.CreateFeature(feature)
```

4. To run the `netcdf2postgis` method from the command line, add the entry point for the script. The code will check whether the script user is correctly using the three required parameters, which are the NetCDF file path, the GDAL PostGIS connection string, and a prefix/suffix to use for table names in PostGIS:

```
if __name__ == '__main__':
  # the user must provide at least three parameters,
  # the netCDF file path, the PostGIS GDAL connection string
  # and the prefix suffix to use for PostGIS table names
  if len(sys.argv) < 4 or len(sys.argv) > 4:
    print "usage: <netCDF file path> <GDAL PostGIS connection
          string><PostGIS table prefix>"
    raise SystemExit
  file_nc = sys.argv[1]
  pg_connection_string = sys.argv[2]
  postgis_table_prefix = sys.argv[3]
  netcdf2postgis(file_nc, pg_connection_string,
                 postgis_table_prefix)
```

5. Run the script. Be sure to use the correct NetCDF file path, GDAL PostGIS connection string (check the format at `http://www.gdal.org/drv_pg.html`), and a table prefix that has to be appended to the table names for tables that will be created in PostGIS:

```
(postgis-cb-env)$ python netcdf2postgis.py
NETCDF:"soilw.mon.ltm.v2.nc"
"PG:dbname='postgis_cookbook' host='localhost'
port='5432' user='me' password='mypassword'" netcdf
Importing from NETCDF:"soilw.mon.ltm.v2.nc":
  climatology_bounds the variable climatology_bounds...
...
Importing from NETCDF:"soilw.mon.ltm.v2.nc":soilw the
  variable soilw...
```

```
Table netcdf_soilw created.
Field band_1 created.
Field band_2 created.
...
Field band_11 created.
Field band_12 created.
Storing a value for variable soilw in point x: 0.25,
        y: 89.75, band: 2, value: -9.96921e+36
Storing a value for variable soilw in point x: 0.25,
        y: 89.75, band: 3, value: -9.96921e+36
...
```

6. At the end of the process, check the results by opening one of the output PostGIS tables using your favorite GIS desktop tool. The following screenshot shows how it looks in the QGIS `soilw` layer with the original NetCDF dataset behind it:

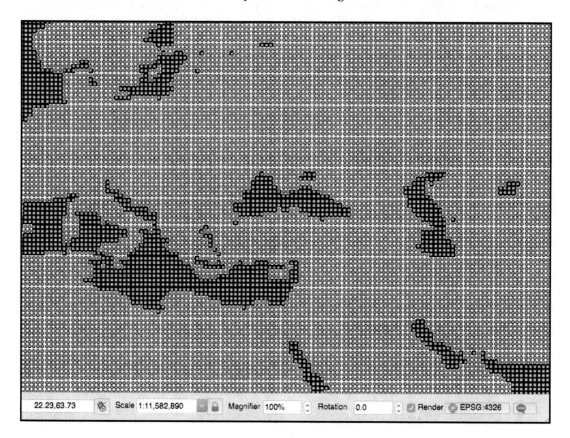

How it works...

You have used Python with GDAL and NumPy in order to create a command-line utility to import a NetCDF dataset into PostGIS.

A NetCDF dataset is composed of multiple subdatasets, and each subdataset is composed of multiple raster bands. Each band is composed of cells. This structure should be clear to you after investigating a sample NetCDF dataset using the `gdalinfo` GDAL command tool.

There are several approaches to exporting cell values to PostGIS. The approach you adopted here is to generate a PostGIS point layer for each subdataset, which is composed of one field for each subdataset band. You then iterated the raster cells and appended a point to the PostGIS layer with the values read from each cell band.

The way you do this with Python is by using the GDAL Python bindings. For reading, you open the NetCDF dataset, and for updating, you open the PostGIS database, using the correct GDAL and OGR drivers. Then, you iterate the NetCDF subdatasets, using the `GetSubDatasets` method, and create a PostGIS table named `NetCDF subdataset variable` (with the prefix) for each subdataset, using the `CreateLayer` method.

For each subdataset, you iterate its bands, using the `GetRasterBand` method. To read each band, you run the `ReadAsArray` method which uses NumPy to get the band as an array.

For each band, you create a field in the PostGIS layer with the correct field data type that will be able to store the band's values. To choose the correct data type, you investigate the band's data type, using the `DataType` property.

Finally, you iterate the raster cells, by reading the correct *x* and *y* coordinates using the subdataset transform parameters, available via the `GetGeoTransform` method. For each cell, you create a point with the `CreateGeometryFromWkt` method, then set the field values, and read from the band array using the `SetField` feature method.

Finally, you append the new point to the PostGIS layer using the `CreateFeature` method.

PostGIS and the Web

9

In this chapter, we will cover the following topics:

- Creating WMS and WFS services with MapServer
- Creating WMS and WFS services with GeoServer
- Creating a WMS Time service with MapServer
- Consuming WMS services with OpenLayers
- Consuming WMS services with Leaflet
- Consuming WFS-T services with OpenLayers
- Developing web applications with GeoDjango – part 1
- Developing web applications with GeoDjango – part 2
- Developing a web GPX viewer with Mapbox

Introduction

In this chapter, we will try to give you an overview of how you can use PostGIS to develop powerful GIS web applications, using **Open Geospatial Consortium (OGC)** web standards such as **Web Map Service (WMS)** and **Web Feature Service (WFS)**.

In the first two recipes, you will get an overview of two very popular open source web-mapping engines, **MapServer** and **GeoServer**. In both these recipes, you will see how to implement WMS and WFS services using PostGIS layers.

In the third recipe, you will implement a **WMS Time** service using MapServer to expose time-series data.

In the next two recipes, you will learn how to consume these web services to create web map viewers with two very popular JavaScript clients. In the fourth recipe, you will use a WMS service with **OpenLayers**, while in the fifth recipe, you will do the same thing using **Leaflet**.

In the sixth recipe, you will explore the power of transactional WFS to create web-mapping applications to enable editing data.

In the next two recipes, you will unleash the power of the popular **Django** web framework, which is based on Python, and its nice **GeoDjango** library, and see how it is possible to implement a powerful **CRUD** GIS web application. In the seventh recipe, you will create the back office for this application using the Django Admin site, and in the last recipe of the chapter, you will develop a frontend for users to display data from the application in a web map based on Leaflet.

Finally, in the last recipe, you will learn how to import your PostGIS data into Mapbox using **OGR** to create a custom web GPX viewer.

Creating WMS and WFS services with MapServer

In this recipe, you will see how to create a WMS and WFS from a PostGIS layer, using the popular MapServer open source web-mapping engine.

You will then use the services, testing their exposed requests, using first a browser and then a desktop tool such as QGIS (you could do this using other software, such as uDig, gvSIG, and OpenJUMP GIS).

Getting ready

Follow these steps before getting ready:

1. Create a schema for this chapter within the `postgis_cookbook` database using the following command:

   ```
   postgis_cookbook=# create schema chp09;
   ```

2. Be sure to have Apache HTTP installed (MapServer will run on it as a CGI) and check whether it is working by visiting its home page at `http://localhost` (typically, an `It works!` message will be displayed if you still have not customized any features).

3. Install MapServer as per its installation guide (`http://mapserver.org/installation/index.html`).

   > A handy way to have MapServer up and running in Apache for Windows is to install the OSGeo4W (`http://trac.osgeo.org/osgeo4w/`) or MS4W (`http://www.maptools.org/ms4w/`) packages.
   > For Linux, there are packages for almost any kind of distribution.
   > For macOS, you can use again the CMake app to build the installation or use Homebrew with the following command (note the flags needed to compile it with Postgres support):
   > ```
   > brew install mapserver --with-postgresql --with-geos
   > ```

4. Check whether MapServer has been installed correctly and has `POSTGIS`, `WMS_SERVER`, and `WFS_SERVER` support enabled, by running it as a command-line tool with the `-v` option.

On Linux, run the $ /usr/lib/cgi-bin/mapserv -v command and check for the following output:

```
MapServer version 7.0.7 OUTPUT=GIF OUTPUT=PNG OUTPUT=JPEG SUPPORTS=PROJ
SUPPORTS=GD SUPPORTS=AGG SUPPORTS=FREETYPE SUPPORTS=CAIRO
SUPPORTS=SVG_SYMBOLS
SUPPORTS=ICONV SUPPORTS=FRIBIDI SUPPORTS=WMS_SERVER SUPPORTS=WMS_CLIENT
SUPPORTS=WFS_SERVER SUPPORTS=WFS_CLIENT SUPPORTS=WCS_SERVER
SUPPORTS=SOS_SERVER SUPPORTS=FASTCGI SUPPORTS=THREADS SUPPORTS=GEOS
INPUT=JPEG INPUT=POSTGIS INPUT=OGR INPUT=GDAL INPUT=SHAPEFILE
```

On Windows, run the following command:

```
c:\ms4w\Apache\cgi-bin\mapserv.exe -v
```

On macOS, use the $ mapserv -v command:

```
WebServer — bash — 80×24
bash-3.2$ mapserv -v
MapServer version 7.0.7 OUTPUT=PNG OUTPUT=JPEG SUPPORTS=PROJ SUPPORTS=AGG SUPPOR
TS=FREETYPE SUPPORTS=CAIRO SUPPORTS=ICONV SUPPORTS=WMS_SERVER SUPPORTS=WMS_CLIEN
T SUPPORTS=WFS_SERVER SUPPORTS=WFS_CLIENT SUPPORTS=WCS_SERVER SUPPORTS=SOS_SERVE
R SUPPORTS=GEOS INPUT=JPEG INPUT=POSTGIS INPUT=OGR INPUT=GDAL INPUT=SHAPEFILE
bash-3.2$
```

5. Now check whether MapServer is working from within HTTPD, using http://localhost/cgi-bin/mapserv (http://localhost/cgi-bin/mapserv.exe for Windows). If you get a No query information to decode. QUERY_STRING is set, but empty response message, MapServer is correctly working as a CGI script in Apache and is ready to accept HTTP requests.

6. Download the world countries shapefile from http://thematicmapping.org/downloads/TM_WORLD_BORDERS-0.3.zip. A copy of this shapefile is included in the book dataset for Chapter 1, *Moving Data In and Out of PostGIS*. Extract the shapefile to the working/chp09 directory and import it in PostGIS using the **shp2pgsql** tool (be sure to specify the spatial reference system, *EPSG:4326*, with the -s option), as follows:

```
$ shp2pgsql -s 4326 -W LATIN1 -g the_geom -I TM_WORLD_BORDERS-0.3.shp
chp09.countries > countries.sql
Shapefile type: Polygon
Postgis type: MULTIPOLYGON[2]
$ psql -U me -d postgis_cookbook -f countries.sql
```

How to do it...

Carry out the following steps:

1. MapServer exposes its map services using `mapfile`, a text file format, with which it is possible to define the PostGIS layers on the web, enable any vector and raster format supported by GDAL, and specify which services (WMS/WFS/WCS) to expose per layer. Create a new text file named `countries.map` and add the following code:

```
MAP # Start of mapfile
NAME 'population_per_country_map'
IMAGETYPE        PNG
EXTENT           -180 -90 180 90
SIZE             800 400
IMAGECOLOR       255 255 255

# map projection definition
PROJECTION
  'init=epsg:4326'
END

# web section: here we define the ows services
WEB
  # WMS and WFS server settings
  METADATA
    'ows_enable_request'            '*'
    'ows_title'                     'Mapserver sample map'
    'ows_abstract'                  'OWS services about
                                    population per
                                    country map'
    'wms_onlineresource'            'http://localhost/cgi-
                                       bin/mapserv?map=/var
                                       /www/data/
                                       countries.map&'
    'ows_srs'                       'EPSG:4326 EPSG:900913
                                    EPSG:3857'
    'wms_enable_request'            'GetCapabilities,
                                    GetMap,
                                    GetFeatureInfo'
    'wms_feature_info_mime_type'    'text/html'
  END
END

# Start of layers definition
LAYER # Countries polygon layer begins here
```

```
NAME            countries
CONNECTIONTYPE  POSTGIS
CONNECTION      'host=localhost dbname=postgis_cookbook
                user=me password=mypassword port=5432'
DATA            'the_geom from chp09.countries'
TEMPLATE 'template.html'
METADATA
  'ows_title' 'countries'
  'ows_abstract' 'OWS service about population per
    country map in 2005'
  'gml_include_items' 'all'
END
STATUS          ON
TYPE            POLYGON
# layer projection definition
PROJECTION
  'init=epsg:4326'
END

# we define 3 population classes based on the pop2005
  attribute
CLASSITEM 'pop2005'
CLASS # first class
  NAME '0 - 50M inhabitants'
  EXPRESSION ( ([pop2005] >= 0) AND ([pop2005] <=
    50000000) )
  STYLE
    WIDTH 1
    OUTLINECOLOR 0 0 0
    COLOR 254 240 217
  END # end of style
END # end of first class
CLASS # second class
  NAME '50M - 200M inhabitants'
  EXPRESSION ( ([pop2005] > 50000000) AND
    ([pop2005] <= 200000000) )
  STYLE
    WIDTH 1
    OUTLINECOLOR 0 0 0
    COLOR 252 141 89
  END # end of style
END # end of second class
CLASS # third class
  NAME '> 200M inhabitants'
  EXPRESSION ( ([pop2005] > 200000000) )
  STYLE
    WIDTH 1
    OUTLINECOLOR 0 0 0
```

```
         COLOR 179 0 0
      END # end of style
   END # end of third class

   END # Countries polygon layer ends here

   END # End of mapfile
```

2. Save the file we just created in a location that is accessible to the Apache user. For example, in Debian, it is `/var/www/data`, while in Windows, it can be `C:\ms4w\Apache\htdocs`; for macOS, you should use `/Library/WebServer/Documents`.

   Be sure that both the file and the directory containing it are accessible to the Apache user.

3. Create a file named `template.html` in the same location as the `mapfile` and enter the following code in it (this file is used by the `GetFeatureInfo` WMS request to output an HTML response to the client):

```
<!-- MapServer Template -->
<ul>
  <li><strong>Name: </strong>[item name=name]</li>
  <li><strong>ISO2: </strong>[item name=iso2]</li>
  <li><strong>ISO3: </strong>[item name=iso3]</li>
  <li>
    <strong>Population 2005:</strong> [item name=pop2005]
  </li>
</ul>
```

4. With the `mapfile` you just created, you exposed the `countries` PostGIS layer, both as a WMS and WFS service. Both of these services expose to the user a series of requests and you will now test them using a browser. First, without invoking any services, test whether the `mapfile` is working correctly by typing the following URL in the browser:
   - `http://localhost/cgi-bin/mapserv?map=/var/www/data/coun tries.map&layer=countries&mode=map` (for Linux)
   - `http://localhost/cgi-bin/mapserv.exe?map=C:\ms4w\Apache \htdocs\countries.map&layer=countries&mode=map` (for Windows)
   - `http://localhost/cgi-bin/mapserv?map=/Library/WebServer /Documents/countries.map&layer=countries&mode=map` (for macOS)

You should see the `countries` layer rendered with the three symbology classes defined in the `mapfile`, as shown in the following screenshot:

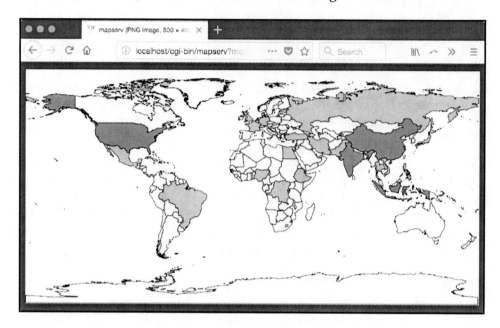

As you can see, there is a small difference between the URLs used in Windows, Linux, and macOS. We will refer to Linux from now on, but you can easily adapt the URLs to Windows or macOS.

5. Now you will start testing the WMS service; you will try running the `GetCapabilities`, `GetMap`, and `GetFeatureInfo` requests. To test the `GetCapabilities` request, type the URL in the browser: `http://localhost/cgi-bin/mapserv?map=/var/www/data/countries.ma p&SERVICE=WMS&VERSION=1.1.1&REQUEST=GetCapabilities`. You should receive a long XML response (as follows) from the server, where the more important fragments are the WMS service definitions in the `<Service>` section, the requests are enabled in the `<Capability>` section, and the layers exposed and their main details (for example, name, abstract, projection, and extent) are in the `<Layer>` section of each of the layers:

```
<WMT_MS_Capabilities version="1.1.1">
  ...
  <Service>
    <Name>OGC:WMS</Name>
    <Title>Population per country map</Title>
```

```
        <Abstract>Map server sample map</Abstract>
        <OnlineResource
         xmlns:xlink="http://www.w3.org/1999/xlink"
         xlink:href="http://localhost/cgi-
         bin/mapserv?map=/var/www/data/countries.map&amp;"/>
        <ContactInformation> </ContactInformation>
      </Service>
      <Capability>
        <Request>
          <GetCapabilities>
            ...
          </GetCapabilities>
          <GetMap>
            <Format>image/png</Format>
            ...
            <Format>image/tiff</Format>
            ...
          </GetMap>
          <GetFeatureInfo>
            <Format>text/plain</Format>
            ...
          </GetFeatureInfo>
          ...
        </Request>
        ...
        <Layer>
          <Name>population_per_country_map</Name>
          <Title>Population per country map</Title>
          <Abstract>OWS service about population per country map
           in 2005</Abstract>
          <SRS>EPSG:4326</SRS>
          <SRS>EPSG:3857</SRS>
          <LatLonBoundingBox minx="-180" miny="-90" maxx="180"
           maxy="90" />
          ...
        </Layer>
      </Layer>
      </Capability>
    </WMT_MS_Capabilities>
```

6. Now test the WMS service with its typical GetMap WMS request, used on many
   clients to display a map to the user. Type the URL
   ```
   http://localhost//cgi-bin/mapserv?map=/var/www/data/countries.m
   ap&SERVICE=WMS&VERSION=1.3.0&REQUEST=GetMap&BBOX=-26,-111,36,-3
   8&CRS=EPSG:4326&WIDTH=1000&HEIGHT=800&LAYERS=countries&STYLES=&
   FORMAT=image/png
   ```

7. Into the browser and check the image that is sent back in response by the MapServer `GetMap` request, as shown in the following screenshot:

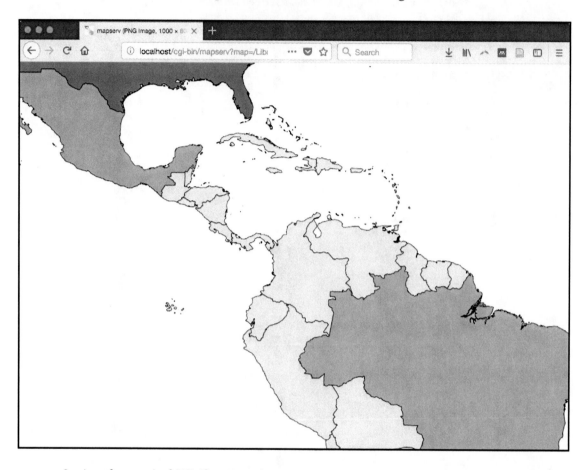

8. Another typical WMS request is `GetFeatureInfo`, used by clients to query the map layer at the given coordinates (points). Type the following URL and you should see the field values for a given feature as the output (the output is built using the `template.html` file):

```
http://localhost/cgi-bin/mapserv?map=/var/www/data/
countries.map&layer=countries&REQUEST=GetFeatureInfo&
SERVICE=WMS&VERSION=1.1.1&LAYERS=countries&
QUERY_LAYERS=countries&SRS=EPSG:4326&BBOX=-122.545074509804,
37.6736653056517,-122.35457254902,37.8428758708189&
X=652&Y=368&WIDTH=1020&HEIGHT=906&INFO_FORMAT=text/html
```

The output should be as follows:

> - **Name:** United States
> - **ISO2:** US
> - **ISO3:** USA
> - **Population 2005:** 299846449

9. Now, you will use QGIS to use the WMS service. Launch QGIS, click on the **Add WMS layer** button (alternatively, navigate to **Layer | Add WMS Layer** or use the QGIS browser), and create a new WMS connection, as shown in the following screenshot. Type something such as `MapServer on localhost` in the **Name** field and `http://localhost/cgi-bin/mapserv?map=/var/www/data/countries.ma p&SERVICE=WMS&VERSION=1.1.1&REQUEST=GetCapabilities` in the **URL** field, and click on the **OK** button (remember to adjust the Apache URL according to the configuration of your OS; check step 4):

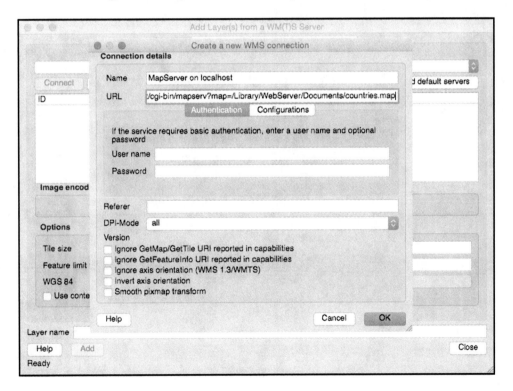

10. Now click on the **Connect** button, as shown in the following screenshot. Then, select the **countries** layer and add it to the QGIS map window using the **Add** button, making sure to select the coordinate system EPSG:4326:

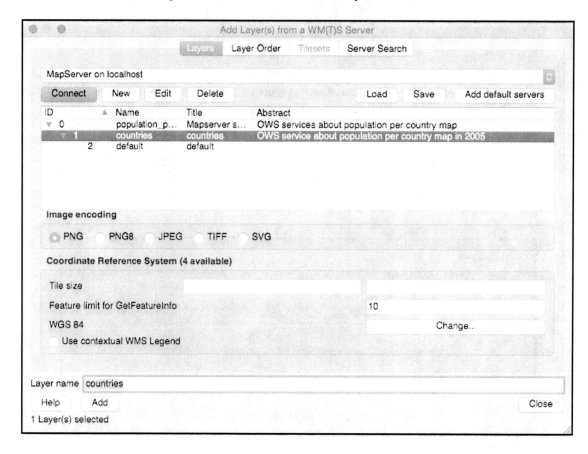

11. Now browse to your WMS countries layer and try to perform some identification operations. QGIS will raise the needed `GetMap` and `GetFeatureInfo` WMS requests for you behind the scenes to give the following output:

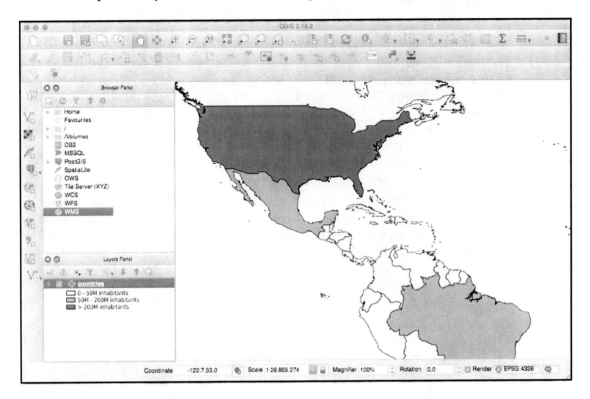

12. Having seen how the WMS service works, you will now start using WFS. Like WMS, WFS offers the user a `GetCapabilities` request as well, resulting in a similar output to the `GetCapabilities` request of WMS. Type the URL `http://localhost/cgi-bin/mapserv?map=/var/www/data/countries.ma` `p&SERVICE=WFS&VERSION=1.0.0&REQUEST=GetCapabilities` into the browser window to inspect the XML response.

13. The main WFS request is `GetFeature`. It lets you query the map layer using several criteria, returning a collection of features in response as **Geography Markup Language** (GML) output. Test the request by typing this URL in the browser: `http://localhost/cgi-bin/mapserv?map=/var/www/data/countries.ma` `p&SERVICE=WFS&VERSION=1.0.0&REQUEST=getfeature&TYPENAME=countri` `es&MAXFEATURES=5`.

14. You should get an XML (GML) response from the browser, as shown in the following code, with a `<wfs:FeatureCollection>` element composed of five `<gml:featureMember>` elements (as indicated in the MAXFEATURES parameter of the request), each representing one country. For each feature, the WFS returns the geometry and all of the field values (this behavior was specified by setting the `gml_include_items` variable in the METADATA layer directive in the `mapfile`). You will see a geometry as follows:

```
<gml:featureMember>
  <ms:countries>
    <gml:boundedBy>
      <gml:Box srsName="EPSG:4326">
        <gml:coordinates>-61.891113,16.989719 -
        61.666389,17.724998</gml:coordinates>
      </gml:Box>
    </gml:boundedBy>

    <ms:msGeometry>
      <gml:MultiPolygon srsName="EPSG:4326">
        <gml:polygonMember>
          <gml:Polygon>
            <gml:outerBoundaryIs>
              <gml:LinearRing>
                <gml:coordinates>
                  -61.686668,17.024441 ...
                </gml:coordinates>
              </gml:LinearRing>
            </gml:outerBoundaryIs>
          </gml:Polygon>
        </gml:polygonMember>
        ...
```

```
          </gml:MultiPolygon>
        </ms:msGeometry>
        <ms:gid>1</ms:gid>
        <ms:fips>AC</ms:fips>
        <ms:iso2>AG</ms:iso2>
        <ms:iso3>ATG</ms:iso3>
        <ms:un>28</ms:un>
        <ms:name>Antigua and Barbuda</ms:name>
        <ms:area>44</ms:area>
        <ms:pop2005>83039</ms:pop2005>
        <ms:region>19</ms:region>
        <ms:subregion>29</ms:subregion>
        <ms:lon>-61.783</ms:lon>
        <ms:lat>17.078</ms:lat>
      </ms:countries>
    </gml:featureMember>
```

15. As a result of the WFS `GetFeature` request executed in the previous step, MapServer has returned only the first five features of the `countries` layers. Now, use the `GetFeature` request to make a query to the layer using a filter and get back the corresponding features. By typing the URL `http://localhost/cgi-bin/mapserv?map=/var/www/data/countries.map&SERVICE=WFS&VERSION=1.0.0&REQUEST=getfeature&TYPENAME=countries&MAXFEATURES=5&Filter=<Filter>` `<PropertyIsEqualTo><PropertyName>name</PropertyName>` `<Literal>Italy</Literal></PropertyIsEqualTo></Filter>`, you will get the feature in the database that has the `name` field set to `Italy`.

16. After testing the WFS requests in a browser, try to open the WFS service in QGIS using the **Add WFS Layer** button (alternatively, navigate to **Layer | Add WFS Layer** or use the QGIS browser). You should see the same **MapServer on Localhost** connection you created a few steps earlier. Click on the **Connect** button and select the **countries** layer, add it to the QGIS project, and browse through it by zooming, panning, and identifying some features. The biggest difference when compared to WMS is that, with WFS, you receive the feature geometries from the server and not just an image, so you can even export the layer to a different format, such as a shapefile or spatialite! The **Add WFS layer from a Server** window is as shown in the following screenshot:

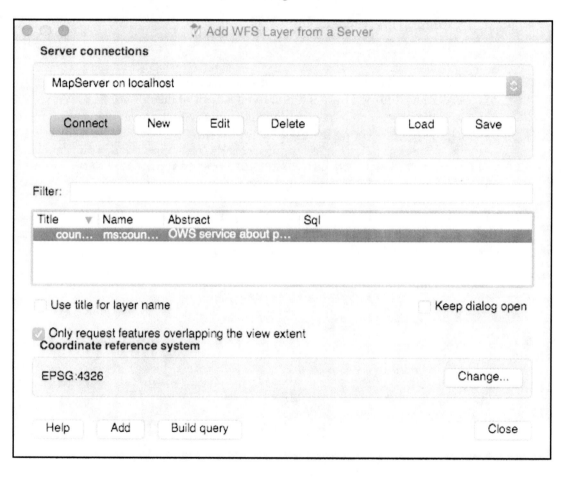

You should now be able to see the vector map in QGIS and inspect the features:

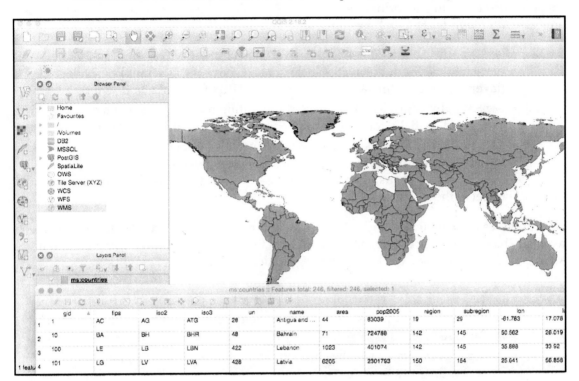

How it works...

In this recipe, you implemented WMS and WFS services for a PostGIS layer using the MapServer open source web-mapping engine. WMS and WFS are the two core concepts to consider when you want to develop a web GIS that is interoperable across many organizations. **Open Geospatial Consortium** (OGC) defined these two standards (and many others) to make web-mapping services exposed in an open, standard way. This way these services can be used by different applications; for example, you have seen in this recipe that a GIS Desktop tool such as QGIS can browse and query those services because it understands these OGC standards (you can get exactly the same results with other tools, such as gvSIG, uDig, OpenJUMP, and ArcGIS Desktop, among others). In the same way, Javascript API libraries, most notably OpenLayers and Leaflet (you will be using these in the other recipes in this chapter), can use these services in a standard way to provide web-mapping features to web applications.

WMS is a service that is used to generate the maps to be displayed by clients. Those maps are generated using image formats, such as PNG, JPEG, and many others. Some of the most typical WMS requests are as follows:

- `GetCapabilities`: This offers an overview of the services offered by WMS, particularly a list of the available layers and some of the details of each layer (layer extent, coordinate reference systems, URI of the data, and so on).
- `GetMap`: This returns a map image representing one or more layers for a specified extent and spatial reference, in a specified image file format and size.
- `GetFeatureInfo`: This is an optional request by WMS that returns, in different formats, the attribute values for the features of a given point in the map. You have seen how to customize the response by introducing a template file that must be set in the `mapfile`.

WFS provides a convenient, standard way to access the features of a vector layer with a web request. The service response streams to the client the requested features using GML (an XML markup defined by OGC to define geographical features).

Some WFS requests are as follows:

- `GetCapabilities`: This gives a description of the services and layers offered by the WFS service
- `GetFeature`: This allows the client to get a set of features of a given layer, corresponding to a given criteria

These WMS and WFS requests can be consumed by the client using the HTTP protocol. You have seen how to query and get a response from the client by typing a URL in a browser with several parameters appended to it. As an example, the following WMS `GetMap` request will return a map image of the layers (using the `LAYERS` parameter) in a specified format (using the `FORMAT` parameter), size (using the `WIDTH` and `HEIGHT` parameters), extent (using the `BBOX` parameter), and spatial reference system (using `CRS`):

```
http://localhost/cgi-bin/mapserv?map=/var/www/data/countries.map&&SERVICE=W
MS&VERSION=1.3.0&REQUEST=GetMap&BBOX=-26,-111,36,-38&CRS=EPSG:4326&WIDTH=80
6&HEIGHT=688&LAYERS=countries&STYLES=&FORMAT=image/png
```

In MapServer, you can create WMS and WFS services in the `mapfile` using its directives. The `mapfile` is a text file that is composed of several sections and is the heart of MapServer. In the beginning of the `mapfile`, it is necessary to define general properties for the map, such as its title, extent, spatial reference, output-image formats, and dimensions to be returned to the user.

Then, it is possible to define which OWS (OGC web services such as WMS, WFS, and WCS) requests to expose.

Then there is the main section of the `mapfile`, where the layers are defined (every layer is defined in the `LAYER` directive). You have seen how to define a PostGIS layer. It is necessary to define its connection information (database, user, password, and so on), the SQL definition in the database (it is possible to use just a PostGIS table name, but you could eventually use a query to define the set of features and attributes defining the layer), the geometric type, and the projection.

A whole directive (`CLASS`) is used to define how the layer features will be rendered. You may use different classes, as you did in this recipe, to render features differently, based on an attribute defined with the `CLASSITEM` setting. In this recipe, you defined three different classes, each representing a population class, using different colors.

See also

- You can find more information about using MapServer by using its extensive documentation at its project home page (`http://mapserver.org/it/index.html`). You will find the mapfile documentation at `http://www.mapserver.org/mapfile/` very useful to read.
- A good tutorial to understand how to generate mapfiles can be found at `http://mapserver.org/tutorial/example1-1.html`.
- In case you want to gain a better understanding of the WMS and WFS standards, check their specifications at the OGC website. For the WMS service, go to `http://www.opengeospatial.org/standards/wms`, whereas for WFS, go to `http://www.opengeospatial.org/standards/wfs`.

Creating WMS and WFS services with GeoServer

In the previous recipe, you created WMS and WFS from a PostGIS layer using MapServer. In this recipe, you will do it using another popular open source web-mapping engine-GeoServer. You will then use the created services as you did with MapServer, testing their exposed requests, first using a browser and then the QGIS desktop tool (you can do this with other software, such as uDig, gvSIG, OpenJUMP GIS, and ArcGIS Desktop).

Getting ready

While MapServer is written in the C language and uses Apache as its web server, GeoServer is written in Java and you therefore need to install the **Java Virtual Machine (JVM)** in your system; it must be used from a servlet container, such as *Jetty* and *Tomcat*. After installing the servlet container, you will be able to deploy the GeoServer application to it. For example, in Tomcat, you can deploy GeoServer by copying the GeoServer **WAR (web archive)** file to Tomcat's `webapps` directory. For this recipe, we will suppose that you have a working GeoServer in your system; if this is not the case, follow the detailed GeoServer installation steps for your OS at the GeoServer website (`http://docs.geoserver.org/stable/en/user/installation/`) and then return to this recipe. Follow these steps:

1. Download the USA counties shapefile from the `https://nationalmap.gov/` website at `http://dds.cr.usgs.gov/pub/data/nationalatlas/countyp020_nt00009.tar.gz` (this archive is included in the book's code bundle). Extract the archive from `working/chp09` and import it to PostGIS using the `ogr2ogr` command, as follows:

   ```
   $ ogr2ogr -f PostgreSQL -a_srs EPSG:4326 -lco GEOMETRY_NAME=the_geom
   -nln chp09.counties PG:"dbname='postgis_cookbook' user='me'
   password='mypassword'" countyp020.shp
   ```

How to do it...

Carry out the following steps:

1. Open the GeoServer administrative interface, which is typically located at `http://localhost:8080/geoserver`, in your favorite browser and log in using your credentials (`admin` as the username and `geoserver` as the password) if you are just using the GeoServer default installation and have not customized things. After starting GeoServer, you should see the following:

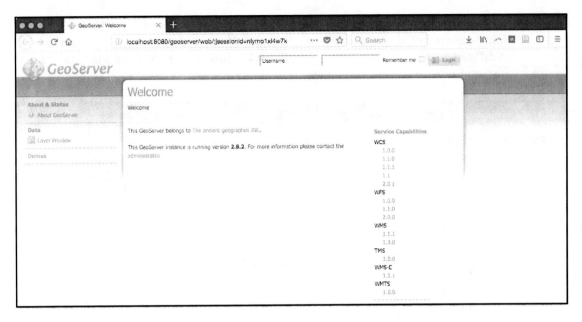

GeoServer welcome screen viewed in a browser

2. After successfully logging in, create a workspace by clicking on the **Workspace** link under **Work** (in the left-hand-side panel of the GeoServer application's main menu) and then click on the **Add new workspace** link. In the text boxes of the form that appears, specify the following values and then click on the **Submit** button:

   - Enter `postgis_cookbook` in the **Name** field
   - Enter the URL `https://www.packtpub.com/big-data-and-business-intelligence/postgis-cookbook` in the **Namespace URI** field

3. Now, to create a PostGIS store, click on the **Stores** link under **Data** (in the left-hand-side panel of the GeoServer application's main menu). Now, click on the **Add new store** link, and then on the **PostGIS** link under **Vector Data Sources,** as shown in the following screenshot:

GeoServer screen to configure new data sources

4. In the **New Vector Data Source** page, complete the form's fields, as follows:
   1. Select **postgis_cookbook** from the **Workspace** drop-down list.
   2. Enter `postgis_cookbook` in the **Data Source Name** field.
   3. Enter `localhost` in the **host** field.
   4. Enter `5432` in the **port** field.
   5. Enter `postgis_cookbook` in the **database** field.
   6. Enter `chp09` in the **schema** field.
   7. Enter `me` in the **user** field.
   8. Enter `mypassword` in the **passwd** field.

The **New Vector Data Source** page is shown in the following screenshot:

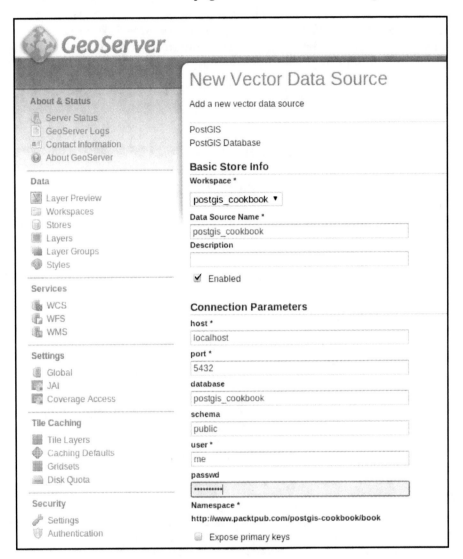

5. Now, click on the **Save** button to successfully create your PostGIS store.

6. Now, you are ready to publish the PostGIS `counties` layer as WMS and WFS. On the **Layers** page, click on the **Add a new resource** link. Now, select **postgis_cookbook** from the **Add layer from** drop-down list. Click on the **Publish** link to the right of the `counties` layer.

7. On the **Edit Layer** page, shown in the following screenshot, click on the links **Compute from data** and **Compute from native bounds**, and then click on the **Save** button:

GeoServer screen to edit the countries layer for publishing

8. Now, you need to define the style used to display the layer to the user. Unlike MapServer, GeoServer uses the OGC-standard **Styled Layer Descriptor (SLD)** notation. Click on the **Styles** link under **Data** and then on the **Add new style** link. Fill the text fields in the form, as follows:

   - Enter `Counties classified per size` in the **Name** field.
   - Enter `postgis_cookbook` in the **Workspace** field

9. In the text area for the SLD, add the following XML code defining the style for the `counties` layer. Then, click on the **Validate** button to check whether your SLD definition is correct and then click on the **Submit** button to save the new style:

```xml
<?xml version="1.0" encoding="UTF-8"?>
<sld:StyledLayerDescriptor xmlns="http://www.opengis.net/sld"
 xmlns:sld="http://www.opengis.net/sld"
 xmlns:ogc="http://www.opengis.net/ogc"
 xmlns:gml="http://www.opengis.net/gml" version="1.0.0">
  <sld:NamedLayer>
    <sld:Name>county_classification</sld:Name>
    <sld:UserStyle>
      <sld:Name>county_classification</sld:Name>
      <sld:Title>County area classification</sld:Title>
      <sld:FeatureTypeStyle>
        <sld:Name>name</sld:Name>
        <sld:Rule>
          <sld:Title>Large counties</sld:Title>
          <ogc:Filter>
            <ogc:PropertyIsGreaterThanOrEqualTo>
              <ogc:PropertyName>square_mil</ogc:PropertyName>
              <ogc:Literal>5000</ogc:Literal>
            </ogc:PropertyIsGreaterThanOrEqualTo>
          </ogc:Filter>
          <sld:PolygonSymbolizer>
            <sld:Fill>
              <sld:CssParameter
               name="fill">#FF0000</sld:CssParameter>
            </sld:Fill>
            <sld:Stroke/>
          </sld:PolygonSymbolizer>
        </sld:Rule>
        <sld:Rule>
          <sld:Title>Small counties</sld:Title>
          <ogc:Filter>
            <ogc:PropertyIsLessThan>
              <ogc:PropertyName>square_mil</ogc:PropertyName>
              <ogc:Literal>5000</ogc:Literal>
            </ogc:PropertyIsLessThan>
          </ogc:Filter>
          <sld:PolygonSymbolizer>
            <sld:Fill>
              <sld:CssParameter
               name="fill">#0000FF</sld:CssParameter>
            </sld:Fill>
            <sld:Stroke/>
          </sld:PolygonSymbolizer>
```

```
            </sld:Rule>
        </sld:FeatureTypeStyle>
      </sld:UserStyle>
    </sld:NamedLayer>
  </sld:StyledLayerDescriptor>
```

The following screenshot shows how the new style looks on the **New style** GeoServer page:

GeoServer screen for creating a new style as an SLD document

10. Now you need to associate the created style with the `counties` layer. Go back to the layer page (**Data | Layers**), click on the `counties` layer link, and then, on the **Edit Layer** page, click on the **Publishing** section. Select **Counties classified per size** in the **Default style** drop-down list and then click on the **Save** button.

11. Now that your WMS and WFS services for the PostGIS `counties` layer are ready, it is time to start using them! First, test the `GetCapabilities` WMS request. To do this, you can click on one of the links on the right-hand-side panel on the GeoServer web application home page. You can click on the link for either WMS version 1.1.1 or WMS version 1.3.0. Click on one of the links or type the `GetCapabilities` request directly in the browser as `http://localhost:8080/geoserver/ows?service=wms&version=1.3.0&r equest=GetCapabilities`.

12. Now, we will investigate the `GetCapabilities` response, shown as follows. You will find a lot of information about WMS is available on your GeoServer instance, such as the WMS-supported requests, projections, and a lot of other information about each published layer. In the case of the `counties` layer, the following code is an extract from the `GetCapabilities` document. Note the main layer information, such as the name, title, abstract (you could redefine all of these using the GeoServer web application), the supported **Coordinate Reference Systems (CRS)**, the geographic extent, and the associated style:

```
<Layer queryable="1">
  <Name>postgis_cookbook:counties</Name>
  <Title>counties</Title>
  <Abstract/>
  <KeywordList>
    <Keyword>counties</Keyword>
    <Keyword>features</Keyword>
  </KeywordList>
  <CRS>EPSG:4326</CRS>
  <CRS>CRS:84</CRS>
  <EX_GeographicBoundingBox>
    <westBoundLongitude>-179.133392333984
    </westBoundLongitude>
    <eastBoundLongitude>-64.566162109375
    </eastBoundLongitude>
    <southBoundLatitude>17.6746921539307
    </southBoundLatitude>
    <northBoundLatitude>71.3980484008789
    </northBoundLatitude>
  </EX_GeographicBoundingBox>
  <BoundingBox CRS="CRS:84" minx="-179.133392333984"
   miny="17.6746921539307" maxx="-64.566162109375"
   maxy="71.3980484008789"/>
  <BoundingBox CRS="EPSG:4326" minx="17.6746921539307"
   miny="-179.133392333984" maxx="71.3980484008789" maxy="-
   64.566162109375"/>
  <Style>
```

```
<Name>Counties classified per size</Name>
<Title>County area classification</Title>
<Abstract/>
<LegendURL width="20" height="20">
  <Format>image/png</Format>
  <OnlineResource
   xmlns:xlink="http://www.w3.org/1999/xlink"
   xlink:type="simple" xlink:href=
   "http://localhost:8080/geoserver/
    ows?service=WMS&amp;request=GetLegendGraphic&amp;
     format=image%2Fpng&amp;width=20&amp;height=20&amp;
    layer=counties"/>
</LegendURL>
  </Style>
</Layer>
```

13. To test the GetMap and GetFeatureInfo WMS requests, the GeoServer web application offers you a very handy way with the **Layer Preview** page. Navigate to **Data | Layer Preview** and then click on the **OpenLayers** link next to the counties layer. The **Layer Preview** page is based on the OpenLayers JavaScript library and lets you experiment with the GetMap and GetFeatureInfo requests.

14. Try to navigate the map; at each zoom and pan action, GeoServer will stream out a new image provided by the response output to a GetMap request. By clicking on the map, you can perform a GetFeatureInfo request and the user interface will display the feature's attributes corresponding to the point on the map on which you clicked. A very effective way to check how the requests are sent to GeoServer as you navigate the map is by using the Firefox Firebug plugin or the Chrome (or Chromium if you are using Linux) Developer Tools. With these tools, you will be able to identify the GetMap and GetFeatureInfo requests that are being sent behind the scenes from the **OpenLayers** viewer to GeoServer. One such map is shown in the following screenshot:

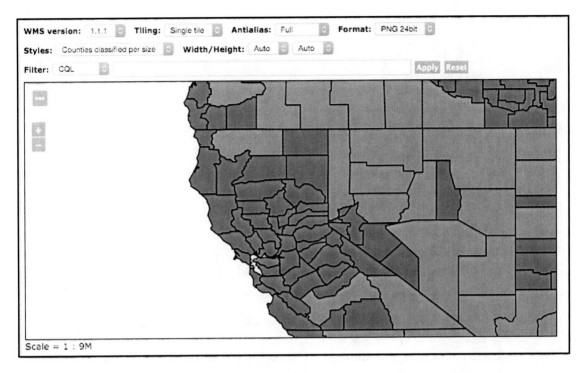

Here is what you get when inspecting the requests with any in-browser developer tool, check the request URL, and verify the parameters sent to geoserver; this is how it looks with Firefox:

15. Now, try a WMS `GetMap` request by typing the URL
    ```
    http://localhost:8080/geoserver/postgis_cookbook/wms?LAYERS=pos
    tgis_cookbook%3Acounties&STYLES=&FORMAT=image%2Fpng&SERVICE=WMS
    &VERSION=1.1.1&REQUEST=GetMap&SRS=EPSG%3A4326&BBOX=-200.5028659
    4033,7.6152902245522,-43.196688503029,81.457450330258&WIDTH=703
    &HEIGHT=330
    ``` in your browser.

16. Try a WMS `GetFeatureInfo` request, as well, by typing the URL
    ```
    http://localhost:8080/geoserver/postgis_cookbook/wms?REQUEST=Ge
    tFeatureInfo&EXCEPTIONS=application%2Fvnd.ogc.se_xml&BBOX=-126.
    094303%2C37.16812%2C-116.262667%2C41.783255&SERVICE=WMS&INFO_FO
    RMAT=text%2Fhtml&QUERY_LAYERS=postgis_cookbook%3Acounties&FEATU
    RE_COUNT=50&Layers=postgis_cookbook%3Acounties&WIDTH=703&HEIGHT
    =330&format=image%2Fpng&styles=&srs=EPSG%3A4326&version=1.1.1&x
    =330&y=158.
    ```

    This will be displayed by prompting the previous URL:

counties								
fid	area	perimeter	countyp020	state	county	fips	state_fips	square_mil
counties.2958	0.456	4.010	2959	CA	Butte County	06007	06	1676.018

17. Now, as you did for the MapService WMS, test the GeoServer WMS in QGIS. Create a WMS connection named `GeoServer on localhost`, pointing to the GeoServer `GetCapabilities` document (`http://localhost:8080/geoserver/ows?service=wms&version=1.3.0& request=GetCapabilities`). Then, connect to the WMS server (for example, from the QGIS browser), select `counties` from the **Layers** list, and add it to the map, as shown in the following screenshot; then navigate the layer and try to identify some of the features:

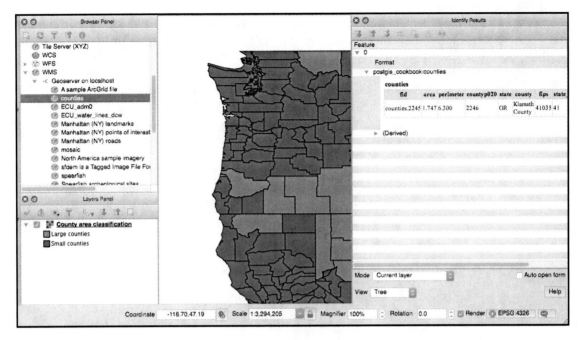

18. Having used WMS, try to test a couple of WFS requests. A typical WFS `GetCapability` request can be executed by typing the URL `http://localhost:8080/geoserver/wfs?service=wfs&version=1.1.0&request=GetCapabilities`. You could also click on one of the WFS links on the home page of the GeoServer web interface.

19. Investigate the XML `GetCapabilities` response and try to identify the information about your layer. You should have a `<FeatureType>` element, such as the following, corresponding to the `counties` layer:

```
<FeatureType>
  <Name>postgis_cookbook:counties</Name>
  <Title>counties</Title>
  <Abstract/>
  <Keywords>counties, features</Keywords>
  <SRS>EPSG:4326</SRS>
  <LatLongBoundingBox minx="-179.133392333984"
   miny="17.6746921539307" maxx="-64.566162109375"
   maxy="71.3980484008789"/>
</FeatureType>
```

20. As shown in the previous recipe, a typical WFS request is `GetFeature`, which will result in a GML response. Try it by typing the URL `http://localhost:8080/geoserver/wfs?service=wfs&version=1.0.0&request=GetFeature&typeName=postgis_cookbook:counties&maxFeatures=5` in your browser. You will receive a GML output composed of a `<wfs:FeatureCollection>` element and a collection of `<gml:featureMember>` elements (possibly five elements, as specified in the `maxFeatures` request's parameter). You will get an output that is similar to the following code:

```
<gml:featureMember>
  <postgis_cookbook:counties fid="counties.3962">
    <postgis_cookbook:the_geom>
      <gml:Polygon srsName="http://www.opengis.net/
      gml/srs/epsg.xml#4326">
        <gml:outerBoundaryIs>
          <gml:LinearRing>
            <gml:coordinates xmlns:gml=
            "http://www.opengis.net/gml"
            decimal="." cs="," ts="">
            -101.62554932,36.50246048 -
            101.0908432,36.50032043 ...
              ...
              ...
            </gml:coordinates>
          </gml:LinearRing>
        </gml:outerBoundaryIs>
      </gml:Polygon>
    </postgis_cookbook:the_geom>
     <postgis_cookbook:area>0.240</postgis_cookbook:area>
    <postgis_cookbook:perimeter>1.967
    </postgis_cookbook:perimeter>
    <postgis_cookbook:co2000p020>3963.0
    </postgis_cookbook:co2000p020>
     <postgis_cookbook:state>TX</postgis_cookbook:state>
    <postgis_cookbook:county>Hansford
     County</postgis_cookbook:county>
     <postgis_cookbook:fips>48195</postgis_cookbook:fips>
    <postgis_cookbook:state_fips>48
    </postgis_cookbook:state_fips>
    <postgis_cookbook:square_mil>919.801
    </postgis_cookbook:square_mil>
  </postgis_cookbook:counties>
</gml:featureMember>
```

21. Now, as you did with WMS, try the **counties** WFS in QGIS (or in your favorite desktop GIS client). Create a new WFS connection by using either the QGIS browser or the **Add WFS Layer** button and then clicking on the **New Connection** button. In the **Create a new WFS connection** dialog box, type `GeoServer on localhost` in the **Name** field and add the WFS `GetCapabilities` URL (`http://localhost:8080/geoserver/wfs?service=wfs&version=1.1.0& request=GetCapabilities`) in the **URL** field.

22. Add the WFS `counties` layer from the previous dialog box and, as a test, select some of the counties and export them to a new shapefile using the **Save As** command from the layer's context menu, as shown in the following screenshot:

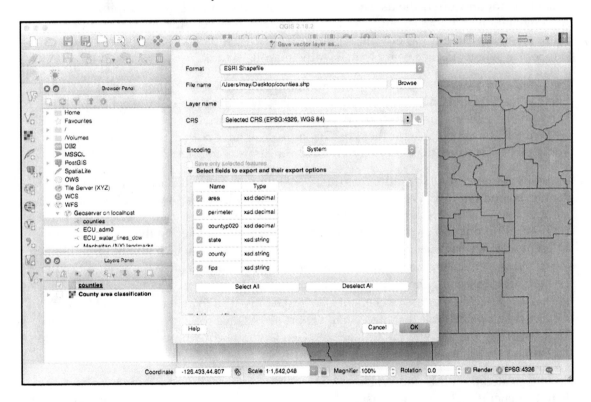

How it works...

In the previous recipe, you were introduced to the basic concepts of the OGC WMS and WFS standards using MapServer. In this recipe, you have done the same using another popular open source web-mapping engine, GeoServer.

Unlike MapServer, which is written in C and can be used from web servers such as Apache HTTP (HTTPD) or Microsoft **Internet Information Server (IIS)** as a CGI program, GeoServer is written in Java and needs a servlet container such as Apache Tomcat or Eclipse Jetty to work.

GeoServer not only offers the user a highly scalable and standard web-mapping engine implementation, but does so with a nice user interface, the Web Administration interface. Therefore, it is generally easier for a beginner to create WMS and WFS services compared to MapServer, where it is necessary to master the mapfile syntax.

The GeoServer workflow to create WMS and WFS services for a PostGIS layer is to first create a PostGIS store, where you need to associate the main PostGIS connection parameters (server name, schema, user, and so on). After the store is correctly created, you can publish the layers that are available for that PostGIS store. You have seen in this recipe how easy the whole process is using the GeoServer Web Administration interface.

To define the layer style to render features, GeoServer uses the SLD schema, an OGC standard based on XML. We have written two distinct rules in this recipe to render the counties that have an area greater than 5,000 square miles an area greater than 5,000 square miles in a different way from the others. For the purpose of rendering the counties in a different way, we have used two `<ogc:Rule>` SLD elements in which you have defined an `<ogc:Filter>` element. For each of these elements, you have defined the criteria to filter the layer features, using the `<ogc:PropertyIsGreaterThanOrEqualTo>` and `<ogc:PropertyIsLessThan>` elements. A very handy way to generate an SLD for a layer is using desktop GIS tools that are able to export an SLD file for a layer (QGIS can do this). After exporting the file, you can upload it to GeoServer by copying the SLD file content to the **Add a new style** page.

Having created the WMS and WFS services for the counties layer, you have been testing them by generating the requests using the handy Layer Preview GeoServer interface (based on OpenLayers) and then typing the requests directly in a browser. You can modify each service request's parameters from the Layer Preview interface or just by changing them in the URL query string.

Finally, you tested the services using QGIS and have seen how it is possible to export some of the layer's features using the WFS service.

See also

If you want more information about GeoServer, you can check out its excellent documentation at `http://docs.geoserver.org/` or get the wonderful *GeoServer Beginner's Guide* book by Packt Publishing (`http://www.packtpub.com/geoserver-share-edit-geospatial-data-beginners-guide/book`).

Creating a WMS Time service with MapServer

In this recipe, you will implement a WMS Time with MapServer. For time-series data, and whenever you have geographic data that is updated continuously and you need to expose it as a WMS in a Web GIS, WMS Time is the way to go. This is possible by providing the `TIME` parameter a time value in the WMS requests, typically in the `GetMap` request.

Here, you will implement a WMS Time service for the hotspots, representing possible fire data acquired by NASA's **Earth Observing System Data and Information System (EOSDIS)**. This excellent system provides data derived from MODIS images from the last 24 hours, 48 hours, and 7 days, which can be downloaded in shapefile, KML, WMS, or text file formats. You will load a bunch of this data to PostGIS, create a WMS Time service with MapServer, and test the WMS `GetCapabilities` and `GetMap` requests using a common browser.

 If you are new to the WMS standard, please check the previous two recipes to get more information.

Getting ready

1. First, download one week's worth of active fire data (hotspots) from the EOSDIS website. For example, Firedata from EOSDIS can be found in this link: `https://earthdata.nasa.gov/earth-observation-data/near-real-time/firms/active-fire-data`. A copy of this shapefile is included in the book code bundle. Use that if you want to use the SQL and WMS parameters that have been used in the following steps.

2. Extract the shapefile from the `Global_7d.zip` archive to the `working/chp09` directory and import this shapefile in PostGIS using the `shp2pgsql` command, as follows:

```
$ shp2pgsql -s 4326 -g the_geom -I
MODIS_C6_Global_7d.shp chp09.hotspots > hotspots.sql
$ psql -U me -d postgis_cookbook -f hotspots.sql
```

3. When the import is completed, check the point fire data (hotspots) you just imported in PostGIS. Each hotspot contains a bunch of useful information, most notably the geometry and the acquisition date and time stored in the `acq_date` and `acq_time` fields. You can easily see that the features loaded from the shapefile span eight consecutive days using the following command:

```
postgis_cookbook=# SELECT acq_date, count(*) AS hotspots_count
FROM chp09.hotspots GROUP BY acq_date ORDER BY acq_date;
```

The previous command will produce the following output:

	acq_date date	hotspots_count bigint
1	2017-12-07	12009
2	2017-12-08	10433
3	2017-12-09	10100
4	2017-12-10	13918
5	2017-12-11	11226
6	2017-12-12	13131
7	2017-12-13	15986
8	2017-12-14	13465

How to do it...

Carry out the following steps:

1. We will first create a WMS for the PostGIS hotspot layer. Create a `mapfile` named `hotspots.map` in a directory accessible to the HTTPD (or IIS) user (for example, `/var/www/data` in Linux, `/Library/WebServer/Documents/` for macOS, and `C:\ms4w\Apache\htdocs` in Windows), by executing the following code after adjusting the database connection settings:

```
MAP # Start of mapfile
  NAME 'hotspots_time_series'
  IMAGETYPE          PNG
  EXTENT             -180 -90 180 90
  SIZE               800 400
  IMAGECOLOR         255 255 255

  # map projection definition
  PROJECTION
    'init=epsg:4326'
  END

  # a symbol for hotspots
  SYMBOL
    NAME "circle"
    TYPE ellipse
    FILLED true
    POINTS
      1 1
    END
  END

  # web section: here we define the ows services
  WEB
    # WMS and WFS server settings
    METADATA
      'wms_name'                'Hotspots'
      'wms_title'               'World hotspots time
                                 series'
      'wms_abstract'            'Active fire data detected
                                 by NASA Earth Observing
                                 System Data and Information
                                 System (EOSDIS)'
      'wms_onlineresource'      'http://localhost/cgi-bin/
                                 mapserv?map=/var/www/data/
                                 hotspots.map&'
```

```
        'wms_srs'                           'EPSG:4326 EPSG:3857'
        'wms_enable_request' '*'
        'wms_feature_info_mime_type'  'text/html'
      END
    END

    # Start of layers definition
    LAYER # Hotspots point layer begins here
      NAME            hotspots
      CONNECTIONTYPE  POSTGIS
      CONNECTION      'host=localhost dbname=postgis_cookbook
                      user=me
                      password=mypassword port=5432'
      DATA            'the_geom from chp09.hotspots'
      TEMPLATE 'template.html'
      METADATA
        'wms_title'                       'World hotspots time
                                          series'
        'gml_include_items' 'all'
      END
      STATUS          ON
      TYPE            POINT
      CLASS
        SYMBOL 'circle'
        SIZE 4
        COLOR          255 0 0
      END # end of class

    END # hotspots layer ends here

  END # End of mapfile
```

2. Check whether the WMS GetCapabilities request for this mapfile is working well by typing the following URLs in the browser:

   - `http://localhost/cgi-bin/mapserv?map=/var/www/data/hotspots.map&SERVICE=WMS&VERSION=1.0.0&REQUEST=GetCapabilities` (in Linux)

   - `http://localhost/cgi-bin/mapserv.exe?map=C:\ms4w\Apache\htdoc\shotspots.map&SERVICE=WMS&VERSION=1.0.0&REQUEST=GetCapabilities` (in Windows)

   - `http://localhost/cgi-bin/mapserv?map=/Library/WebServer/Documents/hotspots.map&SERVICE=WMS&VERSION=1.0.0&REQUEST=GetCapabilities` (in macOS)

In the following steps, we will be referring to Linux. If you are using Windows, you just need to replace
`http://localhost/cgi-bin/mapserv?map=/var/www/data/hotspots.map` with
`http://localhost/cgi-bin/mapserv.exe?map=C:\ms4w\Apache\htdoc\shotspots`
`.map`; or if using macOS, replace it with
`http://localhost/cgi-bin/mapserv?map=/Library/WebServer/Documents/hotsp`
`osts.map` in every request:

1. Now query the WMS service with a `GetMap` request. Type the following URL in the browser. If everything is correct, MapServer should return an image with some hotspots as a response. The URL is
   `http://localhost/cgi-bin/mapserv?map=/var/www/data/hotspots.map`
   `&&SERVICE=WMS&VERSION=1.3.0&REQUEST=GetMap&BBOX=-25,-100,35,-35`
   `&CRS=EPSG:4326&WIDTH=1000&HEIGHT=800&LAYERS=hotspots&STYLES=&FO`
   `RMAT=image/png`.

   The map displayed on your browser will look as follows:

2. Until now, you have implemented a simple WMS service. Now, to make the `TIME` parameter available for WMS Time requests, add the `wms_timeextent`, `wms_timeitem` and `wms_timedefault` variables in the `LAYER METADATA` section, as follows:

```
METADATA
    'wms_title'                         'World hotspots time
                                            series'
    'gml_include_items' 'all'
    'wms_timeextent' '2000-01-01/2020-12-31' # time extent
        for which the service will give a response
    'wms_timeitem' 'acq_date' # layer field to use to filter
        on the TIME parameter
    'wms_timedefault' '2013-05-30' # default parameter if not
        added to the request
END
```

3. Having added these parameters in the `LAYER METADATA` mapfile section, the WMS `GetCapabilities` response should change. Now, the hotspots layer definition includes the time dimension, defined by the `<Dimension>` and `<Extent>` elements. You will get a response, as follows:

```
- <Layer>
    <Name>hotspots_time_series</Name>
  - <Title>
      World hotspots time series
    </Title>
  - <Abstract>
      Active fire data detected by NASA Earth Observing System Data and Information System (EOSDIS)
    </Abstract>
    <SRS>EPSG:4326 EPSG:3857</SRS>
    <LatLonBoundingBox minx="-180" miny="-90" maxx="180" maxy="90"/>
    <BoundingBox SRS="EPSG:4326" minx="-180" miny="-90" maxx="180" maxy="90"/>
  - <Layer queryable="1">
      <Name>hotspots</Name>
      <Title>World hotspots time series</Title>
      <LatLonBoundingBox minx="-175.394" miny="-49.247" maxx="174.895" maxy="67.807"/>
      <BoundingBox SRS="EPSG:4326" minx="-175.394" miny="-49.247" maxx="174.895" maxy="67.807"/>
      <Dimension name="time" units="ISO8601"/>
      <Extent name="time" default="2017-12-12" nearestValue="0">2000-01-01/2020-12-31</Extent>
    </Layer>
  </Layer>
```

4. You can finally test the WMS service with time support. You only need to remember to add the `TIME` parameter in the `GetMap` request (otherwise, `GetMap` will filter out the data using the default date, which is `2017-12-12` in this example) using the URL

```
http://localhost/cgi-bin/mapserv?map=/var/www/data/hotspots.map
&&SERVICE=WMS&VERSION=1.3.0&REQUEST=GetMap&BBOX=-25,-100,35,-35
&CRS=EPSG:4326&WIDTH=1000&HEIGHT=800&LAYERS=hotspots&STYLES=&FO
RMAT=image/png&TIME=2017-12-10.
```

5. Play for a while with the `TIME` parameter in the preceding URL and try to see how the GetMap image response changes day by day. Remember that, for the dataset we imported, the `acq_date` range is from 2017-12-07 to 2017-12-14; but in your case, if you didn't use the hostpots shapefile included in the book dataset, the time range will be different!

   The following are different outputs for the mentioned dates and the full URLs used to query the service:

   - `http://localhost/cgi-bin/mapserv?map=/var/www/data/hots
     pots.map&&SERVICE=WMS&VERSION=1.3.0&REQUEST=GetMap&BBOX
     =-25,-100,35,-35&CRS=EPSG:4326&WIDTH=1000&HEIGHT=800&LA
     YERS=hotspots&STYLES=&FORMAT=image/png&TIME=2017-12-14.`
     The output is as follows (2017-12-14):

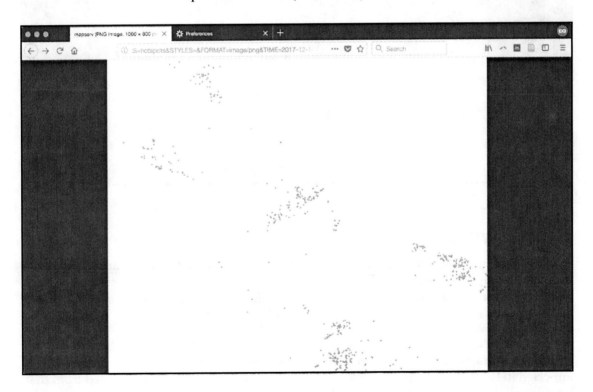

- `http://localhost/cgi-bin/mapserv?map=/var/www/data/h otspots.map&&SERVICE=WMS&VERSION=1.3.0&REQUEST=GetMa p&BBOX=-25,-100,35,-35&CRS=EPSG:4326&WIDTH=1000&HEIG HT=800&LAYERS=hotspots&STYLES=&FORMAT=image/png&TIME =2017-12-07`. **The output is as follows (2017-12-07):**

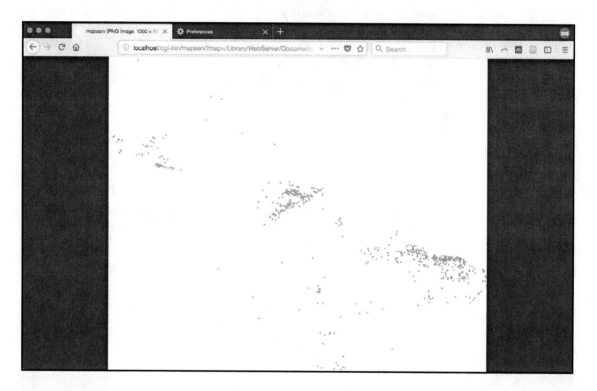

How it works...

In this recipe, you have seen how to create a WMS Time service using the MapServer open source web-mapping engine. A WMS Time service is useful for whenever you have temporal series and geographic data varying in the time. WMS Time lets the user filter the requested data by providing a `TIME` parameter with a time value in the WMS requests.

For this purpose, you first created a plain WMS; if you are new to the WMS standard, mapfile, and MapServer, you can check out the first recipe in this chapter. You have imported in PostGIS a points shapefile with one week's worth of hotspots derived from the MODIS satellite and created a simple WMS for this layer.

After verifying that this WMS works well by testing the WMS `GetCapabilities` and `GetMap` requests, you have time enabled the WMS by adding three parameters in the `LAYER` `METADATA` mapfile section: `wms_timeextent`, `wms_timeitem`, and `wms_timedefault`.

The `wms_timeextent` parameter is the duration of time in which the service will give a response. It defines the PostGIS `table` field to be used to filter the `TIME` parameter (the `acq_date` field in this case). The `wms_timedefault` parameter specifies a default time value to be used when the request to the WMS service does not provide the `TIME` parameter.

At this point, the WMS is time enabled; this means that the WMS GetCapabilities request now includes the time-dimension definition for the PostGIS hotspots layer and, more importantly, the GetMap WMS request lets the user add the `TIME` parameter to query the layer for a specific date.

Consuming WMS services with OpenLayers

In this recipe, you will use the MapServer and Geoserver WMS you created in the first two recipes of this chapter using the OpenLayers open source JavaScript API.

This excellent library helps developers quickly assemble web pages using mapping viewers and features. In this recipe, you will create an HTML page, add an OpenLayers map in it and a bunch of controls in that map for navigation, switch the layers, and identify features of the layers. We will also look at two WMS layers pointing to the PostGIS tables, implemented with MapServer and GeoServer.

Getting ready

MapServer uses *PROJ.4* (`https://trac.osgeo.org/proj/`) for projection management. This library does not exist by default with the *Spherical Mercator* projection (*EPSG:900913*) defined. Such a projection is commonly used by commercial map API providers, such as GoogleMaps, Yahoo! Maps, and Microsoft Bing, and can provide excellent base layers for your maps.

For this recipe, we need to have under consideration the following:

1. Due to security restrictions in JavaScript, it is not possible to retrieve information from remote domains using XMLHttpRequest. You will encounter this issue in the recipe when you send a WMS GetFeatureInfo request to a GeoServer that is typically running on Tomcat at port 8080 and also send a request from an HTML page running on Apache or ISS at port 80. Therefore, unless you run your GeoServer instance using HTTPD URL rewriting, the solution is to create a proxy script.

2. Copy the proxy script included in the book dataset to the web cgi directory of your computer (in Linux, at /usr/lib/cgi-bin/, in macOS, at /Library/WebServer/CGI-Executables, and in Windows, at C:\ms4w\Apache\cgi-bin), open the proxy.cgi file, and add localhost:8080 to the allowedHosts list.

How to do it...

Carry out the following steps:

1. Create the openlayers.html file and add the <head> and <body> tags. In the <head> tag, import the OpenLayers JavaScript library by executing the following code:

```
<!doctype html>
<html>
  <head>
    <title>OpenLayers Example</title>
    <script src="http://openlayers.org/api/OpenLayers.js">
    </script>
  </head>
  <body>
  </body>
</html>
```

2. First, add a <div> element in the <body> tag that will contain the OpenLayers map. The map should be given a width of 900 pixels and a height of 500 pixels, using the following code:

```
<div style="width:900px; height:500px" id="map"></div>
```

3. Just after the map is placed in `<div>`, add a JavaScript script and create an OpenLayers `map` object. In the map constructor parameters, you will add an empty `controls` array and declare that the map has a Spherical Mercator's projection, as shown in the following code:

```
<script defer="defer" type="text/javascript">
  // instantiate the map object
  var map = new OpenLayers.Map("map", {
    controls: [],
    projection: new OpenLayers.Projection("EPSG:3857")
  });
</script>
```

4. Right after the `map` variable is declared, add some OpenLayers controls to the map. For the web GIS viewer you are creating, you will add the `Navigation` control (which handles map browsing with mouse events, such as dragging, double-clicking, and scrolling the wheel), the `PanZoomBar` control (a four-direction navigation using the arrows present above the zooming vertical slider), the `LayerSwitcher` control (which handles the switching on and off of layers added to the map), and the `MousePosition` control (which displays the map coordinates as they change while the user is moving the mouse), using the following code:

```
// add some controls on the map
map.addControl(new OpenLayers.Control.Navigation());
map.addControl(new OpenLayers.Control.PanZoomBar()),
map.addControl(new OpenLayers.Control.LayerSwitcher(
    {"div":OpenLayers.Util.getElement("layerswitcher")}));
map.addControl(new OpenLayers.Control.MousePosition());
```

5. Now create an OSM base layer, using the following code:

```
// set the OSM layer
var osm_layer = new OpenLayers.Layer.OSM();
```

6. Set two variables for the WMS GeoServer and the MapServer URL that you will use (they are the URLs of the services you created in the first two recipes of this chapter):

- For Linux, add the following code:

```
// set the WMS
var geoserver_url = "http://localhost:8080/geoserver/wms";
var mapserver_url = http://localhost/cgi-
bin/mapserv?map=/var/www/data/countries.map&
```

- For Windows, add the following code:

```
// set the WMS
var geoserver_url = "http://localhost:8080/geoserver/wms";
var mapserver_url = http://localhost/cgi-
bin/mapserv.exe?map=C:\\ms4w\\Apache\\
htdocs\\countries.map&
```

- For macOS, add the following code:

```
// set the WMS
var geoserver_url = "http://localhost:8080/geoserver/wms";
var mapserver_url = http://localhost/cgi-
bin/mapserv? map=/Library/WebServer/
Documents/countries.map&
```

7. Now, create a WMS GeoServer layer to display the OpenLayers map the counties from the PostGIS layer. You will set an opacity for this layer, so that it is possible to see the other layer (counties) behind it. The `isBaseLayer` property is set to `false`, since you want to have this layer over the Google Maps base layers and not as an alternative to them (by default, all of the WMS layers in OpenLayers are considered to be base layers). Create the WMS GeoServer layer, using the following code:

```
// set the GeoServer WMS
var geoserver_wms = new OpenLayers.Layer.WMS( "GeoServer WMS",
geoserver_url,
{
  layers: "postgis_cookbook:counties",
  transparent: "true",
  format: "image/png",
},
{
  isBaseLayer: false,
  opacity: 0.4
```

```
} );
```

8. Now, create a WMS MapServer layer to display the countries from the PostGIS layer in the OpenLayers map, using the following code:

```
// set the MapServer WMS
var mapserver_wms = new OpenLayers.Layer.WMS( "MapServer WMS",
mapserver_url,
{
  layers: "countries",
  transparent: "true",
  format: "image/png",
},
{
  isBaseLayer: false
} );
```

9. After creating the OSM and WMS layers, you need to add all of them to the map, using the following code:

```
// add all of the layers to the map
map.addLayers([mapserver_wms, geoserver_wms, osm_layer]);
map.zoomToMaxExtent();
Proxy...
// add the WMSGetFeatureInfo control
OpenLayers.ProxyHost = "/cgi-bin/proxy.cgi?url=";
```

10. You want to provide the user the possibility to identify features of the counties WMS. Add the WMSGetFeatureInfo OpenLayers control (which will send GetFeatureInfo requests to the WMS behind the scenes) that points to the counties PostGIS layer served by the GeoServer WMS, using the following code:

```
var info = new OpenLayers.Control.WMSGetFeatureInfo({
  url: geoserver_url,
  title: 'Identify',
  queryVisible: true,
  eventListeners: {
    getfeatureinfo: function(event) {
      map.addPopup(new OpenLayers.Popup.FramedCloud(
        "WMSIdentify",
        map.getLonLatFromPixel(event.xy),
        null,
        event.text,
        null,
        true
      ));
    }
```

```
    }
});
map.addControl(info);
info.activate();
```

11. Finally, set the center of the map and its initial zoom level, using the following code:

```
// center map
var cpoint = new OpenLayers.LonLat(-11000000, 4800000);
map.setCenter(cpoint, 3);
```

Your HTML file should now look like the `openlayers.html` file contained in `data/chp09`. You can finally deploy this file to your web server (Apache HTTPD or IIS). If you are using Apache HTTPD in Linux, you could copy the file to the `data` directory under `/var/www`, and if you are using Windows, you could copy it to the data directory under `C:\ms4w\Apache\htdocs` (create the `data` directory if it does not already exist). Then, access it using the URL `http://localhost/data/openlayers.html`.

Now, access the `openlayers` web page using your favorite browser. Start browsing the map: zoom, pan, try to switch the base and overlays layers on and off using the layer switcher control, and try to click on a point to identify one feature from the counties PostGIS layer. A map is shown in the following screenshot:

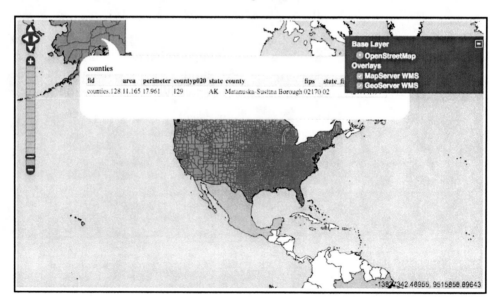

How it works..

You have seen how to create a web map viewer with the *OpenLayers* JavaScript library. This library lets the developer define the various map components, using JavaScript in an HTML page. The core object is a map that is composed of *controls* and *layers*.

OpenLayers comes with a great number of controls (`http://dev.openlayers.org/docs/files/OpenLayers/Control-js.html`), and it is even possible to create custom ones.

Another great OpenLayers feature is the ability to add a good number of geographic data sources as layers in the map (you added just a couple of its types to the map, such as OpenStreetMap and WMS) and you could add sources, such as WFS, GML, KML, GeoRSS, OSM data, ArcGIS Rest, TMS, WMTS, and WorldWind, just to name a few.

Consuming WMS services with Leaflet

In the previous recipe, you have seen how to create a webGIS using the OpenLayers JavaScript API and then added the WMS PostGIS layers served from MapServer and GeoServer .

A lighter alternative to the widespread OpenLayers JavaScript API was created, named **Leaflet**. In this recipe, you will see how to use this JavaScript API to create a webGIS, add a WMS layer from PostGIS to this map, and implement an *identify tool*, sending a `GetFeatureInfo` request to the MapServer WMS. However, unlike OpenLayers, Leaflet does not come with a `WMSGetFeatureInfo` control, so we will see in this recipe how to create this functionality.

How to do it...

Carry out the following steps:

1. Create a new HTML file and name it `leaflet.html` (available in the book source code package). Open it and add the `<head>` and `<body>` tags. In the `<head>` section, import the Leaflet CSS and JavaScript libraries and the jQuery JavaScript library (you will use jQuery to send an AJAX request to the `GetFeatureInfo` from the MapServer WMS):

```
<html>
  <head>
```

```
       <title>Leaflet Example</title>
       <link rel="stylesheet"
        href= "https://unpkg.com/leaflet@1.2.0/dist/leaflet.css" />
       <script src= "https://unpkg.com/leaflet@1.2.0/dist/leaflet.js">
       </script>
       <script src="http://ajax.googleapis.com/ajax/
              libs/jquery/1.9.1/jquery.min.js">
       </script>
     </head>
     <body>
     </body>
   </html>
```

2. Start adding a `<div>` tag in the `<body>` element to include the Leaflet map in your file, as shown in the following code; the map will have a width of 800 pixels and a height of 500 pixels:

```
<div id="map" style="width:800px; height:500px"></div>
```

3. Just after the `<div>` element containing the map, add the following JavaScript code. Create a Leaflet `tileLayer` object using the `tile.osm.org` service based on `OpenStreetMap` data:

```
<script defer="defer" type="text/javascript">
  // osm layer
  var osm = L.tileLayer('http://{s}.tile.osm.org
              /{z}/{x}/{y}.png', {
    maxZoom: 18,
    attribution: "Data by OpenStreetMap"
  });
</script>
```

4. Create a second layer that will use the MapServer WMS you created a few recipes ago in this chapter. You will need to set the `ms_url` variable differently if you're using Linux, Windows, or macOS:

  - For Linux, use the following code:

```
// mapserver layer
var ms_url = "http://localhost/cgi-bin/mapserv?
  map=/var/www/data/countries.map&";
var countries = L.tileLayer.wms(ms_url, {
  layers: 'countries',
  format: 'image/png',
  transparent: true,
  opacity: 0.7
```

```
});
```

- For Windows, use the following code:

```
// mapserver layer
var ms_url = "http://localhost
  /cgi-bin/mapserv.exe?map=C:%5Cms4w%5CApache%5
  Chtdocs%5Ccountries.map&";
var countries = L.tileLayer.wms(ms_url, {
  layers: 'countries',
  format: 'image/png',
  transparent: true,
  opacity: 0.7
});
```

- For macOS, use the following code:

```
// mapserver layer
var ms_url = "http://localhost/cgi-bin/mapserv?
  map=/Library/WebServer/Documents/countries.map&";
var countries = L.tileLayer.wms(ms_url, {
  layers: 'countries',
  format: 'image/png',
  transparent: true,
  opacity: 0.7
});
```

5. Create the Leaflet map and add layers to it, as shown in the following code:

```
// map creation
var map = new L.Map('map', {
  center: new L.LatLng(15, 0),
  zoom: 2,
  layers: [osm, countries],
  zoomControl: true
});
```

6. Now, associate the mouse-click event with a function that will perform the GetFeatureInfo WMS request on the countries layer, by executing the following code:

```
// getfeatureinfo event
map.addEventListener('click', Identify);

function Identify(e) {
  // set parameters needed for GetFeatureInfo WMS request
  var BBOX = map.getBounds().toBBoxString();
```

```
var WIDTH = map.getSize().x;
var HEIGHT = map.getSize().y;
var X = map.layerPointToContainerPoint(e.layerPoint).x;
var Y = map.layerPointToContainerPoint(e.layerPoint).y;
// compose the URL for the request
var URL = ms_url + 'SERVICE=WMS&VERSION=1.1.1&
REQUEST=GetFeatureInfo&LAYERS=countries&
 QUERY_LAYERS=countries&BBOX='+BBOX+'&FEATURE_COUNT=1&
HEIGHT='+HEIGHT+'&WIDTH='+WIDTH+'&
 INFO_FORMAT=text%2Fhtml&SRS=EPSG%3A4326&X='+X+'&Y='+Y;
//send the asynchronous HTTP request using
jQuery $.ajax
$.ajax({
  url: URL,
  dataType: "html",
  type: "GET",
  success: function(data) {
    var popup = new L.Popup({
      maxWidth: 300
    });
    popup.setContent(data);
    popup.setLatLng(e.latlng);
    map.openPopup(popup);
  }
});
}
```

7. Your HTML file should now look like the `leaflet.html` file contained in `data/chp09`. You can now deploy this file to your web server (that is, Apache HTTPD or IIS). If you are using Apache HTTPD in Linux, you could copy the file to the `/var/www/data directory`; if you are running macOS, copy it to `/Library/WebServer/Documents/data` ;and if you are using Windows, you could copy it to `C:\ms4w\Apache\htdocs\data` (create the data directory if it does not already exist). Then, access it with the URL `http://localhost/data/leaflet.html`.

8. Open the web page using your favorite browser, and start navigating the map; zoom, pan, and try to click on a point to identify one feature from the `countries` PostGIS layer, as shown in the following screenshot:

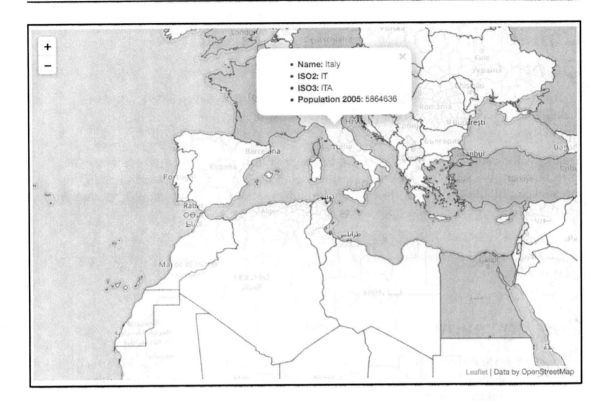

How it works...

In this recipe, you have seen how to use the Leaflet JavaScript API library to add a map in an HTML page. First, you created one layer from an external server to use as the base map. Then, you created another layer using the MapServer WMS you implemented in a previous recipe to expose a PostGIS layer to the web. Then, you created a new map object and added it to these two layers. Finally, using jQuery, you implemented an AJAX call to the GetFeatureInfo WMS request and displayed the results in a Leaflet Popup object.

Leaflet is a very nice and compact alternative to the OpenLayers library and gives very good results when your webGIS service needs to be used from mobile devices, such as tablets and smart phones. Additionally, it has a plethora of plugins and can be easily integrated with JavaScript libraries, such as Raphael and JS3D.

Consuming WFS-T services with OpenLayers

In this recipe, you will create the **Transactional Web Feature Service (WFS-T)** from a PostGIS layer with the GeoServer open source web-mapping engine and then an OpenLayers basic application that will be able to use this service.

This way, the user of the application will be able to manage transactions on the remote PostGIS layer. WFS-T allows for the creation, deletion, and updating of features. In this recipe, you will allow the user to only to add features, but this recipe should put you on your way to creating more composite use cases.

If you are new to GeoServer and OpenLayers, you should first read the *Creating WMS and WFS services with GeoServer* and *Consuming WMS services with OpenLayers* recipes and then return to this one.

Getting ready

1. Create the proxy script and deploy it to your web server (that is, HTTPD or IIS), as indicated in the *Getting ready* section of the *Consuming WMS services with OpenLayers* recipe.

2. Create the following PostGIS points layer named `sites`:

   ```
   CREATE TABLE chp09.sites
   (
     gid serial NOT NULL,
     the_geom geometry(Point,4326),
     CONSTRAINT sites_pkey PRIMARY KEY (gid )
   );
   CREATE INDEX sites_the_geom_gist ON chp09.sites
   USING gist (the_geom );
   ```

3. Now create a PostGIS layer in GeoServer for the `chp09.sites` table. For more information on this, refer to the *Creating WMS and WFS services with GeoServer* recipe in this chapter.

How to do it...

Carry out the following steps:

1. Create a new file named `wfst.html`. Open it and add the `<head>` and `<body>` tags. In the `<head>` tag, import the following `OpenLayers` library:

```
<html>
  <head>
    <title>Consuming a WFS-T with OpenLayers</title>
    <script
     src="http://openlayers.org/api/OpenLayers.js">
    </script>
  </head>
  <body>
  </body>
</html>
```

2. Add a `<div>` tag in the `<body>` tag to contain the OpenLayers map, as shown in the following code; the map will have a width of 700 pixels and a height of 400 pixels:

```
<div style="width:700px; height:400px" id="map"></div>
```

3. Just after the `<div>` tag is made to contain the map, add a JavaScript script. Inside the script, start setting `ProxyHost` to the web location where you deployed your proxy script. Then create a new OpenLayers map, as shown in the following code:

```
<script type="text/javascript">
  // set the proxy
  OpenLayers.ProxyHost = "/cgi-bin/proxy.cgi?url=";
  // create the map
  var map = new OpenLayers.Map('map');
</script>
```

4. Now, in the script, after creating the map, create an `OpenStreetMap` layer that you will use in the map as the base layer, using the following code:

```
// create an OSM base layer
var osm = new OpenLayers.Layer.OSM();
```

5. Now, create the WFS-T layer's `OpenLayers` object using the `StyleMap` object to render the PostGIS layer features with red points, as shown in the following screenshot:

```
// create the wfs layer
var saveStrategy = new OpenLayers.Strategy.Save();
var wfs = new OpenLayers.Layer.Vector("Sites",
{
   strategies: [new OpenLayers.Strategy.BBOX(), saveStrategy],
   projection: new OpenLayers.Projection("EPSG:4326"),
              styleMap: new OpenLayers.StyleMap({
      pointRadius: 7,
      fillColor: "#FF0000"
   }),
   protocol: new OpenLayers.Protocol.WFS({
      version: "1.1.0",
      srsName: "EPSG:4326",
      url: "http://localhost:8080/geoserver/wfs",
      featurePrefix: 'postgis_cookbook',
      featureType: "sites",
      featureNS: "https://www.packtpub.com/application-development/
                postgis-cookbook-second-edition",
      geometryName: "the_geom"
   })
});
```

6. Add the WFS layer to the map, center align the map, and set the initial zoom. You can use the `geometry` transform method to convert a point from `EPSG:4326`, in which the layer is stored, to `ESPG:900913`, which is used by the viewer, as shown in the following code:

```
// add layers to map and center it
map.addLayers([osm, wfs]);
var fromProjection = new OpenLayers.Projection("EPSG:4326");
var toProjection   = new OpenLayers.Projection("EPSG:900913");
var cpoint = new OpenLayers.LonLat(12.5, 41.85).transform(
            fromProjection, toProjection);
map.setCenter(cpoint, 10);
```

7. Now, you will create a panel with a *Draw Point* tool (to add new features) and a *Save Features* tool (to save the features to the underlying WFS-T). We first create the panel, as shown in the following code:

```
// create a panel for tools
var panel = new OpenLayers.Control.Panel({
  displayClass: "olControlEditingToolbar"
});
```

8. Now, we will create the *Draw Point* tool, as shown in the following code:

```
// create a draw point tool
var draw = new OpenLayers.Control.DrawFeature(
  wfs, OpenLayers.Handler.Point,
  {
    handlerOptions: {freehand: false, multi: false},
    displayClass: "olControlDrawFeaturePoint"
  }
);
```

9. Then, we will create the *Save Features* tool, using the following code:

```
// create a save tool
var save = new OpenLayers.Control.Button({
  title: "Save Features",
  trigger: function() {
    saveStrategy.save();
  },
  displayClass: "olControlSaveFeatures"
});
```

10. Finally, add the tools to the panel, including a navigation control, and the panel as a control to the map, using the following code:

```
// add tools to panel and add it to map
panel.addControls([
  new OpenLayers.Control.Navigation(),
  save, draw
]);
map.addControl(panel);
```

11. Your HTML file should now look like the `wfst.html` file contained in the `chp09` directory. Deploy this file to your web server (that is, Apache HTTPD or IIS). If you are using Apache HTTPD in Linux, you could copy the file to the `data` directory under `/var/www`, whereas if you are using Windows, you could copy it to the data directory under `C:\ms4w\Apache\htdocs` (create the `data` directory if it does not already exist). Then, access it using `http://localhost/data/wfst.html`.

12. Open the web page using your favorite browser and start adding some points to the map. Now, click on the **Save** button and reload the page; the previously added points should still be there, as they had been stored in the underlying `PostGIS` table by WFS-T, as shown in the following screenshot:

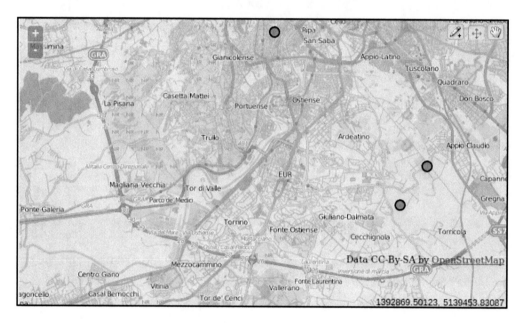

Added points using OpenLayers controls viewed on a browser

How it works...

In this recipe, you first created a point `PostGIS` table and then published it as WFS-T, using GeoServer. You then created a basic OpenLayers application, using the WFS-T layer, allowing the user to add features to the underlying PostGIS layer.

In OpenLayers, the core object needed to implement such a service is the vector layer by defining a WFS protocol. When defining the WFS protocol, you have to provide the WFS version that is using the spatial reference system of the dataset, the URI of the service, the name of the layer (for GeoServer, the name is a combination of the layer workspace, `FeaturePrefix`, and the layer name, `FeatureType`), and the name of the `geometry` field that will be modified. You also can pass to the Vector layer constructor a `StyleMap` value to define the layer's rendering behavior.

You then tested the application by adding some points to the OpenLayers map and checked that those points were effectively stored in PostGIS. When adding the points using the WFS-T layer, with the help of tools such as Firefox Firebug or Chrome (Chromium) Developer Tools, you could dig in detail into the requests that you are making to the WFS-T and its responses.

For example, when adding a point, you will see that an `Insert` request is sent to WFS-T. The following XML is sent to the service (note how the point geometry is inserted in the body of the `<wfs:Insert>` element):

```
<wfs:Transaction xmlns:wfs="http://www.opengis.net/wfs"
 service="WFS" version="1.1.0"
 xsi:schemaLocation="http://www.opengis.net/wfs
 http://schemas.opengis.net/wfs/1.1.0/wfs.xsd"
 xmlns:xsi="http://www.w3.org/2001/XMLSchema-instance">
  <wfs:Insert>
    <feature:sites xmlns:feature="http://www.packtpub.com/
    postgis-cookbook/book">
      <feature:the_geom>
        <gml:Point xmlns:gml="http://www.opengis.net/gml"
        srsName="EPSG:4326">
          <gml:pos>12.450561523436999 41.94302128455888</gml:pos>
        </gml:Point>
              </feature:the_geom>
          </feature:sites>
      </wfs:Insert>
    </wfs:Transaction>
```

The `<wfs:TransactionResponse>` response, as shown in the following code, will be sent from WFS-T if the process has transpired smoothly and the features have been stored (note that the `<wfs:totalInserted>` element value in this case is set to 1, as only one feature was stored):

```
<?xml version="1.0" encoding="UTF-8"?>
<wfs:TransactionResponse version="1.1.0" ...[CLIP]... >
  <wfs:TransactionSummary>
    <wfs:totalInserted>1</wfs:totalInserted>
```

```
    <wfs:totalUpdated>0</wfs:totalUpdated>
    <wfs:totalDeleted>0</wfs:totalDeleted>
  </wfs:TransactionSummary>
  <wfs:TransactionResults/>
  <wfs:InsertResults>
    <wfs:Feature>
      <ogc:FeatureId fid="sites.17"/>
    </wfs:Feature>
  </wfs:InsertResults>
</wfs:TransactionResponse>
```

Developing web applications with GeoDjango – part 1

In this recipe and the next, you will use the **Django** web framework to create a web application to manage wildlife sightings using a PostGIS data store. In this recipe, you will build the back office of the web application, based on the Django admin site.

Upon accessing the back office, an administrative user will be able to, after authentication, manage (insert, update, and delete) the main entities (animals and sightings) of the database. In the next part of the recipe, you will build a front office that displays the sightings on a map based on the **Leaflet** JavaScript library.

 You can find a copy of the whole project that you are going to build in the code bundle under `chp09/wildlife`. Refer to it if a concept is not clear or if you want to copy and paste the code as you go through the steps of the recipe, rather than typing code from scratch.

Getting ready

1. If you are new to Django, check out the official Django tutorial at `https://docs.djangoproject.com/en/dev/intro/tutorial01/` and then return to this recipe.

2. Create a Python *virtualenv* (`http://www.virtualenv.org/en/latest/`) to create an isolated Python environment to use with the web application you will build in this recipe and the next. Then, activate the environment as follows:

   - Use the following commands in Linux:

   ```
   $ cd ~/virtualenvs/
   $ virtualenv --no-site-packages chp09-env
   $ source chp09-env/bin/activate
   ```

   - Type the following commands in Windows (for steps to install `virtualenv` on Windows, refer to `https://zignar.net/2012/06/17/install-python-on-windows/`):

   ```
   cd c:\virtualenvs
   C:\Python27\Scripts\virtualenv.exe
   --no-site-packages chp09-env
   chp09-env\Scripts\activate
   ```

3. Once activated, you can install the Python packages that you will use for this recipe as well as the next, using the `pip` tool (`http://www.pip-installer.org/en/latest/`).

   - In Linux, the command would be as follows:

   ```
   (chp09-env)$ pip install django==1.10
   (chp09-env)$ pip install psycopg2==2.7
   (chp09-env)$ pip install Pillow
   ```

   - In Windows, the command would be as follows:

   ```
   (chp09-env) C:\virtualenvs> pip install django==1.10
   (chp09-env) C:\virtualenvs> pip install psycopg2=2.7
   (chp09-env) C:\virtualenvs> easy_install Pillow
   ```

4. If you haven't done it so far, download the world countries shapefile from `http://thematicmapping.org/downloads/TM_WORLD_BORDERS-0.3.zip`. A copy of this shapefile is included in the code bundle of this book. Extract the shapefile to the `working/chp09` directory.

How to do it...

Carry out the following steps:

1. Create a Django project using the `django-admin` command with the `startproject` option. Name the project `wildlife`. The command for creating the project will be as follows:

```
(chp09-env)$ cd ~/postgis_cookbook/working/chp09
(chp09-env)$ django-admin.py startproject wildlife
```

2. Create a Django application using the `django-admin` command with the `startapp` option. Name the application `sightings`. The command will be as follows:

```
(chp09-env)$ cd wildlife/
(chp09-env)$ django-admin.py startapp sightings
```

Now you should have the following directory structure:

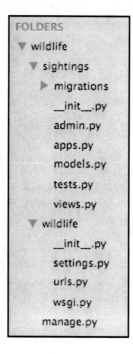

3. You will need to edit some files. Open your favorite editor (**Sublime Text** does the job) and go to the settings in the `settings.py` file in the code bundle under `chp09/wildlife/wildlife`. First, the `DATABASES` settings should be as shown in the following code, in order to use the `postgis_cookbook` PostGIS database for your application data:

```
DATABASES = {
  'default': {
    'ENGINE': 'django.contrib.gis.db.backends.postgis',
    'NAME': 'postgis_cookbook',
    'USER': 'me',
    'PASSWORD': 'mypassword',
    'HOST': 'localhost',
    'PORT': '',
  }
}
```

4. Add the following two lines of code at the top of the `wildlife/settings.py` file (`PROJECT_PATH` is the variable in which you will enter the project's path in the settings menu):

```
import os
PROJECT_PATH = os.path.abspath(os.path.dirname(__file__))
```

5. Make sure that in the `settings.py` file under `chp09/wildlife/wildlife`, `MEDIA_ROOT`, and `MEDIA_URL` are correctly set, as shown the following code (this is to set the media files' path and URLs for the images that the administrative user will upload):

```
MEDIA_ROOT = os.path.join(PROJECT_PATH, "media")
MEDIA_URL = '/media/'
```

6. Make sure that the `INSTALLED_APPS` setting looks as shown in the following code in the `settings.py` file. You will use the Django admin site (`django.contrib.admin`), the GeoDjango core library (`django.contrib.gis`), and the sightings application you are creating in this recipe and the next. For this purpose, add the last three lines:

```
INSTALLED_APPS = (
    'django.contrib.admin',
    'django.contrib.auth',
    'django.contrib.contenttypes',
    'django.contrib.sessions',
    'django.contrib.messages',
    'django.contrib.staticfiles',
    'django.contrib.gis',
    'sightings',
)
```

7. Now, synchronize the database using the Django `migrations` management commands. When prompted to create a *superuser*, answer `yes` and choose a preferred administrative username and password:

```
(chp09-env)$ python manage.py makemigrations
(chp09-env)$ python manage.py migrate
```

8. Now you will add the models needed by the application. Edit the `models.py` file under `chp09/wildlife/sightings` and add the following code:

```
from django.db import models
from django.contrib.gis.db import models as gismodels

class Country(gismodels.Model):
    """
    Model to represent countries.
    """
    isocode = gismodels.CharField(max_length=2)
    name = gismodels.CharField(max_length=255)
    geometry = gismodels.MultiPolygonField(srid=4326)
    objects = gismodels.GeoManager()

    def __unicode__(self):
        return '%s' % (self.name)

class Animal(models.Model):
    """
    Model to represent animals.
    """
```

```
    name = models.CharField(max_length=255)
    image = models.ImageField(upload_to='animals.images')

    def __unicode__(self):
      return '%s' % (self.name)

    def image_url(self):
      return u'<img src="%s" alt="%s" width="80"></img>' %
             (self.image.url, self.name)
      image_url.allow_tags = True

    class Meta:
      ordering = ['name']

class Sighting(gismodels.Model):
    """
      Model to represent sightings.
    """
    RATE_CHOICES = (
        (1, '*'),
        (2, '**'),
        (3, '***'),
    )
    date = gismodels.DateTimeField()
    description = gismodels.TextField()
    rate = gismodels.IntegerField(choices=RATE_CHOICES)
    animal = gismodels.ForeignKey(Animal)
    geometry = gismodels.PointField(srid=4326)
    objects = gismodels.GeoManager()

    def __unicode__(self):
      return '%s' % (self.date)

    class Meta:
      ordering = ['date']
```

9. Each model will become a table in the database with the corresponding fields defined using the `models` and `gismodels` class. Note that the `geometry` variable in the `county` and `sighting` layers will become the `MultiPolygon` and `Point` PostGIS geometry columns, thanks to the GeoDjango library.

10. Create an `admin.py` file under `chp09/wildlife/sightings` and add the following code to it. The classes in this file will define and customize the behavior of the Django admin site when browsing the application models or tables (fields to display, fields to be used to filter records, and fields to order records). Create the file by executing the following code:

```
from django.contrib import admin
from django.contrib.gis.admin import GeoModelAdmin
from models import Country, Animal, Sighting

class SightingAdmin(GeoModelAdmin):
    """
    Web admin behavior for the Sighting model.
    """
    model = Sighting
    list_display = ['date', 'animal', 'rate']
    list_filter = ['date', 'animal', 'rate']
    date_hierarchy = 'date'

class AnimalAdmin(admin.ModelAdmin):
    """
    Web admin behavior for the Animal model.
    """
    model = Animal
    list_display = ['name', 'image_url',]

class CountryAdmin(GeoModelAdmin):
    """
    Web admin behavior for the Country model.
    """
    model = Country
    list_display = ['isocode', 'name']
    ordering = ('name',)

    class Meta:
        verbose_name_plural = 'countries'

admin.site.register(Animal, AnimalAdmin)
admin.site.register(Sighting, SightingAdmin)
admin.site.register(Country, CountryAdmin)
```

11. Now, to synchronize the database, execute the following commands in the Django project folder:

```
(chp09-env)$ python manage.py makemigrations
(chp09-env)$ python manage.py migrate
```

The output should be as follows:

```
(chp09-env) Nina:wildlife may$ python manage.py migrate
Operations to perform:
  Apply all migrations: admin, auth, contenttypes, sessions, sightings
Running migrations:
  Rendering model states... DONE
  Applying contenttypes.0001_initial... OK
  Applying auth.0001_initial... OK
  Applying admin.0001_initial... OK
  Applying admin.0002_logentry_remove_auto_add... OK
  Applying contenttypes.0002_remove_content_type_name... OK
  Applying auth.0002_alter_permission_name_max_length... OK
  Applying auth.0003_alter_user_email_max_length... OK
  Applying auth.0004_alter_user_username_opts... OK
  Applying auth.0005_alter_user_last_login_null... OK
  Applying auth.0006_require_contenttypes_0002... OK
  Applying auth.0007_alter_validators_add_error_messages... OK
  Applying auth.0008_alter_user_username_max_length... OK
  Applying sessions.0001_initial... OK
  Applying sightings.0001_initial... OK
(chp09-env) Nina:wildlife may$
```

12. Now, for each model in `models.py`, a PostgreSQL table should have been created. Check whether your PostgreSQL database effectively contains the three tables created in the preceding commands using your favorite client (that is, `psql` or `pgAdmin`) and whether or not the `sightings_sighting` and `sightings_country` tables contain PostGIS geometric fields.

13. Any web application needs the definition of URLs where the pages can be accessed. Therefore, edit your `urls.py` file under `chp09/wildlife/wildlife` by adding the following code:

```
from django.conf.urls import url
from django.contrib import admin
import settings
from django.conf.urls.static import static
admin.autodiscover()
urlpatterns = [
  url(r'^admin/', admin.site.urls),
] + static(settings.MEDIA_URL, document_root=settings.MEDIA_ROOT)
```

In the `urls.py` file, you basically defined the location of the back office (which was built using the Django admin application) and the media (images) files' location uploaded by the Django administrator when adding new animal entities in the database. Now run the Django development server, using the following `runserver` management command:

(chp09-env)$ python manage.py runserver

14. Access the Django admin site at `http://localhost:8000/admin/` and log in with the superuser credentials you furnished in an earlier step in this recipe (*step 7*).

15. Now, navigate to `http://localhost:8000/admin/sightings/animal/` and add some animals using the **Add animal** button. For each animal, define a name and an image that will be used by the frontend that you will build in the next recipe. You created this page with almost no code, thanks to the Django admin! The following screenshot shows what the **Animals** list page will look like after adding some entities:

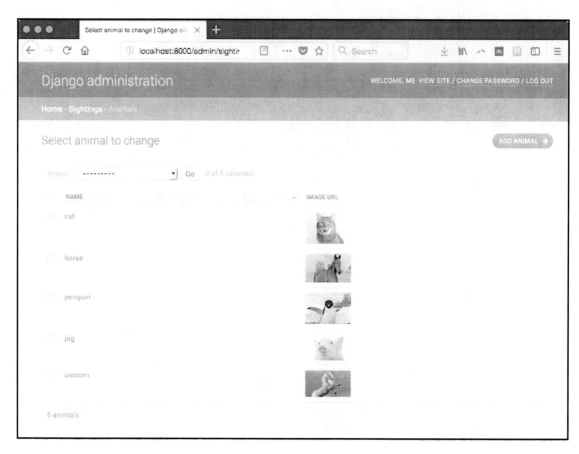

16. Navigate to `http://localhost:8000/admin/sightings/sighting/` **and add some sightings using the Add sighting button. For each sighting, define the Date, Time**, the name of the animal that was spotted, **Rate**, and the location. GeoDjango has added the map widget to the Django Admin site for you, based on the OpenLayers JavaScript library, to add or modify geometric features. The **Sightings** page is shown in the following screenshot:

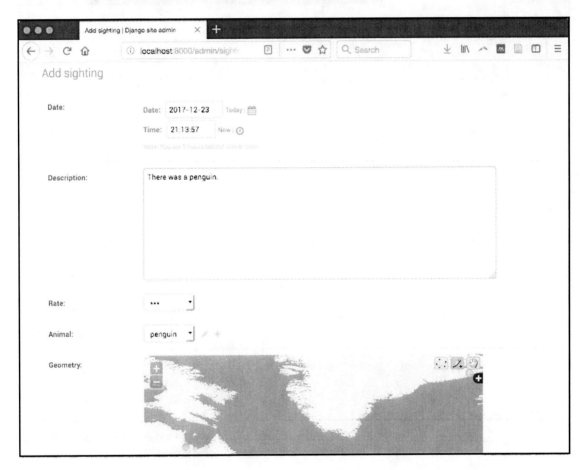

17. The **Sightings** list page, thanks to the Django admin's efficiency, will provide the administrative user with useful features to sort, filter, and navigate the date hierarchy of all of the sightings in the system, as shown in the following screenshot:

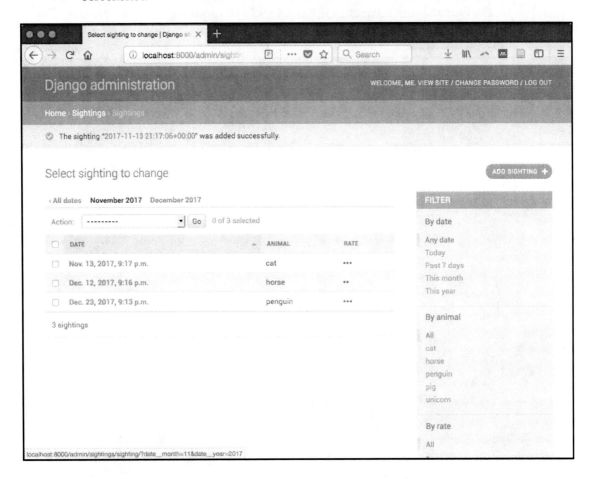

18. Now, you will import the `countries` shapefile to its model. In the next recipe, you will use this model to find the country where each sighting occurred. Before going ahead in this recipe, investigate the shapefile structure; you will need to import just the `NAME` and `ISO2` attributes to the model as the `name` and `isocode` attributes, using the following command:

```
$ ogrinfo TM_WORLD_BORDERS-0.3.shp TM_WORLD_BORDERS-0.3 -al -so
```

```
● ● ●                    Chapter 1 — bash — 80×29

bash-3.2$ ogrinfo TM_WORLD_BORDERS-0.3.shp TM_WORLD_BORDERS-0.3 -al -so
INFO: Open of `TM_WORLD_BORDERS-0.3.shp'
      using driver `ESRI Shapefile' successful.

Layer name: TM_WORLD_BORDERS-0.3
Metadata:
  DBF_DATE_LAST_UPDATE=2008-07-30
Geometry: Polygon
Feature Count: 246
Extent: (-180.000000, -90.000000) - (180.000000, 83.623596)
Layer SRS WKT:
GEOGCS["GCS_WGS_1984",
    DATUM["WGS_1984",
        SPHEROID["WGS_84",6378137.0,298.257223563]],
    PRIMEM["Greenwich",0.0],
    UNIT["Degree",0.0174532925199433]]
FIPS: String (2.0)
ISO2: String (2.0)
ISO3: String (3.0)
UN: Integer (3.0)
NAME: String (50.0)
AREA: Integer (7.0)
POP2005: Integer64 (10.0)
REGION: Integer (3.0)
SUBREGION: Integer (3.0)
LON: Real (8.3)
LAT: Real (7.3)
bash-3.2$ ▊
```

19. Add a `load_countries.py` file under `chp09/wildlife/sightings` and import the shapefile to PostGIS, using the `LayerMapping` GeoDjango utility, using the following code:

```
"""
Script to load the data for the country model from a shapefile.
"""

from django.contrib.gis.utils import LayerMapping
from models import Country

country_mapping = {
  'isocode' : 'ISO2',
  'name' : 'NAME',
  'geometry' : 'MULTIPOLYGON',
}

country_shp = 'TM_WORLD_BORDERS-0.3.shp'
country_lm =  LayerMapping(Country, country_shp, country_mapping,
                           transform=False, encoding='iso-8859-1')
country_lm.save(verbose=True, progress=True)
```

20. You should have the `TM_WORLD_BORDERS-0.3.shp` file placed under `chp09/wildlife` for this code to work. Enter the Python Django shell and run the `utils.py` script. Then, check whether the countries have been correctly inserted in the `sightings_country` table in your PostgreSQL database, using the following command:

```
(chp09-env)$ python manage.py shell
>>> from sightings import load_countries
Saved: Antigua and Barbuda
Saved: Algeria Saved: Azerbaijan
...
Saved: Taiwan
```

Now, you should see the countries in the administrative interface at
`http://localhost:8000/admin/sightings/country/`, while running the
Django server with:

```
(chp09-env)$ python manage.py runserver
```

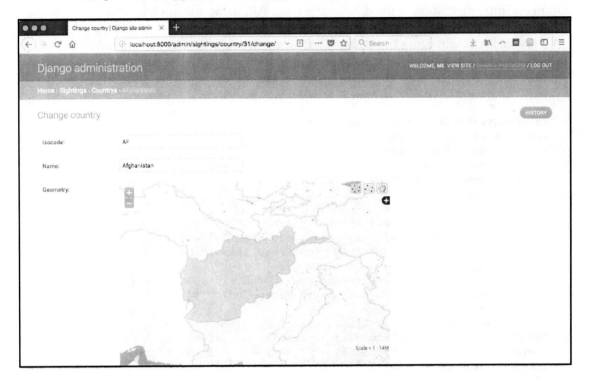

How it works...

In this recipe, you have seen how quick and efficient it is to assemble a back office
application using **Django**, one of the most popular Python web frameworks; this is thanks
to its object-relational mapper, which automatically created the database tables needed by
your application and an automatic API to manage (insert, update, and delete) and query the
entities without using SQL.

Thanks to the **GeoDjango** library, two of the application models, County and Sighting,
have been geo-enabled with their introduction in the database tables of `geometric` PostGIS
fields.

You have customized the powerful **automatic administrative interface** to quickly assemble the back-office pages of your application. Using the **Django URL Dispatcher**, you have defined the URL routes for your application in a concise manner.

As you may have noticed, what is extremely nice about the Django abstraction is the automatic implementation of the data-access layer API using the models. You can now add, update, delete, and query records using Python code, without having any knowledge of SQL. Try this yourself, using the Django Python shell; you will select an animal from the database, add a new sighting for that animal, and then finally delete the sighting. You can investigate the SQL generated by Django, behind the scenes, any time, using the django.db.connection class with the following command:

```
(chp09-env-bis)$ python manage.py shell
>>> from django.db import connection
>>> from datetime import datetime
>>> from sightings.models import Sighting, Animal
>>> an_animal = Animal.objects.all()[0]
>>> an_animal
<Animal: Lion>
>>> print connection.queries[-1]['sql']
SELECT "sightings_animal"."id", "sightings_animal"."name",
"sightings_animal"."image" FROM "sightings_animal" ORDER BY
"sightings_animal"."name" ASC LIMIT 1'
my_sight = Sighting(date=datetime.now(), description='What a lion I have
seen!', rate=1, animal=an_animal, geometry='POINT(10 10)')
>>> my_sight.save()
print connection.queries[-1]['sql']
INSERT INTO "sightings_sighting" ("date", "description", "rate",
"animal_id", "geometry") VALUES ('2013-06-12 14:37:36.544268-05:00', 'What
a lion I have seen!', 1, 2,
ST_GeomFromEWKB('\x0101000020e610000000000000000024400000000000002440'::byt
ea)) RETURNING "sightings_sighting"."id"
>>> my_sight.delete()
>>> print connection.queries[-1]['sql']
DELETE FROM "sightings_sighting" WHERE "id" IN (5)
```

Do you like Django as much as we do? In the next recipe, you will create the frontend of the application. The user will be able to browse the sightings in a map, implemented with the Leaflet JavaScript library. So keep reading!

Developing web applications with GeoDjango – part 2

In this recipe, you will create the front office for the web application you created using **Django** in the previous recipe.

Using HTML and the **Django template language**, you will create a web page displaying a map, implemented with Leaflet, and a list for the user containing all of the sightings available in the system. The user will be able to navigate the map and identify the sightings to get more information.

Getting ready

1. Make sure you have gone through every single step of the previous recipe and have kept the back office of the web application working and its database populated with some entities.

2. Activate the `virtualenv` you created in the *Developing web applications with GeoDjango –Part 1)* recipe, as follows:

   - Use the following command for Linux:

   ```
   $ cd ~/virtualenvs/ $ source chp09-env/bin/activate
   ```

   - Use the following command for Windows:

   ```
   cd c:\virtualenvs > chp09-env\Scripts\activate
   ```

3. Install the libraries that you will use in this recipe; you will need the `simplejson` and `vectorformats` Python libraries to produce a GeoJSON (http://www.geojson.org/) response that will feed the sighting layer in Leaflet:

   - Use the following command for Linux:

   ```
   (chp09-env)$ pip install simplejson
   (chp09-env)$ pip install vectorformats
   ```

- Use the following command for Windows:

```
(chp09-env) C:\virtualenvs> pip install simplejson
(chp09-env) C:\virtualenvs> pip install vectorformats
```

How to do it...

You will now create the front page of your web application, as follows:

1. Go to the directory containing the Django wildlife web application and add the following lines to the `urls.py` file under `chp09/wildlife/wildlife`:

```
from django.conf.urls import patterns, include, url
from django.conf import settings
from sightings.views import get_geojson, home
from django.contrib import admin
admin.autodiscover()
urlpatterns = [
  url(r'^admin/', admin.site.urls),
  url(r'^geojson/', get_geojson),
  url(r'^$', home),
] + static(settings.MEDIA_URL, document_root=settings.MEDIA_ROOT)
  # media files
```

2. Open the `views.py` file under `chp09/wildlife/sightings` and add the following code. The `home` view will return the home page of your application, with the list of sightings and the Leaflet map. The `sighting` layer in the map will display the GeoJSON response given by the `get_geojson` view:

```
from django.shortcuts import render
from django.http import HttpResponse
from  vectorformats.Formats import Django, GeoJSON
from models import Sighting

def home(request):
    """
    Display the home page with the list and a map of the sightings.
    """
    sightings = Sighting.objects.all()
    return render("sightings/home.html", {'sightings' : sightings})

def get_geojson(request):
    """
    Get geojson (needed by the map) for all of the sightings.
    """
```

```
sightings = Sighting.objects.all()
djf = Django.Django(geodjango='geometry',
   properties=['animal_name', 'animal_image_url', 'description',
               'rate', 'date_formatted', 'country_name'])
geoj = GeoJSON.GeoJSON()
s = geoj.encode(djf.decode(sightings))
return HttpResponse(s)
```

3. Add the following @property definitions to the Sighting class in the models.py file under chp09/wildlife/sightings. The get_geojson view will need to use these properties to compose the GeoJSON view needed from the Leaflet map and the information popup. Note how in the country_name property, you are using GeoDjango, which contains a spatial lookup QuerySet operator to detect the country where the sighting happened:

```
@property
def date_formatted(self):
  return self.date.strftime('%m/%d/%Y')

@property
def animal_name(self):
  return self.animal.name

@property
def animal_image_url(self):
  return self.animal.image_url()

@property
def country_name(self):
  country = Country.objects.filter
    (geometry__contains=self.geometry)[0]
  return country.name
```

4. Add a `home.html` file, containing the following code, under `sightings/templates/sightings`. Using the Django template language, you will display the number of sightings in the system, a list of these sightings with the main information for each of them, and the Leaflet map. Using the Leaflet JavaScript API, you add a base OpenStreetMap layer to the map. Then, you make an asynchronous call, using jQuery, to the `get_geojson` view (accessed by adding `/geojson` to the request URL). If the query is successful, it will feed a Leaflet GeoJSON layer with the features from the sighting PostGIS layer and associate with each feature an informative popup. This popup will open any time the user clicks on a point on the map representing a sighting, displaying the main information for that entity:

```html
<!DOCTYPE html>
<html>
  <head>
    <title>Wildlife's Sightings</title>
    <link rel="stylesheet"
    href="https://unpkg.com/leaflet@1.2.0/dist/leaflet.css"
    integrity="sha512-M2wvCLH6DSRazYeZRIm1JnYyh
    22purTM+FDB5CsyxtQJYeKq83arPe5wgbNmcFXGqiSH2XR8dT
    /fJISVA1r/zQ==" crossorigin=""/>
    <script src="https://unpkg.com/leaflet@1.2.0/dist/leaflet.js"
    integrity="sha512-lInM/apFSqyy1o6s89K4iQUKg6ppXEgsVxT35HbzUup
    EVRh2Eu9Wdl4tHj7dZO0s1uvplcYGmt3498TtHq+log==" crossorigin="">
    </script>
    <script src="http://ajax.googleapis.com/ajax/libs
    /jquery/1.9.1/jquery.min.js">
    </script>
  </head>
  <body>
    <h1>Wildlife's Sightings</h1>
    <p>There are {{ sightings.count }} sightings
      in the database.</p>
    <div id="map" style="width:800px; height:500px"></div>
    <ul>
      {% for s in sightings %}
      <li><strong>{{ s.animal }}</strong>,
        seen in {{ s.country_name }} on {{ s.date }}
        and rated {{ s.rate }}
      </li> {% endfor %}
    </ul>
    <script type="text/javascript">
      // OSM layer
      var osm = L.tileLayer('http://{s}.tile.osm.org/{z}/{x}/{y}
                                          .png', {
        maxZoom: 18,
```

```
      attribution: "Data by OpenStreetMap"
    });
    // map creation
    var map = new L.Map('map', {
      center: new L.LatLng(15, 0),
      zoom: 2,
      layers: [osm],
      zoomControl: true
    });
    // add GeoJSON layer
    $.ajax({
      type: "GET",
      url: "geojson",
      dataType: 'json',
      success: function (response) {
        geojsonLayer = L.geoJson(response, {
          style: function (feature) {
            return {color: feature.properties.color};
          },
          onEachFeature: function (feature, layer) {
            var html = "<strong>" +
                        feature.properties.animal_name +
                        "</strong><br />" +
                        feature.properties.animal_image_url +
                        "<br /><strong>Description:</strong> " +
                        feature.properties.description +
                        "<br /><strong>Rate:</strong> " +
                        feature.properties.rate +
                        "<br /><strong>Date:</strong> " +
                        feature.properties.date_formatted +
                        "<br /><strong>Country:</strong> " +
                        feature.properties.country_name
                        layer.bindPopup(html);
          }
        }).addTo(map);
      }
    });
  </script>
 </body>
</html>
```

5. Now that your frontend page is completed, you can finally access it at
   `http://localhost:8000/`. Navigate the map and try to identify some of the
   displayed sightings to check whether the popup opens, as shown in the following
   screenshot:

How it works...

You created an HTML front page for the web application you developed in the previous recipe. The HTML is dynamically created using the Django template language (https://docs.djangoproject.com/en/dev/topics/templates/) and the map was implemented with the Leaflet JavaScript library.

The Django template language uses the response from the home view to generate a list of all of the sightings in the system.

The map was created using Leaflet. First, an OpenStreetMap layer was used as a base map. Then, using jQuery, you fed a GeoJSON layer that displays all of the features generated by the get_geojson view. You associated a popup with the layer that opens every time the user clicks on a sighting entity. The popup displays the main information for that sighting, including a picture of the sighted animal.

Developing a web GPX viewer with Mapbox

For this recipe, we will use the way points dataset from Chapter 3, *Working with Vector Data – The Basics*. Refer to the script in the recipe named *Working with GPS data* to learn how to import .gpx files tracks into PostGIS. You will also need a Mapbox token; for this, go to their site (https://www.mapbox.com) and sign up for one.

How to do it...

1. To prepare the data for Mapbox's GeoJSON format, export the table tracks from Chapter 3, *Working with Vector Data – The Basics* using ogr2ogr with the following code:

```
ogr2ogr -f GeoJSON tracks.json \
"PG:host=localhost dbname=postgis_cookbook user=me" \
-sql "select * from chp03.tracks
```

2. Remove the `crs` definition line on the new `.json` with your favorite editor:

3. Go to your Mapbox account and upload in the Datasets menu the `tracks.json` file. After a successful upload, you will see the following message:

4. Create the dataset and export it to a tileset:

5. Now, create a new style with the outdoors template:

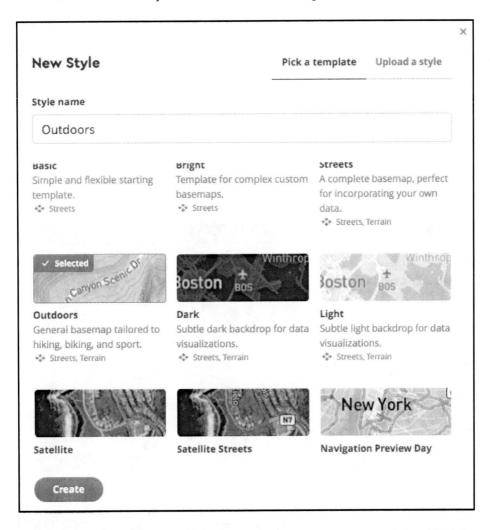

6. Add the tracks layer and publish it. Note the style URL that you can use to share or further develop your map; copy it to use it in your code.

7. Now we are ready to create a mapbox.html file; add the following in the head section to use Mapbox JS and CSS libraries:

```
<script src='https://api.mapbox.com/mapbox-gl-js
        /v0.42.0/mapbox-gl.js'></script>
<link href='https://api.mapbox.com/mapbox-gl-js
        /v0.42.0/mapbox-gl.css' rel='stylesheet' />
```

8. Insert a `map` with your token and the style we've just created in the body:

```
<div id='map' style='width: 800px; height: 600px;'></div>
<script>
  mapboxgl.accessToken = YOUR_TOKEN';
  var map = new mapboxgl.Map({
    container: 'map',
    style: 'YOUR_STYLE_URL'
  });
  // Add zoom and rotation controls to the map.
  map.addControl(new mapboxgl.NavigationControl());
</script>
```

9. That's it, you can double-click and open the HTML with your favorite browser and the Mapbox API will serve your map:

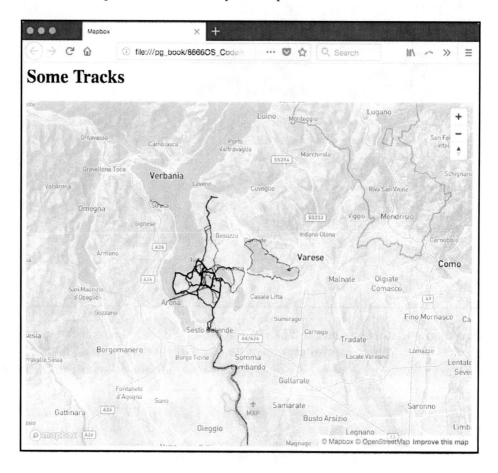

How it works...

To quickly publish and visualize data in a webGIS, you can use the Mapbox API to create beautiful maps with your own data; you will have to keep a GeoJSON format and not exceed the offered bandwidth capacity. In this recipe, you've learned how to export your PostGIS data to publish it in Mapbox as a JS.

Maintenance, Optimization, and Performance Tuning

10

In this chapter, we will cover the following recipes:

- Organizing the database
- Setting up the correct data privilege mechanism
- Backing up the database
- Using indexes
- Clustering for efficiency
- Optimizing SQL queries
- Migrating a PostGIS database to a different server
- Replicating a PostGIS database with streaming replication
- Geospatial sharding
- Paralellizing in PosgtreSQL

Introduction

Unlike prior chapters, this chapter does not discuss the capabilities or applications of PostGIS. Instead, it focuses on the techniques for organizing the database, improving the query performance, and ensuring the long-term viability of the spatial data.

These techniques are frequently ignored by most PostGIS users until it is too late - for example, when data has already been lost because of users' actions or the performance has already decreased as the volume of data or number of users increased.

Such neglect is often due to the amount of time required to learn about each technique, as well as the time it takes implement them. This chapter attempts to demonstrate each technique in a distilled manner that minimizes the learning curve and maximizes the benefits.

Organizing the database

One of the most important things to consider when creating and using a database is how to organize the data. The layout should be decided when you first establish the database. The layout can be decided on or changed at a later date, but this is almost guaranteed to be a tedious, if not difficult, task. If it is never decided on, a database will become disorganized over time and introduce significant hurdles when upgrading components or running backups.

By default, a new PostgreSQL database has only one **schema** - namely, `public`. Most users place all the data (their own and third-party modules, such as PostGIS) in the `public` schema. Doing so mixes different information from various origins. An easy method with which to separate the information is by using schemas. This enables us to use one schema for our data and a separate schema for everything else.

Getting ready

In this recipe, we will create a database and install PostGIS in its own schema. We will also load some geometries and rasters for future use by other recipes in this chapter.

The following are the two methods to create a PostGIS-enabled database:

- Using the `CREATE EXTENSION` statement
- Running the installation SQL scripts with a PostgreSQL client

The `CREATE EXTENSION` method is available if you are running PostgreSQL 9.1 or a later version and is the recommended method for installing PostGIS:

1. Visit the following link to download the shapefiles for California schools and police stations:
   `http://scec.usc.edu/internships/useit/content/california-emergency-fac`
   `ilities-shapefile`.

How to do it...

Carry out the following steps to create and organize a database:

1. Create a database named `chapter10` by executing the following command:

   CREATE DATABASE chapter10;

2. Create a schema named `postgis` in the `chapter10` database, where we will install PostGIS. Execute the following command:

   CREATE SCHEMA postgis;

3. Install PostGIS in the `postgis` schema of the `chapter10` database:
   1. If you are running PostgreSQL 9.1 or a newer version, use the CREATE EXTENSION statement:

      CREATE EXTENSION postgis WITH SCHEMA postgis;

      The WITH SCHEMA clause of the CREATE EXTENSION statement instructs PostgreSQL to install PostGIS and its objects in the `postgis` schema.

4. Check whether or not the PostGIS installation has succeeded by running the following commands:

   ```
   > psql -U me -d chapter10
   > chapter10=# SET search_path = public, postgis;
   ```

   ```
   chapter10=# create extension postgis with schema postgis;
   CREATE EXTENSION
   chapter10=# SET search_path = public, postgis;
   SET
   chapter10=# \dn
     List of schemas
     Name    |   Owner
   ----------+----------
    postgis  | postgres
    public   | postgres
   (2 rows)
   ```

Verify the list of relations in the schema, which should include all the ones created by the extension:

```
chapter10=# \d
                List of relations
   Schema  |        Name        |  Type  |  Owner
-----------+--------------------+--------+----------
   postgis | geography_columns  |  view  |  postgres
   postgis | geometry_columns   |  view  |  postgres
   postgis | raster_columns     |  view  |  postgres
   postgis | raster_overviews   |  view  |  postgres
   postgis | spatial_ref_sys    |  table |  postgres
(5 rows)
```

If you are using `pgAdmin` or a similar database system, you can also check on the graphical interface whether the schemas, views, and table were created successfully.

The `SET` statement instructs PostgreSQL to consider the `public` and `postgis` schemas when processing any SQL statements from our client connection. Without the `SET` statement, the `\d` command will not return any relation from the `postgis` schema.

5. To prevent the need to manually use the `SET` statement every time a client connects to the `chapter10` database, alter the database by executing the following command:

```
ALTER DATABASE chapter10 SET search_path = public, postgis;
```

All future connections and queries to `chapter10` will result in PostgreSQL automatically using both `public` and `postgis` schemas.

Note: It may be the case that, for Windows users, this option may not work well; in version 9.6.7 it worked but not in version 9.6.3. If it does not work, you may need to clearly define the `search_path` on every command. Both versions are provided.

6. Load the PRISM rasters and San Francisco boundaries geometry, which we used in Chapter 5, *Working with Raster Data*, by executing the following command:

```
> raster2pgsql -s 4322 -t 100x100 -I -F -C -Y
C:\postgis_cookbook\data\chap5
\PRISM\   PRISM_tmin_provisional_4kmM2_201703_asc.asc
prism | psql -d chapter10 -U me
```

Then, define the search path:

```
> raster2pgsql -s 4322 -t 100x100 -I -F -C -Y
C\:postgis_cookbook\data\chap5
\PRISM\PRISM_tmin_provisional_4kmM2_201703_asc.asc
prism | psql "dbname=chapter10 options=--search_path=postgis" me
```

7. As we did in `Chapter 5`, *Working with Raster Data,* we will postprocess the raster filenames to a `date` column by executing the following command:

```
ALTER TABLE postgis.prism ADD COLUMN month_year DATE;
UPDATE postgis.prism SET month_year = (
   SUBSTRING(split_part(filename, '_', 5), 0, 5) || '-' ||
   SUBSTRING(split_part(filename, '_', 5), 5, 4) || '-01'
) :: DATE;
```

8. Then, we load the San Francisco boundaries by executing the following command:

```
> shp2pgsql -s 3310 -I
C\:postgis_cookbook\data\chap5\SFPoly\sfpoly.shp sfpoly |
psql -d chapter10 -U me
```

Then, define the search path:

```
> shp2pgsql -s 3310 -I
C\:postgis_cookbook\data\chap5\SFPoly\sfpoly.shp
sfpoly | psql "dbname=chapter10 options=--search_path=postgis" me
```

9. Copy this chapter's dataset to its own directory by executing the following commands:

```
> mkdir C:\postgis_cookbook\data\chap10
> cp -r /path/to/book_dataset/chap10
C\:postgis_cookbook\data\chap10
```

We will use the shapefiles for California schools and police stations provided by the USEIT program at the University of Southern California. Import the shapefiles by executing the following commands; use the spatial index flag `-I` only for the police stations shapefile:

```
> shp2pgsql -s 4269 -I
C\:postgis_cookbook\data\chap10\CAEmergencyFacilities\CA_police.shp
capolice | psql -d chapter10 -U me
```

Then, define the search path:

```
> shp2pgsql -s 4269 C\:postgis_cookbook\data\chap10
\CAEmergencyFacilities\CA_schools.shp
caschools | psql -d chapter10 -U me
```

Then, define the search path:

```
shp2pgsql -s 4269 -I C\:postgis_cookbook\data\chap10
\CAEmergencyFacilities\CA_schools.shp
caschools | psql "dbname=chapter10 options=--search_path=postgis"
me shp2pgsql -s 4269 -I
C\:postgis_cookbook\data\chap10\CAemergencyFacilities\CA_police.shp
capolice | psql "dbname=chapter10 options=--search_path=postgis" me
```

How it works...

In this recipe, we created a new database and installed PostGIS in its own schema. We kept the PostGIS objects separate from our geometries and rasters without installing PostGIS in the `public` schema. This separation keeps the `public` schema tidy and reduces the accidental modification or deletion of the PostGIS objects. If the definition of the search path did not work, then use the explicit definition of the schema in all the commands, as shown.

In the following recipes, we will see that our decision to install PostGIS in its own schema results in fewer problems when maintaining the database.

Setting up the correct data privilege mechanism

PostgreSQL provides a fine-grained privilege system that dictates who can use a particular set of data and how that set of data can be accessed by an approved user. Because of its granular nature, creating an effective set of privileges can be confusing, and may result in undesired behavior. There are different levels of access that can be provided, from controlling who can connect to the database server itself, to who can query a view, to who can execute a PostGIS function.

The challenges of establishing a good set of privileges can be minimized by thinking of the database as an onion. The outermost layer has generic rules and each layer inward applies rules that are more specific than the last. An example of this is a company's database server that only the company's network can access.

Only one of the company's divisions can access database A, which contains a schema for each department. Within one schema, all users can run the SELECT queries against views, but only specific users can add, update, or delete records from tables.

In PostgreSQL, users and groups are known as **roles**. A role can be parent to other roles that are themselves parents to even more roles.

Getting ready

In this recipe, we focus on establishing the best set of privileges for the `postgis` schema created in the previous recipe. With the right selection of privileges, we can control who can use the contents of and apply operations to a geometry, geography, or raster column.

One aspect worth mentioning is that the owner of a database object (such as the database itself, a schema, or a table) always has full control over that object. Unless someone changes the owner, the user who created the database object is typically the owner of the object.

Again, when tested in Windows, the functionalities regarding the granting of permission worked on version 9.6.7 and did not work in version 9.6.3.

How to do it...

In the preceding recipe, we imported several rasters and shapefiles to their respective tables. By default, access to those tables is restricted to only the user who performed the import operation, also known as the owner. The following steps permit other users to access those tables:

1. We need to create several groups and users in order for this recipe to demonstrate and test the privileges set in the `chapter10` database by executing the following commands:

```
CREATE ROLE group1 NOLOGIN;
CREATE ROLE group2 NOLOGIN;
CREATE ROLE user1 LOGIN PASSWORD 'pass1' IN ROLE group1;
CREATE ROLE user2 LOGIN PASSWORD 'pass2' IN ROLE group1;
CREATE ROLE user3 LOGIN PASSWORD 'pass3' IN ROLE group2;
```

The first two CREATE ROLE statements create the groups group1 and group2. The last three CREATE ROLE statements create three users, with the user1 and user2 users assigned to group1 and the user3 user assigned to group2.

2. We want `group1` and `group2` to have access to the `chapter10` database. We want `group1` to be permitted to connect to the database and create temporary tables, while `group2` should be granted all database-level privileges, so we use the GRANT statement as follows:

```
GRANT CONNECT, TEMP ON DATABASE chapter10 TO GROUP group1;
GRANT ALL ON DATABASE chapter10 TO GROUP group2;
```

3. Let's check whether or not the GRANT statement worked by executing the following commands:

```
> psql -U me -d chapter10
```

```
chapter10=# \l
                                       List of databases
     Name    |   Owner   | Encoding |  Collation  |   Ctype    |        Access privileges
-------------+-----------+----------+-------------+------------+------------------------------
 chapter10   | postgres  | UTF8     | en_US.UTF8  | en_US.UTF8 | =Tc/postgres              +
             |           |          |             |            | postgres=CTc/postgres+
             |           |          |             |            | group1=Tc/postgres        +
             |           |          |             |            | group2=CTc/postgres
 postgres    | postgres  | UTF8     | en_US.UTF8  | en_US.UTF8 |
 template0   | postgres  | UTF8     | en_US.UTF8  | en_US.UTF8 | =c/postgres               +
             |           |          |             |            | postgres=CTc/postgres
 template1   | postgres  | UTF8     | en_US.UTF8  | en_US.UTF8 | =c/postgres               +
             |           |          |             |            | postgres=CTc/postgres
|
```

As you can see, `group1` and `group2` are present in the `Access privileges` column of the `chapter10` database:

```
group1=Tc/postgres
group2=CTc/postgres
```

4. There is one thing in the privileges of `chapter10` that may be of concern to us:

```
=Tc/postgres
```

Unlike the privilege listings for `group1` and `group2`, this listing has no value before the equal sign (=). This listing is for the special metagroup `public`, which is built into PostgreSQL and to which all users and groups automatically belong.

5. We don't want everyone to have access to the `chapter10` database, so we need to use the `REVOKE` statement to remove privileges from the `public` metagroup by executing the following command:

    REVOKE ALL ON DATABASE chapter10 FROM public;

6. Let's see what the initial privileges are for the schemas of the `chapter10` database by executing the following command:

```
chapter10=# \dn+
                                 List of schemas
         Name        |  Owner   |  Access privileges   |        Description
---------------------+----------+----------------------+------------------------
 postgis             | postgres |                      |
 public              | postgres | postgres=UC/postgres+| standard public schema
                     |          | =UC/postgres         |

```

7. The `postgis` schema has no privileges listed. However, this does not mean that no one can access the `postgis` schema. Only the owner of the schema - `postgres`, in this case - can access it. We will grant access to the `postgis` schema to both `group1` and `group2` by executing the following command:

    GRANT USAGE ON SCHEMA postgis TO group1, group2;

    We generally do not want to grant the `CREATE` privilege in the `postgis` schema to any user or group. New objects (such as functions, views, and tables) should not be added to the `postgis` schema.

8. If we want all users and groups to have access to the `postgis` schema, we can grant the `USAGE` privilege to the metagroup `public` by executing the following command:

    GRANT USAGE ON SCHEMA postgis TO public;

    If you want to revoke this privilege, use the following command:

    REVOKE USAGE ON SCHEMA postgis FROM public;

9. Before continuing further, we should check that our privileges have been reflected in the database:

```
chapter10=# \dn+
                           List of schemas
    Name   |   Owner   |  Access privileges  |      Description
-----------+-----------+---------------------+------------------------
 postgis   | postgres  | postgres=UC/postgres+|
           |           | group1=U/postgres   +|
           |           | group2=U/postgres    |
 public    | postgres  | postgres=UC/postgres+| standard public schema
           |           | =UC/postgres         |
(2 rows)
```

Granting the USAGE privilege to a schema does not allow the granted users and groups to use any objects in the schema. The USAGE privilege only permits the users and groups to view the schema's child objects. Each child object has its own set of privileges, which we establish in the remaining steps.

PostGIS comes with more than 1,000 functions. It would be unreasonable to individually set privileges for each of those functions. Instead, we grant the EXECUTE privilege to the metagroup public and then grant and/or revoke privileges to specific functions, such as management functions.

10. First, grant the EXECUTE privilege to the metagroup public by executing the following command:

GRANT EXECUTE ON ALL FUNCTIONS IN SCHEMA postgis TO public;

11. Now, revoke the EXECUTE privileges of the public metagroup for some functions, such as postgis_full_version(), by executing the following command:

REVOKE ALL ON FUNCTION postgis_full_version() FROM public;

If there are problems accessing the functions on the postgis schema, use the following command:

REVOKE ALL ON FUNCTION postgis.postgis_full_version() FROM public;

The GRANT and REVOKE statements do not differentiate between tables and views, so care must be taken to ensure that the applied privileges are appropriate for the object.

12. We will grant the SELECT, REFERENCES, and TRIGGER privileges to the public metagroup on all postgis tables and views by executing the following command; none of these privileges gives the public metagroup the ability to alter the tables' or views' contents:

```
GRANT SELECT, REFERENCES, TRIGGER
ON ALL TABLES IN SCHEMA postgis TO public;
```

13. We want to allow group1 to be able to insert new records into the spatial_ref_sys table, so we must execute the following command:

```
GRANT INSERT ON spatial_ref_sys TO group1;
```

Groups and users that are not part of group1 (such as group2) can only use the SELECT statements on spatial_ref_sys. Groups and users that are part of group1 can now use the INSERT statement to add new spatial reference systems.

14. Let's give user2, which is a member of group1, the ability to use the UPDATE and DELETE statements on spatial_ref_sys by executing the following command; we are not going to give anyone the privilege to use the TRUNCATE statement on spatial_ref_sys:

```
GRANT UPDATE, DELETE ON spatial_ref_sys TO user2;
```

15. After establishing the privileges, it is always good practice to check that they actually work. The best way to do so is by logging into the database as one of the users. We will use the user3 user to do this by executing the following command:

```
> psql -d chapter10 -u user3
```

16. Now, check that we can run a SELECT statement on the spatial_ref_sys table by executing the following commands:

```
chapter10=# SELECT count(*) FROM spatial_ref_sys;
```

Of if the schema need to be defined, use the following sentence:

```
chapter10=> SELECT count(*) FROM postgis.spatial_ref_sys;
 count
-------
  5435
(1 row)
```

17. Let's try inserting a new record in `spatial_ref_sys` by executing the following commands:

```
chapter10=# INSERT INTO spatial_ref_sys
VALUES (99999, 'test', 99999, '', '');
ERROR:  permission denied for relation spatial_ref_sys
```

18. Excellent! Now update the records in `spatial_ref_sys` by executing the following commands:

```
chapter10=# UPDATE spatial_ref_sys SET srtext = 'Lorum ipsum';
ERROR:  permission denied for relation spatial_ref_sys
```

19. Run a final check on the `postgis_full_version()` function by executing the following commands:

```
chapter10=# SELECT postgis_full_version();
ERROR:  permission denied for function postgis_full_version
```

How it works...

In this recipe, we granted and revoked privileges based on the group or user, with security increasing as a group or user descends into the database. This resulted in `group1` and `group2` being able to connect to the `chapter10` database and use objects found in the `postgis` schema. `group1` could also insert new records into the `spatial_ref_sys` table. Only `user2` was permitted to update or delete the records of `spatial_ref_sys`.

The GRANT and REVOKE statements used in this recipe work, but they can be tedious to use with a command-line utility, such as `psql`. Instead, use a graphical tool, such as pgAdmin, that provides a grant wizard. Such tools also make it easier to check the behavior of the database after granting and revoking privileges.

For additional practice, set up the privileges on the public schema and child objects so that, although group1 and group2 will be able to run the SELECT queries on the tables, only group2 will be able to use the INSERT statement on the caschools table. You will also want to make sure that an INSERT statement executed by a user of group2 actually works.

Backing up the database

Maintaining functional backups of your data and work is probably the least appreciated, yet the most important thing you can do to improve your productivity (and stress levels). You may think that you don't need to have backups of your PostGIS database because you have the original data imported to the database, but do you remember all the work you did to develop the final product? How about the intermediary products? Even if you remember every step in the process, how much time will it take to create the intermediary and final products?

If any of these questions gives you pause, you need to create a backup for your data. Fortunately, PostgreSQL makes the backup process painless, or at least less painful than the alternatives.

Getting ready

In this recipe, we use PostgreSQL's pg_dump utility. The pg_dump utility ensures that the data being backed up is consistent, even if it is currently in use.

How to do it...

Use the following steps to back up a database:

1. Start backing up the chapter10 database by executing the following command:

```
> pg_dump -f chapter10.backup -F custom chapter10
```

We use the -f flag to specify that the backup should be placed in the chapter10.backup file. We also use the -F flag to set the format of the backup output as custom - the most flexible and compressed of pg_dump's output formats by default.

2. Inspect the backup file by outputting the contents onto a SQL file by executing the following command:

```
> pg_restore -f chapter10.sql chapter10.backup
```

After creating a backup, it is good practice to make sure that the backup is valid. We do so with the pg_restore PostgreSQL tool. The -f flag instructs pg_restore to emit the restored output to a file instead of a database. The emitted output comprises standard SQL statements.

3. Use a text editor to view chapter10.sql. You should see blocks of SQL statements for creating tables, filling created tables, and setting privileges, as shown here:

```
--
-- PostgreSQL database dump
--

-- Dumped from database version 9.6.3
-- Dumped by pg_dump version 9.6.3

SET statement_timeout = 0;
SET lock_timeout = 0;
SET idle_in_transaction_session_timeout = 0;
SET client_encoding = 'UTF8';
SET standard_conforming_strings = on;
SET check_function_bodies = false;
SET client_min_messages = warning;
SET row_security = off;


--
-- Name: postgis; Type: SCHEMA; Schema: -; Owner: postgres
--

CREATE SCHEMA postgis;


ALTER SCHEMA postgis OWNER TO postgres;

--
-- Name: plpgsql; Type: EXTENSION; Schema: -; Owner:
--

CREATE EXTENSION IF NOT EXISTS plpgsql WITH SCHEMA pg_catalog;
```

And the files continue to show information about tables, sequences, and so on:

```
CREATE INDEX caschools_geom_idx ON caschools USING gist (geom);


--
-- Name: prism_st_convexhull_idx; Type: INDEX; Schema: postgis;
Owner: postgres
--

CREATE INDEX prism_st_convexhull_idx ON prism USING gist
(st_convexhull(rast));


--
-- Name: sfpoly_geom_idx; Type: INDEX; Schema: postgis; Owner:
postgres
--

CREATE INDEX sfpoly_geom_idx ON sfpoly USING gist (geom);


--
-- Name: postgis; Type: ACL; Schema: -; Owner: postgres
--

GRANT USAGE ON SCHEMA postgis TO group2;
GRANT USAGE ON SCHEMA postgis TO group1;
```

4. Because we backed up the `chapter10` database using the custom format, we have fine-grained control over how `pg_restore` behaves and what it restores. Let's extract only the `public` schema using the `-n` flag, as follows:

```
> pg_restore -f chapter10_public.sql -n public chapter10.backup
```

If you compare `chapter10_public.sql` to the `chapter10.sql` file exported in the preceding step, you will see that the `postgis` schema is not restored.

How it works...

As you can see, backing up your database is easy in PostgreSQL. Unfortunately, backups are meaningless if they are not performed on a regular schedule. If the database is lost or corrupted, any work done since the last backup is also lost. It is recommended that you perform backups at intervals that minimize the amount of work lost. The ideal interval will depend on the frequency of changes made to the database.

The `pg_dump` utility can be scheduled to run at regular intervals by adding a job to the operating system's task scheduler; the instructions for doing this are available in the PostgreSQL wiki at `http://wiki.postgresql.org/wiki/Automated_Backup_on_Windows` and `http://wiki.postgresql.org/wiki/Automated_Backup_on_Linux`.

The `pg_dump` utility is not adequate for all situations. If you have a database undergoing constant changes or that is larger than a few tens of gigabytes, you will need a backup mechanism far more robust than that discussed in this recipe. Information regarding these robust mechanisms can be found in the PostgreSQL documentation at `http://www.postgresql.org/docs/current/static/backup.html`.

The following are several third-party backup tools available for establishing robust and advanced backup schemes:

- Barman, which is available at `http://www.pgbarman.org`
- pg-rman, which is available at `http://code.google.com/p/pg-rman`

Using indexes

A database index is very much like the index of a book (such as this one). While a book's index indicates the pages on which a word is present, a database column index indicates the rows in a table that contain a searched-for value. Just as a book's index does not indicate exactly where on the page a word is located, the database index may not be able to denote the exact location of the searched-for value in a row's column.

PostgreSQL has several types of index, such as `B-Tree`, `Hash`, `GIST`, `SP-GIST`, and `GIN`. All of these index types are designed to help queries find matching rows faster. What makes the indices different are the underlying algorithms. Generally, to keep things simple, almost all PostgreSQL indexes are of the `B-Tree` type. PostGIS (spatial) indices are of the `GIST` type.

Geometries, geographies, and rasters are all large, complex objects, and relating to or among these objects takes time. Spatial indices are added to the PostGIS data types to improve search performance. The performance improvement comes not from comparing actual, potentially complex, spatial objects, but rather the simple bounding boxes of those objects.

Getting ready

For this recipe, `psql` will be used as follows to time the queries:

```
> psql -U me -d chapter10
chapter10=# \timing on
```

We will use the `caschools` and `sfpoly` tables loaded in this chapter's first recipe.

How to do it...

The best way to see how a query can be affected by an index is by running the query before and after the addition of an index. In this recipe, in order to avoid the need to define the schema, all the tables are assumed to be on the public schema. The following steps will guide you through the process of optimizing a query with an index:

1. Run the following query, which returns the names of all the schools found in San Francisco:

   ```
   SELECT schoolid FROM caschools sc JOIN sfpoly sf
   ON ST_Intersects(sf.geom, ST_Transform(sc.geom, 3310));
   ```

2. The results from the query do not matter. We are more interested in the time it took to run the query. When we run the query three times, it runs with the following elapsed times; your numbers may be different from these numbers:

   ```
   Time: 136.643 ms
   Time: 140.863 ms
   Time: 135.859 ms
   ```

3. The query ran quickly. But, if the query needs to be run many times (say 1,000 times), it will take more than 500 seconds to run it that number of times. Can the query run faster? Use `EXPLAIN ANALYZE` to see how PostgreSQL runs the query, as follows:

   ```
   EXPLAIN ANALYZE
   SELECT schoolid FROM caschools sc JOIN sfpoly sf
   ON ST_Intersects(sf.geom, ST_Transform(sc.geom, 3310));
   ```

Adding EXPLAIN ANALYZE before the query instructs PostgreSQL to return the actual plan used to execute the query, as follows:

```
                                  QUERY PLAN
----------------------------------------------------------------------------------------
 Nested Loop  (cost=0.00..4160.93 rows=4 width=9) (actual time=19.192..152.344 rows=234 loops=1)
   Join Filter: ((sf.geom && st_transform(sc.geom, 3310)) AND _st_intersects(sf.geom, st_transform(sc.geom, 3310)))
   Rows Removed by Join Filter: 13254
   ->  Seq Scan on sfpoly sf  (cost=0.00..1.01 rows=1 width=603872) (actual time=0.016..0.017 rows=1 loops=1)
   ->  Seq Scan on caschools sc  (cost=0.00..551.88 rows=13488 width=41) (actual time=0.006..1.654 rows=13488 loops=1)
 Planning time: 0.126 ms
 Execution time: 153.760 ms
(7 rows)


Time: 154,478 ms
```

What is significant in the preceding QUERY PLAN is Join Filter, which has consumed most of the execution time. This may be happening because the caschools table does not have a spatial index on the geom column.

4. Add a spatial index to the geom column, as follows:

```
CREATE INDEX caschools_geom_idx ON caschools
USING gist (geom);
```

5. Rerun the query from step 1 three times so as to minimize runtime variations. With a spatial index, the query ran with the following elapsed query times:

```
Time: 95.807 ms
Time: 101.626 ms
Time: 103.748 ms
```

The query did not run much faster with the spatial index. What happened? We need to check the QUERY PLAN.

6. You can see whether or not, or even how the QUERY PLAN changed in PostgreSQL using EXPLAIN ANALYZE, as follows:

```
                                  QUERY PLAN
----------------------------------------------------------------------------------------
 Nested Loop  (cost=0.00..4160.93 rows=4 width=9) (actual time=16.714..103.861 rows=234 loops=1)
   Join Filter: ((sf.geom && st_transform(sc.geom, 3310)) AND _st_intersects(sf.geom, st_transform(sc.geom, 3310)))
   Rows Removed by Join Filter: 13254
   ->  Seq Scan on sfpoly sf  (cost=0.00..1.01 rows=1 width=603872) (actual time=0.018..0.018 rows=1 loops=1)
   ->  Seq Scan on caschools sc  (cost=0.00..551.88 rows=13488 width=41) (actual time=0.007..1.352 rows=13488 loops=1)
 Planning time: 0.154 ms
 Execution time: 105.124 ms
(7 rows)


Time: 105,920 ms
```

The QUERY PLAN table is the same as that found in *step 4*. The query is not using the spatial index. Why?

If you look at the query, we used ST_Transform() to reproject caschools.geom on the spatial reference system of sfpoly.geom. The ST_Transform() geometries used in the ST_Intersects() spatial test were in SRID 3310, but the geometries used for the caschools_geom_idx index were in SRID 4269. This difference in spatial reference systems prevented the use of the index in the query.

7. We can create a spatial index that uses geometries projected in the desired spatial reference system. An index that uses a function is known as a **functional index**. It can be created as follows:

```
CREATE INDEX caschools_geom_3310_idx ON caschools
USING gist (ST_Transform(geom, 3310));
```

8. Rerun the query from step 1 three times to get the following output :

```
Time: 63.359 ms
Time: 64.611 ms
Time: 56.485 ms
```

That's better! The duration of the process has decreased from about 135 ms to 60 ms.

9. Check the QUERY PLAN table as follows:

```
                                                           QUERY PLAN
-------------------------------------------------------------------------------------------------------------------------------
 Nested Loop  (cost=0.28..9.56 rows=4 width=9) (actual time=14.589..60.156 rows=234 loops=1)
   ->  Seq Scan on sfpoly sf  (cost=0.00..1.01 rows=1 width=603872) (actual time=0.011..0.012 rows=1 loops=1)
   ->  Index Scan using caschools_geom_3310_idx on caschools sc  (cost=0.28..8.54 rows=1 width=41) (actual time=14.188..59.715 rows=234 loops=1)
         Index Cond: (sf.geom && st_transform(geom, 3310))
         Filter: _st_intersects(sf.geom, st_transform(geom, 3310))
         Rows Removed by Filter: 34
 Planning time: 0.163 ms
 Execution time: 61.467 ms
(8 rows)

Time: 62,336 ms
```

The plan shows that the query used the caschools_geom_3310_idx index. The Index Scan command was significantly faster than the previously used Join Filter command.

How it works...

Database indices help us quickly and efficiently find the values we are interested in. Generally, a query using an index is faster than one that is not, but the performance improvement may not be to the degree found in this recipe.

Additional information about PostgreSQL and PostGIS indices can be found at the following links:

- https://www.postgresql.org/docs/9.6/static/indexes.html
- https://postgis.net/docs/using_postgis_dbmanagement.html#idm2267

We will discuss query plans in greater detail in a later recipe in this chapter. By understanding query plans, it becomes possible to optimize the performance of deficient queries.

Clustering for efficiency

Most users stop optimizing the performance of a table after adding the appropriate indices. This usually happens because the performance reaches a point where it is good enough. But what if the table has millions or billions of records? This amount of information may not fit in the database server's RAM, thereby forcing hard drive access. Generally, table records are stored sequentially on the hard drive. But the data being fetched for a query from the hard drive may be accessing many different parts of the hard drive. Having to access different parts of a hard drive is a known performance limitation.

To mitigate hard drive performance issues, a database table can have its records reordered on the hard drive so that similar record data is stored next to or near each other. The reordering of a database table is known as **clustering** and is used with the CLUSTER statement in PostgreSQL.

Getting ready

We will use the California schools (caschools) and San Francisco boundaries (sfpoly) tables for this recipe. If neither table is available, refer to the first recipe of this chapter.

The psql utility will be used for this recipe's queries, as shown here:

```
> psql -U me -d chapter10
chapter10=# \timing on
```

How to do it...

Use the following steps to cluster a table:

1. Before using the CLUSTER statement, check the time at which the query used in the previous recipe was executed by executing the following commands:

```
SELECT schoolid FROM caschools sc JOIN sfpoly sf
ON ST_Intersects(sf.geom, ST_Transform(sc.geom, 3310));
```

2. We get the following performance numbers for three query runs:

```
Time: 80.746 ms
Time: 80.172 ms
Time: 80.004 ms
```

3. Cluster the caschools table using the caschools_geom_3310_idx index as follows:

```
CLUSTER caschools USING caschools_geom_3310_idx;
```

4. Rerun the query from the first step three times for the following performance timings:

```
Time: 57.880 ms
Time: 55.939 ms
Time: 53.107 ms
```

The performance improvements were not significant.

How it works...

Using the CLUSTER statement on the caschools table did not result in a significant performance boost. The lesson here is that, despite the fact that the data is physically reordered based on the index information in order to optimize searching, there is no guarantee that query performance will improve on a clustered table. Clustering should be reserved for tables with many large records only after adding the appropriate indices to and optimizing queries for the tables in question.

Optimizing SQL queries

When an SQL query is received, PostgreSQL runs the query through its planner to decide the best execution plan. The best execution plan generally results in the fastest query performance. Though the planner usually makes the correct choices, on occasion, a specific query will have a suboptimal execution plan.

For these situations, the following are several things that can be done to change the behavior of the PostgreSQL planner:

- Add appropriate column indices to the tables in question
- Update the statistics of the database tables
- Rewrite the SQL query by evaluating the query's execution plan and using capabilities available in your PostgreSQL installation
- Consider changing or adding the layout of the database tables
- Change the query planner's configuration

Adding indices (the first bullet point) is discussed in a separate recipe found in this chapter. Updating statistics (the second point) is generally done automatically by PostgreSQL after a certain amount of table activity, but the statistics can be manually updated using the `ANALYZE` statement. Changing the database layout and the query planner's configuration (the fourth and fifth bullet point, respectively) are advanced operations used only when the first three points have already been attempted and, thus, will not be discussed further.

This recipe only discusses the third option - that is, optimizing performance by rewriting SQL queries.

Getting ready

For this recipe, we will find the nearest police station to every school and the distance in meters between each school in San Francisco and its nearest station; we will attempt to do this as fast as possible. This will require us to rewrite our query many times to be more efficient and take advantage of the new PostgreSQL capabilities. For this recipe, ensure that you also include the `capolice` table.

How to do it...

The following steps will guide you through the iterative process required to improve query performance:

1. To find a school's nearest police station and the distance between each school in San Francisco and its nearest station, we will start by executing the following query:

```
SELECT
    di.school,
    police_address,
    distance
FROM ( -- for each school, get the minimum distance to a
        -- police station
    SELECT
      gid,
      school,
      min(distance) AS distance
    FROM ( -- get distance between every school and every police
            -- station in San Francisco
      SELECT
        sc.gid,
        sc.name AS school,
        po.address AS police_address,
        ST_Distance(po.geom_3310, sc.geom_3310) AS distance
      FROM ( -- get schools in San Francisco
        SELECT
          ca.gid,
          ca.name,
          ST_Transform(ca.geom, 3310) AS geom_3310
        FROM sfpoly sf
        JOIN caschools ca
          ON ST_Intersects(sf.geom, ST_Transform(ca.geom, 3310))
      ) sc
      CROSS JOIN ( -- get police stations in San Francisco
        SELECT
          ca.address,
          ST_Transform(ca.geom, 3310) AS geom_3310
        FROM sfpoly sf
        JOIN capolice ca
          ON ST_Intersects(sf.geom, ST_Transform(ca.geom, 3310))
      ) po ORDER BY 1, 2, 4
    ) scpo
    GROUP BY 1, 2
    ORDER BY 2
) di JOIN ( -- for each school, collect the police station
```

```
                    -- addresses ordered by distance
SELECT
  gid,
  school,
  (array_agg(police_address))[1] AS police_address
FROM (-- get distance between every school and
        every police station in San Francisco
  SELECT
    sc.gid,
    sc.name AS school,
    po.address AS police_address,
    ST_Distance(po.geom_3310, sc.geom_3310) AS distance
  FROM ( -- get schools in San Francisco
    SELECT
      ca.gid,
      ca.name,
      ST_Transform(ca.geom, 3310) AS geom_3310
    FROM sfpoly sf
    JOIN caschools ca
      ON ST_Intersects(sf.geom, ST_Transform(ca.geom, 3310))
  ) sc
  CROSS JOIN ( -- get police stations in San Francisco
    SELECT
      ca.address,
      ST_Transform(ca.geom, 3310) AS geom_3310
    FROM sfpoly sf JOIN capolice ca
    ON ST_Intersects(sf.geom, ST_Transform(ca.geom, 3310))
  ) po
  ORDER BY 1, 2, 4
) scpo
GROUP BY 1, 2
ORDER BY 2
) po
  ON di.gid = po.gid
ORDER BY di.school;
```

2. Generally speaking, this is a crude and simplistic query. The subquery `scpo` occurs twice in the query because it needs to compute the shortest distance from a school to its nearest police station and the name of the police station closest to each school. If each instance of `scpo` took 10 seconds to compute, two instances of `scpo` would take 20 seconds. This is very detrimental to performance.

Note: the time may vary substantially between experiments, depending on the machine configuration, database usage, and so on. However, the changes in the duration of the experiments will be noticeable and should follow the same improvement ratio presented in this section.

The query output looks as follows:

```
              school                 |      police_address     |      distance
-------------------------------------+-------------------------+--------------------
A. P. GIANNINI MIDDLE                | 1899 Waller St          | 1629.19944804967
ABRAHAM LINCOLN HIGH                 | 461 6th Ave             | 348.311916238521
ADDA CLEVENGER JUNIOR PREPARAT       | 2345 24th Ave           | 1851.38147290568
AIM HIGH ACADEMY                     | 850 Bryant St # 150     | 976.082872160513
ALAMO ELEMENTARY                     | 201 Williams Ave        | 1652.607173246
ALICE FONG YU ELEMENTARY             | 1899 Waller St          | 1588.75288812506
ALVARADO ELEMENTARY                  | 850 Bryant St # 475     | 1030.80925231483
```

...

```
YICK WO ELEMENTARY                   | 301 Eddy St             | 718.415440909486
YOUTH CHANCE HIGH SCHOOL             | 301 Eddy St             | 302.654766715081
ZION LUTHERAN CHURCH SCHOOL          | 461 6th Ave             | 299.087501462243
(234 rows)


Time: 5076,363 ms
```

3. The query results provide the addresses of the schools in San Francisco, the addresses of the closest police station to each of those schools, and the distance from each school to its closest police station. However, we are also interested in getting the answer as fast as possible. With timing turned on in `psql`, we get the following performance numbers for three runs of the query:

```
Time: 5076.363 ms
Time: 4974.282 ms
Time: 5027.721 ms
```

4. Just by looking at the query in step 1, we can see that there are redundant subqueries. Let's get rid of those duplicates using **common table expressions (CTEs)**, introduced in PostgreSQL 8.4. CTEs are used to logically and syntactically separate a block of SQL from subsequent parts of the query. Since CTEs are logically separated, they are run at the start of the query execution and their results are cached for subsequent use:

```
WITH scpo AS ( -- get distance between every school and every
               -- police station in San Francisco
SELECT
  sc.gid,
  sc.name AS school,
  po.address AS police_address,
  ST_Distance(po.geom_3310, sc.geom_3310) AS distance
FROM ( -- get schools in San Francisco
  SELECT
    ca.*,
    ST_Transform(ca.geom, 3310) AS geom_3310
  FROM sfpoly sf
  JOIN caschools ca
    ON ST_Intersects(sf.geom, ST_Transform(ca.geom, 3310))
) sc
CROSS JOIN ( -- get police stations in San Francisco
  SELECT
    ca.*,
    ST_Transform(ca.geom, 3310) AS geom_3310
  FROM sfpoly sf
  JOIN capolice ca
    ON ST_Intersects(sf.geom, ST_Transform(ca.geom, 3310))
) po
ORDER BY 1, 2, 4
)
SELECT
  di.school,
  police_address,
  distance
FROM ( -- for each school, get the minimum distance to a
       -- police station
  SELECT
    gid,
    school,
    min(distance) AS distance
  FROM scpo
  GROUP BY 1, 2
  ORDER BY 2
) di
JOIN ( -- for each school, collect the police station
```

```
      -- addresses ordered by distance
   SELECT
     gid,
     school,
     (array_agg(police_address))[1] AS police_address
   FROM scpo
   GROUP BY 1, 2
   ORDER BY 2
 ) po
   ON di.gid = po.gid
ORDER BY 1;
```

5. Not only is the query syntactically cleaner, but the performance is improved, as shown here:

```
Time: 2803.923 ms
Time: 2798.105 ms
Time: 2796.481 ms
```

The execution times went from more than 5 seconds to less than 3 seconds.

6. Though some may stop optimizing this query at this point, we will continue to improve the query performance. We can use the window functions, which are another PostgreSQL capability introduced in v8.4. Using the window functions as follows, we can get rid of the JOIN expression:

```
WITH scpo AS ( -- get distance between every school and every
              -- police station in San Francisco
  SELECT
    sc.name AS school,
    po.address AS police_address,
    ST_Distance(po.geom_3310, sc.geom_3310) AS distance
  FROM ( -- get schools in San Francisco
    SELECT
      ca.name,
      ST_Transform(ca.geom, 3310) AS geom_3310
    FROM sfpoly sf
    JOIN caschools ca
      ON ST_Intersects(sf.geom, ST_Transform(ca.geom, 3310))
  ) sc
  CROSS JOIN ( -- get police stations in San Francisco
    SELECT
      ca.address,
      ST_Transform(ca.geom, 3310) AS geom_3310
    FROM sfpoly sf
    JOIN capolice ca
      ON ST_Intersects(sf.geom, ST_Transform(ca.geom, 3310))
```

```
      ) po
      ORDER BY 1, 3, 2
)
SELECT
      DISTINCT school,
      first_value(police_address)
            OVER (PARTITION BY school ORDER BY distance),
      first_value(distance)
            OVER (PARTITION BY school ORDER BY distance)
FROM scpo
ORDER BY 1;
```

7. We use the `first_value()` window function to extract the first `police_address` and `distance` values for each school sorted by the distance between the school and a police station. The improvement is considerable, reducing from almost 3 seconds to around 1.2 seconds:

```
Time: 1261.473 ms
Time: 1217.843 ms
Time: 1215.086 ms
```

8. However, it is worth to inspect the execution plan with `EXPLAIN ANALYZE VERBOSE` to see what is decreasing the query performance. Because of the verbosity of the output, we've trimmed it to just the following lines of interest:

```
                                QUERY PLAN
--------------------------------------------------------------------------------------------------------------------------
--------------------------------------------------------------------------------------------------------------------------
Unique  (cost=311.56..311.57 rows=1 width=146) (actual time=1224.805..1226.031 rows=234 loops=1)
  Output: scpo.school, (first_value(scpo.police_address) OVER (?)), (first_value(scpo.distance) OVER (?)), scpo.distance
  CTE scpo
    -> Sort  (cost=311.49..311.49 rows=1 width=48) (actual time=1213.926..1214.563 rows=7956 loops=1)
         Output: ca.name, ca_1.address, (st_distance(st_transform(ca_1.geom, 3310), st_transform(ca.geom, 3310)))
         Sort Key: ca.name, (st_distance(st_transform(ca_1.geom, 3310), st_transform(ca.geom, 3310))), ca_1.address
         Sort Method: quicksort  Memory: 1112kB
         -> Nested Loop  (cost=0.15..311.48 rows=1 width=48) (actual time=15.047..1186.907 rows=7956 loops=1)
              Output: ca.name, ca_1.address, st_distance(st_transform(ca_1.geom, 3310), st_transform(ca.geom, 3310))
              -> Nested Loop  (cost=0.00..302.98 rows=1 width=603921) (actual time=12.959..21.670 rows=34 loops=1)
                   Output: ca_1.address, ca_1.geom, sf.geom
                   -> Nested Loop  (cost=0.00..301.96 rows=1 width=49) (actual time=12.922..21.117 rows=34 loops=1)
                        Output: ca_1.address, ca_1.geom
                        Join Filter: ((sf_1.geom && st_transform(ca_1.geom, 3310)) AND _st_intersects(sf_1.geom, st_transform(ca_1.geom, 3310)))
                        Rows Removed by Join Filter: 946
                        -> Seq Scan on public.sfpoly sf_1  (cost=0.00..1.01 rows=1 width=603872) (actual time=0.013..0.013 rows=1 loops=1)
                             Output: sf_1.gid, sf_1.objectid, sf_1.sde_sfgis_, sf_1.perimeter, sf_1.innerwater, sf_1.shape__are, sf_1.shape__len
, sf_1.geom
                        -> Seq Scan on public.capolice ca_1  (cost=0.00..38.80 rows=980 width=49) (actual time=0.004..0.118 rows=980 loops=1)
                             Output: ca_1.gid, ca_1.objectid, ca_1.policestat, ca_1.efclass, ca_1.tract, ca_1.name, ca_1.address, ca_1.city, ca_
1.zipcode, ca_1.statea, ca_1.contact, ca_1.phonenumbe, ca_1.yearbuilt, ca_1.numstories, ca_1.cost, ca_1.backuppowe, ca_1.area, ca_1.sheltercap, ca_1.k
itchen, ca_1.latitude, ca_1.longitude, ca_1.comment, ca_1.geom
                   -> Seq Scan on public.sfpoly sf  (cost=0.00..1.01 rows=1 width=603872) (actual time=0.002..0.003 rows=1 loops=34)
                        Output: sf.gid, sf.objectid, sf.sde_sfgis_, sf.perimeter, sf.innerwater, sf.shape__are, sf.shape__len, sf.geom
              -> Index Scan using caschools_geom_3310_idx on public.caschools ca  (cost=0.15..8.42 rows=1 width=55) (actual time=0.326..33.462 row
s=234 loops=34)
                   Output: ca.gid, ca.objectid, ca.schoolid, ca.efclass, ca.tract, ca.name, ca.address, ca.city, ca.zipcode, ca.statea, ca.contact
, ca.phonenumbe, ca.yearbuilt, ca.numstories, ca.cost, ca.numstudent, ca.backuppowe, ca.sheltercap, ca.area, ca.district, ca.kitchen, ca.latitude, ca.
longitude, ca.comment, ca.geom
                   Index Cond: (sf.geom && st_transform(ca.geom, 3310))
                   Filter: _st_intersects(sf.geom, st_transform(ca.geom, 3310))
                   Rows Removed by Filter: 34
    -> Sort  (cost=0.07..0.07 rows=1 width=146) (actual time=1224.804..1225.153 rows=7956 loops=1)
```

```
. . .
-> Nested Loop  (cost=0.15..311.48 rows=1 width=48)
   (actual time=15.047..1186.907 rows=7956 loops=1)
   Output: ca.name, ca_1.address,
   st_distance(st_transform(ca_1.geom, 3310),
   st_transform(ca.geom, 3310))
```

9. In the `EXPLAIN ANALYZE VERBOSE` output, we want to inspect the values for the actual time, which provide the actual start and end times for that part of the query. Of all the actual time ranges, the actual time value of 15.047..1186.907 for the `Nested Loop` (highlighted in the preceding output) is the worst. This query step consumes at least 80 percent of the total execution time, so any work done to improve performance must be done in this step.

10. The columns returned from the slow `Nested Loop` utility are found in the value for the output. Of these columns, `st_distance()` is present only in this step and not in any inner step. This means we will need to mitigate the number of calls to `ST_Distance()`.

11. At this step, further query improvements are not possible without running PostgreSQL 9.1 or a later version. PostgreSQL 9.1 introduced indexed nearest-neighbor searches using the `<->` and `<#>` operators to compare the geometries' convex hulls and bounding boxes, respectively. For point geometries, both operators result in the same answer.

12. Let's rewrite the query to take advantage of the `<->` operator. The following query still uses the CTEs and window functions:

```
WITH sc AS ( -- get schools in San Francisco
  SELECT
    ca.gid,
    ca.name,
    ca.geom
  FROM sfpoly sf
  JOIN caschools ca
    ON ST_Intersects(sf.geom, ST_Transform(ca.geom, 3310))
), po AS ( -- get police stations in San Francisco
  SELECT
    ca.gid,
    ca.address,
    ca.geom
  FROM sfpoly sf
  JOIN capolice ca
    ON ST_Intersects(sf.geom, ST_Transform(ca.geom, 3310))
)
SELECT
```

```
        school,
        police_address,
        ST_Distance(ST_Transform(school_geom, 3310),
        ST_Transform(police_geom, 3310)) AS distance
FROM ( -- for each school, number and order the police
        -- stations by how close each station is to the school
    SELECT
        ROW_NUMBER() OVER (
            PARTITION BY sc.gid ORDER BY sc.geom <-> po.geom
        ) AS r,
        sc.name AS school,
        sc.geom AS school_geom,
        po.address AS police_address,
        po.geom AS police_geom
    FROM sc
    CROSS JOIN po
) scpo
WHERE r < 2
ORDER BY 1;
```

13. The query has the following performance numbers:

```
Time: 83.002 ms
Time: 82.586 ms
Time: 83.327 ms
```

Wow! Using indexed nearest-neighbor searches with the `<->` operator, we reduced our initial query from one second to less than a tenth of a second.

How it works...

In this recipe, we optimized a query that users may commonly encounter while using PostGIS. We started by taking advantage of the PostgreSQL capabilities to improve the performance and syntax of our query. When performance could no longer improve, we ran `EXPLAIN ANALYZE VERBOSE` to find out what was consuming most of the query-execution time. We learned that the `ST_Distance()` function consumed the most time from the execution plan. We finally used the `<->` operator of PostgreSQL 9.1 to dramatically improve the query-execution time to under a second.

The output of EXPLAIN ANALYZE VERBOSE used in this recipe is not easy to understand. For complex queries, it is recommended that you use the visual output in pgAdmin (discussed in a separate chapter's recipe) or the color coding provided by the http://explain.depesz.com/ web service, as shown in the following screenshot:

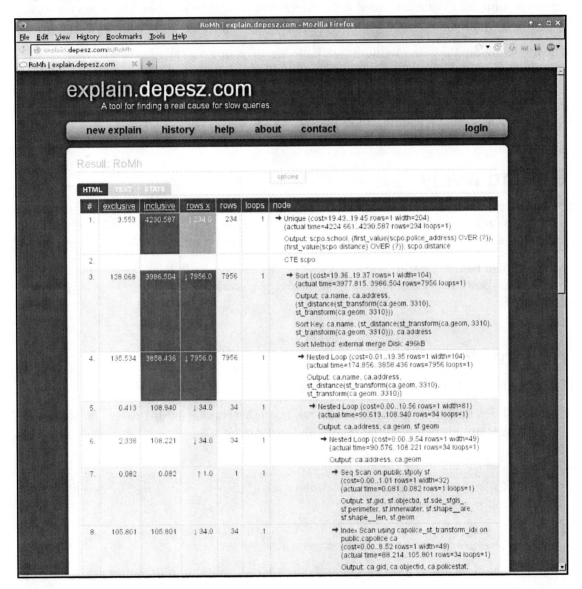

Migrating a PostGIS database to a different server

At some point, user databases need to be migrated to a different server. This need for server migration could be due to new hardware or a database-server software upgrade.

The following are the three methods available for migrating a database:

- Dumping and restoring the database with `pg_dump` and `pg_restore`
- Performing an in-place upgrade of the database with `pg_upgrade`
- Performing streaming replication from one server to another

Getting ready

In this recipe, we will use the `dump` and `restore` methods to move user data to a new database with a new PostGIS installation. Unlike the other methods, this method is the most foolproof, works in all situations, and stores a backup in case things don't work as expected.

As mentioned before, creating a schema specifically to work with PostGIS may not work properly for Windows users. Working on the `public` schema is an option in order to test the results.

How to do it...

On the command line, perform the following steps:

1. Even though a backup file was created in this chapter's third recipe, create a new backup file by executing the following command:

   ```
   > pg_dump -U me -f chapter10.backup -F custom chapter10
   ```

2. Create a new database to which the backup file will be restored by executing the following commands:

   ```
   > psql -d postgres -U me
   postgres=# CREATE DATABASE new10;
   ```

3. Connect to the `new10`, database and create a `postgis` schema as follows:

```
postgres=# \c new10
new10=# CREATE SCHEMA postgis;
```

4. Execute the `CREATE EXTENSION` command to install the Postgis extension in the postgis schema:

```
new10=# CREATE EXTENSION postgis WITH SCHEMA postgis;
```

5. Make sure you set the `search_path` parameter to include the `postgis` schema, as follows:

```
new10=# ALTER DATABASE new10 SET search_path = public, postgis;
```

6. Restore only the `public` schema from the backup file to the `new10` database by executing the following command:

```
> pg_restore -U me -d new10 --schema=public chapter10.backup
```

7. The `restore` method runs and should not generate errors. If it does, an error message such as the following will appear:

```
pg_restore: [archiver (db)] Error while PROCESSING TOC:
pg_restore: [archiver (db)] Error from TOC entry 3781; 03496229
            TABLE DATA prism postgres
pg_restore: [archiver (db)] COPY failed for table "prism":
ERROR:  function st_bandmetadata(postgis.raster, integer[])
        does not exist
LINE 1:  SELECT array_agg(pixeltype)::text[]
         FROM st_bandmetadata($1...
```

We have now installed PostGIS in the `postgis` schema, but the database server can't find the `ST_BandMetadata()` function. If a function cannot be found, it is usually an issue with `search_path`. We will fix this issue in the next step.

8. Check what `pg_restore` actually does by executing the following command:

```
pg_restore -f chapter10.sql --schema=public chapter10.backup
```

9. Looking at the COPY statement for the prism table, everything looks fine. But the search_path method preceding the table does not include the postgis schema as shown here:

```
SET search_path = public, pg_catalog;
```

10. Change the search_path value in chapter10.sql to include the postgis schema by executing the following command:

```
SET search_path = public, postgis, pg_catalog;
```

11. Run chapter10.sql with psql, as follows; the original chapter10.backup file can't be used because the necessary change can't be applied to pg_restore:

```
> psql -U me -d new10 -f chapter10.sql
```

How it works...

This procedure is essentially the standard PostgreSQL backup and restore cycle. It may not be simple, but has the benefit of being accessible in terms of the tools used and the control available in each step of the process. Though the other migration methods may be convenient, they typically require faith in an opaque process or the installation of additional software.

Replicating a PostGIS database with streaming replication

The reality of the world is that, given enough time, everything will break. This includes the hardware and software of computers running PostgreSQL. To protect data in PostgreSQL from corruption or loss, backups are taken using tools such as pg_dump. However, restoring a database backup can take a very long time, during which users cannot use the database.

When downtime must be kept to a minimum or is not acceptable, one or more standby servers are used to compensate for the failed primary PostgreSQL server. The data on the standby server is kept in sync with the primary PostgreSQL server by streaming data as frequently as possible.

In addition, you are strongly discouraged from trying to mix different PostgreSQL versions. Primary and standby servers must run the same PostgreSQL version.

Getting ready

In this recipe, we will use the streaming replication capability introduced in PostgreSQL 9.X. This recipe will use one server with two parallel PostgreSQL installations instead of the typical two or more servers, each with one PostgreSQL installation. We will use two new database clusters in order to keep things simple.

How to do it...

Use the following steps to replicate a PostGIS database:

1. Create directories for the primary and standby database clusters by executing the following commands:

    ```
    > mkdir postgis_cookbook/db
    > mkdir postgis_cookbook/db/primary
    > mkdir postgis_cookbook/db/standby
    ```

2. Initialize the database clusters with `initdb` as follows, defining the user me as the owner of the database:

    ```
    > cd postgis_cookbook/db
    > initdb --encoding=utf8 --locale=en_US.utf-8 -U me -D primary
    > initdb --encoding=utf8 --locale=en_US.utf-8 -U me -D standby
    ```

3. You may opt for avoiding the `--locale=en_US.utf-8` option if an error occurs; in that case, the system will adopt the default locale on your computer.

4. Create directories for the archives of the primary and standby database clusters by executing the following commands:

    ```
    > mkdir postgis_cookbook/db/primary/archive
    > mkdir postgis_cookbook/db/standby/archive
    ```

5. Open the `pg_hba.conf` authentication file of the primary cluster with your preferred editing application.

6. If you're running PostgreSQL 9.0, add the following text to the end of
   `pg_hba.conf`:

```
# TYPE   DATABASE          USER              ADDRESS                   METHOD

# IPv4 local connections:|
host     all               all               127.0.0.1/32              trust
# IPv6 local connections:
host     all               all               ::1/128                   trust
# Allow replication connections from localhost, by a user with the
# replication privilege.
host     replication       postgres          127.0.0.1/32              trust
host     replication       postgres          ::1/128              trust
```

 For PostgreSQL 9.1 or a later version, the configuration lines are already part of the `pg_hba.conf` file. You just need to remove the comment character (#) from the beginning of each matching line.

7. Edit the primary cluster's `postgresql.conf` configuration file to set the streaming replication parameters. Search for each parameter, uncomment and replace the assigned value to the following:

```
port = 5433
wal_level = hot_standby
max_wal_senders = 5
wal_keep_segments = 32
archive_mode = on
archive_command = 'copy "%p"
"C:\\postgis_cookbook\\db\\primary\\archive\\%f"' # for Windows
```

A relative location could also be used:

```
archive_command = 'copy "%p" "archive\\%f" "%p"'
```

When using Linux or macOS type instead:

```
archive_command = 'cp %p archive\/%f'
```

8. Start PostgreSQL on the primary database cluster by executing the following command:

```
> pg_ctl start -D primary -l primary\postgres.log
```

9. Create a base backup of the primary database cluster and copy it to the standby database cluster. Before performing the backup, create an exclusion list file for `xcopy` (Windows only) by executing the following command:

```
> notepad exclude.txt
```

10. Add the following to `exclude.txt`:

```
postmaster.pid
pg_xlog
```

11. Run the base backup and copy the directory contents from the primary to the standby database cluster, as follows:

```
> psql -p 5433 -U me -c "SELECT pg_start_backup('base_backup', true)"
> xcopy primary\* standby\ /e /exclude:primary\exclude.txt
> psql -p 5433 -U me -c "SELECT pg_stop_backup()"
```

12. Make the following changes to the standby cluster's `postgresql.conf` configuration file uncommenting these parameters and adjusting the values:

```
port = 5434
hot_standby = on
archive_command = 'copy "%p"
"C:\\postgis_cookbook\\db\\standby\\archive\\%f"' # for Windows
```

A relative location could also be used:

```
archive_command = 'copy ".\\archive\\%f" "%p"'
```

When using Linux or macOS type instead:

```
archive_command = 'cp %p archive\/%f'
```

13. Create the `recovery.conf` configuration file in the standby cluster directory by executing the following command for Windows:

```
> notepad standby\recovery.conf
```

For Linux or macOS:

```
> nano standby\recovery.conf
```

14. Enter the following in the `recovery.conf` configuration file and save the changes:

```
standby_mode = 'on'
primary_conninfo = 'port=5433 user=me'
restore_command = 'copy
"C:\\postgis_cookbook\\db\\standby\\archive\\%f" "%p"'
```

Or a relative location could be used also:

```
restore_command = 'copy ".\\archive\\%f" "%p"'
```

For Linux or macOS use:

```
restore_command = 'cp %p \archive\/%f"'
```

15. Start PostgreSQL on the standby database cluster by executing the following command:

```
> pg_ctl start -U me -D standby -l standby\postgres.log
```

16. Run some simple tests to make sure the replication is working.

17. Create the `test` database and the `test` table on the primary database server by executing the following commands:

```
> psql -p 5433 -U me
postgres=# CREATE DATABASE test;
postgres=# \c test
test=# CREATE TABLE test AS SELECT 1 AS id, 'one'::text AS value;
```

18. Connect to the standby database server by executing the following command:

```
> psql -p 5434 -U me
```

19. See if the `test` database is present by executing the following command:

```
postgres=# \l
```

```
                                   List of databases
    Name    |  Owner   | Encoding |  Collate   |   Ctype    |   Access privileges
------------+----------+----------+------------+------------+-----------------------
 postgres   | postgres | UTF8     | en_US.utf8 | en_US.utf8 |
 template0  | postgres | UTF8     | en_US.utf8 | en_US.utf8 | =c/postgres          +
            |          |          |            |            | postgres=CTc/postgres
 template1  | postgres | UTF8     | en_US.utf8 | en_US.utf8 | =c/postgres          +
            |          |          |            |            | postgres=CTc/postgres
 test       | postgres | UTF8     | en_US.utf8 | en_US.utf8 |
```

20. Connect to the `test` database and get the list of tables by executing the following command:

postgres=# \c test

```
test=# \d
          List of relations
 Schema | Name | Type  |  Owner
--------+------+-------+----------
 public | test | table | postgres
```

21. Get the records, if any, in the `test` table by executing the following commands:

```
test=# SELECT * FROM test;
 id | value
----+-------
  1 | one
```

Congratulations! The streaming replication works.

How it works...

As demonstrated in this recipe, the basic setup for streaming replication is straightforward. Changes made to the primary database server are quickly pushed to the standby database server.

There are third-party applications to help establish, administer, and maintain streaming replication on production servers. These applications permit complex replication strategies, including multimaster, multistandby, and proper failover. A few of these applications include the following:

- Pgpool-II, which is available at http://www.pgpool.net
- Bucardo, which is available at http://bucardo.org/wiki/Bucardo
- Postgres-XC, which is available at http://postgresxc.wikia.com/wiki/Postgres-XC_Wiki
- Slony-I, which is available at http://slony.info

Geospatial sharding

Working with large datasets can be challenging for the database engine, especially when they are stored in a single table or in a single database. PostgreSQL offers an option to split the data into several external databases, with smaller tables, that work logically as one. Sharding allows distributing the load of storage and processing of a large dataset so that the impact of large local tables is reduced.

One of the most important issues to make it work is the definition of a function to classify and evenly distribute the data. Given that this function can be a geographical property, sharding can be applied to geospatial data.

Getting ready

In this recipe, we will use the postgres_fdw extension that allows the creation of foreign data wrappers, needed to access data stored in external PostgreSQL databases. In order to use this extension, we will need the combination of several concepts: server, foreign data wrapper, user mapping, foreign table and table inheritance. We will see them in action in this recipe, and you are welcome to explore them in detail on the PostgreSQL documentation.

We will use the fire hotspot dataset and the world country borders shapefile used in Chapter 1, *Moving Data in and out of PostGIS*, in order to distribute the records for the hotspot data based on a geographical criteria, we will create a new distributed version of the hotspot dataset.

We will use the postgis_cookbook database for this recipe.

How to do it...

If you did not follow the recipes in Chapter 1, *Moving Data in and out of PostGIS*, be sure to import the hotspots (Global_24h.csv) in PostGIS. The following steps explain how to do it with ogr2ogr (you should import the dataset in their original SRID, 4326, to make spatial operations faster):

1. Start a session in the postgis_cookbook database:

    ```
    > psql -d postgis_cookbook -U me
    ```

2. Create a new schema `chp10` in the `postgis_cookbook` database:

```
postgis_cookbook=# CREATE SCHEMA chp10;
```

3. We need to create the `hotspots_dist` table, that will serve as parent for the foreign tables:

```
postgis_cookbook =# CREATE TABLE chp10.hotspots_dist (id serial
PRIMARY KEY, the_geom public.geometry(Point,4326));
```

4. Exit the `psql` environment:

```
postgis_cookbook=# \q
```

5. Connect to the psql environment as the postgres user:

```
> psql -U me
```

6. Create the remote databases, connect them, create the `postgis` extension and create the foreign tables that will receive the sharded data. Then, exit the `psql` environment. For this, execute the following SQL commands:

```
postgres=# CREATE DATABASE quad_NW;
CREATE DATABASE quad_NE;
CREATE DATABASE quad_SW;
CREATE DATABASE quad_SE;
postgres=# \c quad_NW;
quad_NW =# CREAT EXTENSION postgis;
quad_NW =# CREATE TABLE hotspots_quad_NW (
   id serial PRIMARY KEY,
   the_geom public.geometry(Point,4326)
);
quad_NW =# \c quad_NE;
quad_NE =# CREAT EXTENSION postgis;
quad_NE =# CREATE TABLE hotspots_quad_NE (
   id serial PRIMARY KEY,
   the_geom public.geometry(Point,4326)
);
quad_NW =# \c quad_SW;
quad_SW =# CREAT EXTENSION postgis;
quad_SW =# CREATE TABLE hotspots_quad_SW (
   id serial PRIMARY KEY,
   the_geom public.geometry(Point,4326)
);
quad_SW =# \c quad_SE;
quad_SE =# CREAT EXTENSION postgis;
quad_SE =# CREATE TABLE hotspots_quad_SE (
```

```
    id serial PRIMARY KEY,
    the_geom public.geometry(Point,4326)
);
quad_SE =# \q
```

7. In order to import the fire dataset, create a GDAL virtual data source composed of just one layer derived from the `Global_24h.csv` file. To do so, create a text file named `global_24h.vrt` in the same directory where the CSV file is and edit it as follows:

```xml
<OGRVRTDataSource>
  <OGRVRTLayer name="Global_24h">
    <SrcDataSource>Global_24h.csv</SrcDataSource>
    <GeometryType>wkbPoint</GeometryType>
    <LayerSRS>EPSG:4326</LayerSRS>
    <GeometryField encoding="PointFromColumns"
     x="longitude" y="latitude"/>
  </OGRVRTLayer>
</OGRVRTDataSource>
```

8. Import in PostGIS the `Global_24h.csv` file using the `global_24.vrt` virtual driver you created in a previous recipe:

```
$ ogr2ogr -f PostgreSQL PG:"dbname='postgis_cookbook' user='me'
password='mypassword'" -lco SCHEMA=chp10 global_24h.vrt
-lco OVERWRITE=YES -lco GEOMETRY_NAME=the_geom -nln hotspots
```

9. Create the extension `postgres_fdw` in the database:

```
postgis_cookbook =# CREATE EXTENSION postgres_fdw;
```

10. Define the servers that will host the external databases. You need to define the name of the database, the host address and the port in which the database will receive connections. In this case we will create 4 databases, one per global quadrant, according to latitude and longitude in the Mercator SRID. Execute the following commands to create the four servers:

```
postgis_cookbook =# CREATE SERVER quad_NW
  FOREIGN DATA WRAPPER postgres_fdw OPTIONS
  (dbname 'quad_NW', host 'localhost', port '5432');
CREATE SERVER quad_SW FOREIGN DATA WRAPPER postgres_fdw OPTIONS
  (dbname 'quad_SW', host 'localhost', port '5432');
CREATE SERVER quad_NE FOREIGN DATA WRAPPER postgres_fdw OPTIONS
  (dbname 'quad_NE', host 'localhost', port '5432');
CREATE SERVER quad_SE FOREIGN DATA WRAPPER postgres_fdw OPTIONS
  (dbname 'quad_SE', host 'localhost', port '5432');
```

11. For this example, we will be using local databases, but the host parameter can be either an IP address or a database file. The user who creates these commands will be defined as the local owner of the servers.

12. Create the user mapping in order to be able to connect to the foreign databases. For this, you need to write the login information of the owner of the foreign database in their local server:

```
postgis_cookbook =# CREATE USER MAPPING FOR POSTGRES SERVER quad_NW
   OPTIONS (user 'remoteme1', password 'myPassremote1');
CREATE USER MAPPING FOR POSTGRES SERVER quad_SW
   OPTIONS (user 'remoteme2', password 'myPassremote2');
CREATE USER MAPPING FOR POSTGRES SERVER quad_NE
   OPTIONS (user 'remoteme3', password 'myPassremote3');
CREATE USER MAPPING FOR POSTGRES SERVER quad_SE
   OPTIONS (user 'remoteme4', password 'myPassremote4');
```

13. Create the tables in the foreign databases, based on the local table `chp10.hotspots_dist`:

```
postgis_cookbook =# CREATE FOREIGN TABLE hotspots_quad_NW ()
   INHERITS (chp10.hotspots_dist) SERVER quad_NW
   OPTIONS (table_name 'hotspots_quad_sw');
CREATE FOREIGN TABLE hotspots_quad_SW () INHERITS (chp10.hotspots_dist)
   SERVER quad_SW OPTIONS (table_name 'hotspots_quad_sw');
CREATE FOREIGN TABLE hotspots_quad_NE () INHERITS (chp10.hotspots_dist)
   SERVER quad_NE OPTIONS (table_name 'hotspots_quad_ne');
CREATE FOREIGN TABLE hotspots_quad_SE () INHERITS (chp10.hotspots_dist)
   SERVER quad_SE OPTIONS (table_name 'hotspots_quad_se');
```

14. The name of the table name should preferably be written in lowercase.

15. Create a function that will calculate the quadrant of the point to be inserted in the database:

```
postgis_cookbook=# CREATE OR REPLACE
FUNCTION __trigger_users_before_insert() RETURNS trigger AS $__$
DECLARE
angle integer;
BEGIN
  EXECUTE $$ select (st_azimuth(ST_geomfromtext('Point(0 0)',4326),
    $1)
  /(2*PI()))*360 $$ INTO angle
  USING NEW.the_geom;
  IF (angle >= 0 AND angle<90) THEN
    EXECUTE $$
    INSERT INTO hotspots_quad_ne (the_geom) VALUES ($1)
    $$ USING
```

```
      NEW.the_geom;
   END IF;
   IF (angle >= 90 AND angle <180) THEN
     EXECUTE $$ INSERT INTO hotspots_quad_NW (the_geom) VALUES ($1)
     $$ USING NEW.the_geom;
   END IF;
   IF (angle >= 180 AND angle <270) THEN
     EXECUTE $$ INSERT INTO hotspots_quad_SW (the_geom) VALUES ($1)
     $$ USING NEW.the_geom;
   END IF;
   IF (angle >= 270 AND angle <360) THEN
     EXECUTE $$ INSERT INTO hotspots_quad_SE (the_geom) VALUES ($1)
     $$ USING NEW.the_geom;
   END IF;
   RETURN null;
END;
$__$ LANGUAGE plpgsql;
CREATE TRIGGER users_before_insert
BEFORE INSERT ON chp10.hotspots_dist
FOR EACH ROW EXECUTE PROCEDURE __trigger_users_before_insert();
```

16. Insert the test coordinates (10, 10), (-10, 10) and (-10 -10). The first one should be stored in the NE quadrant, the second on the SE quadrant and the third on the SW quadrant.

```
postgis_cookbook=# INSERT INTO CHP10.hotspots_dist (the_geom)
  VALUES (0, st_geomfromtext('POINT (10 10)',4326));
INSERT INTO CHP10.hotspots_dist (the_geom)
  VALUES ( st_geomfromtext('POINT (-10 10)',4326));
INSERT INTO CHP10.hotspots_dist (the_geom)
  VALUES ( st_geomfromtext('POINT (-10 -10)',4326));
```

17. Check the data insertion in the tables, both the local view and the external database hotspots_quad_NE:

```
postgis_cookbook=# SELECT ST_ASTEXT(the_geom)
FROM CHP10.hotspots_dist;
```

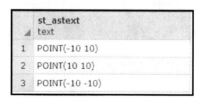

	st_astext text
1	POINT(-10 10)
2	POINT(10 10)
3	POINT(-10 -10)

18. As can be seen, the local version shows all the points that were inserted. Now, execute the query over a remote database:

```
postgis_cookbook=# SELECT ST_ASTEXT(the_geom) FROM hotspots_quad_ne;
```

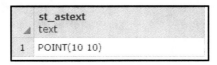

	st_astext text
1	POINT(10 10)

The remote databases only has the point that it should store, based on the trigger function defined earlier.

19. Now, insert all the points from the original hotspot table, imported in step 8. For this test, we will just insert the geometry information. Execute the following SQL sentence:

```
postgis_cookbook=# insert into CHP10.hotspots_dist
   (the_geom, quadrant)
select the_geom, 0 as geom from chp10.hotspots;
```

20. As in *step 15*, in order to check if the results were classified and stored correctly, execute the following queries, to the local table hotspots_dist and the remote table hotsports_quad_ne:

```
postgis_cookbook=# SELECT ST_ASTEXT(the_geom)
FROM CHP10.hotspots_dist;
```

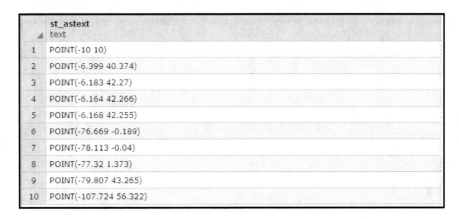

	st_astext text
1	POINT(-10 10)
2	POINT(-6.399 40.374)
3	POINT(-6.183 42.27)
4	POINT(-6.164 42.266)
5	POINT(-6.168 42.255)
6	POINT(-76.669 -0.189)
7	POINT(-78.113 -0.04)
8	POINT(-77.32 1.373)
9	POINT(-79.807 43.265)
10	POINT(-107.724 56.322)

21. The results show the first 10 points stored in the local logical version of the database.

```
postgis_cookbook=# SELECT ST_ASTEXT(the_geom) FROM hotspots_quad_ne;
```

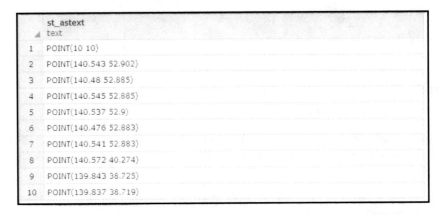

	st_astext text
1	POINT(10 10)
2	POINT(140.543 52.902)
3	POINT(140.48 52.885)
4	POINT(140.545 52.885)
5	POINT(140.537 52.9)
6	POINT(140.476 52.883)
7	POINT(140.541 52.883)
8	POINT(140.572 40.274)
9	POINT(139.843 38.725)
10	POINT(139.837 38.719)

22. The results show the first 10 points stored in the remote database with all the points in the NE quadrant. The points indeed show that they all have positive latitude and longitude values. When presented in a GIS application, the results is the following:

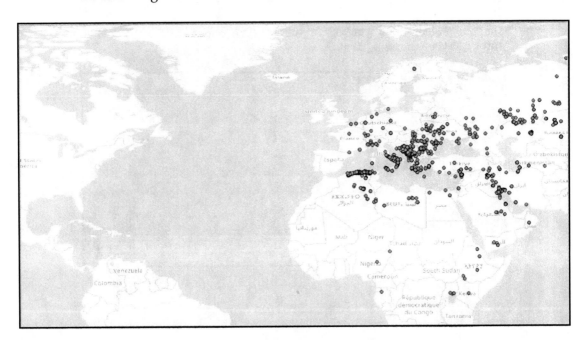

How it works...

In this recipe, a basic setup for geographical sharding is demonstrated. More sophisticated functions can be implemented easily on the same proposed structure. In addition, for heavy lifting applications purposes, there are some products in the market that could be explored, if considered necessary.

The example shown was based partly on a GitHub implementation found at the following link: `https://gist.github.com/sylr/623bab09edd04d53ee4e`.

Paralellizing in PosgtreSQL

Similar to sharding, working with a large amount of rows within a geospatial table in postgres, will cause a lot of processing time for a single worker. With the release of postgres 9.6, the server is capable of executing queries which can be processed by multiple CPUs for a faster answer. According to the postgres documentation, depending of the table size and the query plan, there might not be a considerable benefit when implementing a parallel query, instead of a serial query.

Getting ready

For this recipe, we need a specific version of postgres. It is not mandatory for you to download and install the postgres version that will be used. The reason is that, some developers might have an already configured postgres database version with data, and having multiple servers running within a computer might cause issues later.

To overcome this problem, we will make use of a **docker container**. A container could be defined as a lightweight instantiation of a software application that is isolated from other containers and your computer host. Similar to a virtual machine, you could have multiple versions of your software stored inside your host, and start multiple containers whenever necessary.

First, we will download docker from `https://docs.docker.com/install/` and install the **Community Edition (CE)** version. Then, we will pull an already precompiled docker image. Start a Terminal and run the following command:

```
$ docker pull shongololo/postgis
```

This docker image has PostgreSQL 10 with Postgis 2.4 and SFCGAL plugin. Now we need to start an instance given the image. An important part corresponds to the -p 5433:5432. These arguments maps every connection and request that is received at port 5433 in your host (local) computer to the 5432 port of your container:

```
$ docker run --name parallel -p 5433:5432 -v <SHP_PATH>:/data
shongololo/postgis
```

Now, you can connect to your PostgreSQL container:

```
$ docker exec -it parallel /bin/bash
root@d842288536c9:/# psql -U postgres
psql (10.1)
Type "help" for help.
postgres=#
```

Where root and d842288536c9 corresponds to your container username and group respectively.

How to do it...

Because we created an isolated instance of your postgres database, we have to recreate to use, database name and schema. These operations are optional. However, we encourage you to follow this to make this recipe consistent with the rest of the book:

1. Create the user me in your container:

```
root@d842288536c9:/# psql -U postgres
psql (10.1)
Type "help" for help.
postgres=# CREATE USER me WITH PASSWORD 'me';
CREATE ROLE
postgres=# ALTER USER me WITH SUPERUSER;
ALTER ROLE
```

2. Reconnect to the database but now as user me to create database and schema:

```
root@d842288536c9:/# PGPASSWORD=me psql -U me -d postgres
postgres=# CREATE DATABASE "postgis-cookbook";
CREATE DATABASE
postgres=# \c postgis-cookbook
```

You are now connected to database `postgis-cookbook` as user `me`:

```
postgis-cookbook=# CREATE SCHEMA chp10;
CREATE SCHEMA
postgis-cookbook=# CREATE EXTENSION postgis;
CREATE EXTENSION
```

3. Insert a layer into the database. In this case, we will make use of the `gis.osm_buildings_a_free_1 shapefile` from Colombia. Make sure you have these files within the `SHP_PATH` before starting the container. This database insertion could be run in two forms: First one is inside your docker container:

```
root@d842288536c9:/# /usr/lib/postgresql/10/bin/shp2pgsql -s 3734
-W latin1 /data/gis.osm_buildings_a_free_1.shp chp10.buildings |
PGPASSWORD=me psql -U me -h localhost -p 5432 -d postgis-cookbook
```

The second option is in your host computer. Make sure to correctly set your shapefiles path and host port that maps to the `5432` container port. Also, your host must have `postgresql-client` installed:

```
$ shp2pgsql -s 3734 -W latin1 <SHP_PATH>
/gis.osm_buildings_a_free_1.shp chp10.buildings | PGPASSWORD=me
psql -U me -h localhost -p 5433 -d postgis-cookbook
```

4. Execute parallel query. Using the building table we can execute a `postgis` command in parallel. To check how many workers are created, we make use of the `EXPLAIN ANALYZE` command. So, for example, if we want to calculate the sum of all geometries from the table in a serial query:

```
postgis-cookbook=# EXPLAIN ANALYZE SELECT Sum(ST_Area(geom))
FROM chp10.buildings;
```

We get the following result:

```
Aggregate (cost=35490.10..35490.11 rows=1 width=8)
  (actual time=319.299..319.2 99 rows=1 loops=1)
-> Seq Scan on buildings (cost=0.00..19776.16 rows=571416 width=142)
  (actual time=0.017..68.961 rows=571416 loops=1)
Planning time: 0.088 ms
Execution time: 319.358 ms
(4 rows)
```

Now, if we modify the `max_parallel_workers` and `max_parallel_workers_per_gather` parameters, we activate the parallel query capability of PostgreSQL:

```
Aggregate (cost=35490.10..35490.11 rows=1 width=8)
   (actual time=319.299..319.299 rows=1 loops=1)
-> Seq Scan on buildings (cost=0.00..19776.16 rows=571416 width=142)
   (actual time=0.017..68.961 rows=571416 loops=1)
Planning time: 0.088 ms
Execution time: 319.358 ms
(4 rows)
```

This command prints in Terminal:

```
Finalize Aggregate (cost=21974.61..21974.62 rows=1 width=8)
   (actual time=232.081..232.081 rows=1 loops=1)
-> Gather (cost=21974.30..21974.61 rows=3 width=8)
   (actual time=232.074..232.078 rows=4 loops=1)
Workers Planned: 3
Workers Launched: 3
-> Partial Aggregate (cost=20974.30..20974.31 rows=1 width=8)
   (actual time=151.785..151.785 rows=1 loops=4)
-> Parallel Seq Scan on buildings
   (cost=0.00..15905.28 rows=184328 width=142)
   (actual time=0.017..58.480 rows=142854 loops=4)
Planning time: 0.086 ms
Execution time: 239.393 ms
(8 rows)
```

5. Execute parallel scans. For example, if we want to select polygons whose area is higher than a value:

```
postgis-cookbook=# EXPLAIN ANALYZE SELECT * FROM chp10.buildings
WHERE ST_Area(geom) > 10000;
```

We get the following result:

```
Seq Scan on buildings (cost=0.00..35490.10 rows=190472 width=190)
   (actual time=270.904..270.904 rows=0 loops=1)
Filter: (st_area(geom) > '10000'::double precision)
Rows Removed by Filter: 571416
Planning time: 0.279 ms
Execution time: 270.937 ms
(5 rows)
```

This query is not executed in parallel. This happens because ST_Area function is defined with a COST value of 10. A COST for PostgreSQL is a positive number giving the estimated execution cost for a function. If we increase this value to 100, we can get a parallel plan:

```
postgis-cookbook=# ALTER FUNCTION ST_Area(geometry) COST 100;
postgis-cookbook=# EXPLAIN ANALYZE SELECT * FROM chp10.buildings
  WHERE ST_Area(geom) > 10000;
```

Now we have a parallel plan and 3 workers are executing the query:

```
Gather (cost=1000.00..82495.23 rows=190472 width=190)
   (actual time=189.748..189.748 rows=0 loops=1)
Workers Planned: 3
Workers Launched: 3
-> Parallel Seq Scan on buildings
   (cost=0.00..62448.03 rows=61443 width=190)
   (actual time=130.117..130.117 rows=0 loops=4)
Filter: (st_area(geom) > '10000'::double precision)
Rows Removed by Filter: 142854
Planning time: 0.165 ms
Execution time: 190.300 ms
(8 rows)
```

6. Execute parallel joins. First, we create a point table where we create randomly 10 points per polygon:

```
postgis-cookbook=# DROP TABLE IF EXISTS chp10.pts_10;
postgis-cookbook=# CREATE TABLE chp10.pts_10 AS

SELECT (ST_Dump(ST_GeneratePoints(geom, 10))).geom
  ::Geometry(point, 3734) AS geom,
  gid, osm_id, code, fclass, name, type FROM chp10.buildings;
postgis-cookbook=# CREATE INDEX pts_10_gix
ON chp10.pts_10 USING GIST (geom);
```

Now, we can run a table join between two tables, which does not give us a parallel plan:

```
Nested Loop (cost=0.41..89034428.58 rows=15293156466 width=269)
-> Seq Scan on buildings (cost=0.00..19776.16 rows=571416 width=190)
-> Index Scan using pts_10_gix on pts_10
   (cost=0.41..153.88 rows=190 width=79)
Index Cond: (buildings.geom && geom)
Filter: _st_intersects(buildings.geom, geom)
```

For this case, we need to modify the parameter `parallel_tuple_cost` which sets the planner's estimate of the cost of transferring one tuple from a parallel worker process to another process. Setting the value to `0.001` gives us a parallel plan:

```
Nested Loop (cost=0.41..89034428.58 rows=15293156466 width=269)
 -> Seq Scan on buildings (cost=0.00..19776.16 rows=571416 width=190)
 -> Index Scan using pts_10_gix on pts_10
    (cost=0.41..153.88 rows=190 width=79)
Index Cond: (buildings.geom && geom)
Filter: _st_intersects(buildings.geom, geom)
```

How it works...

As demonstrated in this recipe, parallelizing queries in PostgreSQL allows the optimization of operations that involve a large dataset. The database engine is already capable of implementing parallelism, but defining the proper configuration is crucial in order to take advantage of the functionality.

In this recipe, we used the `max_parallel_workers` and the `parallel_tuple_cost` to configure the desired amount a parallelism. We could evaluate the performance with the `ANALYZE` function.

11
Using Desktop Clients

In this chapter, we will cover the following topics:

- Adding PostGIS layers – QGIS
- Using the Database Manager plugin – QGIS
- Adding PostGIS layers – OpenJUMP GIS
- Running database queries – OpenJUMP GIS
- Adding PostGIS layers – gvSIG
- Adding PostGIS layers – uDig

Introduction

At a minimum, desktop GIS programs allow you to visualize data from a PostGIS database. This relationship gets more interesting with the ability to edit and manipulate data outside of the database and in a dynamic *play* environment.

Make a change, see a change! For this reason, visualizing the data stored in PostGIS is often critical for effective spatial database management—or at least as a now-and-again sanity check. This chapter will demonstrate both dynamic and static relationships between your database and desktop clients.

Regardless of your experience level or role in the geospatial community, you should find at least one of the four GIS programs serviceable as a potential intermediate staging environment between your PostGIS database and end product.

In this chapter, we will connect to PostGIS using the following desktop GIS programs: **QGIS**, **OpenJUMP GIS**, **gvSIG**, and **uDig**.

Once connected to PostGIS, extra emphasis will be placed on some of the more sophisticated functionalities offered by `QGIS` and `OpenJUMP GIS` using the **Database Manager** (**DB Manager**) plugin and data store queries, respectively.

Adding PostGIS layers – QGIS

In this recipe, we will establish a connection to our PostGIS database in order to add a table as a layer in **QGIS** (formerly known as **Quantum GIS**). Viewing tables as layers is great for creating maps or simply working on a copy of the database outside the database.

Please navigate to the following site to install the latest version LTR of QGIS (2.18 – Las Palmas at the time of writing):

`http://qgis.org/en/site/`

On this page, click on **Download Now** and you will be able to choose a suitable operating system and the relevant settings. QGIS is available for Android, Linux, macOS X, and Windows. You might also be inclined to click on **Discover QGIS** to get an overview of basic information about the program along with features, screenshots, and case studies.

Getting ready

To begin, create the schema for this chapter as `chp11`; then, download data from the U.S. Census Bureau's FTP site:

`http://ftp2.census.gov/geo/tiger/TIGER2012/EDGES/tl_2012_39035_edges.zip`

The shapefile is `All Lines` for Cuyahoga county in Ohio, which consist of roads and streams among other line features.

Extract the ZIP file to your working directory and then load it into your database using `shp2pgsql`. Be sure to specify the spatial reference system, EPSG/SRID: 4269. When in doubt about using projections, use the service provided by the folks at OpenGeo at the following website: `http://prj2epsg.org/search`

Use the following command to generate the SQL to load the shapefile in a table of the `chp11` schema:

```
shp2pgsql -s 4269 -W LATIN1 -g the_geom -I tl_2012_39035_edges.shp
chp11.tl_2012_39035_edges > tl_2012_39035_edges.sql
```

How to do it...

Now it's time to give the data we downloaded a look using QGIS. We must first create a connection to the database in order to access the table. Get connected and add the table as a layer by following the ensuing steps:

1. Click on the Add PostGIS Layers icon:

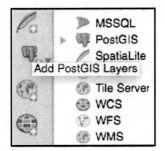

2. Click on the **New** button below the **Connections** drop-down menu.

3. Create a new PostGIS connection. After the **Add PostGIS Table(s)** window opens, create a name for the connection and fill in a few parameters for your database, including **Host**, **Port**, **Database**, **Username**, and **Password**:

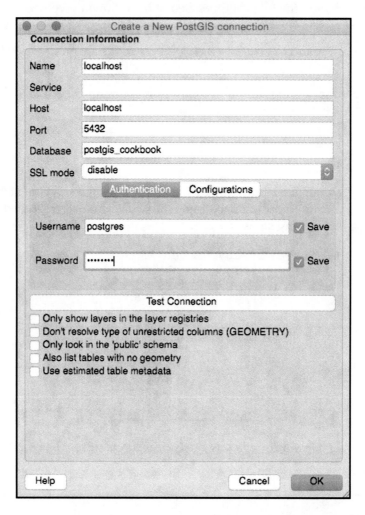

4. Once you have entered all of the pertinent information for your database, click on the **Test Connection** button to verify that the connection is successful. If the connection is not successful, double-check for typos and errors. Additionally, make sure you are attempting to connect to a PostGIS-enabled database.

5. If the connection is successful, go ahead and check the **Save Username** and **Save Password** checkboxes. This will prevent you from having to enter your login information multiple times throughout the exercise.

6. Click on **OK** at the bottom of the menu to apply the connection settings. Now you can connect!

   Make sure the name of your PostGIS connection appears in the drop-down menu and then click on the **Connect** button. If you choose not to store your username and password, you will be asked to submit this information every time you try to access the database.

   Once connected, all schemas within the database will be shown and the tables will be made visible by expanding the target schema.

7. Select the table(s) to be added as a layer by simply clicking on the table name or anywhere along its row. Selection(s) will be highlighted in blue. To deselect a table, click on it a second time and it will no longer be highlighted. Select the tl_2012_39035_edges table that was downloaded at the beginning of the chapter and click on the **Add** button, as shown in the following screenshot:

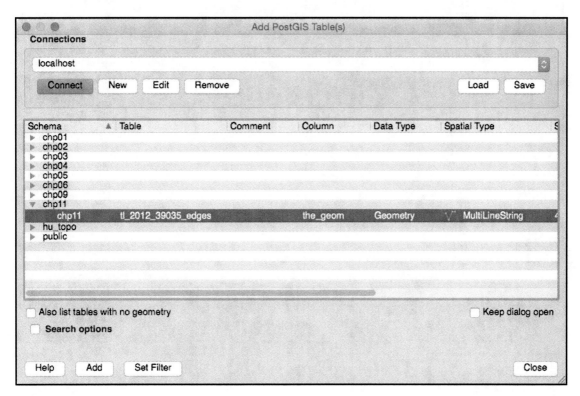

8. A subset of the table can also be added as a layer. This is accomplished by double-clicking on the desired **table name**.

9. The **Query Builder** window will open, which aids in creating simple SQL WHERE clause statements. Add the roads by selecting the records where roadflg = Y. This can be done by typing a query or using the buttons within **Query Builder**:

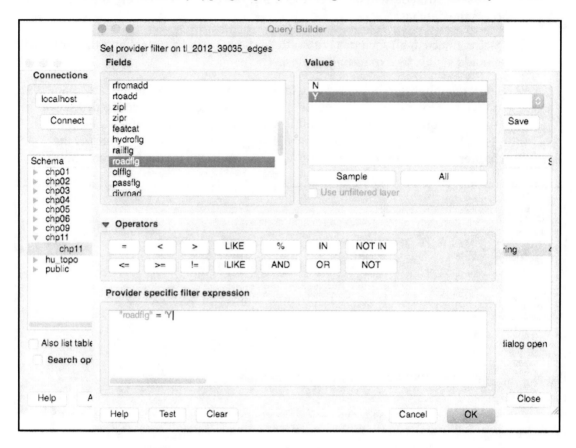

10. Click on the **OK** button followed by the **Add** button. A subset of the table is now loaded into QGIS as a layer. The layer is strictly a static, temporary copy of your database. You can make whatever changes you like to the layer and not affect the database table.

The same holds true the other way around. Changes to the table in the database will have no effect on the layer in QGIS.

If needed, you can save the temporary layer in a variety of formats, such as DXF, GeoJSON, KML, or SHP. Simply right-click on the layer name in the **Layers** panel and click on **Save As**. This will then create a file, which you can recall at a later time or share with others.

The following screenshot shows the Cuyahoga county road network:

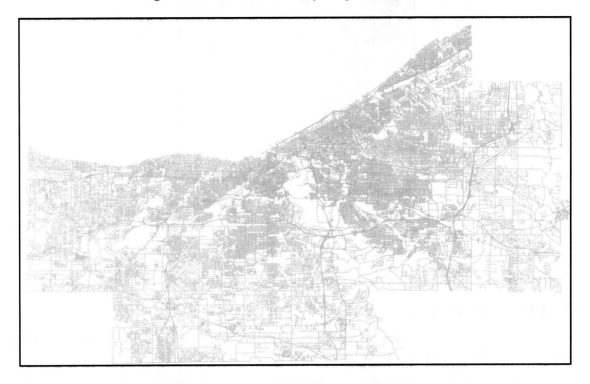

You may also use the QGIS **Browser Panel** to navigate through the now connected PostGIS database and list the schemas and tables. This panel allows you to double-click to add spatial layers to the current project, providing a better user experience not only of connected databases, but on any directory of your machine:

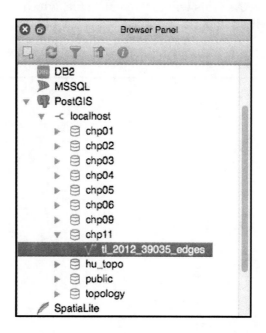

How it works...

You have added a PostGIS layer into QGIS using the built-in **Add PostGIS Table** GUI. This was achieved by creating a new connection and entering your database parameters.

Any number of database connections can be set up simultaneously. If working with multiple databases is more common for your workflows, saving all of the connections into one XML file (see the tip in the preceding section) would save time and energy when returning to these projects in QGIS.

Using the Database Manager plugin – QGIS

Database Manager (**DB Manager**) allows for a more sophisticated relationship with PostGIS by allowing users to interact with the database in a variety of ways. The plugin mimics some of the core functionality of pgAdmin with the added benefit of data visualization.

In this recipe, we will use DB Manager to create, modify, and delete items within the database and then tinker with the SQL window. By the end of this section, you will be able to do the following:

- Navigate to the DB Manager menu
- Create, modify, and delete database schemas and tables
- Run SQL queries to add new QGIS layers or create new tables in the database

QGIS needs to be installed for this recipe. Please refer to the first recipe in this chapter for information on where to download the installer.

Getting ready

Let's make sure the plugin is enabled and connected to the database.

1. Click on the **Plugins** menu located on the QGIS menu bar and select **Manage and Install Plugins** from the drop-down menu, as shown in the following screenshot:

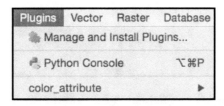

2. The QGIS **Plugin Manager** window will open. Search for **DB Manager** in the list of plugins and make sure it is checked (enabled), as shown in the following screenshot:

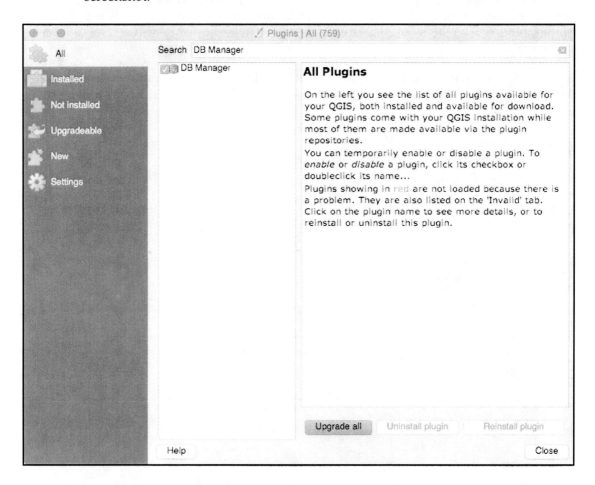

3. Now that **DB Manager** is enabled, let us open the plugin and check the status of the database connection. Open **DB Manager** by navigating to **Database | DB Manager** from the QGIS menu bar, as shown in the following screenshot:

4. Expand the **PostGIS** directory within the **Tree** window of DB Manager. The PostGIS connection created in the last recipe will appear. Expand the connection to view your schema(s) and table(s). You will be asked for a username and password if you opted not to save your credentials.

On the **Info** tab above the main window, you can view information about the data, such as spatial reference, geometry type, field names, field types, and much more, as in the following screenshot:

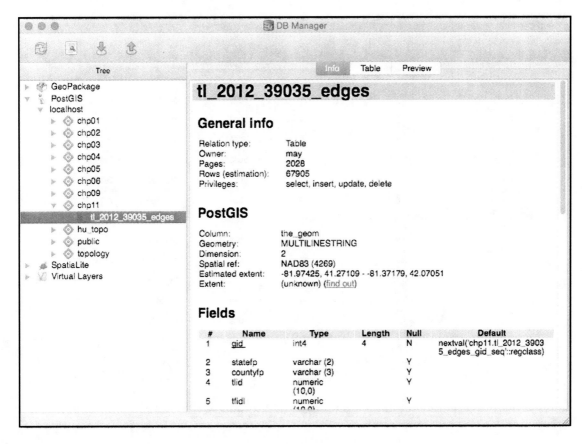

A PostGIS connection is not in place if you are unable to expand the **PostGIS** menu. If you need to establish a connection, refer to *steps 1 to 4* in the *Adding PostGIS layers – QGIS* recipe. The connection must be established before using DB Manager.

How to do it...

Navigate to the **DB Manager** menu and carry out the following steps:

1. Select the `tl_2012_39035_edges` table in the **Tree** window.
2. Next, click on the **Table** tab to view the actual data table, as shown in the following screenshot:

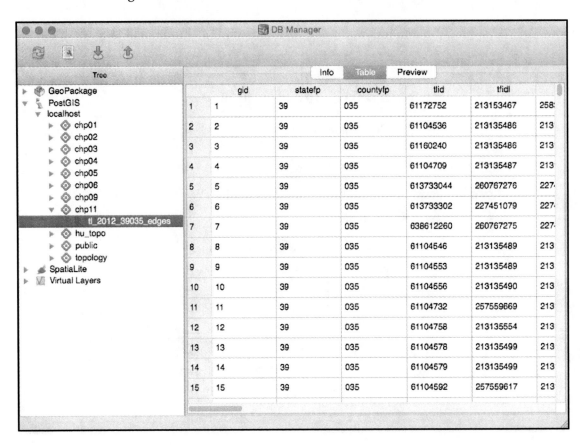

3. The final tab, **Preview**, is for visualizing the data, as shown in the following screenshot:

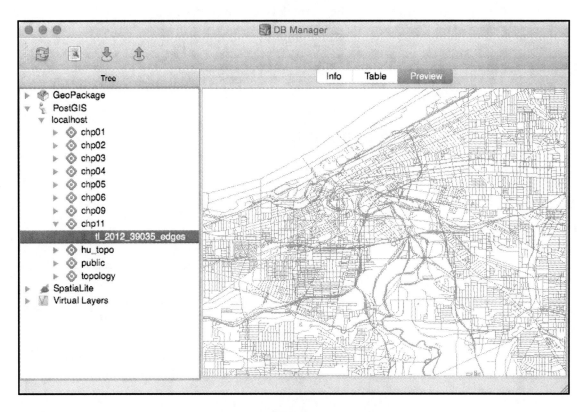

To create, modify, and delete database schemas and tables, follow the ensuing steps:

1. First, create a new schema in the database to store data for this chapter. Select **Schema** | **Create schema** from the menu bar, as shown in the following screenshot:

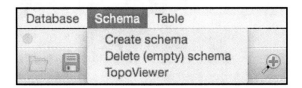

2. Enter `new_schema` as the schema name and then click on **OK**. If you do not see the `new_schema` in the list, you may need to select the database connection in the **Tree** window and click on the **Refresh** button or press *F5* (see the following screenshot):

3. Your new, empty schema will now be visible in the **Tree** window:

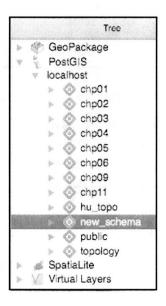

Now let's continue to work with our **chp11** schema containing the t1_2012_39035_edges table. Let's modify the table name to something more generic. How about lines? You can change the table name by clicking on the table in the **Tree** window. As soon as the text is highlighted and the cursor flashes, you can delete the existing name and enter the new name, lines.

Right now, our lines table's data is using degrees as the unit of measurement for its current projection (*EPSG: 4269*). Let's add a new geometry column using EPSG: 3734, which is a State Plane Coordinate system that measures projections in feet. To run SQL queries, follow the ensuing steps:

1. Click on the **SQL window** button in the DB Manager or press *F2*, as shown in the following screenshot:

2. Copy the following query into the SQL window and then click on **Execute**:

```
SELECT AddGeometryColumn ('chp11', 'lines','geom_sp',3734,
                          'MULTILINESTRING', 2);
UPDATE "chp11".lines
SET geom_sp = ST_Transform(the_geom,3734);
```

The query creates a new geometry column named `geom_sp` and then updates the geometry information by transforming the original geometry (`geom`) from EPSG 4269 to 3734, as shown in the following screenshot:

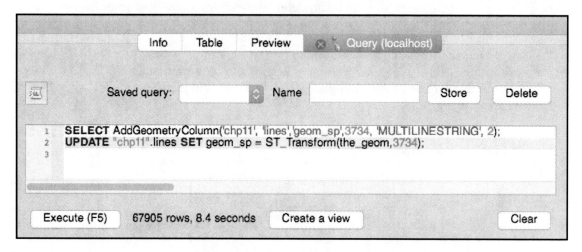

3. Refresh the `chp11` schema and you'll notice that the table in the database now has two geometry columns that are treated independently in the **Tree** window:

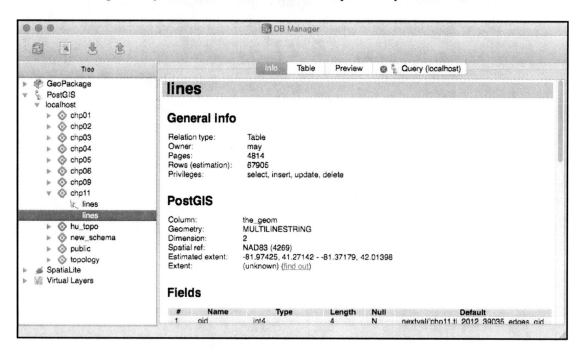

The preceding screenshot shows the original geometry. The following screenshot shows the created geometry:

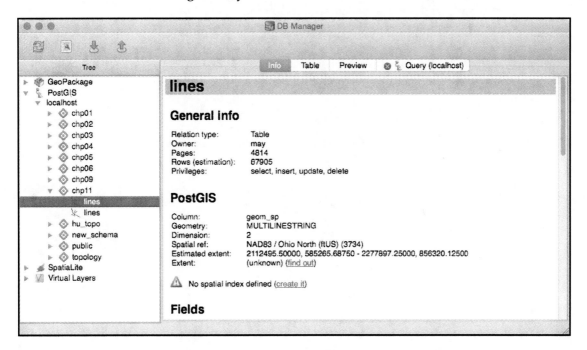

4. For our next query, let us take a subset of the `lines` table. Similar to what we did in the preceding section, we will only look at the data about roads. However, this time, we can limit the columns that we want to load with the layer, as well as perform more complicated spatial queries. We'll apply a buffer of 10 feet using the new geometry column (`geom_sp`) by executing the following command:

```
SELECT gid, ST_Buffer(geom_sp, 10) AS geom, fullname, roadflg
FROM "chp11".lines WHERE roadflg = 'Y'
```

Check the **Load as new layer** checkbox and then select **gid** as the unique ID and **geom** as the geometry. Create a name for the layer and then click on **Load Now!**, and what you'll see is shown in the following screenshot:

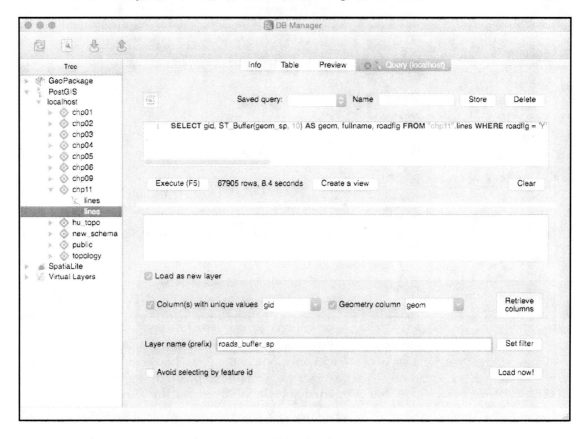

The query adds the result in QGIS as a temporary layer.

5. Now let us modify the query to create a table in the database, rather than load the query as a layer, by executing the following command:

```
CREATE TABLE "chp11".roads_buffer_sp AS SELECT gid,
ST_Buffer(geom_sp, 10) AS geom, fullname, roadflg
FROM "chp11".lines WHERE roadflg = 'Y'
```

The following screenshot shows the Cuyahoga county road network:

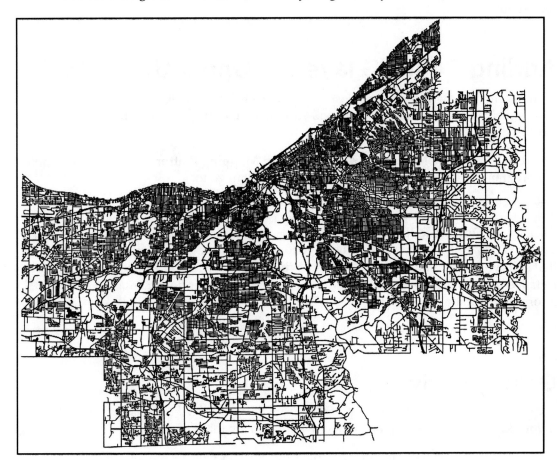

How it works...

Connecting to a PostGIS database (see the *Adding PostGIS layers – QGIS* recipe in this chapter) allows you to utilize the DB Manager plugin. Once DB Manager was enabled, we were able to toggle between the **Info**, **Table**, and **Preview** tabs to efficiently view metadata, tabular data, and data visualization.

Next, we made changes to the database through the query window, running on the table lines of schema `chp11` in order to transform the projection. Note the autocomplete feature in the **SQL Window**, which makes writing queries a breeze.

Changes to the database were made visible in DB Manager by refreshing the database connection.

Adding PostGIS layers – OpenJUMP GIS

In this section, we will connect to PostGIS with OpenJUMP GIS (OpenJUMP) in order to add spatial tables as layers. Next, we will edit the temporary layer and update it in a new table in the database.

The **JUMP** in OpenJUMP stands for **Java Unified Mapping Platform**. To learn more about the program, or if you need to install the latest version, go to:

```
http://www.openjump.org/
```

Click on the **Download latest version** link (`http://sourceforge.net/projects/jump-pilot/files/OpenJUMP/1.12/`) on the page to view the list of installers. Select the version that suits your operating system (`.exe` for Windows and `.jar` for Linux and mac OS). Detailed directions for installing OpenJUMP along with other documentation and information can be found on the OpenJUMP Wiki page at the following link:

```
http://ojwiki.soldin.de/index.php?title=Main_Page
```

Getting ready

We will be reusing and building upon data used in the *Adding PostGIS layers – QGIS* recipe. If you skipped over this recipe, you will want to do the following:

1. Download the following ZIP file from the U.S. Census Bureau's FTP site:

   ```
   ftp://ftp2.census.gov/geo/tiger/TIGER2012/EDGES/tl_2012_39035_edges.zip
   ```

   The shapefile is `All Lines` for Cuyahoga county in Ohio, which consist of roads and streams, among other line features.

2. Extract the ZIP file to your working directory and then load it into your database using `shp2pgsql`. Be sure to specify the spatial reference system, which is *EPSG: 4269*, and name the table `lines`.

How to do it...

The data source layer can be added by performing the following steps:

1. Click on the **Open** (folder) icon or go to **File | Open**.
2. Select **Data Store Layer** from the left-hand-side menu, as shown in the following screenshot:

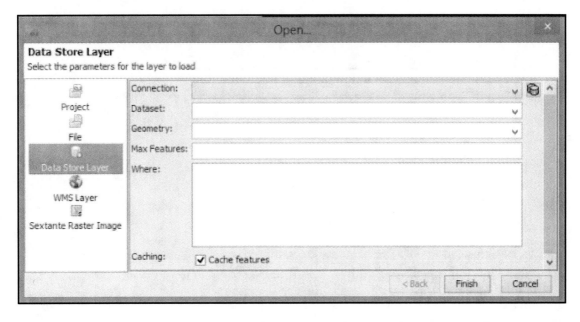

3. Click on the icon to the right of the **Connection** dropdown to open the connection manager.

4. Click on the **Add** button. This will prompt a new window to appear in which you must enter your database parameters:

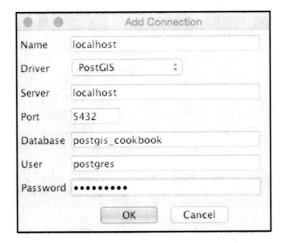

5. Enter a name for the connection and then enter values for the following database parameters:

   - **Server/Host**
   - **Port**
   - **Database**
   - **Username**
   - **Password**

6. Then click on **OK**. You are now connected to the database.

7. Check for typos and errors if a connection error message appears. If the connection is successful, select the connection and click on **OK**.

8. Now you can select the **lines** table to add, as shown in the following screenshot:

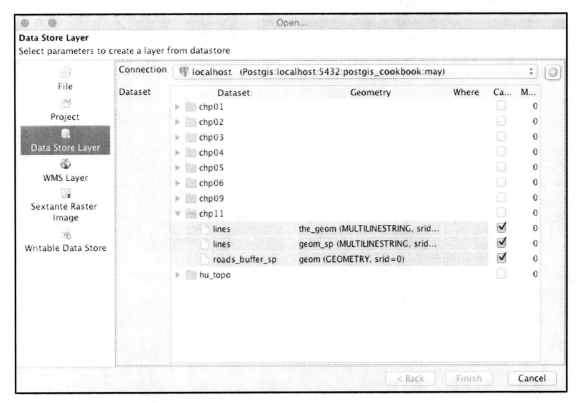

If multiple geometry columns exist, you may choose the one you want to use. Add the data's state plane coordinator geometry (geom_sp), as shown in the *Using the Database Manager plugin – QGIS* recipe.

Simple SQL WHERE clause statements can be used if only a subset of a table is needed.

9. Click on **Finish** to load the dataset into the main window, as shown in the
following screenshot:

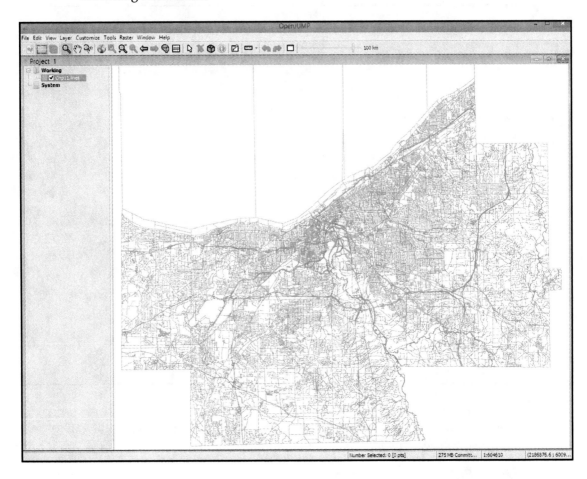

10. Now make a quick edit to the temporary layer and save it back to the database. Select the **Editing Toolbox** button. When the toolbox is loaded, click on the Select Features Tool button (to the top-left corner of the screen), as shown in the following screenshot:

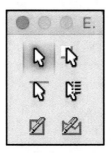

11. Select some of the lines, as shown in the following screenshot, that look out of place on the map. In particular, the lines to the North of the county; these actually jet out into Lake Erie. You can select multiple lines by clicking and dragging a rectangle with the cursor or by holding *Shift* while clicking on line segments. Hit the *Delete* key (or *Fn* + *Delete* on macOS) once you have selected some lines to remove them from the data:

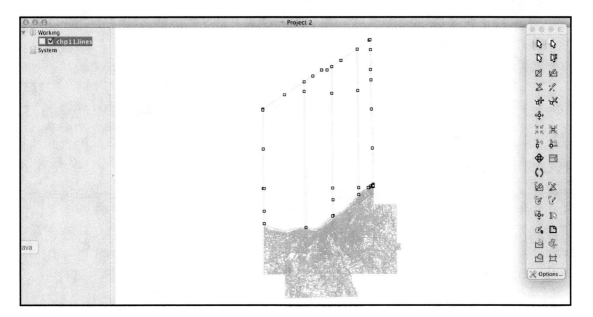

12. Save the changes made to the layer and replace the existing table in the database with the edited copy. Right-click on the layer name on the left panel and then select **Save Dataset As**.

13. Select your PostGIS connection with the **Connection** drop-down menu, choose the appropriate table name, and then make sure that the **Create new or replace existing table** option is selected, as shown in the following screenshot:

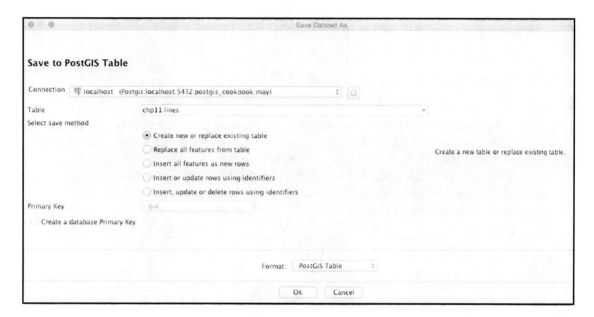

14. Click on **OK**; you have now successfully edited a PostGIS table in OpenJUMP.

How it works...

We added a PostGIS layer in OpenJUMP using the **Open Data Store Layer** menu. This was achieved after creating a new connection and entering our database parameters.

In the example, census data was added which included the boundary of Cuyahoga county. Part of the boundary advances into Lake Erie to the International Boundary with Canada. While technically correct, the water boundary is typically not used for practical mapping purposes. In this case, it's easy to visualize which data needs to be removed.

OpenJUMP allows us to easily see and delete records that should be deleted from the table. The selected lines were deleted, and the table was saved to the database.

Running database queries – OpenJUMP GIS

Executing ad hoc queries in OpenJUMP is simple and offers a couple of unique features. Queries can be run on specific data selections, allowing for the manual control of the queried area without considering the attribution. Similarly, temporary fences (areas) can be drawn on the fly and the geometry of the surface can be used in queries. In this recipe, we will explore each of those cases.

Getting ready

Refer to the preceding recipe if you need to install OpenJUMP or require assistance connecting to a database.

How to do it...

Carry out the following steps to run the data store query:

1. Navigate to **File | Run Datastore Query.** Choose the PostGIS connection from the **Connection** drop-down menu or use the **Connection Manager** utility if you are not linked to the database.

2. We'll create and name a polygon layer of the main streams in the region by executing the following query:

```
SELECT gid, ST_BUFFER("chp11".lines.geom_sp, 75)
AS the_geom, fullname
FROM "chp11".lines WHERE fullname <> '' AND hydroflg = 'Y'
```

The preceding query is shown in the following screenshot:

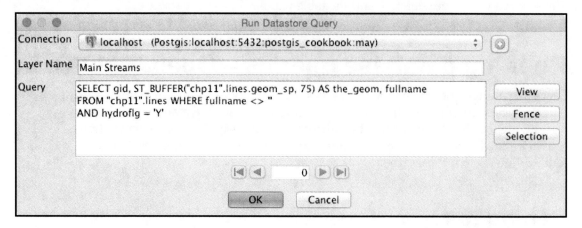

The preceding query selects the lines on the map that represent hydrology units such as "hydroflg" = 'Y' and streams. The selected stream lines (which use the State Plane geometry) are buffered by 75 feet, which should yield a result like that shown in the following screenshot:

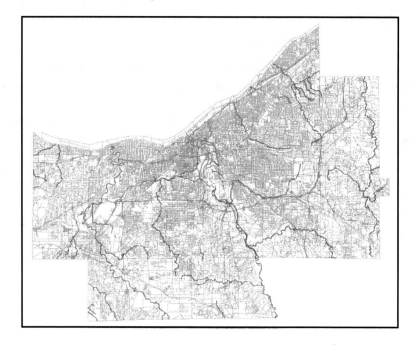

3. The `ST_Buffer` function uses the units of the data projection for buffering. So, if your data still has the original spatial reference *EPSG: 4269*, you will be buffering the lines by 75 degrees, and this will lead to very strange results indeed! Modify the following SQL query to transform your geometry:

```
SELECT AddGeometryColumn('chp11', 'lines','geom_sp',3734,
                         'MULTILINESTRING', 2);
UPDATE "chp11".lines SET geom_sp = ST_Transform(geom,3734);
```

4. You'll then want to go back to *step 2* in order to create the buffer measured in feet.
5. Next, pan and zoom on the map and find two, separate polygons that are near each other.
6. Select the **Fence** icon on the main menu, as shown in the following screenshot:

7. Draw a connection (overlapping a connection is fine) between the two unconnected polygons using the **Fence** tool. Click once on the **Fence** button to create a vertex and double-click on it once your polygon is complete.
8. Switch over to the Select Features Tool, as shown in the following screenshot, and select the polygons that you drew on either side of the **Fence** bridge; select multiple features by holding down the *Shift* key:

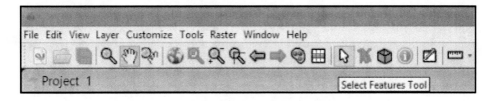

You should now have a fence junction between the selected polygons. You should see something similar to the following screenshot:

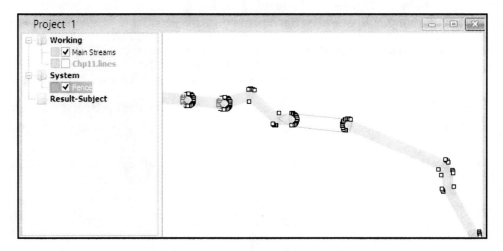

9. Navigate to **File | Run Datastore Query** again.
10. This time, we will utilize the buttons to the right-hand side of the window to connect.

   Run ST_UNION on the selection and fence together so that the gap is filled. We do this with the following query:

   ```
   SELECT ST_UNION(geom1, geom2) AS geom
   ```

   Use the **Selection** and **Fence** buttons in place of geom1 and geom2 so that your query looks as shown in the following screenshot:

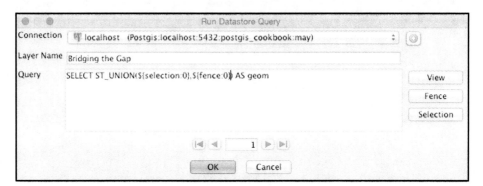

11. Click on **OK** and view the query result by turning off the **Main Streams** and **Fence** layers, as shown in the following screenshot:

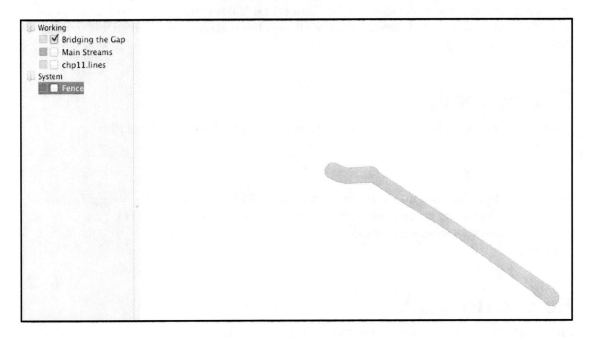

How it works...

We added a buffered subset of a PostGIS layer in OpenJUMP using the **Run Datastore Query** menu. We took lines from a database table and converted them to polygons to view them in OpenJUMP.

We then manually selected an area of interest that had two representative stream polygons disjointed from one another, the idea being that the streams would be, or are, connected in a natural state.

The **Fence** tool was used to draw a freehand polygon between the streams. A union query was then performed to combine the two stream polygons and the fences. Fences allow us to create temporary tables for use in spatial queries executed against a database table.

Adding PostGIS layers – gvSIG

gvSIG is a GIS package developed for the **Generalitat Valenciana (gv)** in Spain. SIG is the Spanish equivalent of GIS. Intended for use all over the world, gvSIG is available in more than a dozen languages.

Getting ready

Installers, documentation, and more details for gvSIG can be found at the following website:

```
http://www.gvsig.org/web/
```

To download gvSIG, click on the latest version (gvSIG 2.0 at the time of writing). The all-included version is recommended on the gvSIG site. Be careful while selecting the `.exe` or `.bin` versions; otherwise, you may download the program in a language that you don't understand.

How to do it...

The GeoDB layer can be added by following the ensuing steps:

1. Select **View** as the document type in the **Project manager** section and then click on the **New** button. A blank view (canvas) will open.
2. Click on the **Add Layer** button on the menu bar, as shown in the following screenshot:

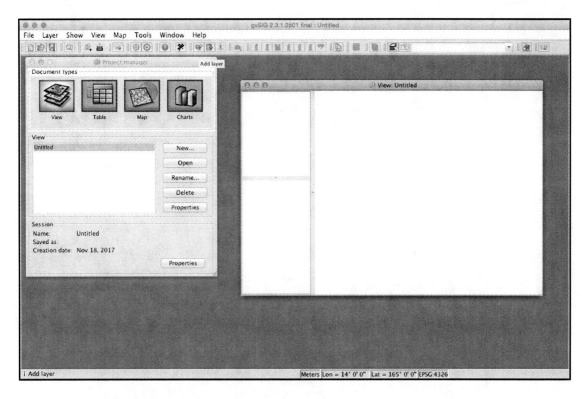

3. Next, select the **GeoDB** tab and click on the button to the right of the **Choose connection** drop-down menu.

4. Enter the values in **Connection parameters** and make sure to select **PostgreSQLExplorer** as the value for **Driver,** as shown in the following screenshot:

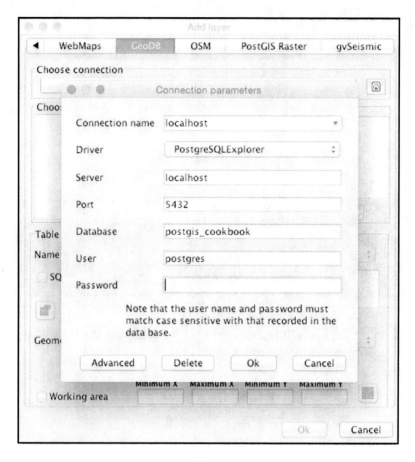

5. Click on **OK**. All of your tables should appear in **Choose table**. One or many tables can be added at a time. You can also do the following:
   - Choose the columns you want to add in each layer
   - Select the geometry column to be used in the event of multiple geometries being present
   - Give each layer a unique name
   - Perform SQL WHERE clause queries to load a subset of a dataset

You can see these steps performed in the following screenshot:

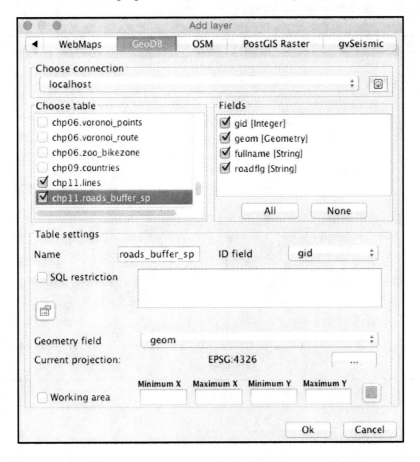

6. Click on **OK** when you're ready. The data will load in the new view that was created, as shown in the following screenshot:

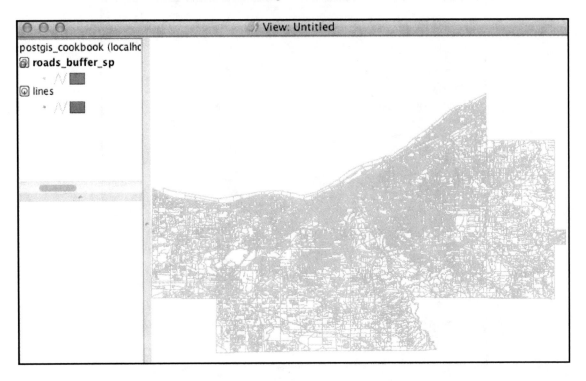

How it works...

PostGIS layers were added to gvSIG using the **Add Layer** menu. The **GeoDB** tab allowed us to set the PostGIS connection. After choosing a table, many options are afforded with gvSIG. The layer name can be aliased to something more meaningful and unnecessary columns can be omitted from the table.

Adding PostGIS layers – uDig

A hallmark of the **User-friendly Desktop Internet GIS (uDig)** program built with **Eclipse** is that it can be used as a standalone application or a plugin for existing applications. Details on the uDig project as well as installers can be found at the following website:

```
http://udig.refractions.net/
```

Click on **Downloads** at the preceding website to view the list of versions and installers. At the time of writing, 2.0.0.RC1 is the latest stable version. uDig is supported by Windows, macOS X, and Linux.

In this recipe, we will quickly connect to a PostGIS database and then add a layer to uDig.

How to do it...

Carry out the following steps:

1. Navigate to **File** | **New Layer** from the main menu, as shown in the following screenshot:

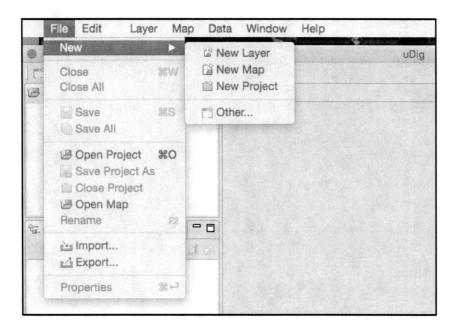

2. Select **PostGIS** as the data source and click on the **Next** button to continue, as shown in the following screenshot:

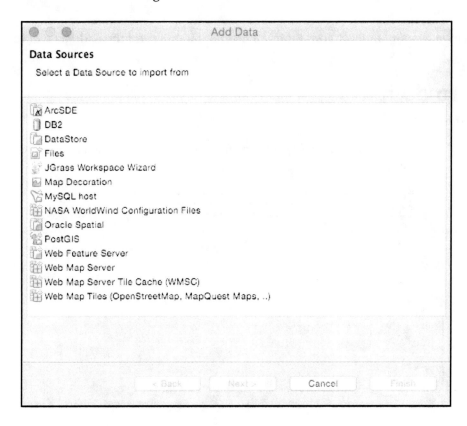

3. Fill in your PostGIS connection parameters and then click on the **Next** button, as shown in the following screenshot:

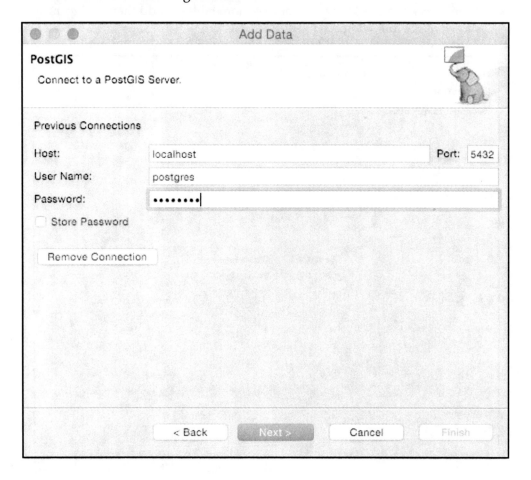

4. Select the target database in the **Database** drop-down menu. Click on the **List** button to view all of the tables from the database that have valid geometries. Then, check the checkboxes for one or more tables to add them as layers, as shown in the following screenshot:

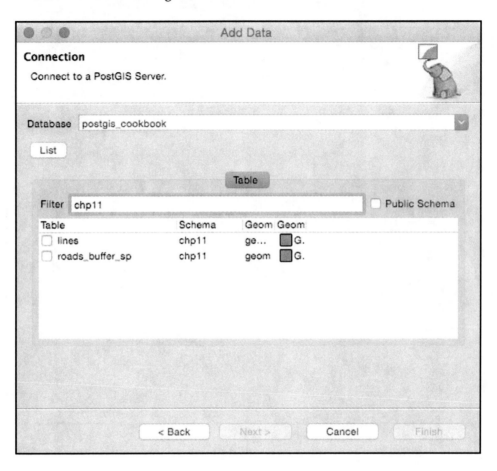

5. Click on **Finish** and your data will be loaded in the **Map** window.

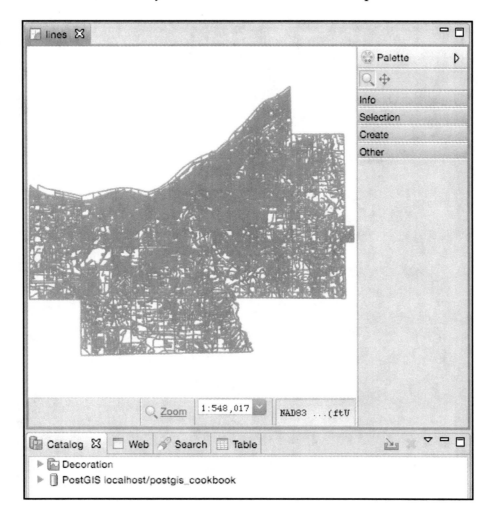

How it works...

The **New Layer** menu in uDig generates a hefty list of possible sources that can be added. PostGIS was set as the database and your database parameters were entered. uDig was then connected to the database. Clicking on **List** displays the total number of tables available in the connected database. Any number of tables can be added at once.

12
Introduction to Location Privacy Protection Mechanisms

In this chapter, we will cover the following recipes:

- Adding noise to protect location data
- Creating redundancy in geographical query results

This chapter includes a set of references to documents (news, laws, academic work, and so on) that will be cited along the text, using a *[#]* format.

Introduction

This chapter is dedicated to an emerging issue in the design and implementation of location-based information systems: LBISs. The increasing use of smartphones in all kinds of applications, and their ability to acquire and report users' locations, has been adopted as a core functionality of many service providers. Enabling access to users' accurate locations throughout the day, which gives context to their requests and allows companies to better know their client and provide any relevant personalized services; however, this information can contain much more about the user than just the context of the service they want to access, such as their weekly routine, frequently visited places, groups of people gathered, and so on. These patterns can be obtained from the phone, and then analyzed and used to categorize or profile customers; this information in the wrong hands, however, could be used against individuals.

Even though there is very little *[1]* to no regulation on how to handle location information in a way that guarantees privacy for users, it is very important that the proper policies and implementation are included at the design stage.

Fortunately, among geoprivacy researchers, there exists a wide variety of mechanisms that can be used to help mitigate the issue of privacy in LBISs.

This chapter is somewhat different from the others because, in order to understand the background of each location privacy technique, we considered important to include the theoretical bases that support these recipes that to the best of our knowledge are only available through academic publications and not yet presented as a hands-on experience.

Definition of Location Privacy Protection Mechanisms – LPPMs

Location privacy can be defined by *Duckham* and *Kulik* in *[2]* as follows: *A special type of information privacy which concerns the claim of individuals to determine for themselves when, how, and to what extent location information about them is communicated to others.* Based on this definition, users should have power over their location information; however, it is well known that this is not the reality in many cases. Often, a service provider requires full access to a user's location in order for the service to become available.

In addition, because there is no restriction on the quality of location information that service providers can record, it's common for the exact GPS coordinates to be acquired, even when it is not relevant to the service itself.

The main goal of LPPMs should be to allow users to hide or reduce the quality of this location information in such a way that users will still have an adequate service functionalities, and that the service provider can still benefit from insights product of spatial analysis .

In order to provide geoprivacy, it is important to understand the components location information, these are: identity, location, and time. If an adversary is able to link those three aspects, location privacy is compromised. These components form an instance of location information; a sequence of such instances that gives historical location information, allowing others to establish behavior patterns and then making it possible for them to identify the user's home, work, and routine. Most LPPMs attack at least one of these components in order to protect privacy.

Suppose an attacker gains access to a user's identity and the time, but has no clear knowledge of what places the user has visited. As the location component has been obfuscated, the attacker would be able to infer very little, as the context is highly-altered and the data has lost its potential usability. (This specific scenario corresponds to location privacy.)

Another popular solution has been the implementation of identity privacy or anonymity, where users' traveled pathways can be accessed, but they provide no information on the identity of the subjects, or even if they are different users; however, this information alone could be enough to infer the identity of a person by matching records on a phonebook, as in the experiments conducted by *[3]*.

Finally, when a user's location and identity are specified, but the time component is missing, the resulting information lacks context, and so pathways may not be reconstructed accurately; however, implementing a model in which this occurs is unlikely, as requests and LBS responses happen at a specific time and delaying queries can cause them to lose their relevance.

Classifying LPPMs

Privacy in location-based services is often viewed as reaching a desirable trade-off between performance and a user's privacy; the more privacy provided, the less likely it is that the service can function as it would under a no-privacy scheme, or without suffering alterations in their architecture or application layer. As LBS offers a great variety of ever-changing features that keep up with users' needs while making use of the latest available technologies and adjusting to social behavior, they provide a similar scenario to LPPMs that aims to cover these services.

In the case of **proactive location-based services (PLBS)**, where users are constantly reporting their location *[4]*, the purpose of LPPMs is to alter the route as much as possible, while still providing a minimum level of accuracy that will allow the LBS to provide relevant information. This can be challenging because many PLBS, like traffic guidance apps, require the exact location of the user. So, unless the original data can be recovered or used in the altered format, it would be very complicated for these applications to implement an LPPM. Other services, like geomarketing or FriendFinder, may tolerate a larger alteration of the data, even if the change cannot be undone.

On the other hand, mechanisms intended for **reactive location-based services (RLBS)** often do not require critical accuracy, and therefore it is tolerable to alter the subject's position in order to provide location privacy.

Some LPPMs require special features alongside the usual client-server architecture, such as special database structures, extra data processing layers, third-party services, proxies, special electronics, a peer-to-peer approach between the LBS users' community, and so on.

Based on this, a proposed way to classify LPPMs is based on the application to PLBS and RLBS. Some of the techniques are general enough that they can be used in both worlds, but each has different implications:

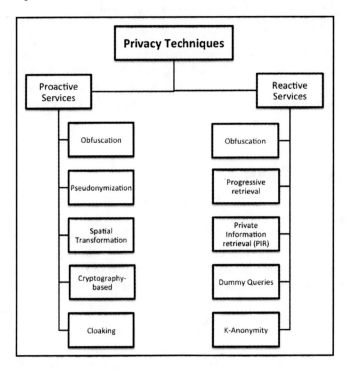

Figure 1. Taxonomy of LPPMs

In this chapter, two examples of LPPM implementations will be shown: noise-based location obfuscation, and private-information retrieval. Each of these imply changes to the design of the LBIS and the geographical database.

Adding noise to protect location data

Some of the mechanisms designed for location privacy protection are based on location obfuscation, which is explained in *[5]* as *the means of deliberately degrading the quality of information about an individual's location in order to protect that individual's location privacy.*

This is perhaps the simplest way to implement location privacy protection in LBISs because it has barely any impact on the server-side of the application, and is usually easy to implement on the client-side. Another way to implement it would be on the server-side, running periodically over the new data, or as a function applied to every new entry.

The main goal of these techniques is to add random noise to the original location obtained by the cellphone or any other location-aware device, so as to reduce the accuracy of the data. In this case, the user can usually define the maximum and/or minimum amount of noise that they want to add. The higher the noise added, the lower the quality of the service; so it is very important to reasonably set this parameter. For example, if a real-time tracking application receives data altered by 1 km, the information provided to the user may not be relevant to the real location.

Each noise-based location obfuscation technique presents a different way to generate noise:

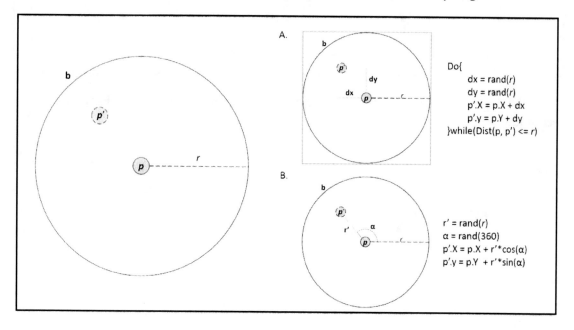

When the noise is generated with polar coordinates, it is more uniformly distributed over a projection of the circular area because both angle and distance follow that distribution. In the case of Cartesian-based noise, points appear to be generated uniformly among the area as a whole, resulting in a lower density of points near the center. The following figure shows the differences in both circular and rectangular projections of 500 random points. In this book, we will work with polar-based random generation:

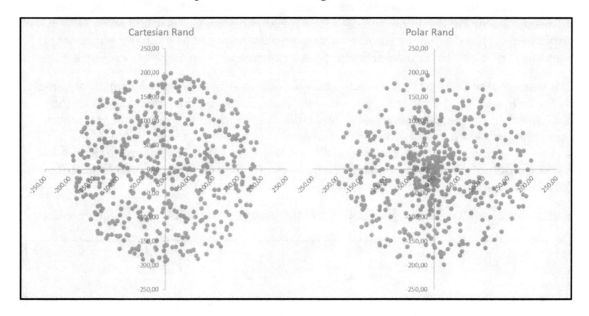

The following figure illustrates the way the **N-RAND** *[6]*, **θ-RAND** *[7]*, and **Pinwheel** *[8]* techniques work:

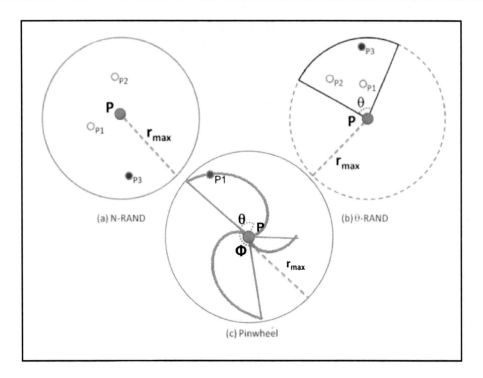

(a) N-RAND

(b) θ-RAND

(c) Pinwheel

N-RAND generates N points in a given area, and selects the point furthest away from the center. **Θ-RAND** does the same, but in a specific sector of the circular area. There can be more than just one area to select from. Finally, the **Pinwheel** mechanism differs from **N-RAND** and **θ-RAND** because it does not generate random distances for the points, and instead defines a specific one for each angle in the circumference, making the selection of the radius a more deterministic process when generating random points. In this case, the only random variable in the generation process is the angle α. The formula to calculate the radius for a given angle, α, is presented in **(1)**, as follows:

$$r_\alpha = (\alpha mod\phi)/\phi . r_{max} (1)$$

Where φ is a preset parameter defined by the user, it determines the amplitude of the wings of geometry, which resembles a pinwheel.

The lower the value of φ, the more wings the pinwheel will have, but those wings will also be thinner; on the other hand, the higher the value, the fewer the number of *wider* wings:

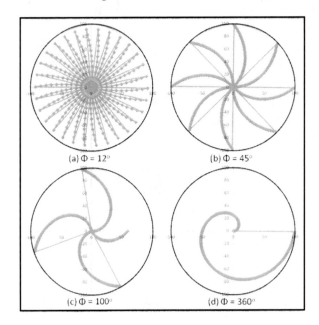

(a) $\Phi = 12°$ (b) $\Phi = 45°$ (c) $\Phi = 100°$ (d) $\Phi = 360°$

Once the locations have been altered, it is very unlikely that you will be able to recover the original information; however, filtering noise techniques are available in the literature that reduce the impact of alterations and allow a better estimation of the location data. One of these mechanisms for noise-filtering is based on an **exponential moving average (EMA)** called Tis-Bad *[9]*.

There is still an open discussion on how much degradation of the location information is sufficient to provide location privacy to users, and moreover, if the resulting obfuscated information remains useful when accessing a LBS. After all, obtaining relevant responses while performing geospatial analysis is one of the main issues regarding LBS and the study of geo-referenced data.

Getting ready

In this recipe, we will create PLPGSQL functions that implement three noise-based obfuscation mechanisms: Rand, N-Rand, and Pinwheel. Then we will create a trigger function for a table in order to alter all newly inserted points. For this chapter, we will reuse the `rk_track_points` dataset used in Chapter 3, *Working with Vector Data – The Basics*.

In this recipe, we will use the ST_Project function to add noise to a single point. Then, we will compare the original data with obfuscated data in QGIS. Finally, we will show the impact of noise filtering on the obfuscated data.

 You will also need to extract the data/chp03/runkeeper-gpx.zip file to working/chp12/runkeeper_gpx.

In the recipe, we will use some of the same steps as in Chapter 3, *Working with Vector Data – The Basics*, but for a new schema.

First, be sure of the format of the .gpx files that you need to import to PostGIS. Open one of them and check the file structure—each file must be in the XML format, composed of one <trk> element, which contains just one <trkseg> element, which contains multiple <trkpt> elements (the points stored from the runner's GPS device).

How to do it...

Carry out the following steps to create the functions:

1. Create a new schema named chp12 to store the data for all the recipes in this chapter using the following command:

   ```
   postgis_cookbook=# create schema chp12;
   ```

2. The implementation of Rand requires the creation of a PLPGSQL function that receives the radius parameter, which defines the maximum distance, and the geometry the_geom to be altered.

   The ST_Project function will move the point to a given distance and angle from its original location. In order to simplify the expression, we will use polar noise generation. Execute the following SQL command:

   ```
   postgis_cookbook=# CREATE OR REPLACE
   FUNCTION chp12.rand(radius numeric, the_geom geometry)
   returns geometry as $$
   BEGIN
     return st_Project(the_geom, random()*radius,
                       radians(random()*360));
   END;
   $$
   LANGUAGE plpgsql;
   ```

3. The implementation of N-Rand requires the n parameter, the number of trials to look for the longest distance from the original point, and the `radius` parameter, which defines the maximum distance, and the geometry `the_geom` to be altered. Execute the following SQL command:

```
postgis_cookbook=# CREATE OR REPLACE FUNCTION chp12.nrand(n integer,
    radius numeric, the_geom geometry)
returns geometry as $$
DECLARE
    tempdist numeric;
    maxdist numeric;
BEGIN
    tempdist := 0;
    maxdist := 0;
    FOR i IN 1..n
    LOOP
      tempdist := random()*radius;
      IF maxdist < tempdist THEN
        maxdist := tempdist;
      END IF;
    END LOOP;
    return st_Project(the_geom,maxdist, radians(random()*360));
END;
$$
LANGUAGE plpgsql;
```

4. The implementation of Pinwheel requires the n parameter, the number of trials to look for the longest distance from the original point, and the `radius` parameter, which defines the maximum distance, and the geometry `the_geom` to be altered. Execute the following SQL command:

```
postgis_cookbook=# CREATE OR REPLACE FUNCTION chp12.pinwheel
    (theta numeric, radius numeric, the_geom geometry)
returns geometry as $$
DECLARE
angle numeric;
BEGIN
  angle = random()*360;
  return st_Project(the_geom,mod(
    CAST(angle as integer), theta)/theta*radius, radians(angle));
END;
$$
LANGUAGE plpgsql;
```

5. Now we will replicate part of the steps in `Chapter 3`, *Working with Vector Data – The Basics*, but for the schema `chp12`. Create the `chp12.rk_track_points` table in PostgreSQL by executing the following command lines:

```
postgis_cookbook=# CREATE TABLE chp12.rk_track_points
(
    fid serial NOT NULL,
    the_geom geometry(Point,4326),
    ele double precision,
    "time" timestamp with time zone,
    CONSTRAINT activities_pk PRIMARY KEY (fid)
);
```

6. As an example, let's use the `nrand` function to create a trigger for all the new points inserted in the `rk_track_points` table. In order to simulate this, we will create a new table that we will use.

   This function will return a new geometry:

```
CREATE OR REPLACE FUNCTION __trigger_rk_track_points_before_insert(
) RETURNS trigger AS $__$
DECLARE
maxdist integer;
n integer;
BEGIN
  maxdist = 500;
  n = 4;
  NEW.the_geom  = chp12.nrand(n, maxdist, NEW.the_geom);
  RETURN NEW;
END;
$__$ LANGUAGE plpgsql;
CREATE TRIGGER rk_track_points_before_insert
BEFORE INSERT ON chp12.rk_track_points FOR EACH ROW
EXECUTE PROCEDURE __trigger_rk_track_points_before_insert();
```

7. Create the following script to import all of the `.gpx` files in the `chp12.rk_track_points` table using the GDAL `ogr2ogr` command.

   The following is the Linux version (name it `working/chp03/import_gpx.sh`):

```
#!/bin/bash
for f in `find runkeeper_gpx -name \*.gpx -printf "%f\n"`
do
  echo "Importing gpx file $f to chp12.rk_track_points
    PostGIS table..." #, ${f%.*}"
  ogr2ogr -append -update  -f PostgreSQL
```

```
PG:"dbname='postgis_cookbook' user='me' password='mypassword'"
runkeeper_gpx/$f -nln chp12.rk_track_points
-sql "SELECT ele, time FROM track_points"
done
```

The following is the Windows version (name it
`working/chp03/import_gpx.bat`):

```
@echo off
for %%I in (runkeeper_gpx\*.gpx*) do (
  echo Importing gpx file %%~nxI to chp12.rk_track_points
    PostGIS table...
  ogr2ogr -append -update -f PostgreSQL
  PG:"dbname='postgis_cookbook' user='me' password='mypassword'"
  runkeeper_gpx/%%~nxI -nln chp12.rk_track_points
  -sql "SELECT ele, time FROM track_points"
)
```

8. In Linux, don't forget to assign an execution permission to it before running. Run the following script:

```
$ chmod 775 import_gpx.sh
$ ./import_gpx.sh
Importing gpx file 2012-02-26-0930.gpx to chp12.rk_track_points
  PostGIS table...
Importing gpx file 2012-02-29-1235.gpx to chp12.rk_track_points
  PostGIS table...
...
Importing gpx file 2011-04-15-1906.gpx to chp12.rk_track_points
  PostGIS table...
```

In Windows, double-click on the `.bat` file, or run it from the command prompt using the following command:

```
> import_gpx.bat
```

9. Once the insertion command is invoked, the trigger call the `nrand` function, alter the incoming geometry in the row and store the new version of the data. If we compare the first 10 values of the original table `chp03.rk_track_points` with the `chp12.rk_track_points`, it can be seen that they are slightly different, due to the added noise. Execute the following query in order to see the results:

```
select ST_ASTEXT(rk.the_geom), ST_ASTEXT(rk2.the_geom)
from chp03.rk_track_points as rk, chp12.rk_track_points as rk2
where rk.fid = rk2.fid
limit 10;
```

The results of the query are as follows:

	st_astext text	st_astext text
1	POINT(12.490049 41.842603)	POINT(12.4956085374046 41.8421401688101)
2	POINT(12.489853 41.842531)	POINT(12.4903858629488 41.83973295932)
3	POINT(12.489683 41.842414)	POINT(12.488238503296 41.8450166403716)
4	POINT(12.489497 41.842331)	POINT(12.4947481426845 41.8409761640323)
5	POINT(12.489404 41.84233)	POINT(12.4886152725506 41.8445327581563)
6	POINT(12.489305 41.842183)	POINT(12.4934162980532 41.8393513242803)
7	POINT(12.489317 41.842018)	POINT(12.485101470889 41.844016256977)
8	POINT(12.489247 41.841869)	POINT(12.4875397731734 41.8379176675626)
9	POINT(12.489026 41.841875)	POINT(12.4900647307263 41.8379892386432)
10	POINT(12.488962 41.841845)	POINT(12.4892071289802 41.8440740069694)

10. In order to evaluate the impact of the noise in the data, we will create two tables to store the obfuscated data with different noise levels: 500 m and 1 km. We will use the previously defined function `rand`. Execute the following SQL commands to create the tables:

```
CREATE TABLE chp12.rk_points_rand_500 AS (
  SELECT chp12.rand(500, the_geom)
  FROM chp12.rk_track_points
);
CREATE TABLE chp12.rk_points_rand_1000 AS (
  SELECT chp12.rand(1000, the_geom)
  FROM chp12.rk_track_points
);
```

11. Load the tables in QGIS or your favorite Desktop GIS. The following figure shows the comparison of the original data and the obfuscated points by 500 m and 1 km:

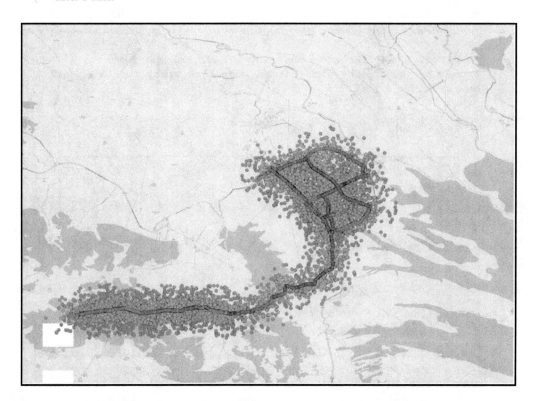

How it works...

In this recipe, we applied three different mechanisms for noise-based location obfuscation: Rand, N-Rand, and Pinwheel, defining PostgreSQL functions in PLPGSQL for each method. We used one of the functions in a trigger in order to automatically alter the incoming data, so that no changes would need to be made on the application on the user's side. In addition, we showed the impact of noise comparing two versions of the altered data, so we can better appreciate the impact of the configuration noise settings

In the following recipes, we will look at an implementation of a private information retrieval-based LPPM.

Creating redundancy in geographical query results

Private information retrieval (**PIR**) LPPMs provide location privacy by mapping the spatial context to provide a private way to query a service without releasing any location information that could be obtained by third parties.

PIR-based methods can be classified as cryptography-based or hardware-based, according to [9]. Hardware-based methods use a special kind of **secure coprocessor** (**SC**) that acts as securely protected spaces in which the PIR query is processed in a non-decipherable way, as in [10]. Cryptography-based techniques only use logic resources, and do not require a special physical disposition on either the server or client-side.

In [10], the authors present a hybrid technique that uses a cloaking method through various-size grid Hilbert curves to limit the search domain of a generic cryptography-based PIR algorithm; however, the PIR processing on the database is still expensive, as shown in their experiments, and it is not practical for a user-defined level of privacy. This is because the method does not allow the cloaking grid cell size to be specified by the user, nor can it be changed once the whole grid has been calculated; in other words, no new PoIs can be added to the system. Other techniques can be found in [12].

PIR can also be combined with other techniques to increase the level of privacy. One type of compatible LPPM is the dummy query-based technique, where a set of random fake or dummy queries are generated for arbitrary locations within the greater search area (city, county, state, for example) [13], [14]. The purpose of this is to hide the one that the user actually wants to send.

The main disadvantage of the dummy query technique is the overall cost of sending and processing a large number of requests for both the user and the server sides. In addition, one of the queries will contain the original exact location and point of interest of the user, so the original trajectory could still be traced based on the query records from a user - especially if no intelligence is applied when generating the dummies. There are improvements to this method discussed in [15], where rather than sending each point on a separate query, all the dummy and real locations are sent along with the location interest specified by the user. In [16], the authors propose a method to avoid the random generation of points for each iteration, which should reduce the possibility of detecting the trend in real points; but this technique requires a lot of resources from the device when generating trajectories for each dummy path, generates separate queries per path, and still reveals the user's location.

The LPPM presented as an example in this book is MaPIR – a Map-based PIR *[17]*. This is a method that applies a mapping technique to provide a common language for the user and server, and that is also capable of providing redundant answers to single queries without overhead on the server-side, which, in turn, can improve response time due to a reduction in its use of geographical queries.

This technique creates a redundant geographical mapping of a certain area that uses the actual coordinate of the PoI to generate IDs on a different search scale. In the MaPIR paper, the decimal digit of the coordinate that will be used for the query. Near the Equator, each digit can be approximated to represent a certain distance, as shown in the following figure:

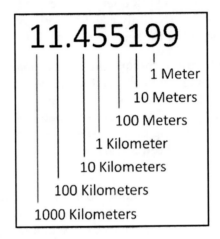

This can be generalized by saying that nearby locations will appear close at larger scales (closer to the integer portion of the location), but not necessarily in smaller ones. It could also show relatively far away points as though they were closer, if they share the same set of digits (nth digit of latitude and nth digit of longitude).

Once the digits have been obtained, depending on the selected scale, a mapping technique is needed to reduce the number to a single ID. On paper, a simple pseudo-random function is applied to reduce the two-dimensional domain to a one-dimensional one:

```
ID(Lat_Nth, Lon_Nth) = (((Lat_Nth + 1) * (Lon_Nth + 1)) mod p) - 1
```

In the preceding equation, we can see that p is the next prime number to the maximum desired ID. Given that for the paper the maximum ID was **9**, the value of p is **11**. After applying this function, the final map looks as follows:

		Lon Nth + 1									
		10	**9**	**8**	**7**	**6**	**5**	**4**	**3**	**2**	**1**
10		1	2	3	4	5	6	7	8	9	10
9		2	4	6	8	10	1	3	5	7	9
8		3	6	9	1	4	7	10	2	5	8
7		4	8	1	5	9	2	6	10	3	7
6		5	10	4	9	3	8	2	7	1	6
5		6	1	7	2	8	3	9	4	10	5
4		7	3	10	6	2	9	5	1	8	4
3		8	5	2	10	7	4	1	9	6	3
2		9	7	5	3	1	10	8	6	4	2
1		10	9	8	7	6	5	4	3	2	1

(Left axis label: Lat Nth + 1)

The following figure shows a sample **PoI ID** that represents a restaurant located at **10.964824,-74.804778**. The final mapping grid cells will be **2, 6,** and **1,** using the scales k = 3, 2, and 1 respectively.

This information can be stored on a specific table in the database, or as the DBA determined best for the application:

(10.964824,-74.804778),					
N	Latitude Nth digit	Longitude Nth digit	Lat Nth + 1	Lon Nth + 1	Id
3	4	4	5	5	2
2	6	0	7	1	5
1	9	8	10	9	1

PoI ID	Type	Coordinates
123456	Restaurant	10.964824, -74.804778

PoI ID	Scale	ID
123456	3	2
123456	2	6
123456	1	1
123456	0	4

Based on this structure, a query generated by a user will need to define the scale of search (within 100 m, 1 km, and so on), the type of business they are looking for, and the grid cell they are located. The server will receive the parameters and look for all restaurants in the same cell ID as the user. The results will return all restaurants located in the cells with the same ID, even if they are not close to the user. Given that cells are indistinguishable, an attacker that gains access to the server's log will only see that a user was in 1 of 10 cell IDs. Of course, some of the IDs may fall in inhabitable areas (such as in a forest or lake), but some level of redundancy will always be present.

Getting ready

In this recipe, we will focus on the implementation of the MaPIR technique as an example of a PIR and dummy query-based LPPM. For this, a small dataset of supermarkets is loaded on the database as PoIs. These points will be processed and stored as explained in MaPIR, and then queried by a user.

The dataset was obtained from the Colombian open data platform *Datos Abiertos* at the following link:

```
https://www.datos.gov.co/Comercio-Industria-y-Turismo/Mapa-supermercados-
Guadalajara-de-Buga/26ma-3v68
```

The points in the dataset are presented in the following figure:

How to do it...

In the preceding recipe, we created temporary tables to store original data, as well as tables containing MaPIR information to be queried later by users. The following steps allow other users to access those tables:

1. First, create the table supermarkets to store the information extracted from the dataset, and the table supermarkets_mapir to store the MaPIR-related information for each supermarket register. Execute the following command:

```
CREATE TABLE chp12.supermarkets (
    sup_id serial,
    the_geom geometry(Point,4326),
```

```
    latitude numeric,
    longitude numeric,
    PRIMARY KEY (sup_id)
);
CREATE TABLE chp12.supermarkets_mapir (
    sup_id int REFERENCES chp12.supermarkets (sup_id),
    cellid int,
    levelid int
);
```

2. Now, create a trigger function that will be applied to all the new registers inserted in the table `supermarkets`, so that the new registers will be inserted in the `supermarkets_mapir` table, calculating the `cellid` and `levelid` values. The following code will create the function:

```
CREATE OR REPLACE FUNCTION __trigger_supermarkets_after_insert(
) RETURNS trigger AS $__$
DECLARE
tempcelliD integer;
BEGIN
  FOR i IN -2..6
  LOOP
    tempcellid = mod((mod(CAST(TRUNC(ABS(NEW.latitude)*POWER(10,i))
    as int),10)+1) * (mod(CAST(TRUNC(ABS(NEW.longitude)*POWER(10,i))
    as int),10)+1), 11)-1;
    INSERT INTO chp12.supermarkets_mapir (sup_id, cellid, levelid)
    VALUES (NEW.sup_id, tempcellid, i);
  END LOOP;
Return NEW;
END;
$__$ LANGUAGE plpgsql;
CREATE TRIGGER supermarkets_after_insert
AFTER INSERT ON chp12.supermarkets FOR EACH ROW
EXECUTE PROCEDURE __trigger_supermarkets_after_insert ();
```

3. Given that the dataset is not properly organized, we extracted the location information of the supermarkets and built the following query. After the execution, both tables `supermarkets` and `supermarkets_mapir` should be populated. Execute the following command:

```
INSERT INTO chp12.supermarkets (the_geom, longitude, latitude) VALUES
  (ST_GEOMFROMTEXT('POINT(-76.304202 3.8992)',4326),
    -76.304202, 3.8992),
  (ST_GEOMFROMTEXT('POINT(-76.308476 3.894591)',4326),
    -76.308476, 3.894591),
  (ST_GEOMFROMTEXT('POINT(-76.297893 3.890615)',4326),
    -76.297893, 3.890615),
```

```
(ST_GEOMFROMTEXT('POINT(-76.299017 3.901726)',4326),
   -76.299017, 3.901726),
(ST_GEOMFROMTEXT('POINT(-76.292027 3.909094)',4326),
   -76.292027, 3.909094),
(ST_GEOMFROMTEXT('POINT(-76.299687 3.888735)',4326),
   -76.299687, 3.888735),
(ST_GEOMFROMTEXT('POINT(-76.307102 3.899181)',4326),
   -76.307102, 3.899181),
(ST_GEOMFROMTEXT('POINT(-76.310342 3.90145)',4326),
   -76.310342, 3.90145),
(ST_GEOMFROMTEXT('POINT(-76.297366 3.889721)',4326),
   -76.297366, 3.889721),
(ST_GEOMFROMTEXT('POINT(-76.293296 3.906171)',4326),
   -76.293296, 3.906171),
(ST_GEOMFROMTEXT('POINT(-76.300154 3.901235)',4326),
   -76.300154, 3.901235),
(ST_GEOMFROMTEXT('POINT(-76.299755 3.899361)',4326),
   -76.299755, 3.899361),
(ST_GEOMFROMTEXT('POINT(-76.303509 3.911253)',4326),
   -76.303509, 3.911253),
(ST_GEOMFROMTEXT('POINT(-76.300152 3.901175)',4326),
   -76.300152, 3.901175),
(ST_GEOMFROMTEXT('POINT(-76.299286 3.900895)',4326),
   -76.299286, 3.900895),
(ST_GEOMFROMTEXT('POINT(-76.309937 3.912021)',4326),
   -76.309937, 3.912021);
```

4. Now, all the supermarkets inserted in the `supermarket` table will have their MaPIR-related information in the `supermarkets_mapir` table. The following query will illustrate the information stored in the `supermarkets_mapir` table for a given register:

```
SELECT * FROM supermarkets_mapir WHERE sup_id = 8;
```

The result of the query is shown in the following table:

	sup_id integer	cellid integer	levelid integer
1	8	0	-2
2	8	7	-1
3	8	5	0
4	8	2	1
5	8	9	2
6	8	5	3
7	8	8	4
8	8	0	5
9	8	2	6

5. Now that the `supermarket` data is ready, assume that a user is at the coordinates `(-76.299017, 3.901726)`, which matches the location of one of the supermarkets, and that they want to use the scale 2 (the second decimal digit corresponding to a grid cell size of approximately 1 km^2 by the Equator).

6. The mobile app should generate a query asking for `levelid = 2` and a `cellid = 9`, calculated from the second decimal digit from `latitude = 0`, and `longitude = 9` on the second decimal digit. This calculation can be verified on the mapping table previously shown, with `Lat Nth +1 = 1` and `Long Nth + 1 = 10`:

```
SELECT sm.the_geom AS the_geom
FROM chp12.supermarkets_mapir AS smm, chp12.supermarkets AS sm
WHERE smm.levelid = 2 AND smm.cellid = 9 AND smm.sup_id = sm.sup_id;
```

Note that there is no need for any geographical information in the query anymore, because the mapping was done during the pre-processing stage. This reduces the query time, because it does not require the use of complex internal functions to determine distance; however, mapping cannot guarantee that all nearby results will be returned, as results in adjacent cells with different IDs may not appear. In the following figure, you can see that the supermarkets from the previous query (in black) do not include some of the supermarkets that are near the user's location (in white near the arrow). Some possible counter-measures can be applied to tackle this, such as double-mapping some of the elements close to the edges of the grid cells:

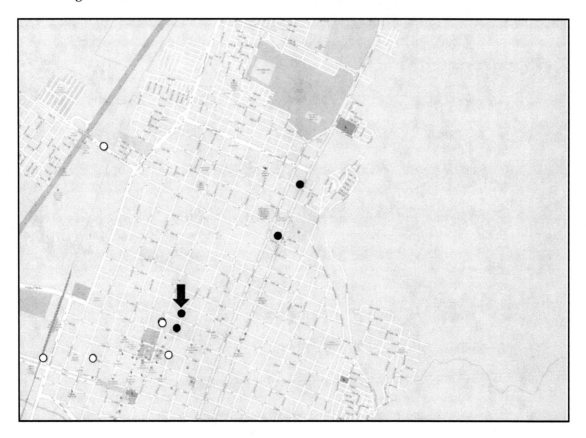

How it works...

In this recipe, we implemented an LPPM that uses PIR and a dummy query called MaPIR. It created a mapping function for points of interest that allowed us to query using different scales. It also included redundancy in the answer, providing privacy protection, as it did not reveal the actual location of the user.

The process required for calculating the mapping of a dataset should be stored in a table that will be used for a user's queries. In the MaPIR paper, it was shown that despite the multiple results, the execution time of the MaPIR queries took less than half the time, compared to the geopraphical queries based on distance.

References

1. European Union Directive on Privacy and Electronic Communications, 2002.

2. *M. Duckham* and *L. Kulik, Location Privacy and Location-aware Computing,* Dyn. Mob. GIS Investig. Chang. Sp. time, vol. 3, pp. 35–51, 2006.

3. *J. Krumm, Inference Attacks on Location Tracks,* in Pervasive Computing. Springer, 2007, pp. 127-143.

4. *M. A. Labrador, A. J. Perez,* and *P. Wightman. Location-based Information Systems: Developing Real-time Tracking Applications.* Boca Raton: CRC Press, 2011.

5. *M. Duckham* and *L. Kulik, A Formal Model of Obfuscation and Negotiation for Location Privacy,* in *Pervasive Computing. Springer,* 2005, pp. 152-170.

6. *P. Wightman, W. Coronell, D. Jabba, M. Jimeno,* and *M. Labrador, Evaluation of Location Obfuscation Techniques for Privacy in Location-based Information Systems,* in Communications (LATINCOM), 2011 IEEE Latin-American Conference on, pp. 1-6.

7. *P. Wightman, M. Zurbarán, E. Zurek, A. Salazar, D. Jabba,* and *M. Jimeno, θ-Rand: Random Noise-based Location Obfuscation Based on Circle Sectors,* in IEEE International Symposium on Industrial Electronics and Applications (ISIEA) on, 2013.

8. *P. Wightman, M. Zurbarán,* and *A. Santander, High Variability Geographical Obfuscation for Location Privacy,* 2013 47th International Carnahan Conference on Security Technology (ICCST), Medellin, 2013, pp. 1-6.

9. *A. Labrador, P. Wightman, A. Santander, D. Jabba, M. Jimeno, Tis-Bad: A Time Series-Based Deobfuscation Algorithm*, in Investigación e Innovación en Ingenierías. Universidad Simón Bolívar. Vol. 3 (1), pp. 1 - 8. 2015.

10. *A. Khoshgozaran, H. Shirani-Mehr, and C. Shahabi, SPIRAL: A Scalable Private Information Retrieval Approach to Location Privacy*, in Mobile Data Management Workshops, 2008. MDMW 2008. Ninth International Conference on, pp. 55-62.

11. *F. Olumofin, P. K. Tysowski, I. Goldberg, and U. Hengartner, Achieving Efficient Query Privacy for Location-based Services*, in Privacy Enhancing Technologies, 2010, pp. 93-110.

12. *G. Ghinita, P. Kalnis, A. Khoshgozaran, C. Shahabi, and K. Tan, Private queries in location-based services: Anonymizers are not necessary*, in Proceedings of the 2008 ACM SIGMOD International Conference on Management of Data, pp. 121-132.

13. *D. Quercia, I. Leontiadis, L. McNamara, C. Mascolo, and J. Crowcroft, SpotME if you can: Randomized Responses for Location Obfuscation on Mobile Phones*, in Distributed Computing Systems (ICDCS), 2011 31st International Conference on, 2011, pp. 363-372.

14. *H. Kido, Y. Yanagisawa, and T. Satoh, An Anonymous Communication Technique using Dummies for Location-based Services*, in Pervasive Services, 2005. ICPS '05. Proceedings. International Conference on, pp. 88-97.

15. *H. Lu, C. S. Jensen, and M. L. Yiu, Pad: Privacy-area aware, dummy-based location privacy in mobile services*, in Proceedings of the Seventh ACM International Workshop on Data Engineering for Wireless and Mobile Access, pp. 16-23.

16. *P. Shankar, V. Ganapathy, and L. Iftode (2009, September), Privately Querying Location-based Services with sybilquery*. In Proceedings of the 11th international conference on Ubiquitous computing, 2009, pp. 31-40.

17. *P. M. Wightman, M. Zurbarán, M. Rodríguez, and M. A. Labrador, MaPIR: Mapping-based Private Information Retrieval for Location Privacy in LBISs*, 38th Annual IEEE Conference on Local Computer Networks - Workshops, Sydney, NSW, 2013, pp. 964-971.

Other Books You May Enjoy

If you enjoyed this book, you may be interested in these other books by Packt:

Mastering PostGIS

Dominik Mikiewicz, Michal Mackiewicz, Tomasz Nycz

ISBN: 978-1-78439-164-5

- Refresh your knowledge of the PostGIS concepts and spatial databases
- Solve spatial problems with the use of SQL in real-world scenarios
- Practical walkthroughs of application development examples using Postgis, GeoServer and OpenLayers.
- Extract, transform and load your spatial data
- Expose data directly or through web services.
- Consume your data in both desktop and web clients

Leave a review - let other readers know what you think

Please share your thoughts on this book with others by leaving a review on the site that you bought it from. If you purchased the book from Amazon, please leave us an honest review on this book's Amazon page. This is vital so that other potential readers can see and use your unbiased opinion to make purchasing decisions, we can understand what our customers think about our products, and our authors can see your feedback on the title that they have worked with Packt to create. It will only take a few minutes of your time, but is valuable to other potential customers, our authors, and Packt. Thank you!

Index

CPSIA information can be obtained
at www.ICGtesting.com
Printed in the USA
LVOW09s0032160418
573614LV00004B/31/P